W9-CPY-378

PUNK.

PUNK.

Stephen Colegrave & Chris Sullivan

THUNDER'S
MOUTH
PRESS

Published in the United States by Thunder's Mouth Press
An Imprint of Avalon Publishing Group Incorporated
245 West 17th Street, New York, NY 10011

First published in Great Britain in 2001 by Cassell & Co

This paperback edition published in 2005 by Cassell Illustrated
a division of Octopus Publishing Group Limited
2-4 Heron Quays, London E14 4JP

Text copyright © 2001 Stephen Colegrave & Chris Sullivan
Design and layout © Cassell Illustrated 2004

The moral right of Stephen Colegrave and Chris Sullivan to be identified as the authors of this work
has been asserted in accordance with the Copyright, Designs and Patents Act of 1988.

All rights reserved. No part of this publication may be reproduced in a material form
(including photocopying or storing it in any medium by electronic means and whether
or not transiently or incidentally to some other use of this publication) without the prior
written permission of the copyright owner, except in accordance with the provisions of
the Copyright, Designs and Patents Act 1988 or under the terms of a licence issued
by the Copyright Licensing Agency, 90 Tottenham Court Road, London W1P 9HE.
Applications for the copyright owner's written permission to reproduce any part of this
publication should be addressed to the publisher.

The picture credits on page 399 constitute an extension of this copyright information.

Library of Congress Control Number: 2005928004

ISBN: 1-56025-769-5

Commissioning editor: John Mitchinson
Project manager: Patricia Burgess
Copy editor: Debbie Kennett
Additional research: John Shearlaw
Consultant: Nils Stevenson
Picture researcher: Frances Topp
Design: Wherefore Art?
(David Costa, Elina Arapoglou, Sian Rance, Alessia Ramaccia)
Index: Tarrant Ranger Indexing

Printed by Toppan Printing Co., Ltd

Colour separations by Fotolito Longo

To everybody who was there,
and especially those that didn't make it.

ACKNOWLEDGEMENTS

We would like to thank everyone who has helped us with this book, particularly the many people we talked to and interviewed. Special thanks go to Nils Stevenson, whose advice and encouragement kept us going; Marco Pirroni, Helen Wellington Lloyd, Leee Childers, Danny Fields, Jayne County, Nat Finkelstein, Dennis Morris, Ray Stevenson, Viv Goldman, Roger Bourton and Joe Corré, who all contributed more than just interviews; Della Lewis, Beth Marissa Sergeant, Natalie Milverton, Siobhan Stanley and Linden Hughes for keeping everything shipshape; Eddie, Gino and Louise for providing the entertainment; Leah Serehsin for sorting out America and much more, and Hilary, Lucy, Rupert and Oliver Colegrave for suffering quietly. We are grateful to John Shearlaw for additional reporting, Tamara Roukaerts for research, Trish Burgess and Debbie Kennett for calmly editing and Frances Topp for picture research. Thanks also to David Costa, Elina Arapoglou, Alessia Ramaccia and Sian Rance at Wherefore Art?, to Michael Dover and David Rowley at Cassells, and particularly to John Mitchinson for having the courage to commission us in the first place.

CONTENTS

Punk is about being 16 and saying no.

Steve Severin, guitarist, Siouxsie and the Banshees

AUTHORS' NOTE

The content of this book is largely based on original interviews conducted by the authors. A full list of interviewees appears on page 385. The authors have also drawn on previously unpublished research from The Filth and the Fury, with kind permission from Julien Temple, and from original interviews with Warhol Factory figures conducted by Nat Finkelstein. A small proportion of material from other sources has been included, mainly to give voice to those now deceased. All sources are acknowledged in situ.

INTRODUCTION

punk n. *1. A youth movement of the late '70s characterized by anti-establishment slogans and outrageous clothes and hairstyles. 2. An inferior, rotten or worthless person or thing. 3. Worthless articles collectively. 4. Short for* punk rock. *5.* Obs. *A young male homosexual; cat. 6.* Obs. *A prostitute –* adj. *7. Rotten or worthless.*

Collins English Dictionary, 2000

In 1977 the dictionary defined punk as many things, but none of them were anything to do with a musical movement. All the definitions were uncompromisingly negative. This absence of acknowledgement at the peak of punk is indicative of its place in contemporary Britain. It was never a comfortable movement; it was not understood by most people over 21; it refused to conform, or to confine itself to a musical trend. No wonder the dictionary tried to ignore it...

Before acquiring its musical connotations, the word had its own hard-edged meaning. For many the term was used by the likes of James Cagney to express derision of someone considered inferior. It was a name rooted in film noir of the 1940s and could not be parted from its origins. The name, though apt, did not immediately catch on in the UK. The Sex Pistols always claimed that they weren't punk – they were the Sex Pistols.

The irony of punk is that virtually as soon as it was named and defined, it was in fact over. However, this does not matter because in this book we are defining punk in terms of the spirit and attitude that epitomized its innovative peak.

Punk was always more than a T-shirt or a piece of loud music: it was an irrepressible attitude. It is this attitude that momentarily rescued the word from its time-honoured place of shame and elevated it to describe a youth movement that dared to rock the status quo beyond the imagination of any previous generation.

Although, for the sake of simplicity, punk is described as a movement, it was only ever a collective of individual free spirits. In fact, it is these individuals who make punk difficult to define: just when you think you have managed to encapsulate the ethos, these free spirits break away and make you think again. This is the essence of the movement and, if nothing else, we hope to demonstrate that the years 1975-9 were a time of intense personal creativity.

Individuality was a quality shared by all the major participants in this story, whether British or American. In the USA it manifested itself principally in music and, arguably, resulted in a richer musical heritage. In Britain the focus was broader, with *people attempting to push out the boundaries of fashion, graphics and design, and to create a politics of subversion. In both countries the roots of punk lay in subversion, which carried the inherent acknowledgement that you were somehow living apart.*

This volatile foundation gave punk its impetus and zest for ridicule, imparting a rawness and freshness previously unseen. We have tried to capture those qualities in the pages of this book.

The sum effect of punk was to create a chasm between the younger and older generations. It was determined that youth should define, annex and follow its own agenda. The confidence it brought to achieving this gave it a bullet-proof brashness that propelled it to victory against record companies, TV hosts and Texan cowboys. Of course, in the unfolding of this story there is much that now appears misguided or even ridiculous, but the essential robustness and relevance of the key theme – that everyone should question authority and do it for themselves – is just as relevant 25 years later.

The importance of being committed to this agenda was most poignantly revealed as the original participants began to drop out of the story. The sense of liberation and personal freedom gave way to tribal tyranny. Spitting, pogoing and racism were never part of the agenda, but they became the hallmarks of those die-hard punk bands that refused to believe it was all over, or to evolve, as the Clash had done. To appreciate the true brilliance of punk you have to dismiss such crass behaviour from your mind.

It is no exaggeration to claim that 1976 was the peak of punk in Britain, as it was for the American bands who came to visit. In fact, the class of '76 went on to become the main movers and shakers in subsequent decades. Punk as a concept set them apart and made it clear that there was a very viable subculture in the UK that was not prepared to settle for what it was given. The only people the younger generation had to look up to were their peers, so it fell to them to run the clubs, own the record labels and design the clothes. It is obvious really when you think about it, but the youth of '76 had to underline these developments with subversion. This book begins with Andy Warhol's Factory in New York, which, although not punk per se, did entertain all its basic principles. As Ronnie Cutrone, a Factory regular, explains in Victor Bockris's book Uptight: The Story of the Velvet Underground, 'Everybody was feeling really cocky and they didn't like anybody. The general attitude was 'Fuck you,' which was very punk, but nobody knew what punk was. The Velvets hated everything. The whole idea was to take a stab at everything.' This was the basic punk maxim. Warhol's Factory is relevant because it condoned subversion and personal anarchy. The Warhol superstars Jackie Curtis, Holly Woodlawn and Candy Darling were right out on a limb, existing in a self-inflicted vacuum that could thrive only within a rarefied environment such as the Factory. In the early days of Malcolm McLaren and Vivienne Westwood's shop Sex, the clientele were pure Warhol – a strange mixture of gay, lesbian, straight, dominant and exhibitionist characters. Just as the Sex Pistols were later to grasp subversity with both hands, so did the Velvet Underground in their day. The main difference was that the British scene was funnier and even younger.

One of punk's greatest influences was the hippie movement because it gave the early protagonists something to rebel against and someone to hate. If it hadn't been for the insipid peace and love philosophy of the hippies, punk would have had nothing to react against. Contentment is the enemy of creation, and we at times need the banal in order to provoke the revolutionary. Punk was no exception. On both sides of the Atlantic apathy was rife.

Twenty-five years later, some people find it hard to recall what the '70s were like in either the US or the UK. Much of the music has lost its sweaty allure. Even so, the Ramones' and the Undertones' punchy two-minute numbers still have the power to shake ex-fans out of middle-aged apathy. But punk always embodied more than music: it dictated how to dress, what drugs to take, where to live and how to survive. To be punk was to be part of an elite that was fighting against the world – a world very different from today's. In post-Vietnam New York and post-three-day-week London there was a feeling that the establishment was irrelevant, old-fashioned and deserved to be shocked.

This book has been created from the actual words of people who were there, and they give a vivid impression of what it was like. To this end we have interviewed a broad range of participants, including band members and their managers, key figures in Warhol's Factory and McLaren's Bromley contingent, owners of the clubs, venues and clothes shops, photographers and journalists, all of whom helped to create what we now call punk.

As with all musical eras, there is a nostalgia industry for punk, which continually re-invents the myths, aggrandizes the trivial and over-estimates the legacy. Unfortunately, the original spontaneity, madness, violent creativity and sheer audacity of the period is in danger of being lost. Mindful of this danger, we have talked to people we know and trust (or their recommended contacts) who have no agenda or axe to grind. This has allowed us to get closer to the truth and avoid rehashes of well-rehearsed stories.

We are keen to tell the story of punk with pictures as well as words. Most of the images have come directly from photographers who have also given us interviews. Some of them, such as Danny Fields, who managed the Ramones, and Leee Childers, who managed the Heartbreakers, were major figures in their own right and have given us many previously unpublished shots. We have also included a number of movie stills, as films such as Jubilee, The Great Rock'n'Roll Swindle and The Punk Rock Movie are incredibly evocative of the era.

Of course, we haven't been able to interview everyone. Many of those we most wanted to talk to are dead. Others weren't prepared to be candid, so we decided to talk instead to people who knew them. We apologize to anyone whom we have inadvertently omitted.

The aim of this book is to do more than just tell a great story. It sets out to convey the feel, the smell, attitude and humour of punk, to allow it to bask in all its brash glory, from its Warhol roots to its eclectic legacy. To show what it was like to live apart –

TO BE PUNK.

Stephen Colegrave & Chris Sullivan
London, June 2001

(and before)

The year 1975 was when punk, as a visible entity, was galvanized into being. Punk was basically an attitude that was expressed mainly through clothing and music. It was anarchic, nihilistic and deliberately confrontational. It questioned the establishment, challenged the status quo and generally posed the question 'Why?'

Quite often the ingredients or influences of a cultural recipe are as interesting as the dish itself, and punk is no exception. That is why in this first chapter we have explored punk's beginnings in New York and London, those who directly influenced it, those who gave punk its unique style, as well as the clubs they played and the places they hung out.

The so-called 'punk' attitude can be traced back to the 19th-century French painter Gustave Courbet, who spearheaded the avant-garde school of Realism that celebrated the common man and his struggles. Courbet and this radical new art form became synonymous with political subversion, an accusation that was also levelled at punk. The similarity does not end there. Just as Courbet believed that anyone could be a painter, so punks believed that anyone could be a musician. Even punk's fondness for sexual deviance, such as rubber and bondage clothing, was nothing new. Courbet himself challenged the sexual mores of his time by portraying subjects that were considered sexually deviant, such as lesbianism. While he didn't have the clothing of a punk, Courbet certainly had the attitude. Early New York punk pioneers have cited some of Courbet's contemporaries – the poets Rimbaud, Baudelaire and Verlaine, and the philosopher Proudhon – as direct influences on their work. But it was Courbet who really started the subversive ball rolling.

In locating the roots of punk, we could also go back to Dada, the highly influential French art movement of the 1920s. Led by a group of radical French painters and poets, Dada condoned anarchy, subversion and provocation, and also employed outrage as a means of self-promotion. Its most famous son was Marcel Duchamp, who, at the Cologne Dada exhibition of 1920, had the patrons enter through the toilets of a café. Once inside, they were met by a young girl in full communion dress reciting obscene verse.

The Dada artist John Heartfield has a particular link with punk because he pioneered montage, the technique of using picture fragments to make a new composite image. This graphic style became synonymous with punk. Another great exponent of Dada and Surrealism was the painter Yves Tanguy, who in 1924 had a spiky punk haircut and whose party trick was to eat live spiders. It is well known that both Malcolm McLaren and Bernie Rhodes (managers of the Sex Pistols and the Clash respectively) applied the ideas of art to rock'n'roll when laying the foundations for British punk, and the art in question was Dada.

Another influence on punk was the Beat movement, which emerged in the USA during the early 1950s with the aim of disrupting the then-stuffy world of literature. Its members included the poets Allen Ginsberg and Gregory Corso, and the writers Jack Kerouac, Charles Bukowski and William Burroughs. They wrote about the highs and lows of urban street life, and drifted into the narcotic-inspired underworld of New York's East Village, where they used and wrote about the virtues of various Class A drugs, amongst other things. This was pretty radical behaviour at the time. Just as Courbet and Duchamp had held the everyday events and objects of their age up to public scrutiny, so the Beat writers laid bare their own experiences, such as heroin addiction. They elevated degradation and the everyday into high literature, appalling many people in the process.

Alongside the Beat movement, the abstract expressionist painters of New York also displayed a Dada/punk attitude to their work. Jackson Pollock had a penchant for peeing in fireplaces at social gatherings, and Robert Rauschenberg found it entirely apt to publicly erase a drawing by William de Kooning. These guerrilla tactics paved the way for a new wave of radical artists, who emerged during the 1960s. One of these was Andy Warhol, who saw that the future of art lay in using a variety of non-traditional media to remain valid. By working with film and music, Warhol was in many ways predicting the future of punk as a multimedia art form.

In this chapter we have gone back to 1960s' New York and Andy Warhol's Factory, as it is they, together with the Velvet Underground, who most clearly lay the foundations for the music and attitude of punk. The Factory, with its mix of gay, straight, lesbian and transvestite artists and performers, was an institution that directly influenced Malcolm McLaren and Vivienne Westwood in the evolution of punk in London. Their shop Sex in the Kings Road was an establishment that Warhol would have been proud of. As Nils Stevenson, Sex Pistols tour manager and McLaren confidant, has said, 'Malcolm would have loved to have been Warhol.' And McLaren himself has acknowledged being influenced by the Factory. It was the nerve centre for a subversive, underground group of malcontents, whose anarchy was entirely personal. At the centre was the Warhol-managed Velvet Underground, a band who sang about sado-masochism, amphetamine abuse and scoring smack. On stage they dressed in black, employed the services of a whip dancer and were deliberately unsettling. As Warhol said, 'Always leave the audience wanting less.' This was in the midst of the Flower Power movement and was truly subversive, even when compared to their musical contemporaries. Warhol had applied the tactics of art to rock'n'roll, and the Velvets were almost an art installation: they were the first to make people question conventional entertainment, and in doing so created an ethic that was at the heart of punk rock.

As the Velvet Underground toured the USA, they left behind a trail of bands inspired by their performance. In Los Angeles they influenced the young film student Jim Morrison, later lead singer with the Doors. More importantly for punk, while playing in Ann Arbor, Michigan, they encouraged two bands that subsequently became highly relevant to the movement – the MC5 and the Stooges. In the early '70s John Cale of the Velvet Underground produced records by the Modern Lovers, the Stooges and Patti Smith, which had all the hallmarks of punk and went on to influence all the main protagonists in the movement. The influence of the Velvet Underground on punk was huge.

Another band that had a profound effect was the New York Dolls, whose members sometimes resembled a cross-dressing street gang and whose tumultuous career and messy demise mirror that of the Sex Pistols. Their music influenced many bands, the Ramones, the Clash and Generation X to name just a few. The Dolls set the tone for 1970s' insurrection and embodied all the excesses associated with rock'n'roll. It was the New York Dolls who provided Malcolm McLaren with the blueprint for the Pistols in all but clothing. They were absolutely essential to the formation of punk.

After the break-up of the Dolls in 1975, punk began to exert itself in New York, with a whole host of bands attempting to replace the now-defunct darlings of the city's underground scene. Centred in the club CBGB's, the whole scene kicked off with bands such as Wayne County's Queen Elizabeth, Richard Hell and Tom Verlaine's Television, Patti Smith, the Dead Boys and, most importantly, the Ramones, all of whom played at the club. Alive but yet unchristened, punk was born. Its name was

acquired shortly afterwards, when illustrator John Holmstrom and writer Legs McNeil started Punk Magazine, a fanzine dedicated to the form, and the name stuck.

The phenomenon did not go unnoticed in the UK. By 1975 Malcolm McLaren and Vivienne Westwood had refurbished their shop Let It Rock and renamed it Sex, the name proudly displayed over the shopfront in big pink plastic letters. The interior was covered in chicken wire and foam rubber and sprayed with quotations from the Scottish writer Alexander Trocchi, who can best be described as a cross between William Burroughs and Albert Camus. The shop sold new stock influenced mainly by fetish wear, but continued to sell the '50s-inspired gems for which Let It Rock had become famous. Slowly the old stock disappeared, making way for the bondage-inspired Sex clothing. The silhouette of the as yet unnamed punk emerged.

Using the shop as a base, McLaren, aided by Bernie Rhodes and influenced by the New York Dolls, started to manage and groom a new young group called the Sex Pistols, who would ultimately change the face of British music. On 5 November 1975 at St Martin's School of Art they played to an audience for the first time, with John Lydon (aka Johnny Rotten) as lead vocalist, Glenn Matlock on bass, Steve Jones on guitar and Paul Cook on drums. They played a mixed set, featuring covers of Faces' songs and a characteristically quirky version of 'Stepping Stone' by the Monkees. Although no one knew it at the time, this was the first punk event in the UK. The circus was about to begin.

The Pistols were not the only band with anarchic pretensions. A Paddington-based outfit called London SS, who acquired Bernie Rhodes as a manager after he and McLaren fell out, were to become very important in the history of the movement. Although the band never played live, its members went on to provide the core of London's other pioneering bands. Tony James formed Chelsea and then Generation X, Mick Jones with Rhodes created the Clash, and Brian James formed the Damned. The scene was up and running.

By the end of 1975, the phenomenon was about to explode into the headlines of newspapers on both sides of the Atlantic. In this chapter we look at the decade that led up to it, examine its stormy gestation and witness the birth of that little rapscallion we all know and love – PUNK.

I stayed at the Factory for close on two years. I watched pop die and saw punk being born.

Nat Finkelstein, photographer

The Factory was just one big single room covered in tin foil on West Forty-Seventh Street in Manhattan. It was Warhol's base. Here he painted his pictures, made his movies. All the people that were hip at the time hung out there and they were quite a hardcore bunch that included all kinds of people – gay, straight, transvestite, you name it. All of them seemed to dress in black – you know, leather jackets, black T-shirt, jeans – and they all loved speed. Most of them were gay, of course, full of unabandoned creative zest.
Leee Childers, ex-manager, the Stooges and the Heartbreakers

Andy Warhol's Factory was an attraction for up-and-coming celebrities. Everybody was there – Salvador Dali, Marcel Duchamp the Dadaist, Bob Dylan, every up-and-coming young rock group. It was obligatory for them to visit the Factory.
Nat Finkelstein

Everybody at the Factory thought they were superstars, and many were…in their own wonderful way.
Leee Childers

Left: Andy Warhol at the Factory

Warhol surrounded himself with three types of people – the rich, the beautiful and the talented. It was even better if you were all three. These were people he could use for whatever purpose. That was his talent – he was good at using people. Nat Finkelstein

The existing central group at the Factory was a bunch of older amphetamine queens who hung out at a bar called the San Remo in the Village, as I did with my younger friends, boys and girls, but it was a *de facto* gay bar. Edward Albee [playwright] was there, Andy Warhol was there, Jasper Johns was there…whatever is now cultural artistic started then…it was *the* artistic faggot bar. About 1961, '62 there were some people who went back and forth between Harvard and New York, and somehow, mainly through me and one or two others, the Harvard people would drift into the orbit of the Factory, like Edie Sedgwick, rich, Protestant, amusing…rich was the most important thing of all, fabulous people… I would have parties and have the Warhol people and the Harvard people meet each other. I was sort of B-list at the Factory because my best friends were there. Andy was not my best friend, but I was always OK with him as for some reason he thought I was rich…the most important and vital bunch of brilliant lunatics in New York in the early '60s were all hanging out.
Danny Fields, ex-manager, the Stooges and the Ramones

Andy was Freud. He was the psychoanalyst. There was that big couch in the Factory and Andy was there. He didn't say anything, you could project anything on him, put anything on him…and he wouldn't put you down. Andy was your father and mother and brother, all of them. That's why people felt so well around him – they could be in those films; they could say and do whatever they wanted because they wouldn't be disapproved [of]. That was his genius.
Jonas Mekas in *Please Kill Me*

Warhol was a man of parts, most of them contradictory, which accounts for his nickname 'Drella, composed equally of Dracula and Cinderella.
Gerard Malanga, poet and Warhol confidant, in his *Secret Diaries*

We all knew something was happening. We just felt it.
Andy Warhol in *Popism: The Warhol '60s*

The Factory was like a sort of human zoo.

Nat Finkelstein

Andy seemed to attract all manner of strange people, a mixture you would never find elsewhere, and that's why a lot of people went there. The uptown people went to look at all the downtown drag queens who were so bitchy and outrageous and they in turn went to see all the rich people. Meanwhile, Andy just sat back and watched the circus.
Jim Fourrat, writer and nightclub owner

Warhol attracted all these outcasts: Edie Sedgwick, the poor little rich kid; Nico, the cool, tall sophisticated beauty; Candy Darling and Holly Woodlawn, both outrageous transvestites; Ondine, the incredibly bitchy queen; La Monte Young [the minimalist composer], who got good drugs. The Velvet Underground were there. They sounded like no other group on earth. Danny Fields, who went on to manage the Stooges, was around, as was Valerie Solanis, this nutty lesbo-feminist hooker, who went on to shoot Andy. And there was me. I took photographs and wore a hat…all at the same time.
Nat Finkelstein

The Factory was similar to the shop Sex in London – the transvestites and the queens – though the art was on the T-shirts instead of on canvas. McLaren had the Pistols and Warhol the Velvets. The big difference was that the Factory was first.
Nils Stevenson, Sex Pistols' tour manager, 1976

They were all elitist assholes. If Andy decided you were not part of his gang, he had the cheek to say you were 'excommunicated'. They all lived in their own fantasy world.
Nat Finkelstein

Paul Morrissey had a sign up on the door [of the Factory] that said, 'Absolutely no drugs allowed'. Meanwhile, everybody was shooting up on the staircase. Nobody actually took drugs in the Factory, except Andy, who took Obetrol, those little orange speed pills. He took one a day to paint, because he was a workaholic. That was really his thing. Everybody else shot up on the staircase.
Ronnie Cutrone, painter and Factory assistant, in *Please Kill Me*

Heroin was around. It was really bullshit. They were doing like three per cent heroin and then saying, 'I'm a junkie, I'm a junkie.'
Nat Finkelstein

When we first showed up, we were downer people – pill people who took thorazine and all the barbiturates. Seconal and thorazine were big favourites. You could get thorazine from doctors – someone always had a prescription. It was good pharmaceutical and drugstore stuff. They used to give thorazine to dangerous psychotics – it definitely subdues you. It puts you into a catatonic-like state. I'd wash it down with alcohol and see if I was alive the next morning.
Sterling Morrison of the Velvet Underground in *Please Kill Me*

Drugs destroy the creative process, they ruin relationships, and they kill people. Most of all, they kill the user's ability to reason, to make decisions and to control his destiny.
Jim Fourrat

Basically, nobody had any money except Andy, and he wasn't giving any of it out. It was just gay politics. Warhol was a manipulating son of a bitch, but he was a genius artist.
Nat Finkelstein

Of course, everybody wanted the attention of Andy, and he would just sit there. Everybody was so bitchy and paranoid, especially with all that amphetamine. It was awful. You'd turn your back and you knew they were all talking about you. Each word could go a thousand ways. You'd have to back out facing everyone.
Jayne County, singer, actress and DJ

Opposite, right to left: Andy Warhol, Ingrid Superstar and Gerard Malanga, 1964 • Above, top row: Baby Jane Holzer, Betsey Johnson and friend • Centre, clockwise: Andy Warhol, Paul Morrissey, Gerard Malanga and Lou Reed • Bottom: Factory toilet, 1965

A painting that doesn't shock isn't worth painting. Marcel Duchamp, artist

Marcel Duchamp was a true gentleman. You could push him this way, you could push him that way and he always had a smile on his face because he'd made it. He was Duchamp and these guys wanted to be near to him. He was the first, he was the man behind the Dada and Surrealist movements that all and sundry, and especially Andy, were so enamoured of. He was *the* Marcel Duchamp and he treated everybody with respect.
Nat Finkelstein

Andy Warhol must have been ecstatic when Marcel Duchamp visited the Factory. Duchamp was a leading light in the Dada art movement, which set the tone of cultural subversion within the arts for the whole of the twentieth century. Warhol's veneration of ordinary objects, such as Campbell's soup cans, was just a watered-down rehash of Duchamp's elevation of the common object to high art, the most notable being the urinal

he exhibited signed R. Mutt. Duchamp was the man who disestablished art in the 1920s, grabbing the art world by the neck and shaking it until it emerged with a new set of rules, divorcing it from the purely aesthetic and giving it an almost philosophical role in society. Duchamp visiting the Factory was like God appearing to Moses on Mount Sinai. He gave it a seal of approval that no one else was qualified to do.
Chris Sullivan, author

Duchamp was the first artist to take everyday objects out of their conventional settings and place them in galleries, therefore altering their meaning. Warhol also did this with commercial art, taking a leaf out of Duchamp's book and raising the banal to the level of high art.
Steve Walsh, guitarist, the Flowers of Romance

It has to be said once and for all to art critics, artists, etc. that they need expect nothing from the new surrealist images but disappointment, distaste and repulsion.

Salvador Dali, surrealist artist

Salvador Dali was an absolute wanker. He wanted to meet me, so Andy summoned me to the St Regis (Hotel), where we were supposed to have dinner. We were sitting at the bar waiting for our table and Dali's whispering in Andy's ear. Andy said, 'Guess what Dali would like you to do? He wants to make a living tableau on the ground and wants you to jump out of a plane in a parachute and photograph it from above. I said, 'Well, it seems to be a nice idea. Here's my agent's telephone number. We'll set the rates and see how much it's going to cost.' Gala, Dali's wife, looked up and said, 'But this is Dali.' I said, 'Yeah, and this is Nat Finkelstein. I'm a professional photographer. If I get hurt, I can't earn a living any more. You guys are just going to walk away and leave me. If you want to hire me, you pay me.' Dali was shocked. Andy laughed, and Gala said, 'This is Dali. You must remember this is Dali.' Then they got up and left me with the bill.

Nat Finkelstein

Most teenage would-be artists venerate Dali. When they get to about 20, they realize that he, like Andy Warhol, perfected a certain formula and then basically repeated it until he died. He used the same techniques and references throughout his life, and towards the end employed a group of students to create 'new' Dalis. His work has as much relevance today as Woolworth's wallpaper, probably less, and maybe that was the point. He was also a true skinflint and a total fascist – he supported General Franco right up to his death.
Chris Sullivan

There were many similarities between the Dada and Surrealist camps and the Factory. Both were small groups that held parties, both had a coterie of rich and beautiful followers, both venerated the disposable items that were part of everyday existence. For Duchamp, it was the urinal; for Warhol, it was the Campbell's soup can. Both factions used shock tactics and delighted in the bizarre. They both used poetry as part of their expression. The Factory poetry was set to the music of Lou Reed and the Velvet Underground. The big difference was that the Dadaists were first.
Nils Stevenson

The Factory was basically the decadent, soft underbelly of the upper bourgeoisie.

Nat Finkelstein

EDIE SEDGWICK

Edie wasn't happy with the way her career was progressing with Andy… Of course, she had gotten into amphetamime crystal stuff with me and Ondine and Brigid Polk [Factory members], and that really devastated any possible career… You would stay in your place and get ready for six hours.
Billy Name, Factory manager and photographer, in *Please Kill Me*

Edie was your typical poor little rich girl, spoiled and pampered her whole life. She never needed anything, but was always wanting more attention. She came into the scene, it sucked her up and it bit her in the ass. I must say Edie could always find the best wine in New York City at 1 a.m.
Nat Finkelstein

Before Nico came along, Edie Sedgwick was the face of the Factory. She is the one we all think of. She was the icon and, as such, was almost destined to die young.
Steve Walsh

Edie was born to die from her pleasures. She would have to die from drugs whoever gave them to her.
Nico in *Nico: The Life and Lies of an Icon*

HOLLY WOODLAWN

Holly once said, 'We didn't think we were…women. We didn't want to look like women. We just wanted to get high and get laid.'
Leee Childers

I still speak to Holly. Her life is so dramatic – every day there's some drama, some excruciating episode. I think she likes it that way.
Jayne County

Holly Woodlawn wore anything, and I mean anything. She would steal clothes, or find things in the trash. If she couldn't find anything to wear, she'd get out of bed and wrap a sheet around herself, put on her make-up and go out. She got in a lot of trouble with the welfare. We were all on welfare, but the difference was that she would show up at the welfare office in ostrich feathers, false eyelashes and, of course, the high heels. They took her to one side and said, 'Sir, this is the welfare office and you are turning up in evening gowns and ostrich feathers. The other welfare recipients are getting very upset.' She said, 'Buy me some blue jeans and I'll wear them. Otherwise I'll spend my own money as I please, and I please to spend it on ostrich feathers.'
Leee Childers

GERARD MALANGA

He was one of the originals, a very handsome guy with a great look, all dressed in black leather head to foot. He started out acting in Warhol's version of *A Clockwork Orange*. He used to get on stage with the Velvet Underground and do a dance with the whip that he always carried around with him. I think he might have been arrested for carrying that whip, but I could be wrong.
Gene Krell, Factory figure

Gerard Malanga was a friend and, in every sort of way, he was a gentleman, but he was always trouble.
Nat Finklestein

Jim Morrison [of the Doors] came to see us at the Trip [an LA club] because he was a film student in LA at the time. That's when, as the theory goes, he adopted my look – the black leather pants – from seeing me dancing on stage at the Trip.
Gerard Malanga in *Please Kill Me*

JACKIE CURTIS

Jackie was always speeding her head off…she was a writer, so she'd take speed and then write page after page after page and some of it made absolutely no sense whatsoever. A lot of it was put on stage, yet it still made no sense.
Jayne County

Jackie was in front of the mirror preparing herself. Silver glitter on her eyelids, red glitter on her lips, dyed red hair, old lady's dress, black stockings with holes in them, old lady's orthopaedic shoes spray-painted silver. She laughs loudly, turning to Jayne County and me, and doubles up with laughter. She straightens up and says, 'Haha! One day everyone will look like me.'
Leee Childers

Jackie Curtis was fantastic in *Femme Fatale*. At the end of the play she was crucified to an IBM card [a computer program punchcard]. We had this giant IBM card and we stapled her to it.
Jayne County

Jackie had been working in an underground play and had fallen out with the director, John Vaccaro. Dramatic as ever, she went and threw some of her clothing and stuff into the river and then showed up at my house asking if I could hide her so everyone would think that she'd committed suicide. So I said, 'Sure.' We would still go up to Max's to eat every night, and Holly Woodlawn, who was living with us, decided

that she had to dress in mourning – her version of mourning, because they were the only clothes she had – turkey feather boas, black feathers sprouting out the top of her head and all this black glitter over her face. People would say, 'Holly, what are you dressed like that for?' And she'd say, 'I'm in mourning.'
Leee Childers

CANDY DARLING

Candy was the most beautiful of all the Warhol drag queens, with her blonde hair, snow white skin and ruby red lips. Born Richard Slattery in Long Island, she soon gravitated to Greenwich Village, falling in with the bizarre underground community that was rapidly becoming a major artistic movement. She became friends with Jackie Curtis and they'd panhandle the money to go and sit in darkened movie theatres for hours and hours until they knew the pictures off by heart – every move, affectation and line of dialogue. Candy's favourite movie stars were Kim Novak and Beverley Michaels. She was envied by all the other Village queens, but she'd just say, 'Why must they envy me? I can't help it if I was born beautiful and they weren't.' She became one of Andy's favourites, appeared in the movie *Flesh* and then in *Women in Revolt*. She became a good friend of Jane Fonda and had a small part in *Klute*. She was given a starring role on Broadway by Tennessee Williams in *Small Craft Warnings*. Candy was particularly proud of this part as she was playing a woman…no allusions were ever made to the truth. She was still a man.
Leee Childers

Andy Warhol can make anybody a star.
Candy Darling in the movie *I Shot Andy Warhol*

On New Year's day John Vaccaro, director of the Playhouse of the Ridiculous, kicked Candy down the stairs, right the way down two flights. It was so cold and it was really snowing – the snow was about three feet thick and there was a blizzard, and he kicked her right out into the snow in her evening gown. The next day I'm sure she went back as if nothing had happened. She just lived for drama. I loved her.
Leee Childers

The Factory was a gay, male-dominated society. The women were there to be used. No girls ever hung around for very long. The boys were real and touchable… Andy never touched the girls.
Nat Finkelstein

Opposite (main picture): Gerard Malanga, Danny Williams, Ingrid Superstar, Andy Warhol; • (small pictures): Jackie Curtis; Edie Sedgwick; Holly Woodlawn

Punk as a concept began with the Beat poets. William Burroughs has been called the grandfather of punk.

Jim Fourrat

The hipster bebop junkies never showed at 103rd Street. The 103rd Street boys were all old timers – thin, sallow faces; bitter, twisted mouths; stiff-fingered, stylized gestures. (There is a junk gesture that marks the junkie like the limp wrist marks the fag: the hand swings out from the elbow palm up.) They were of various nationalities and physical types but they all looked alike somehow. They all looked like junk. There was Irish, George the Greek, Pantopon Rose, Louie the Bellhop, Eric the Fag, the Beagle, the Sailor, and Jor the Mex. Several of them are dead now, and others are doing time.
Excerpt from *Junkie* by William Burroughs

Richard Hell, Debbie Harry, they all read Allen Ginsberg, William Burroughs and Jack Kerouac. From them they learned a certain style and attitude. I read an article about the last days of Allen Ginsberg. His doctor had told him that he had terminal cancer and had about three months left to live. So Allen would call up people and say, 'Hi, I'm dying. Do you need any money?' How cool!
Leee Childers

Lou Reed always had a certain Beat sensibility. In many ways he took what Burroughs and Ginsberg had done, added his own unique edge and put it to music. He was a great songwriter.
Chris Sullivan

I thought a punk was someone who took it up the ass.
William Burroughs in *Please Kill Me*

Left: Gerard Malanga, Allen Ginsberg and Timothy Leary at an East Village Other Benefit Party, 1965 • Overleaf: Lou Reed in front of a projected image of Nico at the Dom, 1966

It has been said that everyone who listened to the Velvet Underground started a band... I know I did.

Steve Severin, bass player, Siouxsie and the Banshees

I think it started with the Velvets,
the whole thing, in about 1965.
No one was writing about real experiences —
the Velvets did. Legs McNeil, writer on *Punk Magazine*

Our favourite quote [about the Velvets] was: 'The flowers
of evil are in bloom. Someone has to stamp them out before they spread.'
Lou Reed

They got their name from the title of a cheap paperback that they found literally in the gutter.
It was called *The Velvet Underground* and was all about suburban sex. Great name…
Nat Finkelstein

Mo Tucker went to Lou Reed and John Cale's apartment in Ludlow Street on the lower East
Side and was totally impressed. She had a limited repertoire, which aided the Velvets no end.
Chris Sullivan

Mo Tucker was just fabulous. She'd stand there with these mallets and these big drums,
and no one knew whether she was male or female.
Leee Childers

Eventually we found some more [garbage cans] and took them back, stood them
onstage, and put some mikes under them. That's what I played for a week or so. The
audience loved it. At the end of every night we'd have to clean up the little piles of
garbage that got loose during the set. One of the reviewers called it 'garbage music'.
Maureen Tucker in *Uptight: The Story of the Velvet Underground*

No chicks in the band.
No chicks.

John Cale in *Lou Reed: The Biography*

Mo Tucker was super-cool, androgynous and really ahead of her time. She could very
well have been a man. It was no secret she was a dyke. It was so cool having her as a
drummer…Andy had to sign the band .He got them a place to stay, managed them,
which was both a help and a hindrance. The Warhol thing scared a lot of people.
Jayne County

Sterling Morrison just kinda stood there looking awkward and tall.
Leee Childers

Al Aronowitz was managing them. He was old-school music business – had a lot of contacts.
He put them on at some high school in Jersey, and then got them a residency at an ice-
cream parlour in Greenwich Village called Café Bizarre. Then Barbara Rubin brought the
Warhol crowd down and Andy took them on. They went for Andy because he was famous
and they wanted to be famous too.
Nat Finkelstein

I gave the Velvet Underground their first gig. I put them on as the opening act at the Summit High School in New Jersey and they stole my wallet-sized tape recorder first thing. They were junkies, crooks, hustlers; most of the musicians came with high-minded ideals, but they were all full of shit… But I'd committed myself. So I put them into the Café Bizarre and I said, 'You work here and you'll get some exposure, build up your chops, and get it together.'
Al Aronowitz in *Please Kill Me*

The story goes that Gerard Malanga, seized by the moment, dived onto the empty dance floor and started to perform this rather slow, oscillating cobra-like dance, liberally cracking his whip as he went. Apparently, the band were rather taken by this and invited him to come back next time. Malanga, seeing the opportunity, thought that the Velvets would be the perfect band for Warhol.
Stephen Colegrave, author

Malanga's dance was a set-up. Andy loved it. Paul Morrisey asked Lou if he had a manager. Lou said, 'Maybe, yes – oh…well, no' and in true rock'n'roll tradition, Aronowitz was ditched.
Nat Finkelstein

I didn't discover the Velvet Underground; Gerard Malanga did. He found them in a club in the West Village, brought them to the Factory and they became the Factory band. I fell in love with Lou and I fell in love with their music.
Danny Fields

What really happened was that I had this idea that Andy could make money not from underground films but from putting the movies in some sort of rock'n'roll context. Discovering the Velvets, bringing them up to the Factory and working with them was done purely for commercial reasons.
Paul Morrissey in *Uptight: The Story of the Velvet Underground*

The band needed Nico. Lou was a terrible front man: he just stood there and the rest played their instruments. Nico stood there and was beautiful against this drone of noise. Of course, Lou didn't want her. He fought against it all the way, but she made the group.
Nat Finkelstein

Nico was Andy Warhol's idea, but who else could have sung 'All Tomorrow's Parties' or 'Chelsea Girl'? They're classics.
Steve Severin

The Velvets hated everything.
The whole idea was to take a stab

We had no idea what Nico would bring to the band. It was just something Andy came up with and it was very difficult to accept.

John Cale in *Lou Reed: The Biography*

Nico was interested in nothing. Actually, that's not true – she was interested in heroin. She told me that it was her reason for getting up in the day, which was kind of sad because in many respects she was a very kind person. She just lived with this constant cloud over her. She was also an incredibly violent person. She broke my nose.
Gene Krell, Nico's husband

As far as I'm concerned Nico was the shining star in the Velvet Underground. When they came back to do gigs without her, people really missed Nico. I remember one night seeing the Velvet Underground upstairs at Max's with no Nico and someone in the audience started shouting, 'We want Nico, we want Nico.' Lou was not amused – not amused at all.
Jayne County

[Nico] was a schmuck from the first. She was this beautiful person who had travelled through Europe being a semi-star. Her ego had grown very large.
Maureen Tucker in *Lou Reed: The Biography*

Nico called me up at 2.a.m. She said, 'Nat, I need to see you…I must see you' – you know, in that voice. So I went all the way across town and she said, 'Nat, I much prefer the smell of women to men…' Man, what a prick teaser!
Nat Finkelstein

She's 23 and she's got a very, very cute German accent.
Ingrid Superstar, Factory figure

Nico hooked up with the Velvet Underground and the rest is history, but prior to that Nico had already had a past of her own. She was no fool and she was amazingly hip. She'd been a top model in Paris, and she'd had affairs with Bob Dylan and Brian Jones [of the Rolling Stones]. She had a son, Ari, by Alain Delon, then the biggest and hippest star in France. She'd also had a part in Fellini's *La Dolce Vita*. She was quite a catch for the band.
Gene Krell

Nico was a real person. She was the only one who wasn't sucking up to people. She was a complete human being. She was polite and nice to everybody, and she didn't kiss ass like the rest of them.
Nat Finkelstein

Nico was tall, blonde, a northern European goddess. She was amazingly stylish, she would wear either a black or white pants suit. Everybody thought she was just gorgeous. And of course there was the voice.

Danny Fields

Opposite: Nico • Above, left to right: Gerard Malanga, Mary Woronov, Andy Warhol, Sterling Morrison, Mo Tucker, Lou Reed, John Cale

35

Honey, I'm a cocksucker. What are you?

Lou Reed in *Intransit: The Andy Warhol–Gerard Malanga Monster Issue*

I was terrified of Lou. I was always trying to think of things to say to him that would be sharp. Everybody was in love with him. He was the sexiest boy in town.
Danny Fields in *Lou Reed: The Biography*

Lou was very full of himself and faggy in those days. We called him Lulu, and I was Black Jack. Lou wanted to be queen bitch and spit out the sharpest rebukes of anyone around. Lou always ran with the pack, and the Factory was full of queens to run with.
John Cale in *Nico: The Life and Lies of an Icon*

I loved Lou Reed but he could be very nasty. We all loved him. He was so sexy in those days.
Danny Fields

Andy was grooming Lou to be a star and Lou wanted it. They wanted to make as much money as possible. If they could have, they would have made films like *Lou Reed in Hawaii, Lou in the Navy* – you know, like Elvis.
Nat Finkelstein

Our music's for the pretty people – all the beautiful people.
Lou Reed

We were playing together a long time ago, in a $30 a month apartment, and we really didn't have any money. We used to eat oatmeal all day and all night and give blood, among other things, or pose for these nickel or 15 cent tabloids… When I posed for them, my picture came out and the caption said I was a sex maniac that had killed 14 children and tape-recorded it and played it in a barn in Kansas at midnight. And when John's picture came out in the paper, it said he had killed his lover because his lover was going to marry his sister and he didn't want his sister to marry a fag.
Lou Reed

Lou Reed was a nasty, nasty person but he's been okay with me recently. He does write great songs. Back then there were all these bands singing about flowers and beads and love and grooving, but Lou was singing about black boots and people being beaten by whips and shooting heroin. They were going totally against the grain.
Jayne County

Hey, don't be afraid. You'd better take drugs and learn to love PLASTIC. All different kinds of plastic – pliable, rigid, colored, colorful, nonattached plastic.
Lou Reed in *Intransit: The Andy Warhol–Gerard Malanga Monster Issue*

Lou tried to put the make on me once. It didn't go anywhere.
Gerard Malanga in *Lou Reed: The Biography*

John Cale can't make his mind up whether he wants to be Frankenstein, Elvis Presley or Chopin.
Nat Finkelstein

I use cracks on the sidewalk to walk down the street. I'd always walk on the lines. I never take anything but a calculated risk, and do it because it gives me a sense of identity. Fear is a man's best friend.
John Cale in *Lou Reed: The Biography*

John Cale is a fucking elitist. He did not like the people he was playing for. He's Welsh, and they're all nasty bastards.
Nat Finkelstein

John Cale? Good grief! I couldn't begin to describe him. He's just funny-looking… He looks like the devil.
Ingrid Superstar

John Cale is from Aberdare in Wales and went to the local grammar school. It's a hard, rough and surprisingly violent place, where huge bar brawls and street fights are considered normal. To grow up as the son of a teacher, play the cello and then be a child prodigy must have been hard work for Cale, and no mistake.
Chris Sullivan

John Cale is fantastic, and he made the sound of the Velvet Underground.
Jayne County

I liked him personally, and we got up to all kinds of adventures. I remember once I hid his whole band at our flat in Oakley Street, London. It was when the weird rumours were going round that he was biting the heads off chickens and things like that. He did do something on stage, but I can't remember what it was. In any case, his band were all vegetarians. They showed up at my flat in the middle of the night and said, 'Can you hide us from John? We've left the band, we're hiding out.' So I took them in and hid them. He came to the house and looked in through the window, but the band were all huddled behind a column on the other side of the living-room so he couldn't see them. He knocked at the door. I answered and told him, 'They're not here and we're all asleep.' He knew they were there. 'Let me in,' he said. 'No,' I said. He laughed about it later.
Leee Childers

John Cale gave the Velvet Underground that strange, romantic sound. Without John Cale there would be no edge. The sound of the Velvet Underground was Cale.
Stephen Colegrave

I was staying at the Tropicana Hotel in Hollywood. One day we heard all this noise. We looked across the parking lot to the other side where the noise was coming from and suddenly the whole door of this room came flying out onto the balcony, and there stood John Cale. He couldn't work the doorknob, so he just knocked the door down, right off the hinges.
Leee Childers

John Cale, as far as the British punk is concerned, is very important. He produced the first Stooges' album, the Modern Lovers' first album with 'Roadrunner' on it, and Patti Smith's first album *Horses*. These were very influential.
Marco Pirroni, guitarist, Siouxsie and the Banshees

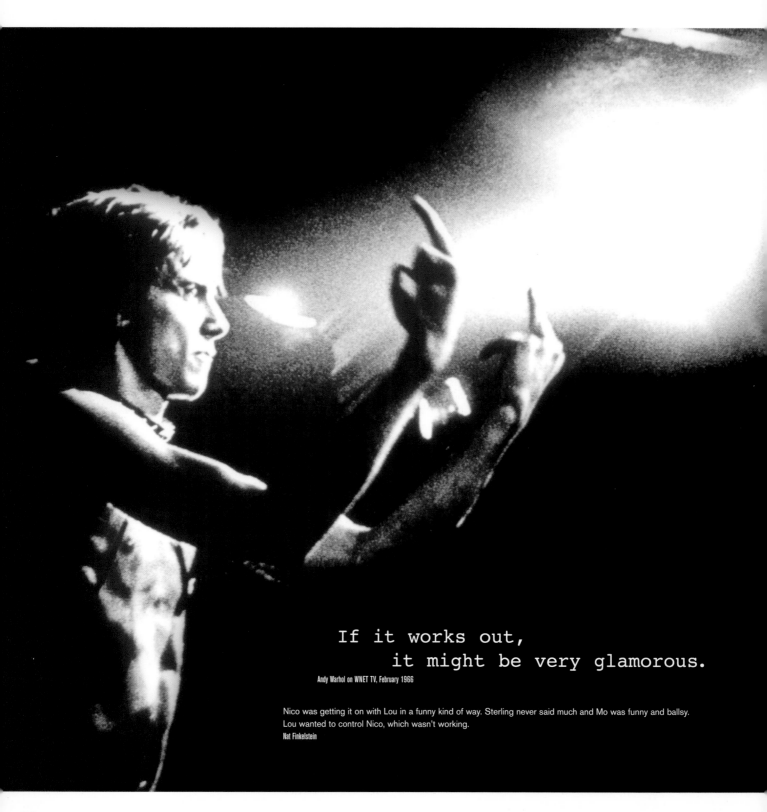

If it works out,
    it might be very glamorous.

Andy Warhol on WNET TV, February 1966

Nico was getting it on with Lou in a funny kind of way. Sterling never said much and Mo was funny and ballsy.
Lou wanted to control Nico, which wasn't working.
Nat Finkelstein

Above: Iggy Pop on stage • Opposite: Nico

Anybody who made love to our music wouldn't necessarily need a partner.
Lou Reed

In March we left for Ann Arbor and the University of Michigan… Ann Arbor was crazy.
          At least the Velvets were a smash. I'd sit on the steps in the lobby during intermissions and people from the local papers would interview me, ask about my movies, what we were trying to do. 'If they can take it for 10 minutes, then we play it for 15,' I'd explain. 'That's our policy – always leave them wanting less.'
Andy Warhol in *Lou Reed: The Biography*

Ann Arbor was very important. Iggy Pop was there. That's how he came in contact with the Velvets. They also had a big effect on Wayne Kramer of the MC5, who were also there. You could say everything came from the Velvets.
Nat Finkelstein

I didn't like
that peace and love shit.
Maureen Tucker in *Please Kill Me*

Flouncing out of the club on the first night, a terrified Cher snapped that the music would replace nothing, except suicide.
Victor Bockris, *Lou Reed: The Biography*

The Velvet Underground were into hard drugs, but the West Coast preferred soft.
Nat Finkelstein

I love LA. I love Hollywood. They're beautiful. Everybody's plastic – but I love plastic. I want to be plastic.
Andy Warhol in *Uptight: The Story of the Velvet Underground*

The Velvet Underground hated hippies… They didn't want to go to California, but they did make the album there.
Nat Finkelstein

This shoe salesman [called] Dolph put up the money [to make a record, *The Velvet Underground and Nico*]…and he got a deal at Cameo-Parkway Studios… We went in there, and the floorboards were torn up, the walls were out, there were four mikes working. We set up the drums where there was enough floor [space], turned it all up and went from there.
John Cale in *Lou Reed: The Biography*

I think Andy was interested in shocking, in giving people a jolt and not letting them talk us into making compromises. He said, 'Oh, you've got to make sure you leave all the dirty words in.' He was adamant about that.
Lou Reed in *The Velvet Underground*

Lou was starting to act funny. He brought in this real snake, Steve Sesnick, to be our manager, and all this intrigue started to take place.
John Cale in *Please Kill Me*

Before the Velvet Underground split from Andy there was all this talk about Lou going behind his back to find another manager.
Jayne County

I don't think Andy had much to do with Lou after the split. He was polite, as always, but he was…well…excommunicated.
Jim Fourrat

Nico apparently walked in one day and said, 'I cannot make love to Jews any more,' referring to Lou Reed. Shortly after that she left the band and had an affair with Iggy Pop.
Chris Sullivan

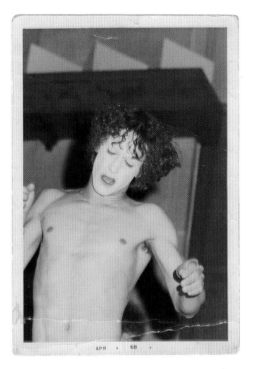

RAW POWER. Second album by Iggy and the Stooges

The first time I heard *The Velvet Underground and Nico* was at a party on the University of Michigan campus. I just hated the sound. You know, 'How could anybody make a record that sounds like such a piece of shit? This is disgusting! All these people make me fucking sick! Fucking disgusting hippy vermin! Fucking beatniks! I wanna kill them all! This just sounds like trash!' Then, about six months later, it hit me. 'Oh, my God! Wow! This is just a great fucking record!' That record became very key for me, not just for what [it was], and for how great it was, but also because I heard other people who could make good music without being good at music. It gave me hope.
Iggy Pop in *Please Kill Me*

In '68 I went to Detroit and saw the Stooges and the MC5. Elektra Records was just starting out. I had the ear of the company president, so I called him up and said, 'I just saw two great bands. One of them is very popular – they draw two to three thousand people. The other one is a baby band, but they're really great. They've got a wonderful, primitive sound and an incredible front man. The company president said, 'I'll tell you what. I don't want to phone the two managers at home.' Tell them I offer the big band $20,000 and the little band $5,000.' It was more money than the bands had ever heard of, and in 1968 it was worth eight or 10 times what it is today. The first MC5 album was then recorded in September 1968.
Danny Fields

Danny Fields and I went to see the MC5 in Detroit…the opening act was the Stooges and I fell in love with them.
John Cale in *The Velvet Underground*

I took John Cale to see the MC5, but he was more impressed by the Stooges, and wanted to produce them, which was fine. When Nico said she wanted to go along, I should have seen it coming. I mean, she and Iggy were so totally opposite, so different, yet perfectly suited… I'm sure he satisfied her. She loved the brilliant, the insane and the addicted – it was perfect. I just thought, 'Ho hum, another day, another poet,' but Iggy and Nico became a big deal.
Danny Fields

Whoever came up with the idea that John Cale should produce the Stooges was a genius, and whoever came up with the idea of Iggy and Nico was insane.
Leee Childers

Of course we all loved the Stooges and the Velvets. At the time we had no idea of who slept with whom and who produced what; we just got on with listening to the records. When we discovered this intricate web of incest that bound together all our favourite music we thought, 'Fuck, now I get it…now it makes sense.
Nils Stevenson

Opposite, top: Iggy Pop's childhood bedroom • Opposite, bottom: Montage of Iggy Pop's childhood home. • Above: Early photos of Iggy Pop

41

KICK OUT THE JAMS

MC5 album title

The MC5 supported the Velvet Underground at the Boston Tea Party 1968, watched by Bostonian Jonathan Richman. John Cale had left, Nico had left and there was a near-riot involving a politically motivated bunch of mad bastards called the East Village Motherfuckers: SNAFU – Situation Normal All Fucked Up – for the MC5.
Chris Sullivan

The MC5 were very influential in London. When we started the Pistols, apart from the English stuff like the Faces, the MC5, Jonathan Richman, the New York Dolls and the Stooges were all we listened to. *Kick Out the Jams* was massive with us.
Glen Matlock, bass player, the Sex Pistols

The Motor City Five, or the MC5 as they came to be known, were more than a band. They were a totally mad concept. They were the 'house' band for a political organization by the name of the White Panthers. MC5 were managed by the radical left-wing poet John Sinclair, who founded the White Panther Party. The WPP lived in a commune within a fraternity house on the Michigan University Campus in Ann Arbor, and had all the trappings of a political party, including their own ministers and cultural attachés. In essence, the party was a bunch of hippies, and the MC5 were a motley crew of youthful hustlers who got involved because they saw money in the hippy scene. By all accounts, they had a whale of a time. In the words of Wayne Kramer, the band's leader, 'We were sexist bastards. We were not politically correct at all.'
Chris Sullivan

I just loved the MC5. In fact, I loved all the Detroit bands so much that I named myself Wayne County after Wayne County, Michigan, which, as you may or may not know, has a very famous women's prison.
Jayne County

Chicago was in chaos after the famous riots at the Democratic Convention. The MC5 were the only band to play there, and now it's part of their legend. This was one of the things that made them so glamorous. The riots were one of the biggest political events of the '60s. It did not have much to do with them, but it was an event and they glamorized it.
Danny Fields

They [MC5] were the official band of the White Panthers. I was interviewed once by a college kid, who was asking me about the White Panthers. He was under the impression that they were a racist white power group. People, in the main, don't understand that they were a parody of the radical groups at the time because their political platform included not wearing any underwear and fucking in the streets. It was crazy.
John Holmstrom, editor, *Punk Magazine*

We were trying to be a show band [and] had all these spangly clothes and sequins. …the Velvets were plain-looking.
Wayne Kramer of MC5 in *Uptight: The Story of the Velvet Underground*

I first met John Sinclair and the MC5 in the autumn of 1968. They picked me up at the airport, and we went to their headquarters in this wonderful big mansion at 1510 Hill Street, Ann Arbor. It was a fraternity house – all the students had their own bedrooms and there was a common area downstairs. The White Panthers managed to get two neighbouring big old houses. John Sinclair had the master bedroom, while the basement had printing presses and served as a darkroom and a studio where artists worked and the band rehearsed. The Panthers had their own 'politicians' – a minister of defence, a minister for culture… The Black Panthers came to visit to give talks and things. It was like a sort of Viking commune. You had all the hippy liberal stuff – equality, revolution, liberation – but then you had all these women in long dresses cooking up great big meals of meat for the men. They didn't eat together. The men were in one room and the women in the other, seen and not heard.
Danny Fields

We were telling people at our shows to smoke reefers, to burn their bras, to fuck in the streets.
Wayne Kramer in *Please Kill Me*

The MC5 were not political radicals, and nor were the kids of the people who worked in the car factories, though they were politically motivated. Robin Tyner [of MC5] was the most educated and middle class of them all, and he was indoctrinated by Sinclair, whose parents were also professionals. The leaders of the '60s radicals…were all rich kids. They were rebelling against their parents by being anarchists and communists.
Danny Fields

I was the White Panthers' minister of culture for New York. It was a political time, and there was something very erotic, very beautiful and very moving about the Black Panther Party… I went to meet with Bobby Seale [founder of the Black Panthers]. It was really quite serious, and this is something most people at Max's Kansas City were not.
Jim Fourrat

Ironically, the day I saw the MC5 and got so excited about them, Wayne Kramer [of MC5] said to me, 'If you like us, you'd really like our baby brother band, the Stooges.' They were playing that weekend at the Student Union. It only takes me a few seconds to know if I like what I'm hearing and seeing, and they sounded great.
Danny Fields

Wayne Kramer of the MC5 was caught in possession of five or six ounces of 88 per cent cocaine. He was dealing and got busted by the Feds. He was in for about four years from '75 to '79 and missed out on the whole scene. When he got out, he started playing with Johnny Thunders. He's the real thing, man.
Legs McNeil

'I Wanna Be Your Dog'

Song by Iggy Pop and the Stooges

The Stooges were wonderful. 'I Wanna Be Your Dog' became the standard song of a new generation. Bands would audition a new member and they would say they were going to do 'I Wanna Be Your Dog'. They would assume that everybody knew it. The song has just one hypnotic melodic riff that is repeated over and over, and the lyrics are just wonderful. I think when the Sex Pistols started, it was the only song they knew how to play.

Danny Fields

We invented some instruments that we used that first show. We had a blender with a little bit of water in it and put a mike right down onto it and just turned it on. We played that for like 15 minutes before we went on stage. It was a great sound, especially going through the PA all cranked up. Then we had a washboard with contact mikes [and] Iggy would put on golf shoes and…kind of shuffle around.

Ron Asheton of the Stooges in *Please Kill Me*

You know, if I had never been into music, I'd have liked to be a professional golfer.

Iggy Pop, *Melody Maker*, 1973

I was close to Ron Asheton. He was friendlier than his brother Scott, who was always scary and mysterious to me. Scott was the drummer and Ron was like, 'Let me show you my collection of Nazi overcoats.' I was independent. I don't think he believed in the Nazi philosophy per se, but he thought their artefacts were very stylish, which they are. There was a bond between us, and I became the Stooges' manager when their manager retired. It was difficult because I lived in New York and they lived in Detroit. The radio refused to play their records and the promoters wouldn't book them. That's why all of their dates are really remembered – they didn't occur that often. They had a record company, but the record company saw that the stuff wasn't getting played on the radio, so they dropped them.

Danny Fields

There are things I don't remember. I used to reach blackout point really easily and still be walking around. I'd wake up with bumps on the head, blood on my shirt and green coming out of my penis.

Iggy Pop, the *Guardian*, 1996

I don't think I ever heard the Stooges on the radio in America. It was all shit music by bands like Bachmann-Turner Overdrive or a 14-minute opus on the existential power of the mushroom by Tonto's Expanding Head Band.

Paul Durden, former Jeff Beck roadie, now scriptwriter

I think I am a little different upstairs, yeah…but so are a lot of people.

Iggy Pop, *Sounds* magazine, 1986

We put on a concert in New York, at the 1964 World's Fair, with MC5, the Stooges and another one of my signings for Elektra Records. The promoter's wife said Iggy was so

shocking that she miscarried during his performance. The promoter got on the phone and said, 'Watch out for this band called the Stooges. They cause the death of unborn babies.' After that they were blackballed. The same thing happened years later to the Ramones, who were tarnished by association with the Sex Pistols. Everybody thought the Sex Pistols would vomit on you, stab the Queen with safety-pins and that sort of thing. The Ramones were seen as a parallel phenomenon in the USA and considered dangerous. The same with the Stooges – no one would touch them until they became popular.

Danny Fields

I know it for a fact that if anyone is going to be next to go, it'll be me. I'm not afraid to die.

Iggy Pop in *Iggy Pop*

I almost saw the Stooges at St Mark's Place [New York] in 1971 when I was on tour with Jeff Beck. We waited for ever and, in the end, we left before they came on. I heard afterwards that they did play and the reason for their late performance was that Iggy had locked himself in the toilet and wouldn't come out. Apparently, he couldn't find a vein to shoot his heroin into and wouldn't go on until he did. When he did come on, he apparently threw up all over the stage. I wished I'd stayed.

Paul Durden

At one point I'd had enough. They were just too far gone, especially Iggy. He's a brilliant artist and a fantastic performer, but he was getting too stoned. They became too hard to manage. In fact, it became impossible. I went on to get a real job at *Sixteen Magazine* and, as a result, met and managed the Ramones.

Danny Fields

The music drives me into a peak freak. I can't feel any pain or realize what goes on around me, and when I dive into the sea of people, it is the feeling of the music, the mood.

Iggy Pop, *Rolling Stone*, 1970

We were big Stooges' fans. When I first heard the Stooges, I thought they were some avant-garde version of the Rolling Stones. It was like some cubic form of the Stones. I thought their music was fantastic. I just loved it.

Tommy Ramone

I can do a very nice steak *provençale*, using a little sage.

Iggy Pop, *Q* magazine, 1996

Opposite: The Stooges (James Williamson, Iggy Pop, Ron Asheton, Scott Asheton)

Max's **Kansas City**

was at the intersection of everything.

William Burroughs in *High on Rebellion*

Of course there was the time when Iggy rolled all over the floor and cut himself to pieces in Max's. Apparently, Jackie Curtis was shouting 'I want to see blood tonight,' but I don't remember that.
Leee Childers

Andrea ['Whips' Feldman, New York socialite] growled in her deep, demonic rasp, her beautiful wobbly legs straddling the huge bowl of salad in the middle of the table. It's 'showtime!' And she began to strip. This was New York in the '60s. This was 'the backroom' of Max's Kansas City, the melting pot of New York's pop and avant-garde elite. This was Andy Warhol's neighborhood bar.
Cherry Vanilla, singer, in *High on Rebellion*

You weren't being angry and bold in the back of Max's Kansas City – you were getting blow jobs and trying to be fabulous. I remember we used to have to guess who or what was giving us a blow job under the table.
Jim Fourrat

Max's was *the* place. Everybody went there, even Robert Kennedy.
Jayne County

I first went to Max's in 1965. It was a bar created in a neighbourhood of insurance companies that didn't exist after the nine to five working day ended. Now you can just walk over to Park Avenue South and it's booming with trendy restaurants, bars and stores, but then there was nothing; it was dead. It couldn't have been in a more convenient location, so it was very smart of Mickey Ruskin to open Max's. Mickey had mainly been involved with artists' bars, like Stanley's, Avenue B and the Night Circle (before it was a gay bar). His artist friends were the first customers, then, with the artists, came the poets. Then painters and sculptors started to go there, along with some underground fashion designers. I brought the music people in. The Warhol people came because the Factory had moved from 47th Street to just across Union Square, which was just about a block away from Max's. With Warhol's presence it was immediately ambisexual. The waitresses were all beautiful – Debbie Harry was a waitress there. The bus boys were beautiful; Mickey knew they would keep the faggots like me interested. We called the bus boys 'Phoebes'. Another group we called the skinnies: they were thin and pale and dressed all in black.
Danny Fields

You never knew who would turn up at Max's. Today the New York scene is just too scattered and too weird. In those days, you went along to Max's…whoever was with you, and that fluctuated from night to night. Sometimes it would be underground actors, sometimes it would be poets, sometimes it would be writers, sometimes it would be famous people; most of the time it would be influential people. Something outrageous would always happen there. I remember seeing Nico hit a man over the head with a champagne bottle. Champagne bottles, unlike the ones in the movies, don't break, they just knock you out. Andrea 'Whips' Feldman would get up on the table and take all her clothes off and it would be 'showtime'. There'd be constant sex in the telephone booths – it was a totally outrageous place. In some ways, though, it was an innocent time. Brigid Polk would fill up a hypodermic needle and wait for you. You'd walk past the round table and the next thing you knew, she'd stabbed you and you were on speed.
Leee Childers

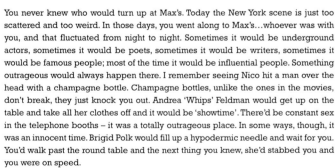

Max's was the exact spot where Pop art and Pop life came together in the '60s.

Andy Warhol in *High on Rebellion*

My places have always been my living-room, and every night I throw a party. But at Max's it went from being just an ordinary little salon, and turned into magic.
Mickey Ruskin, owner, Max's Kansas City, in *High on Rebellion*

At the door was Dorothy Dean, a short, ferocious-looking black woman, who considered herself a faggot trapped in the body of a woman. She had gone to Radcliffe and was a bridesmaid at Nelson Rockefeller's wedding. She was in that crowd. She had almost no black friends, unless they were criminals or something. Once, a black guy at the bar was causing a problem. Dorothy was sent to deal with him. She said, 'So who are you?' and he said, 'Yo sister, black is beautiful!' She said, 'Don't call me Yo. I am not your sister and black is not beautiful, it's pathetic.' She sat at the door and she'd give you a look. You either belonged or you didn't, and it was quite enough.

Patti Smith and [photographer] Robert Mapplethorpe heard about Max's and started going there. The underground theatre people, the Playhouse of the Ridiculous, were there. When the Cockettes came to New York, that's where they hung out. Drag queens went there. As long as someone there knew you and you could behave yourself, it didn't matter who you were. Everybody was connected. Bobby Kennedy would go there to see what was happening. He knew he wouldn't be mobbed or attacked by reporters. It was downtown and it was cool.
Danny Fields

Around the time of Max's Kansas City and the Factory there were three doctors in New York, who were called the Vitamin Doctors. Robert Kennedy was known to go to one of them. I was in a Broadway play with a famous actress named Jean Arthur, and I became the Vitamin Doctors' client. You got vitamin 1, vitamin 2, vitamin 3 and vitamin B4; speed was an extra.
Jim Fourrat

Towards the end of Mickey's era cocaine was just starting to show up in Max's. MDA and poppers were the latest thing, but heroin was still very much taboo. People we knew had started to die – Janis Joplin, Jimi Hendrix, Edie Sedgwick – all drink and drug-related deaths. The old 'turn on and trip out' attitude had lost its innocence. No one was cutting back at all on their intake. Everyone was still having a good time, but some did see that Warhol's era was passing and that things would change.
Yvonne Sewall-Ruskin

One year Andrea 'Whips' Feldman had her birthday party at Max's and arrived wearing a stunning black and white dress that Cecil Beaton had designed for 'My Fair Lady'. In no time at all, she had taken it off and was on the table naked, shoving the necks of champagne bottles up her vagina and then serving her giggling guests from them.

Leee Childers

Opposite, clockwise from top left: Holly Woodlawn and friend; Candy Darling; Via Valentina; dancing at Max's; Alice Cooper • Above: Alice Cooper and David Cassidy at Max's

Max's was like one of the lower circles of Dante's Inferno filled with Bosch and Brueghel characters.

Terry Southern, writer, in *High on Rebellion*

In Max's I played the music I wanted to hear and, luckily, that was what everybody else wanted as well. The crowd varied, but on any one night you could see Iggy, Bowie, Jane Fonda, Warhol, Gram Parsons, Emmy Lou Harris, Willem de Kooning, Roy Lichtenstein, René Ricard, Mick Jagger, Taylor Mead, Gregory Corso, Lou Reed, just about everybody. It really was fantastic. Jayne County **Jayne has always known her music. She'd play the Hullabaloos, the Searchers, Count Five and all sorts of great music. She loves so many different kinds of music, but she hates requests. There's a famous time at Max's when this girl kept nagging her to play James Brown. Jayne just loves James Brown, but the girl kept nagging. Finally, Jayne got out this James Brown LP and said, 'Is this who you mean? Is this it? Is this James Brown?' The girl says, 'Yeah, that's a good album. Play something from that.' Jayne went 'crack!' and smashed it over her knee into thousands of little pieces.** Leee Childers My policy at Max's when I DJ'd was if it rocked, I'd play it. I'd play Velvet Underground, the Seeds, Strawberry Alarm Clock, the Nuggets, the Castaways. I'd play a lot of '60s garage psychedelic, Count Five, Psychotic Reaction and then later on, when the glam thing happened, I was the first one to play the Dolls 'Acetate'. I played it to death. Later on I was the first person in America to play 'Anarchy in the UK' and records by the Damned. DeeDee Ramone got very upset, screaming at me, 'Why are you playing these English bands? They're ripping us off.' Jayne County **Only looking back can one see how the glitter that had once looked so blithe and beguiling on Jackie Curtis (and others)…was beginning to look rather common and clichéd on the new glitter rockers. A lot of it had to do with drugs. Glitter looks so rich and magical when seen through psychedelic eyes, but becomes so gritty and garish when one is high on opiates or cocaine.** Yvonne Sewall-Ruskin, *High on Rebellion* Everyone knew the age of innocence was dying, and everyone was about to give it its last hurrah. It was a divine inspiration which could not go on for ever, for soon the very air of it would be gone. Cherry Vanilla in *High on Rebellion* **Of course it all changed when Tommy Dean took over Max's. He did it to make money, whereas Mickey did it for fun. Tommy just didn't have what it takes for that kind of bar. Then Peter Crowley walked in and said to Tommy, 'This place stinks, but I can make you a lot of money. Get rid of the stained glass, the waitresses in the bow-ties and let's do rock'n'roll here.' Peter started a tradition of bands playing at Max's and other bands coming down to hang out. We were all swept along with the flow. This was really the beginning of punk.** Leee Childers

The Theatre of the Ridiculous was an extremely camp, downtown theatre group led by this director John Vaccaro. They took show tunes and changed the lyrics from the banal to the offensive, and they were very effective.

Jim Fourrat

The Theatre of the Ridiculous was great. When I think back, a lot of it was so innocent compared to what goes on now. The people were just outrageous cartoon characters on stage. There was a lot of simulated sex, which didn't involve any nudity at all, just a lot of bumping people from behind and stuff like that. There were a lot of wild faces and wonderful songs like 'He's Got the Biggest Balls in Town'. The shows were nearly always musicals and they were amazing.
Leee Childers

Leee started getting more and more involved in the underground arts scene, and he took me along to see the shows and meet the people. He was always much better at making friends than I was, and he was always ready to try something new. He was also totally obsessed with Andy Warhol, and he knew the Theatre of the Ridiculous stuff. He took me to see my first Ridiculous play, which Jackie Curtis was in: *The Life of Lady Godiva*, directed by John Vaccaro, written by Warhol's screenwriter Ronnie Tavel and starring Ruby Lynn Reiner, another big underground star. Vaccaro was the founder of the Theatre of the Ridiculous. Charles Ludlam [the playwright], who became a lot more famous, started out with Vaccaro. Jackie had to come out and sing hymns, while Ruby, as Lady Godiva, had sex with a wooden horse. I was completely in shock. I didn't know whether to laugh or scream. I was never the same after seeing *The Life of Lady Godiva*. It really clicked with me.
Jayne County

We went to see *Heaven Grand in Amber Orbit* by Jackie Curtis, which was more extreme than Lady Godiva. The play started in the lobby. Everyone was standing around waiting to go in and, all of a sudden, these characters appeared in the lobby covered in glitter singing a song called 'Thalidomide Baby'. Then this character came out with no arms and lurched around the lobby. Me and Leee were standing there with our mouths open going, 'Wow! The nerve!' We just couldn't believe that anyone would take the piss out of a thalidomide baby. We were astounded.
Jayne County in *Man Enough to Be a Woman*

Yeah, the Theatre of the Ridiculous could be pretty…how can I put? Well…sick.
Jim Fourrat

Cherry Vanilla was originally a nice Irish Catholic girl from Queens called Kathy Dorritie. She moved to New York and started hanging out at Max's and mixing with the rich, uptown crowd. She went along to these underground theatre performances and soon heard that Tony Ingrassia was casting for a production of Wayne County's *World: The Birth of a Nation*. She went for the audition. I was stage-manager and had to interview her. I couldn't believe that this cultured, expensively attired lady was seeking a role in an underground play. I tactfully explained that she would very likely be required to indulge in profanity and humiliating sex acts, plus there was no pay involved. She said, 'Fine'. She told me she was thinking of changing her name to Party Favour, and asked me what I thought. So Party Favour got a role where, among other things, she simulated sex with a dead puppy and pretended to drink piss. She loved it. So did her rich friends, who invited us to lavish uptown dinner parties, where we soon learned that bizarre sex acts are not always simulated.
Leee Childers

Above: The Theatre of the Ridiculous

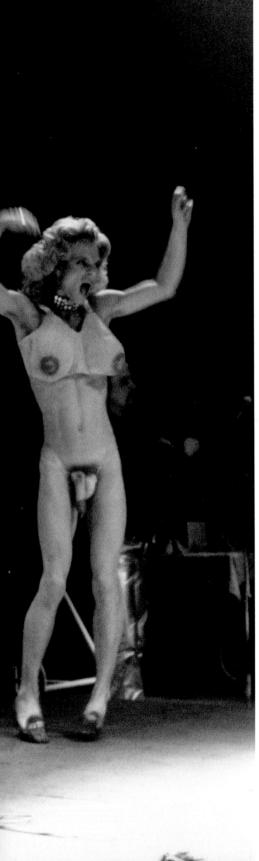

PORK

Play by Tony Ingrassia based on Andy Warhol tapes

Pork was Andy Warhol's play. It was directed by Tony Ingrassia and opened at Café la Mama in 1971. In the play were Harvey Fierstein, Tony Zanatta, Cyrinda Foxe, Jamie Andrews, Suzanne Smith and me in the starring roles. It was wild, and soon the backroom at Max's was a-buzz again with the talk of *Pork*, but this time *Pork* was a play.
Jayne County

Andy Warhol came to see some of the shows [at the Theatre of the Ridiculous]. He would come every night to see this one called *Island*. Andy said to Tony Ingrassia, the director, 'I've got a bunch of tapes. Maybe they would make a good play.' In those days Andy carried around a cassette recorder with a little microphone, and he was taping everything. Tony said OK, so Andy delivered six big boxes full of cassette tapes. Somehow Tony listened to them and got together what was really a very funny play [*Pork*]. It was really cool. It contained lots of talk about various kinds of shit. It was really weird. The people in the play didn't talk to each other directly. They all had a telephone, and the dialogue was actually done into a phone. They were talking with each other on the phone on stage. This, of course, was all done on regular phones as cell phones weren't around then. In a way, I guess he was predicting the future because now you just have to walk down the street and you see everyone talking into their phones. Back when I was a kid, if you saw someone talking to themselves on the street, you'd think they were crazy.
Leee Childers

A lot of *Pork* was to do with shit for some reason. In one scene Pork [the lead character, who was based on Brigid Polk] talked about doing a 'plate' job. This involved a guy lying down with a Pyrex plate over his face, and Pork had to squat down and shit on the plate while the guy moaned. We used dog food, I think, and it really looked like big blobs of shit. I had lots of speeches about different types of shit, and I had one scene that used to cause us a lot of trouble. I sat there while one of the boys spoonfed me beans. We'd kiss and mush the beans all over our faces, then I'd talk about shit and he'd feed me some more and

kiss me. After I'd eaten all the beans, I got up, pulled my dress up and bent over, and the guy stuck his nose up my butt. Then I made a loud farting noise, he inhaled and went into ecstasy and the lights went down.
Jayne County, *Man Enough to Be a Woman*

A producer from London was negotiating with Andy and Tony to take the play over there. So in the summer of '71, when the play went to the Roundhouse in London, he replaced her [the original Pork] with Cherry Vanilla. Andy had apparently admired Cherry's humping of dead dogs and castrating raw hot dog cocks when he saw her in WORLD. Then, when she sang 'Dear Lady of Fatima' for him at her audition, and told him everything he wanted to know about TV commercials, he immediately decided she should be a superstar. Leee Childers was *Pork*'s production manager…he and Cherry became a really notorious team on the London scene, interviewing and photographing the city's young musicians for American rock'n'roll magazines – some real and some fictitious! Cherry invented a column called 'Cherry Vanilla with Scoops for You' and created a scandal when she did some blowing of her own with the horn section on a BB King recording session. At one point she had a whole young band called Bronco living in her bedroom.
Yvonne Sewall-Ruskin, *High on Rebellion*

My character was based on Viva, the Warhol star, but the name was changed to Vulva Lips. *Pork* got a big write-up in *The New York Times,* with a big photograph of me and Tony Zanatta. It was picked up by other papers across the country; my mother saw it. People were stopping me in the street and congratulating me. Then Ira Gale, an art dealer who handled a lot of Andy's paintings in London, announced that he wanted to take *Pork* to London.
Jayne County

It caused quite a sensation in London. All these articles were coming out about how outrageous we were. It really was big news. There were people picketing the play. We had no idea how incredibly, wonderfully trashy the British were, or we could have really had a ball. The only one who played up to it was Cherry Vanilla, who had big silicone breasts. She had ambitions of being a model of some kind. A photographer took her down to The Mall, posed her in front of Clarence House and she popped her tits out. The police came along and arrested her and she said, 'What's the matter with tits? The Queen's got them.' That made headlines.
Leee Childers

Main picture: Performance of *Pork* • Inset: Patti Smith, Jackie Curtis and Penny Arcade

Malcolm McLaren and David Bowie are both cultural vampires. David is a nice vampire and Malcolm isn't.

Danny Fields

Back at 'pig mansions' [where the cast of *Pork* was living] everyone was trying to be as outrageous as possible. Cherry Vanilla gave an interview to a journalist from *Rolling Stone* while giving a blow job to some guy she'd picked up. Rod Stewart and Ron Wood came to visit us. She was running around going, 'Rod Stewart and Ron Wood are here. Should I blow them? Should I blow Ron Wood first or should I blow both of them at the same time?'
Jayne County, *Man Enough to Be a Woman*

To pass the time Cherry Vanilla and I decided to pretend we were rock journalists from America. I pretended to be the photographer and Cherry pretended to be the writer. It was so easy, and probably still is. We just called up and said, 'We are from America' and we would be right on the guest list of all these bands. We met Marc Bolan, Rod Stewart and all the people who were very trendy at that time. But David Bowie wasn't. I was looking through *NME* trying to decide what we were going to do, and there was this little ad that said David Bowie. I said, 'Cherry, I remember reading an article about this guy who wore dresses,' and Jayne said, 'Let's go see him.' He was playing in a place called the Country Club, which was, I think, in north London. We called up the club and they just said, 'Yes, come on down.' So we went down, me and Cherry Vanilla and Jayne County.
Leee Childers

David Bowie had just released *Hunky Dory*, but the live show was really lame. It was just folk music with acoustic guitars. Bowie was sitting on a stool for much of the time, Mick Ronson looked like a hippy and all the audience were squatting on the floor with their legs crossed.
Jayne County

David Bowie was thrilled because, as far as he was concerned, we were representatives of Andy Warhol, so he introduced us to the audience. Cherry, being Cherry, stood up

and popped a tit out – that's what everybody was doing in those days. Jayne didn't have any tits, not then at least. If she had, she would have popped both of them out. But she was still a man then. David had this long hippy hair, and he was wearing a large kaftan with a big old hat. We all thought Mick Ronson was cute though. We met Angie [Bowie] that night at the show. We loved her. She was outrageous and trashy and talked dirty. Angie and David came to see *Pork* at the Roundhouse, and they kept coming back night after night. David wouldn't dance. He'd just sit there. Angie would dance with anybody: male, female, dog, cat, duck. We just loved her, but we figured that was the last time we'd see either of them.
Leee Childers

David and Angie had had Tony Zanatta over for dinner, but it didn't stop there. We were all laughing, saying, 'Tony, you did not go to bed with those two! You're crazy.' He was so embarrassed.
Jayne County

At that time, my hair was cut in this out-of-control quiff, which was standing up everywhere. It was dyed with some crazy colour. In those days you just had to dye your hair with anything you could get – food colouring and all kinds of stuff. I'd managed to make my hair a really disgusting shade of purply red. Later, we all went back to America and I went to work for *Sixteen Magazine* with Danny Fields. One day the phone rang and it was Tony Defries [David Bowie's manager at the time], who said that he was bringing David to America and he wanted staff – people like us who were more colourful. We went up to the Windsor Hotel [in New York] and there was the new album *Ziggy Stardust*. Cherry, Jayne, Tony [Zanatta] and I looked at it and all looked at each other and went, 'Well, look at that! What a transformation!'
Leee Childers

He'd come backstage and say how much he enjoyed our performance [in *Pork*]. Very serious. But all the while he was studying our make-up for his own future use.
Wayne County, *Man Enough to Be a Woman*

He had mainly hoisted the look and the clothes from us individually. I remember on that very first American tour, we were standing out in the audience watching the show and David came on stage. Cyrinda Foxe was standing with me and she said, 'Oh, look, David's wearing clothes just like… Oh! David's wearing my clothes.' And he was. His whole costume was a copy of Cyrinda's clothes – the skin-tight black pants with rhinestones, the woman's blouse tied in a little knot. It was all Cyrinda, right down to the earrings even.
Leee Childers

David Bowie just stole everything. His whole look came from us and the cast of *Pork*. He then signed me to MainMan and kept me under wraps with one excuse or another, both me and Iggy. Of course it would not have looked at all good if people could see where he got his ideas from.
Wayne County, *Man Enough to Be a Woman*

Tony Defries decided to take us on the road [on the Ziggy Stardust tour with Bowie]. RCA, a big record company, were really taken for a ride. David was going through that fiction then that he couldn't fly, though we all knew that he'd flown from London to New York. When we got to Hollywood, they booked us in to the Chateau Marmont. I called Lisa Robinson and told her where we were staying. She said, 'Oh, no, you can't stay there. Demand the Beverly Hills Hotel.' So of course we did. They moved all 40 of us to the Beverly Hills Hotel. I went and got a lounger by the pool, the whole routine. The roadies would take a car on the bill up to Hollywood Boulevard and bring tourists back to the hotel, order them lavish room-service dinners, worth $400, charge them $50, then take them back to Hollywood Boulevard. Then they'd pick up another load. We did that for a month. We made a fortune.
Leee Childers

I always wondered how or why David Bowie suddenly transformed himself from acoustic guitar-playing hippy to androgynous space-age superstar Ziggy Stardust.
Chris Sullivan

David had met Iggy and imported him to London. Iggy was taking a lot of drugs. He was out to shock. Iggy abused his welcome a great deal with David. I used to tell him to hold off a bit and go for the big score, but he couldn't resist the quick kill. Iggy had his blue and silver hair at the time, but nobody saw him live. Tony Defries had a thing that I am sure was instigated by David: they would sign up people who David was influenced by. They would be supported and have a place to live, but you'd never see them. They would never gig. There would always be a reason why they shouldn't – they weren't considered ready by MainMan or whatever. Meanwhile, David was developing his style on stage.
Leee Childers

Then David Bowie started turning up at Dolls' shows, like you know, with a notebook.
Wayne County, *Man Enough to Be a Woman*

'Personality Crisis' Song by the New York Dolls

All these other bands started up around the Max's scene, like the New York Dolls, Ruby and the Rednecks, the Harlots of 42nd Street and Jayne County's band Queen Elizabeth. They were really the precursors of punk. All these little kids would come and see them and then start their own bands. One of the great things about this music was that anyone could play it. Then you had the Ramones, Television, and so on.
Leee Childers

Johnny Thunders of the Dolls used to share a flat with me on First Avenue in New York. He would drive us crazy practising his guitar for hours on end. He was determined to be a star. His girlfriend, Janis, was my cousin and we used to drive all over to see bands like the MC5, the Velvets and Janis Joplin, and because we were…well…cheeky we would end up meeting them. We used to go to this bar on Fifth Avenue and 13th Street and people like Jagger, Keith Richard and Lennon used to go there. We would sit around talking to all the stars. Johnny used to say, 'I want to be a pop star. I want to be like Keith Richard.' He even kept Keith's cigarette packet.'
Gail Higgins Smith, Heartbreakers' tour manager

Another curious tale in this cross-cultural exchange between London and New York is that Syl Sylvain, a guitarist with the New York Dolls, actually had a clothing company with Billy Murcia, the original drummer, who came from Colombia. They specialized in hippy woollens, based on the traditional dress in Colombia. They sold their designs to a manufacturer for a large amount. Syl went to London and Billy to Amsterdam. After a year they met up again, Syl having met Trevor Miles, a purveyor of antique clothing, who owned a shop at 430 Kings Road known as Paradise Garage. This was 1970. About a year later Malcolm McLaren and Vivienne Westwood moved into the premises. Some years later the pair would clothe the Dolls and Malcolm would manage them after a fashion. Syl, influenced by his trip, would buy a grey Jaguar and a load of Mickey Mouse T-shirts.
Chris Sullivan

When the Dolls played at the Mercer Arts Center [in New York] they used to attract all the right people. They managed to attract both the art and the music scenes. The crowd really dressed for the occasion. There were two guys who I worked with in a department store who called themselves the Tois Sisters. One was the heir to the Heinz fortune. I saw him at a Dolls' gig and he was in a dress. That was the influence of the Dolls. There was one guy who used to wear an open black vest with clothes pegs on his nipples, two Tibetan girls covered in tattoos, plus all the Warhol transvestites, like Jackie Curtis and Holly Woodlawn. They were wild.
Gail Higgins Smith

The Dolls could certainly be uneven, to say the least. They'd do two sets a night and one would be the worst show you'd ever seen and the other would be the best. Maybe that was to do with the amount of alcohol you'd drunk. The first time I saw them play, which was the first show I ever saw in New York, was at Club 82, a drag place on East Fourth Street. The Dolls had this idea of playing in drag because of it being a drag club. They were all wearing dresses and I thought maybe that was their regular outfit – short, strapless dresses, wigs and high heels. The Dolls were so not gay, almost the opposite of that: real out-of-borough guys, with these set-me-up accents from Queens and Brooklyn. They had a really hard time getting Jerry Nolan into a dress. He was probably about 10 years older than the others, but he looked really good, so it didn't matter. If you believe his stories, he had this history going back more to Elvis and the '50s.

The Dolls hadn't played for a long time and, you know, everybody rewrites history, but 'The Red Leather Show' was the stupidest thing they ever did. Maybe people should have taken it lighter. Johnny Thunders was asked, 'Are you communists?' And he said, 'What of it?' David [Johansen] was trying to soft-pedal and say it was Malcolm's idea, but Johnny was like, 'Fuck you!' Like Marlon Brando in The Wild Ones.
Roberta Bayley, photographer

The Dolls were very heterosexual. When I met them I was impressed by how macho they were and how on the make for women. There wasn't anything gay about them at all. People tend to misinterpret a little when they say they dressed up like women because back then anybody who put on a halter top or high heels would be accused of wearing women's clothes. The Dolls did wear some items that might have been from the women's department – high heels and the like – but there were no women that dressed like them. They never once looked like women. They always looked like macho guys with make-up. It's like when Iggy Pop was arrested. His friend bailed him out. Iggy staggered out of jail, still stoned, and his friend looked at him and said, 'Iggy, you're wearing a lady's dress,' and Iggy said, 'I beg your pardon. This is a man's dress.' That's what it's about. Iggy's never been gay, but he might have had a dress on.
Bob Gruen, photographer

The New York Dolls wore effeminate clothing, but they were all tough street kids from the suburbs. The Dolls could only have been born and bred in New York. It really was this trashy-drag-queen-meets-the-mods ideology. They were very brash. The New York Dolls to me were the modern-day equivalent of the Bowery Boys in drag. I think the most fascinating thing about them, which really captured most people's interest, was that they looked like drag queens, but if you referred to them as such, they'd beat the stuffing out of you. They were tough kids – real leathernecks. Except for Syl – he wasn't much like that. David [Johansen] remained quite streetwise, and Johnny was a thug. Of all the bands that came out of New York, the New York Dolls were certainly the most interesting. They preceded the movement which would follow – the whole scene at CBGB's.
Gene Krell

Opposite: The New York Dolls • Above, left to right: David Johansen, Johnny Thunders, Arthur Kane, Syl Sylvain, Billy Murcia

'Night of the Living Dolls'

Song by the New York Dolls

The New York Dolls were an inspiration to a lot of the people in the punk scene. Before the New York Dolls were around music seemed distant. All the musicians and bands seemed to be organized by a record company or a manager or somebody. When people saw the New York Dolls, they had a different take on it. The Dolls were so chaotic, and they were having so much fun. When people saw them they said, 'Well, I can do that.' It didn't seem so hard any more. I think they inspired a lot of people. The band Kiss told me they went to a New York Dolls' show and the Dolls were so beautiful that they thought they couldn't really compete and try to be a better-looking band, so they did the opposite and tried to look like monsters.

Bob Gruen

Johnny Thunders met Arthur Kane and Rick Rivets in less typical Dolls fashion. He was hanging out on Bleeker Street [New York] and saw the drunken Kane and Rivets trying to steal a motorbike, which was hanging out of their van. The two dropped the bike and advanced towards Thunders. About to run, Thunders recognized them and then embarked on what was to become a beautiful friendship, aka the New York Dolls.
Chris Sullivan

I was with Rick Rivets [the first Dolls' guitarist] when I saw him [Johnny Thunders] outside a pizza place. We were across the street and I said, 'Why don't we go over and find out what's going on with him?' I went over and said, 'I hear you play guitar or bass or something. Do you want to get together?'
Arthur Kane of the New Yorks Dolls in *Too Much Too Soon*

I saw the New York Dolls on *The Old Grey Whistle Test* [UK music programme] and I was knocked sideways. They were all over the place – mad hair, platform boots, tripping over each other. It was really funny, and they didn't give a shit. 'Whispering' Bob Harris [the presenter] just looked shocked and said, 'Tut, tut, mock rock.' It was great.
Paul Cook, drummer, the Sex Pistols

We'd all heard about this band called the New York Dolls. Everybody in the UK was expecting something really special. Then I saw them on *The Old Grey Whistle Test* and thought they were really shit, really old hat. It was just these guys acting like the Stones and falling about. They were rubbish.
Kevin Rowland, Dexy's Midnight Runners

They were like the worst striptease rock act you can imagine. I loved their awkward, trashy vibe. We [from Too Fast to Live, Too Young to Die] became part of their entourage and followed them to Paris.
Malcolm McLaren in *Too Much Too Soon*

Opposite: Johnny Thunders and David Johansen • Above: Syl Sylvain and Arthur Kane

When Malcolm used the Dolls as the prototypes for the Sex Pistols, he forgot to erase their proclivity for misadventure.

Nina Antonia, *Too Much Too Soon*

The Dolls were the beginning of it all. This was pre-CBGB's, and the Dolls were at the centre of everything. In the early '70s they were the band of our lives. They were the band we all wanted to see, and when they played, the backroom of Max's emptied out. They had such enormous influence. Everybody was influenced by them in one way or another.
Danny Fields

The similarities between the New York Dolls and the Pistols are endless. Neither of them could play at the beginning. They were all street kids. The Dolls could not get radio play. They caused a riot in Memphis, where they were seen as evil. Mothers boycotted the show. Billy Murcia, the original drummer, died of a drug overdose while depressed, a bit like Sid [Vicious]. They also caused controversy wherever they went and made headlines – bad headlines.
Marco Pirroni, guitarist, Siouxsie and the Banshees

The Dolls went to Memphis and, like the Pistols, caused a riot. The police came out in force, and an organization called the Mothers of Memphis boycotted their show, shouting, 'Mothers, keep your children away from the New York Dolls. They will corrupt your children. They are evil.' Thing is, they were right.
Stephen Colegrave

The New York Dolls were a handful. They were wild by anybody's measure. They went to France, and Johnny threw up at the airport in front of everyone. The press in France branded them drug-addicted faggots. In London Syl and Arthur were caught changing labels over in Biba and were almost charged with shoplifting. Even David Johansen was charged with lewd public behaviour and put in jail for the night, though it wasn't his fault. And then, of course, there was the drugs and the booze.
Leee Childers

The New York Dolls played what was possibly one of the worst sets I've seen [Wembley, October 1973]. Their glamour bit brought wolf whistles and shouts to go long before a note had been played, and by the time a string had broken on Johnny Thunders' plexiglass guitar, they had lost what sympathy they had.
Mark Plummer, *Melody Maker*, October 1973

The Dolls played great rock'n'roll music the way I like to hear it – kinda sloppy. I was a real big fan of the Faces, but they were a bit more controlled, more like good-time music. The Dolls were seriously crazy, and I'd never seen anything like that. I don't think anyone had. The audience [at Wembley] hated them and started slinging shit at them, but they kept on playing. They were great.
Steve Jones of the Sex Pistols in *Too Much Too Soon*

Me, my cousin and Johnny all moved into an apartment on First Avenue between Ninth and Tenth Street. In those days that part of East Village was like no man's land. When we moved in, we found someone had left a load of furniture in the place, including an old piano that we didn't have room for. As we tried to move the piano, the front came off and we saw all these big bits of pot inside. Johnny was sort of scared going, 'Oh, what are we gonna do?' We decided we couldn't just throw it away. We thought we could maybe make some money on it. So Johnny called up a friend of his from Queens and sold it. As far as I know that was his first involvement with drugs. When he got into something, he went the whole way.
Gail Higgins Smith

Apparently, the New York Dolls were taking smack on a daily basis. A recipe for disaster if ever there was one.
Chris Sullivan

A lot of speed freaks seem to go straight from that onto smack. Maybe they need to catch up on their sleep.
Steve Walsh

The New York Dolls – womanizing, drug-addled, alcoholic, ministers of pure rock'n'roll. How did they go wrong?
Chris Sullivan

Above: Sleeve detail from *Live In New York* by the New York Dolls • Opposite: Sleeve for *Live In New York* by the New York Dolls

Some observers are going as far as saying the Dolls' demise is a carbon copy of the Velvet Underground story in New York.

Chris Charlesworth, *Melody Maker,* August 1973

The New York Dolls walked down the Kings Road in high-heeled shoes and lipstick and everything, but they were fucking hard. They were the New York Dolls and they were in Malcolm's shop. He thought they were the best things he had ever seen, and somehow they got chatting. He decided to try to get involved in their management. I dunno how he convinced them that he was able to do it, but somehow he did. Joe Corré, son of Vivienne Westwood and Malcolm McLaren **So I tried to throw politics into the mill.** Malcolm McLaren in *Please Kill Me* When they played, Malcolm put a red flag behind them with a hammer and sickle on it. Someone asked Johnny if he was a communist. He said, in typical Johnny style, 'Hey, what of it?' Gail Higgins Smith **Malcolm just stole that whole red book communist thing he did with the Dolls from the MC5. It was so blatant.** Danny Fields I remember that he went over to New York. There's a picture of him on a ladder, putting up this great big flag with a hammer and sickle on it. He's behind the set and there's the guitarist, Johnny Thunders, looking up puzzled. Joe Corré **Johnny Thunders and the Dolls didn't know what a goddamn hammer and sickle were even used for. They're American, for God's sake.** Gail Higgins Smith Jerry Nolan would say, 'Johnny, look at this guy…how [are] we gonna become like the Beatles with this schmuck?' And Johnny would think, 'He's right. This guy's an idiot.' They didn't take Malcolm seriously, which was a mistake. Sylvain in *Please Kill Me* **I don't think either Jerry or Johnny liked Malcolm. They thought he was a goofy nerd.** Gail Higgins Smith The New York Dolls had huge problems by the end of '74 and McLaren tried his best to help them. Unfortunately, they were too far gone. The Dolls split and Thunders and Nolan went on to form the Heartbreakers. McLaren, once bitten but not at all shy, returned to London in '75 and, with Bernie Rhodes, started to groom the Sex Pistols, combining the Dolls' attitude with what he'd observed of the New York punk scene. Chris Sullivan

CBGB's braved the world of music and we braved the smell of urine to go there.

Leee Childers

CBGB's [in New York] had a wonderful atmosphere. It had the best sound of any club I've ever been to in the world, and the people were fabulous. Hundreds of thousands of dollars were spent on the club to make it better. For me and the audience it never got better, and it never got worse; it was born perfect. Nothing mattered as much as the way the music sounded. If it was a good band, like Television or the Ramones or the Dictators, and you were a fan, you were swept up in the music. You drowned in the music. That's what it was all about. It wasn't about being seen or getting in for nothing. You went to hear the bands.
Danny Fields

Before CBGB's I managed the Vanguard, which was a famous jazz venue. Before that I was producing college concerts. We did folk and jazz from '63 onwards till about '69. There wasn't any punk. I didn't do it deliberately.
Hilly Kristal, owner, CBGB's

CBGB's was a really funky place. It smelled like piss. Unbelievably, they actually served food. Somebody asked me just the other day, 'Did you know that people used to jack off in the chilli?' and I said, 'Yes.' They said, 'Well, did you eat it?' and I said, 'Yes, I've eaten worse things.' I'm not sure who it was who did that. Probably Hilly Kristal could tell you better than me.
Leee Childers

CBGB OMFUG stands for Country, Blue Grass, Blues and Other Music for Uplifting Gourmandizers. Close, but no cigar.
Chris Sullivan

When CBGB's started up in New York it was a lot of fun. Some interesting new bands used to play there, like Television and Patti Smith. Back then a band would play just one or two nights a week. Once CBGB's started getting to be a place for bands, they could play four nights a week, doing two sets on Thursdays and Fridays and three sets on the weekend. Nowadays a band plays one set a month and they think they're playing regular. A lot of us used to go back and forth from CBGB's to Max's. It was very easy as they were only about 15 blocks apart. If you weren't really into the band at CBGB's, or there weren't too many girls around you were interested in, you'd take a quick cab ride up to Max's and hang out there for an hour or two, before going back to CBGB's.
Bob Gruen

We were the first band to play CBGB's, even before Television. I played there with my band Queen Elizabeth just after I played the transvestite bar the 82 Club, where I'd debuted the song that was to become my anthem: 'If you don't want to fuck me, baby, fuck off.'
Jayne County

I don't know who really broke the rock'n'roll barrier. CBGB's was meant to be just a country and blues place, so it was either the Ramones or Patti Smith. I think it was the Ramones who started it. Patti soon figured out she had a place to play, and then everybody started going, despite how really seedy it was. In those days going that far down the Bowery was quite an adventure. Me and Jayne and Cyrinda and people like that were used to it because the theatre where we put on the underground shows was only a block from there, but Danny Fields and Lisa Robinson were afraid to go that far downtown. CBGB's was right next door to the Palace Hotel, which was a traditional 25-cent flophouse. People would come reeling out of there drunk on meths, looking like they were from the moon. The music at CBGB's was so completely different from anything we were hearing elsewhere, and it was even different from the Dolls. CBGB's braved the world of music, and we braved the smell of urine in order to go there.
Leee Childers

It wasn't expanding consciousness, it was getting fucked up. I woke up a lot of mornings on the floor. I was the guy you stepped over. Hilly was passed out by 10.30 on the couch. It was like the adults had gone to sleep. You could just reach around the bar and steal the beers. Everybody knew the trick, and it was so easy. And the bartenders never charged anyway. It was cool.
Legs McNeil

Above, left to right: David Johansen, Danny Fields, James Sliman (bending), Joey Ramone, Earl McGrath, Arturo Vega (in doorway), Jimmy Destri (extreme right)

I was interested in the fact that they [Television] were doing their own thing. They were original, and that's what made it exciting. Each band was different from the next one. I think Television were there at the beginning. Tom Verlaine and Richard Hell did some wonderful things.
Hilly Kristal

Richard Hell to me was kind of in between the serious and the cynical. He was into symbolist poets and everything, but he was also writing songs like 'Fuck Rock'n'Roll, I'd Rather Read a Book'. He had much more of a sense of humour about it.
Roberta Bayley

The first few times Television played I didn't like what they were doing. I let them play because some of these bands were just interesting. Their music didn't quite make sense at the beginning, but soon after, when they got it together, it did.
Hilly Kristal

I thought Television had a great look. It was the hippie era, the glam glitter era. Then along came Television with a totally new look. I thought it was a brilliant move on their part to break away from everything and start something fresh.
Tommy Ramone, drummer, the Ramones

Television looked quite extraordinary, with their spiked hair and ripped clothes. The idea was that, in contrast to all these bands like Yes, who were doing 20-minute drum solos, their songs would be very quick. In one set they'd literally do maybe 20 songs, all two or three minutes long. It was Richard Hell who gave birth to the term 'Blank Generation'. They actually had a song '(I Belong to the) Blank Generation'.
Gene Krell

Above: Television (Richard Hell, Billy Ficca, Richard Lloyd, Tom Verlaine) performing in New York, 1974

We felt like we were living in some post-apocalyptic ruin.

The radio in America was really good in the '60s. We'd all grown up with this really great rock'n'roll stuff. It was wonderful. The music just kept getting better and better, and no one thought it was going to stop. Then, suddenly, it was gone, and you had this awful folk rock stuff with John Denver singing some shit. What happened? Legs McNeil **It was hippie heaven. Everyone wore bellbottoms or velvet pants and leather-fringed jackets. Punk slowly changed all that. You'd dig up an old pair of those nice velvet pants and rip the shit out of them.** Walter Lure, the Heartbreakers You had Watergate, and then Nixon resigned in '74. The war in Vietnam was over, but had haunted all of us as we were growing up – your brother would have to go register for the draft. It really was a big thing that was hanging over everybody, and then we lost! We were glad it was over, but this losing thing…you know? Legs McNeil **A lot of people forget that we had suffered all kinds of political upheaval – the end of the war, Watergate. New York City was bankrupt. The city was tough.** Jim Fourrat A lot of white people left Manhattan after World War II. It was their dream to get a house in the suburbs, so from the late '40s to the end of the '60s everybody was leaving the city. It was abandoned. No one wanted to live there. Then, in 1975, New York City went bankrupt. They asked for a loan to bail them out and President Ford told them to drop dead. I remember the cover of the *New York Post*: 'Ford to New York: Drop Dead'. No one now knows if he actually said those words, but they became the popular myth. There was this really decrepit kind of crumbling, decaying feeling. The East Village had lots of burned-out buildings from fires and stuff. It really was a slum. The buildings were just façades – store fronts with nothing behind them. This all subconsciously added to the aesthetic. We just felt like we were living in some post-apocalyptic ruin. New York looked like the set of a *film noir* movie. It was dirty. It wasn't clean like the rest of America. It was wonderful, and you could do anything you wanted. Legs McNeil **We were the first generation to grow up with television. I remember watching the Marines landing in Saigon in '65. Then you'd turn the channel and there'd be police dogs chewing on some little black kid, or Timothy Leary [counterculture guru] in Greenwich Village. I think television made people aware of everything. The Vietnam War had ended and the punks were just getting going, so they don't really refer to it very much. Everybody was so poor. No one had any money. Nobody could pay for a drink.** Leee Childers There were a lot of very violent fights. These guys coming in from Queens would pick on the punks. New York was scary. There was a sense of foreboding, an element of the city and the night. It was dangerous, not like it is now, but it was fun too. Legs McNeil

The Ramones weren't an art band: they were trying to be heavy metal bubblegum. John Holmstrom

I was trying to do a compilation of all-time punk classics, and when I finished I saw I had the whole of the Ramones' first album, every bloody song.
Nils Stevenson

Johnny Ramone and I went to high school together. Johnny, Joey, Dee Dee and I all knew each other. We're from the same middle-class neighbourhood in New York – Forest Hills – where they used to have the tennis tournament. Later on I became a recording engineer. During the '70s we found that we weren't hearing the music we liked on the radio any more. It was all progressive rock and stuff like that, and we were missing the fun, exciting, rock'n'roll songs. So we decided to put the band together and try to do it ourselves.
Tommy Ramone

Joey became lead singer, Johnny was on guitar and Tommy Ramone, who was managing us, finally had to sit down behind the drums because no one else wanted to. That completed the original Ramones' line-up.
Dee Dee Ramone, bass player, in *Please Kill Me*

We threw around names. We had like 40 names to choose from. Dee Dee came up with the Ramones. I guess he got it from Paul McCartney, who at one time called himself Paul Ramone. We didn't know that at the time. We just liked the sound of the name. We thought it was interesting and ridiculous enough to work.
Tommy Ramone

Minimalism was a very powerful influence on what was happening in New York, and the Ramones were a definite attempt to do something. They weren't trying to be an art band; they were trying to be heavy metal bubblegum.
John Holmstrom

We were influenced by comic books, movies, the Andy Warhol scene, and avant-garde films. I was a big Mad magazine fan myself.
Tommy Ramone

I went down to CBGB's to see them that summer and I was just knocked out from day one. As advertised, they only played 20 minutes, but it was like my week to your year all in 20 minutes. They were fantastic, and that was why I wanted to start a magazine, so I could write about bands like the Dictators and the Ramones. They had this very politically incorrect attitude.
John Holmstrom

I didn't think the Ramones played very well at first. I don't think Dee Dee could play the bass at all; it just sounded awful. Tommy was a good drummer. Joe, of course, sang, though he didn't have a marvellous voice. The problem with them was they'd keep stopping and starting, then the amp would break down or something, and it would all be over. They were very loud and they'd just yell at each other. After a while, I was persuaded to keep putting them on, and they started to get better. I still don't know whose idea it was, but when they started doing the 17 minutes of music – 20 songs in 17 minutes without stopping – it became interesting. Joey always wrote some nice little lyrics and good melodies. As they learned to play better, they began to sound very good. They had a lot of energy and they never stopped. Soon everybody was talking about them. I remember once Linda Ronstadt came in here with a couple of people. I guess she wanted to see what all the fuss was about. It was too much for her. I think she stayed for about five minutes, and then she fled.
Hilly Kristal

We were playing at CBGB's for about half a year with absolutely nobody showing up. Then Hilly Kristal, the owner, decided to have a festival of bands, which got a lot of publicity. We'd already had some good write-ups in *The Village Voice* and the *SoHo Weekly News*, so when he had the festival, everybody came down to see what all the hubbub was about. That's how the world discovered us. We were happy they showed up.
Tommy Ramone

Hey! Ho! Let's go.

Title of Ramones' anthology

Above left, top to bottom: The Ramones (Johnny, Tommy, Joey, Dee Dee) in Washington, DC; in the studio; in concert • Main picture: The Ramones in a television studio • Opposite: Joey Ramone promoting the Ramones' album

I like the Ramones a lot. I saw them first in a rehearsal studio. It was just the most bizarre thing I'd ever heard – very short songs played really loud and really fast. It seemed like conceptual art or something.

Roberta Bayley

We were huge fans of the New York Dolls. They made it clear at the time that musical virtuosity wasn't necessarily the most important thing any more. Virtuosity was so common by that point, with everybody playing like Led Zeppelin or Eric Clapton. The New York Dolls were the most exciting band around at that time. They could only just play, but they put on a great show. They were clever and original. They loved being on stage and doing their thing – they gave off this excitement and had a great attitude. They really got me thinking, 'Hey, wow! This is something new. This is a great direction to go for.'
Tommy Ramone

The Dolls showed the Ramones how to have fun, and the Ramones showed the Dolls how to do it fast. I remember the first time I saw the Ramones showcasing 10 or 12 songs in like 16 or 18 minutes. It was unbelievable. One song was over, and the next one beginning, and you didn't even know it, it was so fast.
Bob Gruen

I was hired to DJ at a party where the Ramones were playing, and a friend of mine said, 'Who is this fucking band? They're like the New York Dolls on speed,' which was true in a way. They were fantastic.
Jayne County

The Ramones called me up, and they kept pestering me to come down and see them. The whole set was only 15 minutes long, but I loved them in the first five seconds. I said, 'Here I am. I came to see you. I love you, in fact I love you so much I want to manage you.' Joey Ramone said, 'We need $3,500 for equipment.' That was literally their response. I said, 'And if you get that, you'll let me

manage you?' They all said, 'Well, yeah.' They knew who I was. I had the Iggy connection and impeccable credentials, but they needed money. So I went to Florida and told my mother I'd found this great band that would be very big and make me rich. I said, 'Mom, I need some money to get them started,' and she said 'OK.' If it wasn't for my mother, who knows what history would have been?
Danny Fields

We loved all the garage bands of the '60s, like the Shadows of the Night and the Knickerbockers. They could have come up with better names but they were still great bands. We loved bubblegum music. Later on we loved the MC5 and the Stooges. I think John and Dee Dee were into Grand Funk Railroad. We all loved '50s rock. We loved Little Richard, Chuck Berry and Elvis Presley. We were like rock'n'roll connoisseurs. We knew that Danny Fields was involved with the Stooges and the Doors, who we also liked. Danny ran a rock gossip column in the *SoHo Weekly News*, so we got in touch with him. We kept sending him invitations to come see us, and eventually he did. That's how we got together.
Tommy Ramone

They were trying to break into *Sixteen Magazine* 'cause their manager was Danny Fields and he thought they could be like the Partridge Family or something.
John Holmstrom

I just don't get it. Malcolm McLaren thought the Pistols would be the next Bay City Rollers, *Punk Magazine* featured the Rollers, and the Ramones started off playing their songs. Why? The Rollers were shit, or am I mistaken?
Chris Sullivan

The Ramones took things one step further.

Marco Pirroni

Here was a band who were very genuine, appealing and funny. If you had a room of six people sitting down, Joey Ramone would be the least likely candidate to front a band and that was what made them so accessible.

Gene Krell

I loved Dee Dee. He was always so stoned. I remember one day when I was at Max's in the upstairs dressing-room, getting ready to go on stage. He came in and said, 'You don't mind, but I gotta piss.' He took out his cock and started peeing. He had a huge cock and he insisted on showing me the scars where a girlfriend had tried to cut it off with a knife. 'Look at my dick, Wayne. Look at the scars!'

Jayne County

All the other bands were in some way derivative. The Ramones were out there on their own and they'd missed the bus back.

Chris Sullivan

The Sex Pistols distilled the sound. They simplified it and made it more punchy. The Ramones took things one step further and simplified it even more. They wrote fucking great songs. There's no getting away from that. The first three albums are just brilliant.

Marco Pirroni

The Ramones always put a few drops of piss in anything they give their guests as a little joke. When Johnny Rotten came to see the Ramones at the Roundhouse [in London], he asked…if he could come backstage to say hello. Johnny Ramone said it was all right. [He] was very friendly to Johnny Rotten when they met. He shook his hand, patted him on the back and asked if he wanted a beer. Ha, ha, ha. Johnny Rotten took it and drank it down in one gulp. We were all holding our breaths and going blank. So he just left.

Dee Dee Ramone in *Please Kill Me*

It was a great idea to have Phil Spector produce the Ramones. They were the perfect partnership.

Leee Childers

We were, of course, huge Phil Spector fans, so we were thrilled when we were invited over to his house. Then he locked the door and wouldn't let us out. He kept us there all night, getting us drunk and waving guns around. We eventually calmed him down and had a nice talk with him. I have no idea why he wanted to kidnap us. I think he just wanted to produce us.

Tommy Ramone

Phil Spector was wacko. He always carried a gun and had fully armed twin bodyguards with him constantly. He did, however, produce some absolutely brilliant records. Where would we be without the Shangri-Las, for God's sake? Spector producing the Ramones: what a fantastic idea!

Steve Holloway, DJ

The Ramones were really right-wing. They named one of their albums *Rocket to Russia*, which is quite an astonishing statement, but they got away with it. Tommy's family had escaped from Hungary in '68 when the communists marched in. Johnny was brilliant – one of the smartest people I've ever known in my life, but a complete Archie Bunker [Alf Garnett]. He hated communists. Joey became a liberal because he was Jewish. Dee Dee was in a class by himself – an army brat.

Danny Fields

We walked into CBGB's and it was like 'We are home'. The Ramones came on stage, they counted off, '1, 2, 3, 4' and they all started playing a different song. They threw down their guitars in disgust and walked off the stage. It was the best concert I'd ever seen in my life. I thought, 'This is it, this is what I want.'

Legs McNeil

Lisa Robinson called me up. Blue Oyster Cult were playing Madison Square Garden. She told me it was her time of the month and asked me if I could go and photograph them and give a report on the show in her place. I said, 'I'm sorry, I can't. I've got flu or something. I don't know what it is, but I can't move. Why don't you call Bob [Gruen]?' She said, 'I've already called Bob and he's sick too. There must be flu going around. Who am I going to get to cover for me?' About an hour later, Lisa, me and Bob all ran into each other at a Ramones' show at CBGB's. No one has a bad word to say about the Ramones.

Leee Childers

That's one of the things about punk rock. Joey was not your typical good-looking idol, and yet a lot of girls adored him. He was a very special person. That's one of the things punk rock really changed. You didn't have to be a glamorous product of a corporation. You could just be the geek you were in high school and still be a star. Punk kind of opened it up for everybody, and inspired a lot of people.

Bob Gruen

Top left: The Ramones outside a record shop in New York • Above: The Ramones in London • Opposite: Joey Ramone in bed with Debbie Harry

The Stilettos played a mixture of old tunes and show tunes, but with an outrageous twist.

Leee Childers

I loved the Stilettos. They were very influenced by those underground plays and musicals that we did. The people who wrote the plays weren't songwriters, so they used old tunes and put new words to them. The words were often outrageously dirty – 'Thalidomide Baby' and stuff like that. The Stilettos played a mixture of old tunes and show tunes, but with an outrageous twist. They would go from dirty songs to pop songs. The band was a good training ground for Debbie Harry.
Leee Childers

The Stilettos were a really good band. They were fronted by the three girls – Debbie, Elda Gentile and Rosie Ross. They were a lot of fun; it was a camp kind of thing. They did a couple of covers, but it was mostly their own music, which Debbie wrote. They would change the lyrics to other songs and they did their own. They changed a lot of things. It was pretty original.
Hilly Kristal

The Stilettos were the original band that turned into Blondie. They did a campy cabaret type of act. There were three girls, who were basically very good to look at. It was a fun act, but then the girls broke up and it was just Debbie Harry that lasted. Then it became Blondie, and it went from a cabaret-type act to a sort of pop band.
Tommy Ramone

Blondie were good. In the early days they were just a three-girl band.
Walter Lure

They must have known what they were doing because they were the ones that made it commercially.
Tommy Ramone

Debbie was very nervous about being able to sing. She also didn't think she was pretty.
Leee Childers

Debbie was our *Punk Magazine* centrefold in issue 4, and everybody loved that. People think that Patti Smith was the hip chick, but actually it was Debbie because she was so beautiful. And, more importantly, she was funnier. She had her Mustang parked out the front of CBGB's and she'd give me a ride home. I remember when Debbie and Chris had a fire in their apartment and Chris's *Plastic Man* comics were destroyed. As part of Blondie's stage act Debbie used to put up these cartoon images – Godzilla and giant ants from space – on big backdrops and then they'd smash them down. They were into Japanese horror movies and stuff, which was a big thing, so there was that aesthetic to it. The first two Blondie albums, before they got a number one, were really quite good. The first album was great.
Legs McNeil

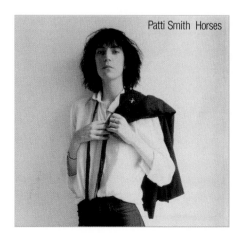

Patti Smith Horses

Patti Smith, of course, had been a poet, but I think her music was very expressive.

Hilly Kristal

Patti Smith and Robert Mapplethorpe couldn't get into the backroom at Max's at first. They looked like hippies, and Mickey [Ruskin] didn't want any hippies in there. They would sit on the kerb and we'd feel sorry for them. We used to sneak them out glasses of wine and stuff under our coats. Eventually their persistence paid off and Mickey started to let them in.
Leee Childers

I think Patti Smith and Tom Verlaine [of the band Television] were friendly. They used to have tea and stuff. Patti and Lenny [Kaye] decided to form a band. Clive Davis [an A & R man] was interested in seeing her, so they decided to play here [at CBGB's]. Jane Friedman was their manager. She booked them for one day, and they went over so well that we decided to put them in for a week. They did two sets a night for four days a week, and I let Television open for them. They lasted seven weeks. When they first played, Patti had not been a singer before, but she was just wonderful. The music and the lyrics were very domineering, the sets were wonderful and Patti was dominant on stage. Lenny and Ivan Kral were good musicians. She came back many times. That was very exciting. She had a reputation as a poet and a lot of people knew her, so a lot of famous people came in. I think Andy Warhol was here. A lot of people came in to see her who were interested in poetry and wanted to know what was happening. John Cale produced her first record, which was wonderful.
Hilly Kristal

I remember the look on Patti's and Tom's faces when they were caught kissing behind CBGB's… Tom blushed and Patti went 'Fuck off'.
Debbie Harry in *Please Kill Me*

The first night at Max's nobody could believe that Wayne County was going to take the piss out of Patti Smith. I came on stage in white and spat on the floor and started going 'Television, Television' because Patti was having an affair with Tom Verlaine of Television and she was always ranting on about the band. Then I'd do my own version of 'Horses', about Jimmy who goes down to the locker room where all these football players rip his clothes off and wank all over him. Jimmy would shout, 'Yeah man, I ain't queer. I just like to be jerked off on by football players! Yeah! Sperm! Come! Cock! Balls! Asshole! Fuck! Shit! Horses! Horses! Horses! Horses! Chickens! Chickens! Wildebeest! Wildebeest! Giraffes! Giraffes!' And so on. I don't think Patti ever saw it.
Jayne County

Left: Pattie Smith • Above: Album sleeve for *Horses* by Patti Smith • Opposite: Jonathan Richman

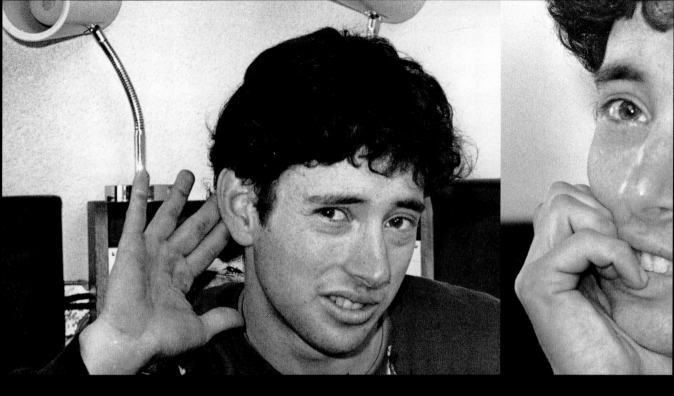

The Modern Lovers

'Roadrunner' was on the jukebox at Sex [the Kings Road shop in London]. We all thought it was fantastic. It was one of the first proper punk records. What's amazing was that it was recorded in 1971 and not released till years later. *The Modern Lovers* album was produced by John Cale and was so influential for everybody.
Nils Stevenson, the Sex Pistols' tour manager, 1976

I loved Jonathan Richman. I managed him for a little while. I've known him since he was a little kid. He worshipped Lou Reed and the Velvet Underground. He was in the band the Modern Lovers in the early '70s and they were very hot. Jerry Harrison was in the band too – he became part of the Talking Heads. The drummer [Dave Robinson] went on to be in the Cars. Ernie Brooks was the bass player. I don't remember what happened to him, but he'll always be fabulous. That was the Modern Lovers. I very much wanted to manage them.
Danny Fields, ex-manager, Jonathan Richman and the Modern Lovers

Jonathan Richman was fun. He's got quirky, kind of fun songs. His protests were always in a much lighter vein. 'Roadrunner' has a great feeling of escapism – being out on the road, listening to rock'n'roll music and getting away from everything. It was great in the sense that anybody could do that sort of thing…
Bob Gruen

Their first album sat in a can for many years before Warner Brothers finally released it. I attacked Mo Ostin [record company executive] on a plane once on a Warner Brothers' trip. They were flying us back and forth from Memphis to see something called the Doobie Brothers, and I said, 'Mo, you've got this famous record, *The Modern Lovers*.' They were so hot, and the record was just sitting there. 'Roadrunner' and 'Pablo Picasso' were two of the best tracks ever.
Danny Fields

Jonathan Richman for me stands alone. The first album was produced by John Cale. Its innocence and naivety were the anthem for the whole punk movement. 'Pablo Picasso' has some great lyrics about people trying to pick up girls and getting called an asshole, which would never have happened to Pablo Picasso because girls couldn't resist him. I mean, this is at a time when people were singing these abstract kind of lyrics, a psychedelic version of 'Summertime Blues' or Emerson Lake and Palmer or whatever their incarnation was. Then Jonathan Richman came along and sang songs that were sheer poetry in what they had to express. Cale found that very appealing.
Gene Krell

The Modern Lovers…they had it all.
Chris Sullivan

The Dead Boys were from Cleveland, Ohio, and they were fucking crazy, man. I mean, all that industrial angst. If ever a band could be called Punk with a capital P, they were it.

Gene Krell

The Dead Boys, of course, had something to rebel against. They were from Cleveland.
Gail Higgins Smith

We met Stiv Bators when we went to Cleveland. He was a very exciting, very charismatic guy, but he was totally mad. He invited us over to a party. We were following his car and, as he was driving, he climbs out of the window onto the roof of the car and moons us. Then he gets back in. That's how we met Stiv Bators.
Tommy Ramone

The Dead Boys were pre-punk and continued to live the life up till the mid-'80s.
Gene Krell

The Dead Boys were a very good rock'n'roll band. Cheetah Chrome was wonderful, and Stiv was a great front person. Both he and Cheetah really were terrors. And Johnny Blitz was a very strong drummer. Cheetah, Jimmy [Zero] the guitarist, and Stiv wrote most of the songs, and then they finally picked up a bass player [Jeff Magnum]. They were one of the most exciting things I'd ever heard. They had tremendous energy… Of course,

attitude-wise they were definitely punks…rebelling against the 'Yes sir, no sir' stuff they grew up with. Things changed and, in the end, after a couple of records, they were just yelling and screaming at each other. I was friendly with Cheetah and still see him. He married a Kennedy and they went to Ireland for their honeymoon.
Hilly Kristal

The Dead Boys didn't know New York. It almost killed them.
Gene Krell

Somebody had told me to go to CBGB's to see the greatest band in the world – the Dead Boys. So I went down [there] one night when they were playing, and…the first thing I [saw was] Stiv getting head on stage.
Bebe Buell, Liv Tyler's mother, in *Please Kill Me*

Stiv Bators was getting a blow job off some waitress at CB's in the middle of his set. I don't think he came or anything – I mean he had to stay in tune.
Leee Childers

Above: The Dead Boys (Cheetah Chrome, Jimmy Zero, Stiv Bators, Johnny Blitz) • Opposite: Jayne County

Mad drag queen attacks poor defenseless wrestler.

The Village Voice

The Dictators were a rowdy bunch. 'Handsome' Dick Manitoba was supposedly a wrestler. They drank a bit. One night at CBGB's, Jayne County was doing her thing on stage. She was wearing her big dress, her wig and the whole thing. I guess Dick was sitting at the end of the bar, which was near the stage at that point. I think he was probably yelling things. He says he was just having a good time. He came over to the stage and Jayne County thought he was about to attack her, so she picked up a microphone stand and hit him really hard. He ended up with a broken bone.
Hilly Kristal

I went on stage at CBGB's and everything was going just fine until I heard someone calling from the audience, 'Queer! Queer! You fucking drag queen!' I ignored him, I did another song and the same man started shouting abuse again. So I said, 'Who the fuck is that? Why don't you come up here and say it, you fucking asshole?' All of a sudden, up comes this short, fat, ugly thing with this horrible black curly hair. It was 'Handsome' Dick Manitoba of the Dictators. I started screaming at him, calling him all these names like 'fat pig'. Then he jumped on stage with a beer mug in his hand. I knew he'd been a professional wrestler and I was scared. I thought he was going to hit me, so I picked up my microphone stand, one of those with the heavy circular base, and hit him with it right on the collar-bone. He went flying and banged his head on the corner of a table, cutting it open. He picked himself up and attacked me again. I got him on the floor, sat on his chest and began hitting him in the face with my fists. They had to pull me off him. I was in full drag with make-up and a wig. My dress was ripped and there was blood all over me. People were screaming, 'Finish him off. Kill him.' I got back on stage and was still singing when the ambulance took him to hospital. The headlines in *The Village Voice* said: 'Mad drag queen attacks poor defenseless wrestler'. It was the worst thing I'd ever done, and I still very much regret it to this day. I was arrested after a few weeks and taken to the Tombs. They put me in a cell and charged me with assault. Eventually, after Dick failed to appear in court for the third time, the charges were dropped.
Jayne County

It was a huge deal and it was spontaneous. Manitoba's not a bad person at all, and I don't think he knew what came over him. I don't think he had any idea. He's a smart enough and sensitive enough guy, and I'm sure if he'd known what he would provoke, he wouldn't have done it. It became something of a *cause célèbre*. As a gay man, it certainly was powerful for me to see this drag queen beat the shit out of this wrestler. It caused a real divide in the scene, with people taking sides. He said he was just going to the bathroom, which was behind the stage. I'm not so sure. Jayne was very pivotal to the New York sound of rock'n'roll and stayed very consistent, and still is today.
Jim Fourrat

It turned into more than just a fight in a bar. Here we are 25 years later and we're still talking about it. In light of that, you should also mention that last summer they had a show together, where Manitoba got on stage with Jayne, did a duet with her and gave her a big kiss. Jayne is a DJ at Manitoba's club now and bygones are bygones.
Bob Gruen

'Chinese Rocks'

Song by Johnny Thunders and the Heartbreakers

When the New York Dolls broke up, Richard Hell formed the Heartbreakers because he wanted to be more in control of the group. He brought Johnny [Thunders] and Jerry [Nolan] with him so that he could have a guitar player and a drummer in his band. He didn't realize that one of the reasons the Dolls broke up was because Johnny wanted to lead a group, so within a couple of weeks they were having their differences. Richard then went on to form his own group – the Voidoids. Richard Hell wrote 'Blank Generation' when he was in Television, one of the first bands playing at CBGB's.
Bob Gruen

Jerry and John were a team: Jerry was like the father and John was the wild little brat. John was a sod, and Jerry would let him get away with it, up to a point. Jerry was about the only one that John ever respected because Jerry would pick him up and whack him, and John would shut up or stop acting up.
Walter Lure

I think the Heartbreakers played at CBGB's when Richard Hell was with the band. I was really anti-drugs and tried not to allow them. They got pretty deeply into that scene, so I set down rules. I didn't care what anybody did outside, but I didn't want drugs here. When Richard and Johnny and Nolan were all together, it was a great band. Johnny Thunders put a lot of energy into what he did. I don't know how he could do two shows – I don't know if he was drunk or high for the second show but he still did it. It's hard to explain what it was that he created, but he had a certain flair. He played the guitar well, and had his own way of playing. They were especially good, as far as I'm concerned, when he and Richard were together. It was wonderful. Richard was always good, very exciting; on key or off key he sounded good, though he wasn't a very good bass player.
Hilly Kristal

Our first show was at CBGB's…like a one-off show. I'd never seen such a mob as were there to see us. It was good fun, but we fucked up. We couldn't remember the songs. John was like nodding off on the walls. He had this white Falcon guitar, but the thing was all fucked up and wouldn't stay in tune. John thought his guitar looked really cool, and he didn't care what it sounded like.
Walter Lure

Richard Hell was a junkie who got out of bed with his hair messed up. He didn't notice, and everyone thought he looked good. He is credited with the idea of holding clothes together with safety-pins. The way I understand the story is that a girlfriend was angry with him and cut all his clothes up. He wanted to go out that night and he had nothing to wear, so he put his clothes together with safety-pins. Malcolm McLaren happened to be in the club that night and saw it and thought it was a fantastic style, 'a fascinating style' as Malcolm put it.
Bob Gruen

I never liked Richard Hell's versions of the songs we played, but Richard was in another world. He was in love with himself. It's not hard to find people like that in the industry, but he considered himself to be the only thing that was like serious art. His attitude really kept you away from a lot of his stuff. Some of the songs were good, and the lyrics were great. He was a funny guy. I just never wanted to follow him around because he was an obnoxious idiot. Walter Lure

Opposite: The Heartbreakers (Jerry Nolan, Richard Hell, Walter Lure, Johnny Thunders)

Richard Hell was probably one of the great geniuses of his generation, but he was just too smart for his own good. He couldn't get along in a band. He couldn't get along with Tom Verlaine when he was in Television, and he couldn't get along with Johnny Thunders. It was already that old thing: 'Go see the Heartbreakers tonight. It might be the last night they ever play because one of them will be dead soon.' A lot of people would go for that reason. Johnny and Richard Hell would physically fight on stage. When it broke up, and there was just Johnny, Jerry and Walter left, Johnny called me up and asked me if I would be interested in managing them. I called a friend and said I'd decided to manage the Heartbreakers, and he said, 'Are you crazy? They're junkies, they're nuts.' At least while I had the Heartbreakers I kept them alive. I got them a record contract, and they never ever missed a gig. **There were times when I had to push Johnny on stage, and I had to put a bucket out so he could throw up between songs, but you just deal with that reality. I never went into it thinking I was going to change them.** Leee Childers

Drugs fuelled a sense of
invincibility and immortality.

Legs McNeil

Poverty was one of the big influences on the scene. Everybody was incredibly poor. Mary Harron [the director of *American Psycho* and a contributor to *Punk Magazine*] was telling me recently about Tom Katz, who was one of the publishers of *Punk Magazine* and a good friend of Legs McNeil's. His budget was a dollar a day: he'd spend 50 cents on cigarettes and 50 cents on a slice of pizza and that's what he lived on. People didn't really have enough money to buy drugs. As the scene progressed, some women found ways to make money. Strippers could make $200 a day and, as a result, they were very desirable to have as girlfriends, and could probably help to sustain a drug habit. Within each band there may have been one person, or possibly two, who had a drug problem.
Roberta Bayley

It was very Melvillian – there's that line from *Moby Dick* where it says, 'If the sun offends thee, I would pluck it from the sky.' There was something about going against the grain, you know, driving the car off the cliff, which drugs certainly fuelled – a sense of invincibility and immortality.
Legs McNeil

I don't think there were any bands on hard drugs until Richard Hell and Johnny Thunders formed the Heartbreakers. Drugs were always running through the scene from the Velvet Underground to the Stooges, the Stooges probably being the worst offenders. But even the Velvet Underground weren't all heroin addicts. They wrote a song about heroin, but then they're artists. They write songs about the things that are out there in the world, and heroin is one of them. In the early days of Television there were a couple of people in the band who did heroin. On Sunday night, when you got paid your $25 for the gig, you might go to Avenue D and cop heroin and shoot up, but then you wouldn't have any money for another week or two.
Roberta Bayley

I think Richard Hell was the first person who shot up in front of me. I never did any heroin. Dee Dee [Ramone] and Connie were doing heroin, Richard was doing heroin, Johnny Thunders was doing heroin, as were a lot of other people. The scene seemed to me very hardcore. It was whisky and heroin, not pot and psychedelics. Some people smoked pot, but the punk scene had more of a drunk drug addict feel to it.
Legs McNeil

A lot of people aspired to doing drugs, but I didn't think it was really the defining element of the scene. I think Budweiser was much more the drug of choice. Mary Harron was saying she would get a Coke for $1 and nurse it all night, as she couldn't afford liquor. Danny Fields had a great line when he was asked, 'What is your drug of choice?' He said, 'Whatever's free.' If somebody offered you coke, you'd just do it. If somebody offers you a Rolls-Royce, you'll drive it away, so what's the problem? It wasn't like somebody was going to turn tricks so they could become a cocaine addict.
Roberta Bayley

The reason why us girls used to dress the way we did is because we were topless dancers and we had to wear the stilettos, the make-up, the hair, the feathers, and the gloves to hide our track marks.
Gyda Gash in *Please Kill Me*

The people that were into drugs were probably aware of all the people that did drugs, and the people that weren't into drugs were probably oblivious to it. Most people were just kids going down to a club and having fun.
Roberta Bayley

The sexual revolution supposedly happened in the '60s, but it didn't really filter down to anybody in the '70s. Some people in California were having sex in the '60s, but most people in America weren't. People weren't looking for relationships. They weren't looking to get married. I think the things they were looking at really made people horny. You just wanted a fuck. And that seems to be the point. Rock'n'roll, fucking and drugs – that's what I wanted.
Legs McNeil

The worst thing was that you wasted a lot of time getting fucked up with drugs. I suppose if the drugs weren't there, people might have been a lot more boring, but then not every band went through the same routine that we did. We were just known for it and took to it like ducks to water. If a band wasn't on drugs, they'd have some other problem. Rock'n'roll bands were supposed to have these problems. The fact is, I've been through all that and I'm still alive. I can pass on my knowledge. I would say a lot of time was wasted. You don't just stop it overnight. It takes quite a few years of running around like a lunatic to stop it. It's a waste.
Walter Lure

Left: Johnny Thunders

Punk was a massive insult

to anyone who'd been in the prison system, but fairly innocuous to anyone else. Nat Finkelstein

The name 'punk' came from me. John [Holmstrom] wanted to call the magazine *Teenage News*, which I thought was a stupid title. Years later, I found out it was from this unreleased New York Dolls' song. I didn't know this at the time. I just thought he was being stupid.
Legs McNeil

Punk Magazine came out before any English fanzines. Legs McNeil came up with the name but, more important than that, Legs was also the first person to call himself a punk. This was before anybody in England called themselves punks or was even aware of the phenomenon. At that time the term only existed in the United States. I knew there was punk rock, so when Legs thought of the name Punk, I thought it was perfect because I loved punk rock so much. I don't think Legs knew what punk rock was at the time, although I talked about it. The first issue of the magazine was an instant success. We got written up in the press, such as *The Village Voice*, and within a week everyone was clamouring for it everywhere.
John Holmstrom

I didn't want to do the magazine. I thought it was stupid. It seemed like work! John was a cartoonist,

and he had strips in magazines. I would write the script. I think I got paid $75 for each one, which was a lot of money. We got $150 per script between us. He was always bugging me, 'Come on, write some scripts.' And he'd always have to hold out a six-pack. It was kind of like that when he did the magazine. When he said he was going to call it *Teenage News*, I said why don't we call it *Punk*. In the early '70s there were all these TV shows like *Kojak* and *Columbo*. When they caught the bad guy at the end, they'd say, 'Hey, punk.' I was always running from the cops as a kid, and I got picked up by them a lot. If they caught you, they'd say, 'You're just nothing but a punk.'
Legs McNeil

The word 'punk' goes back to the '60s, but we were calling it punk rock in 1974, and in '75 they were referring to garage rock revival. Groundsville Station was punk rock, and Alice Cooper was punk rock. I remember getting copies of *NME* in the summer of '75 and they were calling AC/DC, the Bay City Rollers and Eddie and the Hot Rods punk rock. I remember seeing a big article on Eddie and the Hot Rods saying, 'Here comes punk,' but they weren't punk rock then, they were doing 'Woolly

Bully'. Here in the States, in 1975, *Creem* magazine would call anything remotely hard 'punk', and that included Alice Cooper, the MC5 and the Dictators.
John Holmstrom

So we were going to start the magazine, and John said, 'OK, I'll be the editor. There was another guy, Ged Dunn, who had the money, and he said he'd be the publisher. Then they looked at me and said, 'What are you going to do?' and John said, 'You can be the resident punk.' They were laughing hysterically, and I was kinda like, 'OK, gimme some beer.' That's how it started.
Legs McNeil

Within a few months there was huge demand for *Punk Magazine* in England. That's where we had our biggest market, and by the spring of '76 we were sending thousands of copies to Rough Trade [a London record shop]. They cost so much to airfreight that even though we were selling them at a great discount (we were trying to put them out as cheaply as possible), they were still selling for like $10 a piece. We were getting this reputation over there of ripping everyone off, but all the money was going into the airfreight. Rough Trade was trying to get the

magazine as quickly as they could because it was selling so fast. Then they came up with the great idea of photocopying everybody else's English fanzines, which kind of put us out of business. Suddenly, they didn't want our *Punk Magazine* any more. That first year, 1975, we brought out six or seven issues that were all over the UK.
John Holmstrom

We put together everything we liked – Lou Reed, the Ramones and the Dictators. We thought everybody was going to love it because we loved it. It was all about bad TV and comic books: everybody read comic books. I think we asked the Ramones what their favourite comic books were. We all had the same aesthetic without knowing each other. We all had the same taste. Chris Stein, the Ramones and everybody were huge fans of *Tales from the Crypt* [an American comic book]. It was very naive, but we just thought that what we were doing was better and more interesting than anything else.
Legs McNeil

At the time *Punk Magazine* said everything that needed to be said about the New York scene.
Leee Childers

In London McLaren and Westwood had opened Let It Rock in 1972, Too Fast to Live in '73 and Sex in '74. The latter would define the style of punk.

Chris Sullivan

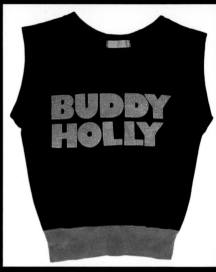

The metamorphosis of Let It Rock is an interesting story. There was a fellow named Trevor Miles, who was fascinated with Americana. He opened a small shop on the Kings Road in London called Paradise Garage. Everyone said the shop lacked a certain authenticity, so he discovered Malcolm McLaren and Vivienne Westwood, or rather they discovered him. Malcolm was still in art school or had just graduated. Malcolm and Vivienne sold old radios and repaired them in the back of Trevor's shop. Eventually, they started to sell records. Trevor then agreed to let them sell some clothes in the shop. When Paradise Garage failed, Malcolm and Vivienne appropriated the shop and started selling '50s Teddy boy clothing. Malcolm's contention was that Billy Fury was more important than Bob Dylan. He thought that rockabillies walked on water, but in most cases they walked on him. They refused to pay for anything.
Gene Krell

I first went to Let It Rock for a pair of creepers. That's what everybody did – it was the only place that sold them. I was really young. I think I was still in school. They sold clothes like hound's-tooth drapes with velvet collars, with big turn-ups, which I really liked. All the clothes seemed very classy, and the fabrics were really nice. At the time everywhere else sold stuff made out of horrible manmade fibres. Let It Rock used proper tailoring techniques, and the shop itself was very tactile. I think that's why people remember it so well. It kind of smelt good and everything was nice to touch – the rubber curtains, all the cloths, the mohair jumpers and all that. It wasn't like that scratchy horrible Lurex feel that all the other shops had.
Marco Pirroni

There was something surreal about it. He would have drag queens and Teddy boys in the same shop, which

was, and still is, unheard of. The shop had more incarnations than Shirley MacLaine. It started out selling '50s gear, and from that it evolved into Too Fast to Live, Too Young to Die, which was a bikers' shop. That was the beginnings of punk. Then it was called Sex, with the wonderful Jordan. After that I think it became Seditionaries, and then, ultimately, World's End.
Gene Krell

All these weird people shopped there. You could never figure out who the fuck they were. There were all the people left over from the end of the '60s – these Kings Road groovers who'd stopped being hippies, like Dougie Fields [artist] and Andrew Logan [sculptor]. Obviously they were much older than me and they were dressed in the stuff, but you could never figure out what they did. It's not like now, when everyone's stylish and fashionable.
Marco Pirroni

I think that's why people remember Let It Rock so well – it smelt good. Marco Pirroni

I walked in and wanted to buy **everything.**

Steve Severin

Malcolm was certainly the ideas person. He knew exactly what he wanted the shop to look like. Vivienne would then finesse the whole thing. I guess it started with Paradise Garage, which was owned by Trevor Miles, who used to import American stuff. The shop was all done out like a jungle, with '50s bamboo lettering on the front. Trevor sublet a little bit out the back of the shop to Malcolm and Vivienne. They used to sell old seven-inch singles and rocker stuff. Then they started to sell clothing, creepers and drapes. Roger Bourton, clothing supplier to the film industry

When I first went into Sex I thought, 'I want everything!' It was like a dream come true; there was nowhere else like it. Every week there'd be something new, and you'd go. 'That's just brilliant!' Malcolm sort of encouraged you to hang out there and get into the whole thing. Everyone would save up what they could to get the one item they felt was most important to them. This was way before all the bondage stuff and that. Everything was individual, and you'd think, 'That's it! That's exactly what I've been looking for.' It was way beyond the Bowie stuff, which we couldn't possibly live up to anyway. Everybody was young and trying to make their mark, going to jumble sales to find odd bits and pieces to put their own look together, all very cheap and nasty. We wanted to look a bit different, a bit more stylish than the Bay City Rollers. Then along comes this shop and it's just beyond anything we'd hoped for. Steve Severin When I was working at Let It Rock, they were doing a lot of Ted stuff. Then, because a lot of the Teds wanted stuff to be made up, they moved into made-to-measure – what Malcolm called 'Alan Ladd' suits, sort of early '50s two-button, wide-lapelled jackets with big shoulders made in beautiful pale gabardine. Then they moved onto these single-breasted zoot suits that Malcolm called jazz suits, with the sharp, nipped-in waist and peg trousers that ballooned right out. For the time it was totally new. Glen Matlock **At the time there were certain**

rumblings that were inherently '50s in character. Bryan Ferry and Andy [Mackay] of Roxy Music both sported quiffs and '50s attire on the inner cover of their first album, albeit somewhat glam. Let It Rock and Too Fast to Live Too Young to Die brought a definite authentic street edge to the '50s look. The shop was filled with both retro and replica '50s garments, some of which were imported from the US – flecked jackets, peg trousers, hand-painted ties, gabardine shirts. These items became the stock in trade for all the hip clothing stores of the Kings Road – Acme Attractions, Retro, Marx, American Classics – for the next 10 years. These shops clothed every self-respecting style-monger, from the Soul Boys to the swing fraternity at the Goldmine in Canvey Island and the hyper-trendies of the Kings Road. In 1971 the whole concept of '50s clothing in the midst of hippie nonsense was totally radical, and Let It Rock was the shop that defined and perfected the look. They did Edwardian-style drapes and perfectly tailored late '40s double-breasted suits in pale gabardine, and were probably the first to revive the zoot suit, albeit refined. The '50s as a style is now commonplace, but Malcolm McLaren and Vivienne Westwood were probably the first to do it second time around at Let It Rock. Chris Sullivan The other

thing I could never work out was when it was open. I'd go down there at midday and it would be shut. I'd go back at 4.00 p.m. and it would still be shut. It was even closed on Saturday mornings. Maybe that's another reason why it was so hip – you had to be a part of some inner circle to know when it was open. I don't know how they made any money. Marco Pirroni

I first came across pictures of Let It Rock in a girlie magazine called *Club International*, and they literally changed my life. To this day I have yet to see a better fashion spread. It featured Malcolm McLaren, amongst others, modelling these superb American early '50s suits and hand-painted ties against period billboards and cars. Alongside him was a girl in pink pedal-pushers with a matching pink poodle. Dave Parkinson, a friend of McLaren's who later killed himself, took the photos. The man was a genius. It affected me so much that I've spent my life collecting these clothes. Superb. Chris Sullivan

MALCOLM SAID THAT HE WAS MANAGING THIS BAND WHO WOULD BE THE NEXT BAY CITY ROLLERS...

Nils Stevenson

Left to right: Glen Matlock, Johnny Rotten, Paul Cook, Steve Jones

The Sex Pistols are about as subtle as
a sawn-off shotgun.

Record Mirror, 10 December 1976

We wanted to shake things up. We grew up with three-day weeks and power cuts, sitting with candles. Corrugated iron everywhere, like the war was happening. Nobody considered the future really. It was just a crack…but we did influence a lot of people, not just music – fashion, and even comedy.
Paul Cook

They looked and sounded like nothing I'd ever seen before. Absolutely stunning, but disturbing at the same time.
Mark Perry, *The Essential Punk Accessory*

I remember that St Martin's gig. I went into Sex that day and they had flyers with the pistol on the front, remember? They were brilliant. I couldn't say musically they were brilliant, but it was just a shock to see. They were nothing like you'd ever seen before. They captured all the things you really wanted to do and say…they did it with style. Everybody was incredibly young at the time. I think it was coincidental that the Pistols were actually good. They did write good songs. I don't know what would have happened if their songs had been crap – if they'd been average sort of punk fare. Although you couldn't really hear them, that didn't matter when you saw them. You just saw the attitude of the singer, who didn't really give a fuck. That was just anti.
Marco Pirroni

The Sex Pistols' audience at the beginning didn't go to watch bands. They didn't like them. It was not a band scene.
Chris Sullivan

Above, left to right: Glen Matlock, Johnny Rotten, Paul Cook and Steve Jones on stage • Opposite: Original Sex Pistols' poster

We thought pop stars came from outer space and we couldn't do it. Paul Cook

We were all based around Shepherd's Bush. We all went to the same school, Christopher Reading, right next to the White City Estate, which is where we all come from. I'd known Steve Jones since about 10. Our mums knew each other. Jonesy was always the loose cannon, getting into trouble even from a really young age. He never went to school, so he was sent away to boarding-school when he was young.

We all grew up in the early '70s when it was all glam rock stuff – Marc Bolan, David Bowie, Roxy Music, Gary Glitter. But we used to go and see all kinds of bands. Wally [Warwick Nightingale] was really into the Faces. We always bunked in, never paid to get in anywhere. It was so easy in those days. We'd always find a way round. It was a big adventure getting in – all part of it really.

It was our last summer at school. We had bunked off and were sitting around in Wally's back garden when he said, 'Let's start a band.' God knows what we were going to play. We thought Jonesy, being the loose cannon, would have to be singer… Wally would be on guitar, Jim [Mackin] was going to play keyboard, Steve was meant to play bass and myself on the drums, and that's how it went for a little bit. Steve started strumming along on the guitar as well. Eventually the bass and keyboard player baled out, and I carried on with the drums and Wally was on guitar.

We'd always be up the Kings Road hanging around Malcolm's shop. At the time it was called Let It Rock, I think. Steve would be up there a lot. He didn't go to school. We ended up becoming quite good friends with Malcolm because it was the only place where you could go and hang out.

Glen [Matlock] was working in the shop then. We were looking for a bass player. Steve came back one day and said, 'I've got a bass player,' and I said, 'Where from?' He said, 'He works in the shop, as Malcolm's assistant,' and I just thought, well, great, you know, go and meet him, and that worked out fine. He did play bass and he was quite a competent musician, more so than we were at the time. Paul Cook

When I worked in the shop, Steve and Paul used to come in. Paul used to chat Malcolm up, saying, 'Be our manager, be our manager.' Paul's brother-in-law was the bass player and he never used to turn up, so they needed a bass player… We used to rehearse in a place in Hammersmith, which later became the Riverside Studios. Wally's old man was an electrician and he got the contract to strip out anything worthwhile from this place. He got us a set of keys cut and we had a studio. It had the best sound-room in Europe. Steve used to turn up with all the best equipment. Glen Matlock

Steve had a mission really, to get equipment now. Before, he was nicking anything. Now he knew he had to go and get musical equipment. We didn't have any money at the time – we'd never be able to afford to buy it anyway – and we managed to get a whole back line-up, guitars, drums and everything. I mean, we didn't nick it all; we bought some of it, but not much. People were quite impressed with our line-up, and we could barely play.

Once Glen was involved in the band, we thought he might be able to help us become a real band. At that time, Malcolm didn't know much about music. He had this jukebox with all this rock'n'roll stuff and was still selling Teddy Boy retro stuff, so he was kind of stuck in the past. I suppose we dragged him into the '70s. He started to come down to see us. He was kind of interested in what we were up to because Steve was always in the shop, virtually all week. He didn't live very far away from the Kings Road.

Malcolm started to come down then and see us rehearse and, at the time, we could barely play. We were playing old Faces' numbers or whatever. Anything with three chords. We were doing all this stuff and we were a bit confused. We were along the way of falling out with Wally. Malcolm saw that and said, 'I don't think he's the right one. He doesn't have the right attitude.'

I must say Wally pissed us all off. He was a bit precious about everything. We thought eventually we

Above: David Bowie c. 1973 • Opposite, top to bottom: Paul Cook; Steve Jones, Paul Cook, Johnny Thunders and Leee Childers; Johnny Rotten and Glen Matlock; Paul Cook and Tracey O'Keefe

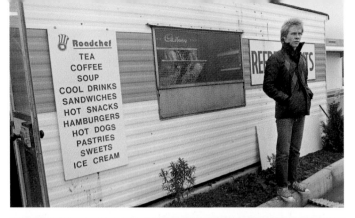

must get rid of him. And of course we lost our rehearsal place because that was down to Wally's dad. Wally was outed rather unceremoniously, and then we thought, 'We've got to look for a front man.' It was quite clinical really, but we knew what we had to do. I didn't see Wally for a long time after the Pistols. I think I might have bumped into him once and he was always very bitter about it. I mean, that's the way things worked out. He died eventually – took loads of pills or something. He always used to be on pills.
Paul Cook

Malcolm's first real task as our manager was to find us a singer, and this was at the tail end of when Wally was still in the band. He'd invite people to have a jam at the studios. I mean, one bloke came down and then another bloke stayed, looked the part but couldn't sing. John [Lydon] was always one of the crowd down the Kings Road, but it was funny, we were still trying out other people, perhaps four or five.

   The most important thing Malcolm did was provide us with a sort of base at his shop. People with lots of money used to come, much older than us. He used to laugh at them. But he always gave us a place to hang out when we needed it most.
Glen Matlock

The first time I met Steve Jones and Paul Cook at the pub I thought they were just two hoodlums. They had nothing to do with my world at all. They looked like villains, and they were kind of scary, like skinheads. But when I started speaking to them, they were really nice, like two working-class sort of funny blokes.
Nils Stevenson

The band, when we started, was a school band really, with mates from school, myself, Jonesy and Wally.

Paul Cook

Chicken wire, Cambridge Rapist masks, inflatable foam rubber with things sprayed on it, shoes that looked like orthopaedic wear, and a dwarf.

Steve Walsh

Sex was a bit freakish, wasn't it? Leather on one side, rubber on the other. At the back you had your Teddy boys' stuff.
Helen Wellington Lloyd, assistant in Sex and McLaren muse

I heard there was a shop on the Kings Road that sold brothel creepers. I went down and walked in there thinking, 'What an amazing place!' It was like a sitting-room. Either I was going to get the elbow or I was going to have to leave. I said, 'Do you want anybody to work here?' and they said, 'We do actually.'
Glen Matlock

It was very intimidating you know – the whole atmosphere. It was like a weird mixture of sexual slogans and things on the wall. What made it for me was that, at the time, I was ready for a bit of fetish, bondage stuff, but when I walked in, Jordan was there and I thought, 'Oh, weird-looking girl, a bit on the large side,' but then there was the dwarf, Helen. That really did it for me for some reason. I was hooked.
Steve Walsh

Sex became the place to hang out, to find out what was going on, if there was a party or whatever. Things weren't like now – there was nowhere to go. It was gay clubs or parties. So all these people used to pop into the shop, all types of people from all over. But the clothes were very expensive: most came in just to have a look. There were '50s types in their suits and '60s types in winkle-pickers and, of course, the perverts in their macs. The police came and investigated the shop as there was a rumour that the Cambridge rapist had bought his mask there.
Helen Wellington Lloyd

At the time Jordan was working there, Steve was already working in the shop. Every Saturday, without exception, we'd get on a number 11 bus and get off at World's End, march up and down the Kings Road and then end up in Malcolm's shop and basically just hang around.
Paul Cook

Saturdays, we'd parade the Kings Road in the same clothes we wore to clubs, full of our own superiority. We'd walk slowly from Sloane Square to World's End and hang around outside Malcolm McLaren and Vivienne Westwood's shop, Sex, daring each other to step inside. Entering was like testing the water of a freezing pool. Jordan, the psycho-hived manageress, was every bit as intimidating as the premises, a small dark shop with sloping wooden floor and blacked-out windows. She dressed like a sadistic Tiller girl, carried a whip and hissed at customers. Hers was a very modern sales technique .
Boy George in *Take It Like a Man*

Sex had a definite ideology. It wasn't about selling anything; it was about creating attitude. It wasn't some fucking middle-of-the-road golden oldies shop. It was nothing quite like anything in New York. Nobody in New York was selling rock'n' roll culture, in the form of dress and music, in one particular place.
Malcolm McLaren in *Please Kill Me*

I went into Sex in the Kings Road in '75. I thought it felt a bit…lonely.
Paul Durden

I first saw the shop Sex in a magazine called *Forum* that I pinched from a newsagent (as one does). It was an erotic sort of readers' letters/advice mag. There were these black and white photos of Vivienne Westwood, Chrissie Hynde, Alan Jones (who worked in the shop) and Steve Jones, who was later in the Sex Pistols. They were all bent over with the word Sex written on their rear ends. At first I ignored the article as I was looking for the good bits. Then, on one of my trips to the Kings Road, I left Beaufort Market and took a little detour to World's End and there it was – Sex. I must admit, it took courage to go in as it was not at all inviting, but when I did, I found it a bit creepy. You felt as if you were under the scrutiny of the rather extreme assistants who, as far as I could gather, were not there to help but to put you off. It took me a while to buy something – about four visits.
Chris Sullivan

Sex was brilliant. I absolutely loved it. When it opened, there were only a few of us who went there: the Bromley lot, Anne Ferris, the first girl in London to have green hair, Little Debbie, Sue Catwoman, Linda Ashby, not a lot more. It was like a little club. At first no one wore the stuff it sold. It took a lot of guts to wear it all those years ago.
Phillip Salon, club promoter

I was at Granny Takes a Trip just down the street and we used to dress all the big rock bands. It was really quite odd all the people that went there. I used to see Jeremy Thorpe all the time, the Sensational Alex Harvey Band, Chris Spedding, Nick Kent the writer. I think when it was Too Fast To Live it even clothed Kilburn and the High Roads because Tommy Roberts, who made the Bowie pin-ups suit, knew Malcolm and managed Ian Dury. I remember one day Mick Jagger came in to Granny's after having been in Let It Rock and just didn't get it. He'd seen Malcolm and overheard him talking and couldn't work out why someone who looked like a Ted spoke so eloquently. I don't think Jagger ever got it.
Gene Krell

Sex was more than a shop – it was a concept.
Steve Severin

Opposite and above: Unidentified girl, Alan Jones, Chrissie Hynde, Vivienne Westwood, Jordan

As a child, whenever they used to tell me to write 'I will not be bad', I changed [it] to 'I will be so bad.' And that amused me no end. Malcolm McLaren in *Please Kill Me*

Malcolm never went to school in his life. He went for one day, came back and told his grandmother that they were all imbeciles. He refused to go after that. He led this insular life – never had any idea how to relate to other people in a family way. He had this completely mad upbringing, but yet he has a kind of genius and a sense of energy that was just unbelievable. Joe Corré **Alan Jones introduced me to this shop. It was a very intimidating place. You really had to be brave to go in there because the shop assistants treated you like shit. It looked very, very hardcore, a Teddy boy kind of place. Nevertheless, I was besotted with Vivienne because she looked extraordinary, with spiky white hair. There was no other girl around who looked like that. I got a couple of dates with Vivienne. We used to go off in her puke-green Mini to various places and I managed to snog her a few times. I was quite chuffed about it. She seemed quite schoolgirlish about the whole thing. As this relationship between Vivienne and me started developing, I think Malcolm may have actually cottoned on because suddenly I found him arriving at my house in Richmond. I shared the house with a bunch of hippie drug smugglers. It became like this *ménage à trois* without any sex. We'd hang out together in a platonic kind of fashion.** Nils Stevenson Sometimes Malcolm would go missing for days and we'd ask Vivienne where he was. She'd say, 'Oh, I've locked him in a cupboard under the stairs.' We all laughed, but then we realized she was serious. There was something rather odd going on. Alan Jones, assistant in Sex, 1975-7 **There wasn't anything kinky about it. He'd just be locked in under the stairs, sitting there trying to get out.** Marco Pirroni Soon Malcolm managed to push himself between Vivienne and me and I found myself much more interested in him. We talked and talked drunkenly about doing this club together. Then, one night, he mentioned that he managed this band who he said were going to be the next Bay City Rollers. I thought, 'That sounds like shit. What are you talking about?' Nils Stevenson **I was this strange guy with this mad dream. I was trying to do with the Sex Pistols what I had failed to do with the New York Dolls. I was taking the nuances of Richard Hell, the faggy, pop side of the New York Dolls, the politics of boredom, and mashing it all together to make a statement, maybe the final statement, and piss off this rock'n'roll scene. That's what I was doing. I wasn't doing anything new. I was waiting my turn to make the statement I'd been trying to make since I was 14.** Malcolm McLaren in *Please Kill Me* No matter what Malcolm or Vivienne say, it was basically a fashion, a scene with about 30 or so people…at the start. Alan Jones

Johnny Rotten just hangs from the mike stand…
burns the crowd
with his glassy, taunting, cynical eyes.

Tony Parsons, *New Musical Express*, 9 December 1976

I'd seen Johnny in the shop. He used to hang about with a gang of guys. They all had shaved hair at the time, dyed green and red. You didn't have to do much to stick out in those days. He kind of stuck out. We would eye him up. He had a look about him. He even came into the shop with that look.
Paul Cook

John was one of the crowd that used to stop at pubs on the way down the Kings Road on a Saturday. He looked exactly like Richard Hell. John always looked like that. Malcolm had nothing to do with it. John was the first person to use safety-pins.
Glen Matlock

Malcolm just said to him, 'We're looking for a singer. Can you sing?' He just came out with something like, 'Yeah, really badly and out of tune.' Malcolm said, 'Well, that will do.' He came down that night and we met him in the pub just round the corner. We sat there and chatted with him for a few hours. You know, I liked him straight away. Steve was a bit more suspicious of him than me. I thought he would be great. He certainly had an attitude about him.
Paul Cook

At one point they were going to have this guy called David sing in the band – a very handsome guy but with no charisma, and he may have even been gay. Imagine that, man, the Sex Pistols with a gay singer…
Gene Krell

Rotten looked the part with his green hair, but he couldn't sing. Then again, we couldn't play, so it was OK.
Steve Jones

He came round the shop the next day. Malcolm had the jukebox there and we said, 'What can you do?' We put on Alice Cooper's 'Eighteen' and said, 'Go on, sing.' He just went into an act in front of the jukebox, going into spasms. This was late at night, about one in the morning. He wailed and screamed. I was in stitches. I thought, yeah, he's great. We said, 'Come down. We'll try it out.' That's basically how it happened. That's how we met him. Malcolm didn't really know what to make of Johnny's act, but he knew we needed a front man.

Paul Cook

Left and opposite: Johnny Rotten

Ro**en's not **e **ind of bloke who looks at someone else and thinks he'll copy them. I think he's unique.

Nils Stevenson

thought John was great. I really liked him because he was always trying to stretch himself intellectually. He wanted, and needed, new ideas. He tapped into people. I think I was one, as were Malcolm and Vivienne. He was like a sponge, just soaking up every fucking idea everybody had.
Nils Stevenson

Rotten had incredible taste.
Steve Walsh

You'd play him something like Herbie Hancock and he'd think it was brilliant. He'd always have a point of view. He liked difficult music because there was a sort of snobbishness about John. If it was difficult, he'd be interested. He didn't want to know about Rod Stewart or all the stuff that Paul and Steve liked. But you could stretch him…he was great.
Nils Stevenson

Johnny was a little odd because he had this real negative nastiness about him, like he was working very hard at it. He would say off-the-wall, sarcastic, cynical things like: 'Wow, excuse me for being in your life.'
Bob Gruen

He wanted to know everything that I knew. Although I was only a couple of years older than him, I had lived in San Francisco. I had been through a lot of weird shit and he wanted to soak it all up. He wanted to know what I listened to. He was particularly obsessed with music.
Nils Stevenson

Whatever you think about Johnny Rotten, he had something that was very special. The whole attitude and delivery that he had was fantastic really. There was nothing else like it. He had an attitude that was genuine. He never liked me but I was only eight at the time.
Joe Corré

On stage, great front man; off stage, total fucking arsehole.
Frank Kelly, Sex Pistols aficionado

John's mother would ring up and say in her broad Irish accent, 'Now do look after my Johnny because he never has been well. He was very ill as a child and he's very

contrary. If he likes you, he will say he hates you. He always says the opposite of what he really means.'
Helen Wellington Lloyd

We did the 100 Club and there was nobody there, sort of a midweek thing. John was really out of it. I don't know what happened. I think he'd shot himself up with speed or something. He sang all the words perfectly, but to all the wrong songs. So we were doing 'Pretty Vacant' and I was singing 'You're just, you're just a wanker' to John, and he said to me, 'Do you want a fight?' and I said, 'We're doing a gig. After the gig, yeah, definitely' and he stormed off. He walked up the stairs, out of the club and waited for the number 73 bus outside while we were still playing. Malcolm followed him up the stairs and told him, 'Get back on stage or you're out.'
Glen Matlock

He was one of the smartest people I had ever met – someone very young who had a vision and for whatever reason was absolutely at the centre of this spinning record, because they embody the thing they are representing… Certainly, of all the interviews I've ever done, Johnny Rotten was the most impressive.
Mary Harron, journalist, in *Please Kill Me*

I remember we had to take Johnny to the dentist in Streatham. He was just shitting himself the whole way there. He was so nervous…he hadn't been to a dentist for 20 years or so. He had these completely rotten teeth. That's why he was called Johnny Rotten. The dentist took a picture for his records to show that this could happen to your teeth – like a textbook case.
Joe Corré

John comes on now like he was a sort of stud in those days. He wasn't, you know. It's just rubbish. He used to claim to hate sex, but obviously he was fascinated by it. He and Sid had a squat in Hampstead, and all over the walls there were beaver shots cut out of magazines. They were just everywhere. John's take on it was: 'We're taking the piss, you know – everything's crap and pathetic.' But he didn't really think that. He was obsessed with it. He was in denial with all this Catholic guilt about sex and stuff, whereas Steve Jones didn't have any of those problems at all.
Nils Stevenson

He was an asshol a total asshole, a jerk-off. It wasn't that I didn't like him; no one liked him.

Eliot Kidd, lead singer of the Demons

When I first saw Steve Jones play, I thought, 'Fuck, I could do that,' but I didn't do it first. I didn't think of it. That's the important bit.

Marco Pirroni

Steve Jones came to stay with me at Richmond when my flatmates, the hippie drug smugglers, went off to India on one of their regular visits. He couldn't stand the studio in Denmark Street. It was disgusting. He nicked a load of jewellery belonging to the hippies, so got kicked out. I had to move into the hell-hole in Denmark Street. But, you know, Steve was fantastic. He supported Paul and me. He stole food for us and everything. It was great. We would have died without him. We would have starved.

Nils Stevenson

I always thought Steve Jones's guitaring made your hair stand on end. It was the thing that really got to you. It was just the way he did that. It was electrifying. It just drove the whole place mad. There was something in here, some magic, some raw nerve that it touched and you couldn't help yourself.

Joe Corré

I love Steve to death. I just love him. He had this thing with music. His guitar was just like sex. That's what his guitaring says: 'There are no fiddly bits. I'm just going to stick it in your mouth and that's it.' There's nothing else. It's really direct, it's really fucking serious, and if you don't like it, tough shit. He made a powerful partner for John. The front man, Rotten, was terrified of sex, and the guitarist, Steve, was this knob on legs. They were two powerful things, two ends of a spectrum.

Nils Stevenson

Steve was a thief and had real flair and loved clothes. He was always in the shop trying to nick a jumper or whatever. Basically, nicking from Malcolm and running down the road with something or other. But I remember Malcolm telling my mum, 'Watch that boy. Watch what he goes for because he's got something, you know. Watch what he gets because he's good and he knows what's good.'

Joe Corré

Steve stole all of David Bowie's mikes before the Last Stand concert at Hammersmith, the Ziggy Stardust thing. Before us Bowie was huge, but we stole his equipment... and his thunder.

Glen Matlock

When we started out, we liked the Dolls and the Faces. In fact, we wanted to BE the Faces.

Steve Jones

What is punk music?

It's disgusting, degrading, ghastly, sleazy, prurient, voyeuristic and nauseating...

Most of these groups would be vastly improved by sudden death.

Bernard Brook Partridge, member of the Greater London Council, 25 December 1976

Opposite, left to right: Johnny Rotten and Steve Jones; Paul Cook, Steve Jones and Johnny Rotten; Paul Cook and Steve Jones • Above: Steve Jones and Glen Matlock

It all started with a band me and Mick Jones had called London SS, which was a New York Dolls thing.

Tony James, bass player, Generation X

Punk should be remembered if only to illustrate how influential a small group of people can be. Chris Sullivan We wanted to be the New York Dolls. We had long hair, platform shoes, tight satin trousers. I have a London SS tape that has us playing 'Road Runner' by Jonathan Richman, 'Barracuda' by the Night Breeds, 'Rambling Rose' by the MC5, and a track by the Flaming Groovies – our influences at the time. Tony James **The New York Dolls were already passé by the time punks started in Britain.** Kevin Rowland, Dexy's Midnight Runners The inner core of the early punk phenomenon seemed to stem from two places – a shop in a seedy part of Chelsea and a café in the seedier Praed Street in Paddington. It seems to have been the result of a conspiracy between two managers and a handful of young musicians. Chris Sullivan **We were advertising in *Melody Maker* for people into the New York Dolls, the Stooges and MC5. No one else was advertising for anything like that. It was as if it was a world that didn't exist, and like two people would phone up and we'd go and meet them and generally they either looked terrible or just wrong or didn't know what we were talking about. There was one guy who sent us a letter from Manchester who said how much he loved the New York Dolls and he wanted to be a singer. We never took him seriously; we never thought he'd be any good. How could a bloke called Morrissey from Manchester ever make it? We never did go and meet him. Brian James [of the Damned] answered the advert. He was playing in a group called Bastard in Croydon, so he joined. So many people came through the ranks of that place.** Tony James London SS provided the nucleus of the three main acts on the scene apart from the Pistols – the Clash, the Damned and Chelsea, who became Generation X. Stephen Colegrave **Bernie Rhodes started managing the group after a rather odd confrontation. I'd been to Sex in the Kings Road and bought one of those T-shirts that says 'One day you'll wake up and know what side of the bed you've been lying on'. Mick Jones and I were standing at the gig watching the show, and this little bloke in a hat that was standing next to us and he was wearing the very same T-shirt as me. So I sort of leant over and went, 'Excuse me, mate, can you stand over there wearing the same T-shirt? You're making us look bad here.' He went, 'You cunt. I fucking invented this T-shirt. I designed it. What do you know about rock'n'roll?' So we started talking and said we had this group called London SS. He thought it sounded interesting and said, 'My mate's got a group called the Sex Pistols. They're these three young kids and we're putting it all together. They live in Chelsea.' So we suggested he come and see us, and then Bernie started working for London SS.** Tony James Bernie Rhodes, with his constant questioning and confrontational

...three weeks after the T-shirt episode, Bernie called and said, 'I need to meet you both.' Me and Mick met him in a pub called the Bush in Shepherds Bush Green, which was then a very heavy area. So we're sitting in the bar of this straight working-man's pub and Bernie opens his bag and starts slapping Nazi regalia on the table – swastikas, flags and daggers. We're like, 'Bernie, we're gonna be killed here.' He went, 'What you've got to understand if you're going to call your group London SS is that you'd better be ready for that, otherwise you're not for real.' That kind of shook our belief in what seemed to us to be just a provocative name. Looking back on it, London SS would have been a huge burden. We thought it was OK because Kiss had used SS, and they were another group that we liked at the time.
Tony James

A lot of the credit for the whole punk explosion has gone, for whatever reason, to Malcolm McLaren, but in fact Bernie Rhodes was equally responsible, and in traditional terms infinitely more successful as a manager.
Chris Sullivan

What Bernie gave us was an understanding. In the '60s mods were synonymous with the Two I's coffee bar, and in the '70s the Sex Pistols were synonymous with the shop Sex in the Kings Road. Bernie made us understand that you've got to have a base, a place where you hang out. We said, 'Well, we all live in Paddington,' so Bernie said 'Let's meet in Praed Street. That's where all the hookers go.' So we walk down this street and there's this place called the Praed Street Café, so that became our base. For weeks and weeks Mick and I hung out in this café on our own. We auditioned all the people for London SS in the café – it was our scene. Bernie infiltrated the café and put his records on the juke box. So here we were single-handedly trying to create a coffee bar scene in the middle of a red light district. Next thing Bernie says, 'You've got to have your own rehearsal place, your own PA, your own posters on the walls.' Two weeks later he says, 'I've found you a place, it's perfect. I'll show you where it is.' We walk out the door of the café, we turn right, right and right again, then we go in through a little door under the café. It's a dingy basement 20 foot square, really low ceiling. He says, 'This is the place.' Two weeks later he turns up with PA equipment and microphones, which we subsequently found out Steve Jones had stolen from backstage at the Mick Ronson/Ian Hunter gigs. So we then had our equipment and our base.
Tony James

We rehearsed and rehearsed for about a year with London SS, but it never really got off the ground. We couldn't find a singer or a drummer. When we did find a drummer (Rat Scabies), the others didn't want him, so me and Rat went and formed the Damned.
Brian James, guitarist, the Damned

The main nucleus of the group was me, Mick Jones, Brian James and various occasional drummers. Bernie

really liked the idea of having this bloke from Purley, and his idea was to call the drummer Chain Pain and to keep him chained to his drum kit. He'd be really red and sweating and we'd have girls coming on and they'd whip him while he was playing drums. When you look back, it was a very Bernie/Malcolm idea.
Tony James

I thought being in a band was about pulling birds and having a right grin, not bloody politics.
Frank Kelly

Bernie Rhodes was our manager. We were being groomed by him and he used to make our lives a misery because he would always say to us, 'Tell me what you're about,' and we didn't know what he meant. He used to say, 'I haven't heard one statement from you that's anything different,' and we'd go, 'What do you mean, statement? What do you mean, what we're about?' because we didn't understand art. On several occasions Bernie said to me, 'You don't know what's happening, you don't know what's going on. One day, when you know what's going on, then you'll be happy in yourself.' This was the riddle that Bernie would always say to us. He would phone me up at all hours in my middle-class house in Twickenham and go, 'Have you got any ideas?' and I'd go, 'We want to be in a band.' He'd say, 'Yeah, but what's your ideas? What are you about? What are you saying?' We didn't understand what he meant. No one had ideas or something to say as they do now. In those days it was a radical thing. Bernie was very clever at tutoring us through this maze. It was almost like a Zen thing. It was like, 'I can't tell you the answer to the riddle. You have to find it out yourself. I can only pose the riddle. When you can answer the riddle, then you'll be happening.' It took us a long time to understand. Bernie would give me reading lists: 'You should read Sartre, you should go and read about modern art, you should read about Jackson Pollock,' and I dutifully trotted to the library and got all the books out and read about all this stuff and gradually I began to understand. I began to ask, 'What is a modern artist's idea? What's his theme? What's he saying? What does his work say to you?'
Tony James

It's amazing how many people involved in punk actually came from art school.
Clive Langer, songwriter and producer

They all came from an art school background, applying the ideas of art to rock'n'roll. It took us a long time to understand it because they would always say, 'I can't tell you what it is.' We were all very much rock'n'roll fans and had read all the books about the Rolling Stones' parties, so one night Bernie took me and Mick and Brian James, who was then playing with London SS, in his little car to this grand party in Hamilton Terrace. We parked outside and watched all these famous and

groovy bohemian people going in. Then Bernie said, 'I could take you to this party 'cause I know the people' and we thought that would be great, then he went, 'But I'm not going to because you're not ready for it' and he drove us away. I remember sitting in a café in Praed Street and Bernie saying, 'What are your songs about?' I said, 'Sort of love songs' and he said, 'That's not good enough – you've got to be about something.' This is pre-'Anarchy in the UK' pre-political, although you could say the MC5 were political, but we didn't get it for a long time.
Tony James

As guided by McLaren and Rhodes, the initial punk thing was extremely well thought out. They were all very knowledgeable about existential literature, art and philosophy. It was deliberately confrontational – that was the point.
Chris Sullivan

Mick and I used to go see the 101ers every week with Joe singing, little knowing that Mick would one day end up in one of the greatest song-writing partnerships ever with Joe Strummer.
Tony James

There was this guy I knew at college who was a drummer, and he said he was accosted in the street by a couple of characters who said, 'Are you a drummer?' (He probably had drumsticks poking out of his pockets.) He told me he'd got an audition with their group and asked if I wanted to come along. I said OK so we turned up at this really dingy place in Paddington and there was Mick Jones, Tony James, Brian James and Bernie Rhodes. The guy I went with sat down to try out for the drums. Mick said to me, 'Are you a singer?' and I was like, 'No, not at all.' They said 'Do you want to have a go?' and I said, 'Yeah, why not?' So basically I did an audition, which was completely atrocious because first of all they were really into the New York Dolls and stuff like that and I wasn't. There was one song called 'Young Barracuda' that I'd never heard of, and another by Jonathan Richman who I'd never heard of. They wanted me to sing these songs without knowing the melody or whatever. I was completely fucked. I was more familiar with reggae, the Who or the Kinks, so basically it was a disaster. Bernie was sitting at the rehearsal and after I did my stint I sat down with him and said, 'Are you the manager?' and he went, 'Why, what's it to you?' Nice and friendly! 'OK, fair enough,' I said. 'I'm not bothered either way.'
Paul Simonon, bass player, the Clash

After a while, London SS foundered and Mick Jones went on to form the Clash with Paul Simonon. Tony James joined the band Chelsea that John Krevine of Acme Attractions had put together with singer Gene October. It was then that he met Billy Idol, which would lead to Generation X.
Chris Sullivan

They were dreadful.
They were fucking dreadful.

Chris Duffy, bass player, Bazooka Joe

We'd been rehearsing hard. I'd been accepted to do my degree in fine art at St Martin's, but we'd all decided to take the band seriously. So I was like a man of principle when I walked into college on the first day. I said, 'Oh, you know, I'm not going to come to your stupid art college,' thinking they would say, 'Please come.' I told them I was joining a rock'n'roll band and they went, 'All right.' But at the time I became social secretary of the St Martin's College Union because nobody else wanted to do it... So I went in on the first day; I booked the Pistols for a gig, and that was that.
Glen Matlock

At the St Martin's gig there was a buzz because the Sex Pistols were going to support us. A lot of hype was starting to happen. I don't think I'd actually heard of them up to that point. As far as we were concerned, they were just some band that was going to support us. If I remember rightly, they actually used our gear. They were dreadful. They were fucking dreadful.
Chris Duffy

The Sex Pistols play their first gig at St Martin's Art College, very near their cramped rehearsal space… Five songs into a blistering set, the plug is pulled on the band. They play covers of the Who's 'Substitute' and the Small Faces' 'Whatcha Gonna Do About It?' On the latter song, they changed the lyric to sing 'I want you to know that I *hate* you baby, want you to know I don't care.'
George Gimarc, *Punk Diary 1970-1979*

I was at the St Martin's gig, man, and the other band actually pulled the plug on them. They were making a racket. They sucked musically, but they had something. There was a great potential – no one was sure for what, but they had something. I remember Malcolm looking perplexed and then curious. I think he could see what a lot of the clued up amongst us could see – this raw talent that was just bursting to get out.
Gene Krell

It was our first gig. I'd had a few pints and a couple of Mandies [uppers]. We were all over the place. They pulled the plug after 15 minutes.
Steve Jones

We were running on adrenaline. We were really pumped up. It was mad, the gig. They pulled the plug on us. They actually turned us off – 'cause of the racket, I suppose. Big Steve was out of his head. We were all going mad, and that was our way of getting through the first gig. So, yeah, we were running on high energy. Malcolm was there, and I think he made a decision to get more involved. I don't know what he thought about the music. I don't think he knew much about music, myself. But he did know we were able to shock, more probably than we did.
Paul Cook

It was in the air. *You could smell it. All over Britain young fashionable types, who had recently shown a penchant for David Bowie and Roxy Music, liberally peppered with soul and funk, were secretly listening to Lou Reed, the Velvet Underground, the Stooges and Patti Smith. Those who last year wore brightly coloured peg trousers, plastic sandals and '50s garb were keeping a determined eye out for clothing that gave them an edge, that placed them just out of reach of Joe Public's comprehension, that put them…out there. The race was on to look more and more bizarre, but without looking foolish. People were scouring jumble sales for drainpipes and getting their mothers to knit them oversized mohair jumpers. The same youths were getting two, three, four or more earrings in one ear, cropping their hair and then bleaching it. For the last few years, a certain retro sensibility had stood your common or garden trendsetter in good stead, but by 1976, those days were numbered. This peculiar style was now becoming increasingly evident, but the music to accompany it was but a fledgling. Its main UK protagonists, the Sex Pistols, had played to only a handful of people. In other words, nobody had heard of them, or, for that matter, the word 'punk'.*

But it was early days. Situationist Malcolm McLaren and designer Vivienne Westwood, together with their small gang of devoted customers, had led the way until now. By 1976 it was time for their protégés, the Sex Pistols, to spearhead both the stylistic and musical changes that were to come.

What had been a whisper in 1975 would develop into a roar in '76, easily accommodating style-mongers nationwide, who found themselves disenchanted with former favourites, who could now best be described as stadium acts. Bowie, as if in the act of waving goodbye to his thousands of devoted supporters, played at Wembley in May 1976, which in his eyes may have seemed like a celebration of his newly acquired superstar status, but it only illustrated the fact that he was now, quite literally, out of touch. The crowd that assembled at Wembley were the movers and shakers on the British scene, some of whom had travelled from all corners of the UK. Later that night, those in the know, those who would play a huge part in the emergent punk scene, went on either to Louise's or Chaguarama's. The latter became the Roxy, the first venue to showcase totally punk acts, while the former became the meeting-place for the Sex crowd, which included the Pistols and the Bromley contingent. At that Wembley performance, those who for years had ruled their respective roosts by carbon-copying either Bowie or Ferry now appeared nothing less than old hat. Something else was stirring, something that was slowly becoming known as punk.

Meanwhile, the Sex Pistols were making news. In February the New Musical Express had led with the headline: 'Watch out – the Sex Pistols are coming'. Only the foolish debated the point.

After a series of London events, the Pistols had become the darlings of the fashion crowd, playing at Andrew Logan's Valentine's Day ball, where the predominantly gay, fashion-loving audience regarded the Pistols as naughty boys demolishing Logan's trendy loft apartment. A fight involving Vivienne Westwood and the band at their Nashville date in west London assured them another damning headline in the NME. The saying 'There's no such thing as bad publicity' could well have been employed, but in the Pistols' case, this was to be the first in a series of damning reports that would dub them and their small band of followers as rowdy, uneducated thugs, when in fact the opposite was true. The scene at the time was drawn from the ranks of London's small and intimate coterie of fashion victims, emanating in part from many of inner London's most prestigious art colleges and hairdressing salons. The general public would prove to be only too ready to accept the image created by punk's bad publicity, but this general attitude of revulsion only served to galvanize the scene. After a series of performances, the Sex Pistols embarked on their recording career, with legendary guitarist Chris Spedding producing, before most other punk acts had even formed.

In 1976, however, the British thunder was stolen, in part, as punk's New York originators displayed their wares in the UK. Patti Smith released the ground-breaking single 'Gloria' in April, and the mighty Ramones played the Roundhouse in July, showing the UK protagonists how it was done. Although it was the Sex Pistols' very existence that influenced many of the scene's up-and-coming young bands, it was the Ramones who delivered the musical blueprint that all others would follow.

Even though '76 was very much the Sex Pistols' year, other bands were forming that were to play a huge part in the oncoming movement. The Clash, under the tutelage of Bernie Rhodes, were now fully up, running and exploring another side of the punk coin. Howard Devoto and Pete Shelley, who had travelled down from Manchester to see the Pistols, then went back north to form the Buzzcocks, while the Damned had embarked on a career as a punk cabaret act. The seed that McLaren and the Pistols had planted was now beginning to flourish in the UK.

Just as the Velvet Underground had inspired others, so it seems that almost everyone who saw the Sex Pistols started their own band. When they played at the Lesser Free Trade Hall in Manchester, a gig organized by the Buzzcocks, the audience was full of future stars, including Mark E. Smith of the Fall, Morrissey of the Smiths, Bernard Sumner of New Order, Mick Hucknall of Simply Red and Peter Hook of Joy Division. Up until that point, none had considered a career in music. Wherever the Pistols played, they left behind a gang of hopefuls who thought, 'I can do that.' Unfortunately, most could not.

The Pistols' great achievement was to spread the word and create little fledgling scenes all over the country, each one slightly different from the next.

What had begun purely as a fashion movement now manifested itself in other ways. In July Mark Perry, seeing a gap in the market, started the fanzine called Sniffin' Glue…and Other Rock'n'Roll Habits, taking the name from a Ramones' song title that signposted the lacklustre depths punk would eventually sink to.

As the weather became hotter and the ladybirds multiplied, so did the punk scene, and on 29 August the Sex Pistols, the Clash and the Buzzcocks played at Screen on the Green in London's Islington. Many would argue that this was the scene's zenith and that the bands involved were the best it would produce. True or not, this was the last of the 'closed' events that only the inner coterie had access to: the scene would now burst open to infiltrate the furthest corners of the UK.

September was the month when the word 'punk' became a new and visible entity. It was a term that each and every one of the original protagonists hated. As Glenn Matlock said, 'We hate the term punk. We're not punk – we're the Sex Pistols.' In fact, any term to categorize them would have been an annoyance. A label that would attract yobs of all persuasions was against their belief.

In other camps, however, all was fine and dandy now that the movement had a name and could be pigeon-holed. The music paper Melody Maker, seeing itself left behind in the furore, devoted a whole page to 'Punk Rock'. On 4 September the Sex Pistols played 'So It Goes' on national television, giving the youth of Britain the chance to see the band they had, until then, only heard about. Jordan, the Pistols' muse, had to cover her swastika armband, and Rotten demolished the sarcastic Clive James in an on-screen 'debate'. From that moment forth, the writing was on the wall: punk was going to be huge and the momentum was gaining.

On 20 September the 100 Club in London's Oxford Street held the first Punk Festival, featuring the Sex Pistols, Subway Sect, the Clash, the Banshees, the Damned, the Vibrators and, from France, the Stinky Toys. Unfortunately, the two-night festival served only to bolster punk's ever-growing image as a violent and loutish movement. During a performance by the Damned, Sid Vicious, hurled a glass at the band. It missed, but hit a young girl, causing her to lose an eye. The tabloid press seized on the incident to brand punk a danger to society and a blot on the landscape. Many of those who would like to have been just that joined its ranks. The rot was, already, beginning to set in.

On 9 October EMI, seeing an opportunity to cash in on this new phenomenon, signed the Sex Pistols, and the band went into the studios to record their first single. Unfortunately, its release was pipped at the post by the Damned's 'New Rose'. The Damned were, in many people's eyes, an aberration, a punk cartoon, but 'New Rose' was undeniably the first British punk single. This was supremely irritating to the Pistols and their fans.

The Damned had thrown down the gauntlet, and the Pistols responded on 19 November by releasing 'Anarchy in the UK'. It would soon become punk's overriding theme tune. It was the single of the decade, the song that defined the whole scene; the lyrics said all that needed to be said. And maybe that, in hindsight, was the problem.

Punk's reputation was growing, and the establishment started to respond. On 29 November college authorities banned the Sex Pistols from appearing at Lancaster Polytechnic, but the shit really hit the fan when, two days later, the band appeared on Bill Grundy's Today show at 6 p.m. Pushed and provoked by the pixilated host, the band responded with a string of four-letter words, causing uproar and outrage. The press needed no urging to sensationalize the event. By the morning every household's newspaper had a headline that branded punk and the Pistols as obscene and degenerate. Of course, this bad press did nothing to hinder punk's growth. Just as with Elvis, it served only to stimulate interest.

As the year came to a close, the Sex Pistols, the Clash, the Heartbreakers and the Damned embarked on the ill-fated Anarchy tour. The tabloid propaganda, that punk was indeed a serious threat to civilization, had done its work, and 14 out of 19 tour dates were cancelled amidst much publicity. Meanwhile, 'Anarchy in the UK' had entered the charts; Generation X (with Billy Idol) had formed; and the Roxy, the venue that was to become the epicentre of the punk movement, had opened. Then, as now, young people listened neither to the press or their parents, and thank God for that.

Although British punk was not born in 1976, that was the year when it reared its colourful and controversial head and screamed into the country's consciousness. By the end of the year, the word 'punk' was on everybody's lips, and by the end of the following year, it would be in every young person's record collection.

I just knew instantly I had to be involved in it. I thought they were fantastic.

Nils Stevenson, Sex Pistols' tour manager, 1976

In the New Year the Pistols went on the offensive. Prior to Christmas they had played some of London's most prestigious art colleges — St Martin's, Central, Chelsea and Ravensbourne. On 12 February they played the Marquee, supporting Eddie and the Hot Rods, and trashed the stage. They then played before the London fashion fraternity at Andrew Logan's Valentine's Day ball and again caused havoc. The name was growing but not, unfortunately, because of the music. People turned up mainly because the band was fashionable. The music was secondary; they were like an art installation. Stephen Colegrave, author

Malcolm said, 'You've got to come and see the Pistols.' Vivienne, Chrissie Hynde and Malcolm came to pick me up in the old Mini and we trekked off to the Marquee. It was the first time I saw the Pistols and I was entranced. They were extraordinary. Rotten reminded me very much of Iggy Pop, who I saw in 1972. He had the same sort of irreverence and craziness. He was running across the stage, spitting in girls' faces and pulling them by the hair. The songs sounded the same as Iggy's. Rotten went and sat in the audience with a really long microphone lead, saying, 'I've always wanted to watch my band play.' Then he started throwing chairs about, got hold of Jordan, the shop assistant from Sex, and started pulling her clothes off and throwing her on the floor. Nils Stevenson

They were playing at the Marquee, supporting Eddie and the Hot Rods. There were probably only about 10 people, but Johnny still managed to smash up the stage and threw the front row of seats all over the place. Steve Severin, bass player, Siouxsie and the Banshees

Malcolm didn't realize how fantastic they were. He wanted them to be the next Bay City Rollers. When he said, 'Do you wanna be involved?' I said, 'Yes, I think they're brilliant.' He replied, 'Why don't you come and manage them with me?' So I closed down the stall that I had with Lloyd Johnson and spent all my time working with Malcolm on the band. Shortly afterwards, he left Vivienne and moved in with Helen Wellington Lloyd (the dwarf). Nils Stevenson

It was seriously the worst dive you've ever come across — the El Paradiso strip club.

Alan Jones, assistant in Sex, 1975-7

We played in High Wycombe, opening for Screamin' Lord Sutch. Ron Watts was in the audience and booked us for the 100 Club. The Paradiso was the key date: it was a strip joint in Soho owned by Vince, a Maltese gangster. Malcolm was four hours late to the meeting with him. He knocked on the door and just pushed me inside. I was fucking terrified. There was all these hard characters, smoking and drinking, and they all looked at me like I was a freak. I thought, 'I'm gonna get my fucking head kicked in.' The deal was £90 hire for the club. Malcolm just stood behind me, silently watching all this going on, crapping himself. We left and Malcolm said, 'You're fucking useless. That's far too much money you paid. It's extortionate.' So I went, 'Where the fuck were you?' He said, 'I thought I'd leave it to you, to see if you could do it.'
Nils Stevenson

When we arrived at the Paradiso, there were like five Maltese gangsters and their girlfriends with the whole glamour number – piled-up hair, glitter – sitting there

chewing. It was like the biggest cliché. The place was falling apart. We had to go into the toilets and hose the shit off the walls, and there were like three scruffy broken seats in the entire venue. It was seriously the worst dive you could ever come across. But it was still my favourite Pistols' show.
Alan Jones

At the Paradiso Rotten had an audience who understood what the band were on about. He sort of kicked some lightbulbs in at the front of the stage, and just as he did that Vince turned up with his henchmen. Rotten clocked him and started trying to behave. Before that, some irate stripper turned up who'd been booked to perform by the club. She was really gross and ugly – you'd pay not to see her. So she went on and the audience were just pissing themselves and telling her to get 'em on. The band came on and they were absolutely brilliant. We paid £90, took £240. Alan Jones was taking the money on the door with this Cambridge Rapist leather

mask on. Jordan, of course, was there with Michael Collins, and spiked this punch, and we were all terrified that Vince might find out and we'd all get our kneecaps broken as it was a Sunday and there was no licence. Luckily Vince had been paid. Then Malcolm disappeared with the rest of the takings and I thought, 'Fucking hell, what was all that about? I set it up.'
Nils Stevenson

I remember going with Malcolm to buy this enormous plastic drum-like thing, like a drinks dispenser. There used to be a chemist near Sex in the Kings Road and Malcolm had just got loads of speed off this guy. He made this cocktail and poured all the speed into it. It was one of the first Sex Pistols gigs [El Paradiso]. He served up the cocktail and they didn't know it had speed in it. He just put it in there so that he'd get everyone fucking mad. For him it was an interesting experiment, but I remember him coming back and saying they'd sold it all.
Joe Corré, son of Vivienne Westwood and Malcolm McLaren

Above: Glen Matlock, Johnny Rotten and Steve Jones • Top right: Flyer from El Paradiso featuring Jordan and the Sex Pistols

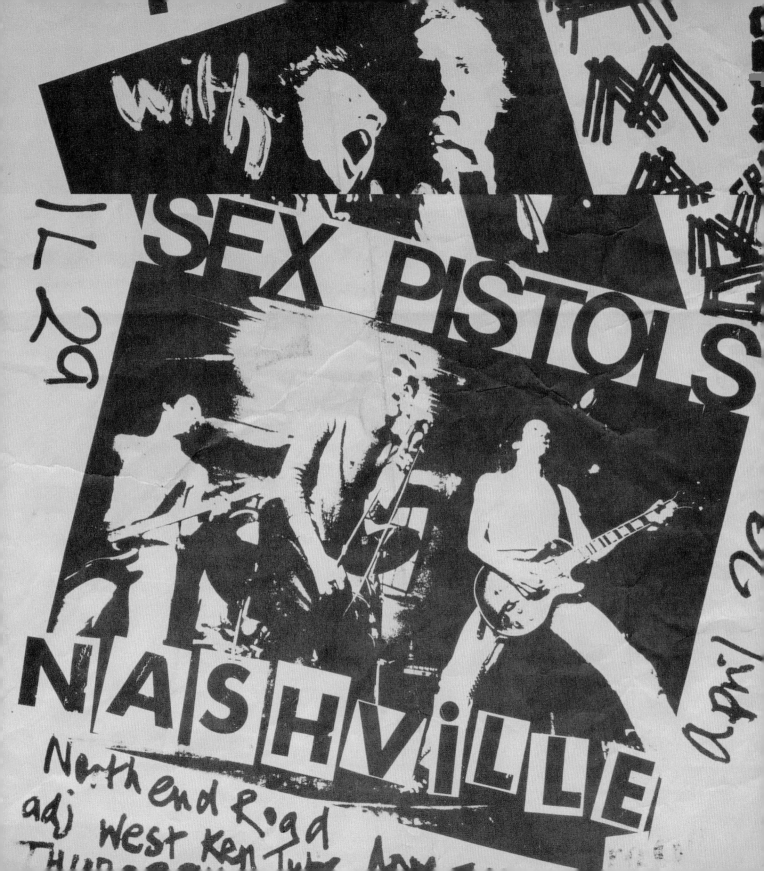

When the Pistols took to the stage, it was cultural **year zero.** Don Letts, film-maker and DJ

Of course the gig that got the first press for the Pistols was at the Nashville with the 101ers, Joe Strummer's band.
Gene Krell, punk clothing entrepreneur

At the Nashville I was operating the follow spot. A fight broke out because someone had taken Vivienne's chair. She slapped the bloke and it went off. Even Malcolm steamed in, which amazed me. Naturally, I turned the spot on the fight. The band jumped in and I think Glen hit someone over the head with his bass. It all ended up in the bloody *Melody Maker*.
Nils Stevenson

The Nashville was fun. It just seemed normal for us for something to go wrong at that point. My dream of being like the Faces went right out the window even then.
Steve Jones, guitarist, the Sex Pistols

Vivienne was pissed. She went to get a drink and somebody nicked her seat, so she took a swing at this bloke. Sid hated Vivienne, so he used this as an excuse to lay into her. She thought it was this other bloke. Then all the people who came to the shop thought the bloke

was laying into her and dived in too.
Glen Matlock, bass player, the Sex Pistols

The picture of the fight with John, Malcolm and Glen all trying to hit this bloke was on the front page of *Melody Maker* with the headline 'Don't Look Over Your Shoulder, the Sex Pistols are coming'. Later Vivienne claimed she'd done it on purpose to get publicity, but I don't believe that.
Nils Stevenson

We tried to break up the fight... The picture makes it look like we started it, but we were trying to stop it.
Glen Matlock

As you know the Pistols are composed of three nice, clean middle-class art students and a real live dementoid, Johnny Rotten. Now, on Friday night El Dementoid wasn't really on top form, although the rest of the band were doing their best to compensate. Johnny's heart wasn't in the music. His lack of interest was naturally reflected by the audience who, disapointed, weren't reacting sufficiently to the band. So how do the Pistols create their atmosphere when their music has failed? By beating

up a member of the audience, how else?
Neil Tennant (later of the Pet Shop Boys) in a letter to the *NME*, 18 April 1976

You were never looking to...see a good rock'n'roll band, you were...hoping to see the most...wonderful...energy ...that could be described as your first fuck really.
Malcolm McLaren in *I Swear I Was There*

Violence at a Sex Pistols gig is not only accepted, it is expected –
George Gimarc, *Punk Diary 1970-1979*

In June the Pistols played in Manchester, as organized by the Buzzcocks. This gig had a strong influence on many future musicians, including Morrissey and Mick Hucknall. Up until that point, they hadn't considered a career in music.
Chris Sullivan, author

All the dates until then had been building up to the Screen on the Green. That was when it all came together – the band, the audience, the event.
Nils Stevenson

Opposite: Poster advertising the Sex Pistols at the Nashville • Above: Poster advertising the Sex Pistols at the Screen on the Green

115

The Screen on the Green was an attempt by Malcolm and me to tap into our '60s kind of happening experiences. We'd both been at UFO and the Arts Lab, all those sort of places that were around in 1967 and 1968. We thought a cinema was great because we could show some films. We could have these fabulous people, who we'd got to know during this period. Malcolm's favourite film was *Scorpio Rising*, and that sat OK with me. It was arty, gay and fetishistic, although it was a bit too queer for my liking. I couldn't think of anything better, other than the obvious Cabaret, which everyone knew anyway. I thought *Scorpio Rising* was more hard core, so we banged that on.
Nils Stevenson

The first time at the Screen on the Green was really good because the Clash and the Buzzcocks were on. It seemed like a really big place to us, but it is actually tiny and only holds about 500 people. It was the first time you thought there was something happening. I just felt this is where I wanted to belong, this was where I wanted to be. I didn't care whether the outside world got it or not. In fact, I preferred it because this wasn't the outside world, it was our own scene. Everyone thought like me. Everyone liked the same things as me and, more importantly, everyone hated the same things.
Marco Pirroni, guitarist, Siouxsie and the Banshees

Siouxsie turned out resplendent in a big swastika with her tits hanging out. It was a fucking fantastic event. Nils Stevenson

Following El Paradiso, the Sex Pistols played the Screen on the Green. This was much more than a traditional gig, it was more of an art college-inspired event. Kenneth Anger films punctuated the bands as they played from midnight to dawn. The Bromley contingent were very visible in a Warholian menagerie, resplendent in Vivienne Westwood's best designs. The Sex Pistols were joined by the Clash and the Buzzcocks, both of whom were playing their first public gig in London – the first of many.
Stephen Colegrave

The Buzzcocks had been inspired by the Pistols, so they were part of it. I think they played first and then they were followed by the Clash. There was some antagonism between Malcolm and Bernard [Rhodes] over the Pistols and the Clash. The Clash were only allowed to play if they built the stage. (Being a cinema, there was no stage.) They spent all day erecting scaffolding and were pretty knackered by the end of it. But they were allowed to play.
Nils Stevenson

We'd played with the Pistols before, but as there'd been some friction in the past between Malcolm and Bernie, they made us build the stage. I don't mind a bit of manual work, but to do that all day with the scaffolding and stuff and then go and play was a bit much, I thought.
Paul Simonon, bass player, the Clash

I turned up at the Screen on the Green dressed in a nightie, sunglasses, a housecoat, turban and bedroom slippers, and got on stage. A lot of them just did not get it, but isn't that what it was all about?
Phillip Salon, club promoter

All the characters were there – Phillip Salon, Jordan, Siouxsie obviously. Steve [Jones] always had this habit of spewing up before he went on stage. I think that was the night he spewed up in a filing cabinet.
Nils Stevenson

We had already done a gig with the Pistols at the Mucky Duck in Sheffield. There had been quite a few hip characters there, who'd picked up on what the Pistols had been doing. I used to enjoy those early gigs. Me and Joe Strummer used to leap off the stage to hit people. I remember one time we came back afterwards and said to Mick, 'How come you didn't jump off and join in?' He said, 'Well, somebody's got to be in time,' which was a fair point. Our drummer had his cymbals flat to protect himself because he couldn't move. We were used to ducking and moving out of the spotlight to see who was there and who was chucking stuff.
Paul Simonon

It was great and everybody was broke. All the punters were broke. The Screen on the Green finished at God knows what time in the morning. Everybody had to walk home. There were no night buses. The degree of commitment from Marco and Siouxsie and everyone else was quite extraordinary. There was something fabulous going on. We felt connected.
Nils Stevenson

Siouxsie was wearing fishnet stockings, a black cupless bra, a swastika armband and mismatched leather shoes. She and Steve Severin approached Pistols' manager Malcom McLaren about the possibility of their new band playing with the Sex Pistols at the upcoming 100 Club Punk Rock Festival in September.
Sniffin' Glue, issue 12, August 1976

Opposite: Vivienne Westwood on stage with the Sex Pistols • Above left: Siouxsie and Debbie Juvenile • Above right: Siouxsie (far left), Phillip Salon (far right) and assorted revellers on stage at the Screen on the Green

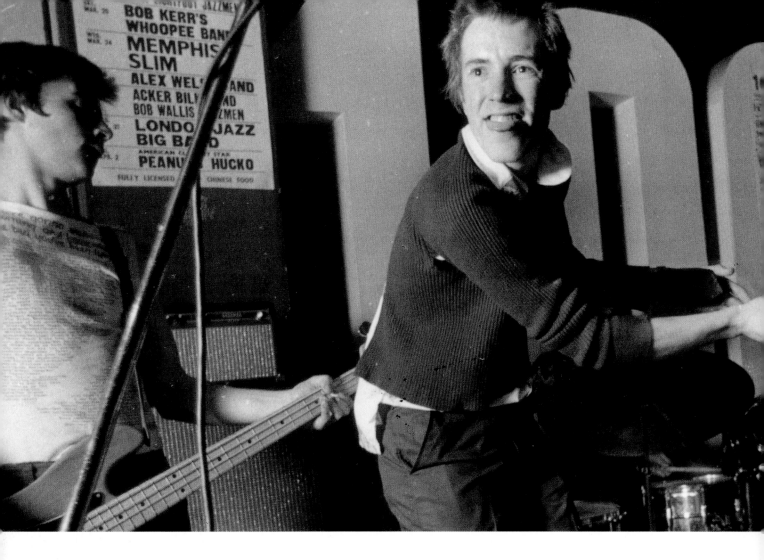

Maybe I was the only promoter tough enough to do it.
I wasn't frightened of anybody.

Ron Watts, promoter, the 100 Club

Above and opposite: Glen Matlock and Johnny Rotten

The Sex Pistols' following was drawn from London's most prestigious art colleges, hairdressers and clothes shops... as well as the band's mates. Chris Sullivan

I'd heard about the Nashville gig and the trouble there, but I'd already made up my mind. I wanted the 100 Club to be a punk venue. I could see that the state of the music industry wasn't right, that the young people were very fed up. They weren't coming to gigs – it was old men like me, old hippies, people like that, big guys with beards like you'd see down the rugby club. These were the kind of people who were going to gigs at the time – you just didn't see the 17- to 20-year-olds who should have been at gigs. They were all indoors – spiking up their hair or something, getting ready. They should have been the ones that were going to clubs and they weren't. They didn't want to see Yes, or Van Der Graaf Generator…a load of bollocks, like the Pistols said. I mean, rock was being seen as arty and farty and

middle class. These young kids wanted their own music, their own heroes – heroes from the same background.
Ron Watts

The 100 Club reminded me of a northern working men's club. It was a shit hole. I loved it.
Chris Sullivan

Every gig there were a few more and a few more. You'd see people come down in new outfits, stuff they were creating themselves, like Cambridge Rapist masks.
Sue 'Catwoman' Lucas, early Sex aficionado

It was liberating. Punk definitely made that happen.
Johnny Rotten in *The Filth and the Fury*

I was enjoying punk so much. I could see that it was going to be huge. I wanted to make some money out of it. Making money out of it is what being a promoter is all about. I thought the way to make that money was to bring some other bands on quickly so there could be a roster of bands to perform. I needed to bring some other bands into the limelight and move the whole thing on. The two-day festival was just the extension of that idea, with Malcolm helping me out with the Manchester bands.
Ron Watts

Bernie told me that it was he who organized the whole 100 Club event. He said he got Malcolm in and that it was his idea.
Chris Sullivan

We went to the Screen on the Green in August, where the Pistols played with the Buzzcocks. They'd come down from Manchester for the first time, and after that Malcolm was talking about doing a two-night punk festival at the 100 Club. He said he needed to fill a slot. I think it was probably Billy [Idol] who said leisurely he'd do it. We were probably three weeks away from the actual gig, maybe even less. We went away thinking, 'Oh, my God, what have we done?' So Malcolm said yes, and it was all sorted out…except we didn't really know how to go about it. We'd committed ourselves and it just got closer and closer.

Then came the evening down at Louise's [a lesbian club in Poland Street], where we met Sid, and of course we still didn't have a drummer. Sid already had a band called the Flowers of Romance that were sort of rehearsing. They weren't really started, so Sid agreed to play drums. In theory, we had a four-piece band. We'd already thought of the name – Siouxsie and the Banshees. In fact, I think the original poster spelt it Susi and the Banshees. So the posters were done and we were ready. We'd also met this guy Nils [Stevenson] who was Malcolm's right-hand man. He did everything for the Pistols. He was taking an interest even at that point. He later became our manager.

We were expected to go on before the Clash, so they quickly said, 'We'll give you rehearsal time and you can borrow our gear.'

Billy was already in this band called Chelsea. Then, a week before the gig was meant to happen, Tony James took him to one side and said, 'You can't possibly do this Siouxsie and the Banshees thing because you'll damage your chances with Chelsea.' He persuaded Billy he should pull out, so right at the last moment he did. We thought, 'Fuck, what are we gonna do?' We were down at Louise's, and Nils introduced us to this guy Marco. Now we were a four-piece again, with the same set-up. Marco could actually play guitar. We did one rehearsal for about 10 minutes. Sid got bored and said, 'Oh, that'll do. Let's just make a racket. Who cares?' We all agreed, and then we went down the 100 Club and did the first show.
Steve Severin

The first night of the festival was cracking. The only problem I had was a bunch of punks from Manchester who weren't hitting it off socially with the London punks. The Manchester lot thought they were just as big at being punks as the London lot. I had to sort it out a couple of times, but they all calmed down eventually. The first night was an amazing success.
Ron Watts

I went to the 100 Club. It was shit – not a decent bird in the whole gaff.
Frank Kelly, Sex Pistols' aficionado

We came up with the idea of just making a load of noise. Siouxsie

recited the Lord's Prayer and threw in other lyrics from horrible songs, like the Bay City Rollers, 'Twist and Shout' and 'Knocking on Heaven's Door'. Then Marco would break into 'Smoke on the Water'. It was just a huge piss-take. About 10,000 people claim they were there, but in reality there were less than 150. But for us it was a defining moment, and 20 minutes later we just walked off the front of the stage back into the audience…it was one 20-minute barrage of sound. It was horrible.
Steve Severin

There was no 'If we do this, we'll be famous' because we didn't think we would be. We just got away with it.
Marco Pirroni

I was trying to work out whether we were plugged in.
Steve Severin

I was following this bird to the bog to try and pull her. By the time she decided that I was indeed a total wanker, the gig was all over.
Chris Sullivan

Caroline Coon came from the *Melody Maker* to review the gigs. She was a convert anyway, but she was also there because she'd discovered that all the guys in the office were too scared to come. They knew something was happening, but they were putting off facing up to it.
Ron Watts

It was the most horrendous thing I'd ever heard.
Marco Pirroni

We did get the best reviews, didn't we?
Steve Severin

We said what we wanted to say. We walked straight off the stage and I never spoke to them again for years.
Marco Pirroni

I am still convinced to this day that the reason this bird turned me down was that she couldn't hear me over this horrendous racket.
Chris Sullivan

The Banshees – a great rock'n'roll band.
Ian Dickson, rock photographer

They reminded me of Yoko Ono's album *Fly*. Everybody hated them. I wanted to manage them. Bernard [Rhodes, manager of the Clash] wouldn't let the Banshees use the Clash's equipment because of Sid and Siouxsie's swastikas. This incensed Sid, who berated Bernard from the stage, calling him a tight old Jew.
Nils Stevenson

Siouxsie and the Banshees were an absolute joke. A Lydon-copier. Fucking useless band. I can't believe they carried on playing. But it happened.
Keith Levene, guitarist, London SS and the Clash

There were four of us: two on the door, one on the stage and one in the club. I preferred to sort the trouble out myself. That way people wouldn't get hit.
Ron Watts

**Siouxsie who can't sing, Steve Severin who can't play bass,
Marco Pirroni who can play guitar and Sid Vicious who can't play drums.**
They make a wonderful racket
for about 15 minutes.

Nils Stevenson

Above, clockwise from top left: Siouxsie, Steve Severin, Marco Pirroni and Sid Vicious; Siouxsie, Steve Severin and Marco Pirroni; Johnny Rotten, Steve Severin, Jonh Ingham and Siouxsie

100 Club Festival: first night Pistols, Clash, Subway Sect and the Banshees – it doesn't get much better than that.

Mark McCarthy, Sex Pistols fan

Having formed just in time to support the Pistols in Manchester, we were asked back to play Screen on the Green, and then for the two-day festival in London. When we arrived they asked us if we wanted to play last – or second last. We thought about this for a while. Like, do they actually mean they want us to headline the punk festival? This was progress indeed. We opted for last, which in retrospect was a mistake. By the time we got on stage, half the audience seemed to have disappeared off in the direction of the buses and tubes, or wherever it was punks in London went in 1976.
Howard Devoto, the Buzzcocks

From the music press point of view, the story of the Sex Pistols was already out there by the time of the festival. The big thing was the sheer number of bands – and the fact it was the first real showcase gig for the Clash, who had only just come into being. Joe [Strummer] had disbanded the 101ers – who the music press had been very keen on – straight away after he'd seen the Sex Pistols for the first time. Now his new band were playing the same bill as the Pistols.
John Shearlaw, music journalist

The Clash at the 100 Club? I don't remember them.
Nils Stevenson

Unfortunately, we played a really good set at that first 100 Club night. I think we played better than the rest…for once. We were tight.
Paul Simonon

The Pistols and the Clash pretended to get on, but they hated each other.
Roadent, aka Steve Connolly, Pistols' and Clash roadie

The Buzzcocks are still one of my favourite bands. I did a lot of gigs with them [when I was with] Adam and the Ants and I thought they were great, probably the best to come out in the wake of the Pistols, and they were in a different league really. They had the same independence and the same power, but they made something new…and it wasn't just a rehash. I didn't like the Clash very much: I think they preached a sort of poverty-stricken, downtrodden story in their songs, nothing heroic.
Jordan, assistant in Sex, in *I Swear I Was There*

Top: The Clash (left to right) Joe Strummer, Mick Jones and Paul Simonon • Bottom: Subway Sect (left to right) Paul Myers, Paul Smith, Vic Godard and Robert Simmons • Opposite: 100 Club poster advertising the Sex Pistols

It was the worst thing that ever happened to me in my promoting career. It really broke my heart.

Sid was arrested.

Ron Watts

Sid Vicious – what a pest!

Frank Kelly

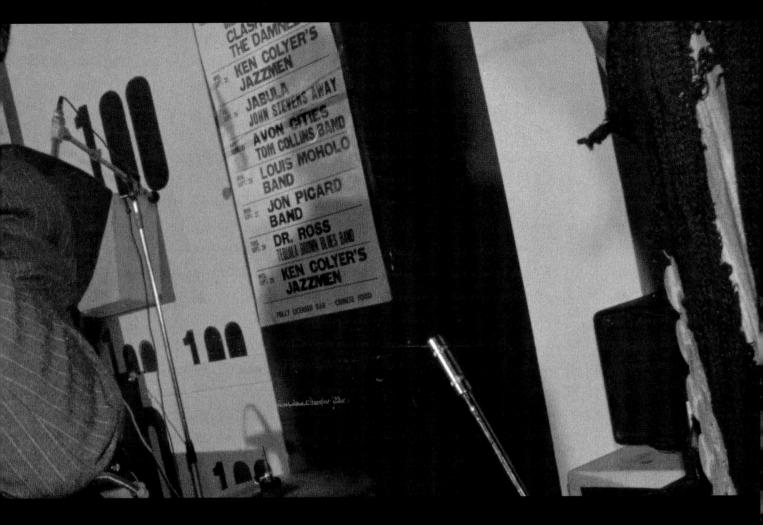

Sid misbehaved on the first night. He threw a knife and threatened to impale the French band, the Stinky Toys. I had to take the knife off him backstage.
Ron Watts

Vicious was throwing bottles and arsing about. What a wanker! The bloke was a total fucking nuisance. The police could have arrested him for getting on people's nerves.
Frank Kelly

The second night, Sid launched a pint pot at the Damned. It missed them, hit the central pillar, and a shard of glass went into a girl's eye. Sid was arrested, put on remand and a lot of punks went to get him out. Sid being Sid, it all went wrong.
Ron Watts

I was with Sid at the 100 Club. He did throw the glass, but he fucked it up as usual. Sid was inadequate in most things, especially glass-throwing. He wasn't very good at drumming either, but he was sort of endearing, like a naughty 12-year-old.
Steve Walsh, guitarist, the Flowers of Romance

Caroline Coon said it was an accident. I'm sure stabbing Nancy was an accident too. Chaining Nick Kent was an accident. Sid's whole life was a fucking accident.
Nils Stevenson

Jonesy and I visited Sid in Ashford Remand Centre, where he was taken after his arrest for allegedly throwing a glass and partially blinding a girl at the 100 Club. Sid claims he didn't do it.
Nils Stevenson

I knew John and Sid from early on and liked them both. They were like Laurel and Hardy to me. I'd call them that. They really made me laugh. I let Sid come and live with me after he came out of Ashford as he had nowhere else to stay. I'd cook him food and talk. I'm from a family of 12 brothers, so I was used to it. And we'd go to gigs. I'd get home safe because I was with Sid. When he left, he just told me, 'It's been nice poncing off you for the last few months.' That was Sid. Like, 'I'll see you later and I'll push your face in.' The real Sid had a great sense of humour.
Sue 'Catwoman' Lucas

I banned Sid. Then he got his mum to come down and get him in. I relented because of her. But Sid never behaved. On one occasion, he attacked the journalist Nick Kent. I picked Sid up from behind. I held him up in the air. I said, 'Sid, are you going to calm down?' Eventually he said he would, so I put him down. Then it would happen again. He would always have to start some sort of shit, but I was always able to handle him. I was a boxer; I could handle myself.
Ron Watts

Sex was all about breaking down taboos and, if you think about it,

they really did do that. There had never been such provocative clothes before — clothes that really changed the way you thought about things. Marco Pirroni

Above: Jordan outside Sex in the Kings Road

SEX – Specialists in Rubberwear, Glamourwear, and Stagewear.

Business card for Sex

Jordan at the time was the icon of the moment. She looked better than anyone on the scene. She looked like a character out of some '50s S&M B-movie. She was the one many girls aspired to, and Michael Collins, the other assistant in Sex, was the aspirational figure for men. He was the first bloke I saw with multiple earrings. They did it with taste and looked great…all the time.
Chris Sullivan

I'd been, for want of a better description, the front person of Vivienne's shop. A lot of glossy girl magazines used to come and take photos and talk to me about what the shop was all about. I was dressing very crazy at that time…bouffant, black eyeliner, sort of 'Cleopatra goes '50s'…with lots of ripped tights, stilettos and Perspex clothes. I was doing my own thing, buying my own clothes, down in Sussex, which was really comparable with what Malcolm and Vivienne were doing up in London.
Jordan in *I Swear I Was There*

Jordan – she was amazing. She used to commute every day from near Brighton in this see-through lingerie and corsets and rubber dresses, which caused havoc on the train. In the

end I think British Rail gave her a first-class pass, and when she ran into trouble with the Teds, she'd get a police escort to Sloane Square tube station.
Gene Krell

To regular people you looked like aliens. To Teddy boys you looked like targets.
Tony James, bass guitarist, Generation X

I commuted for about two years. I had some real bad do's on the train. I had tourists trying to pay me for my photo…worse than that, mothers saying that I'm upsetting their children and debauching them and how dare I get on a train looking like that. Somebody tried to throw me off the train one day, literally out the door, so British Rail told me to go sit in first class, get out of trouble. Me sitting on the train in my rubber gear and what have you, a few men used to get a bit het up as well. I think that might have caused a bit of a stir.
Jordan in *I Swear I Was There*

The people in the streets were like shit. They came in one colour, which was beige, and they sort of bristled with

static electricity. Everything was nylon and crappy. It was all brown or beige. Everything was shit – shit-coloured.
Marco Pirroni

I went to the Sex Pistols' gig at Andrew Logan's party. They were doing Small Faces and Stooges numbers. That was the first party where the Pistols played as the focal point, and that was the happening creative scene in London at the time. That was when Jordan got on the stage for the first time with the Pistols.
Tony James

Jordan appeared on stage with the Sex Pistols and gave it another edge; she was a big face on the scene and gave them extra credibility, not that they needed it. Then she was on that Tony Wilson show, *So It Goes*, with the Pistols, which was their first TV. I'm sure that she would have become a massive artist had she taken the Siouxsie route, but I suppose she was a big star already on that scene.
Chris Sullivan

Everything changed – the world went flare-shaped.
Paul Simonon

TOO FAST
TO LIVE,
TOO YOUNG
TO DIE

Growing bored with the '50s just as mainstream fashion caught up with his designs, Malcolm happened upon a catalogue for a Walthamstow lingerie shop. This, unusually for the times, openly advertised 'scandalous lingerie and glamour wear'. Changing the name of the shop to 'Sex', Malcolm sprayed its interior...with slogans from Valerie Solanis's 'Scum Manifesto'. Then, looting Soho porn shops for design ideas, he and Vivienne gradually assembled the range of bizarre, fetishistic clothing, which turned into the punk rock look.
Fred and Judy Vermorel, *The Sex Pistols: The Inside Story*

As you walked down the Kings Road, it got weirder – Acme Attractions, pink peg trousers and dub, Beaufort Market, drainpipes, pickers and mohair,

as dance to funk in clubs like Crackers, Chag's and the Sombrero. The style was there way before the band were popular on the scene.
Frank Kelly

I used to go down the Kings Road and thieve a lot out of those bullshit shops like Take Six, and I always ended up in Let It Rock. They had a couch and a jukebox and you could hang out there. Then I got friendly with McLaren. The prices were a bit steep but being a tea leaf like myself, you didn't pay for much. Then it changed to Sex after the Pistols got going, which was a lot more original than Let It Rock, and a little strange at first with all the rubber gear and that. Of course, all my mates thought I was a poof to wear it. The clientele was a combination of punks and pervs, sort of businessmen. I wasn't hip to all that at first, but hanging round there really opened my eyes. I soon realized there are a lot of nonces around.
Steve Jones

I certainly think as far as Malcolm and Vivienne were concerned, there was always a conscious effort to shock, to see how far they could push it. Everybody else was jumping on the bandwagon but they were always off on their own tangents.
Roger Bourton, clothing supplier to the film industry

It was about pushing ideas as far as they could go. We had a little flat in Clapham, and the whole hallway was piled high with boxes of lurex socks and these underpants with 'People of Rock' on them or whatever. They did this 'Let It Rock' concert at Wembley that was like a rock'n'roll reunion. People like Jerry Lee Lewis and Chuck Berry came over for it. Malcolm was like, 'Right, we're going to do these T-shirts with the signatures of all the artists,' then he did all these underpants to match. He went all the way up to

L'Age d'or on it in handwriting. It was simple and I knew what it meant. Luis Buñuel, who made the surrealist fim *L'Age d'or*, was a foot fetishist, and that's the code. Not many people would know that, and I thought, 'Whoever did this T-shirt knows that I'm privy to that information' and you felt connected. I bought that T-shirt for £15, which was a week's wages.
Nils Stevenson

When I first went into Sex, there was all this chicken wire and writing on the wall. I later found out that the writing was from the SCUM [Society For Cutting Up Men] Manifesto by Valerie Solanis, the woman who shot Warhol. I now find that very interesting, but think just how deliberate, contrived and really clever it all was, in the best possible way. No one does that now, or seems capable of it.
Chris Sullivan

Because it was high fashion you did get some nice birds at the start. Everyone else was in flares, had centre partings and were really belligerent. It was like 'Oy, fucking weirdo' all the bleeding time. I thought, 'Fuck 'em. I'll wear what I want. I'll pull all the nice birds and they can keep their ugly ones.' Of course, it changed later.
Frank Kelly

Everybody else looked like Richard Beckinsale off *Rising Damp* or Reg Varney from *On the Buses*.
Chris Sullivan

I was thinking about working in Vivienne's shop, although I was kinda worried about the dress code. I didn't see Don Letts in rubber.
Don Letts

A lot of the Soul Boys were prepared for the shop Sex because of Bowie's *Young Americans*, but not quite.

Sex was great. I loved it.
Phillip Salon, club promoter

then you hit Sex and thought...um, OK, I can handle this...I think.
Chris Sullivan

I'd say there was a small core of about 50 people who had either the guts to go into Sex, or to wear the Sex gear. I mean wearing a Cambridge Rapist T-shirt really pissed people off, but Sex was the hippest shop at the time in London. You had all the hip London designers, all the faggot fashion bods, the type of people who today would buy Prada if it was more underground. Before the Pistols we'd listen to Lou Reed, the Velvets, the Stooges, as well

Wembley and sold like...two, you know what I mean? We had literally thousands of these fucking T-shirts hanging around our house for years. I have this vivid picture of the old man walking around the house in these black 'People of Rock' underpants.
Joe Corré

I thought the most extraordinary thing about Sex was the coding. Codes in clothes were really important. What attracted me to Malcolm and Vivienne was the shirt with the appliquéd soft porn pictures. They were cut out of magazines and stuck on under plastic. There was one of a woman's foot in a stiletto shoe and it said

One day it was wedge haircuts and plastic sandals, and the next it would be the very same blokes in gay stuff like the cowboy T-shirt, leather trousers, cropped white hair and multiple earrings. No wonder the public couldn't handle it and got a bit aggressive.
Mark Powell

The windows of Sex were always getting broken, so we put grids over them. One day we took them off 'cause I kept telling Vivienne it looked like a fucking sex shop: you couldn't see in. Ten minutes later the windows were broken. She said, 'Alan it's your fault.'
Alan Jones

I'm serious. You can't make this stuff up. Gene Krell

So many people came into the shop, not to buy, just to look. Sometimes, if we felt up for it, Jordan especially would try on the rubber suits for the old men who'd come in. Then they'd go into the changing room and we could hear them coming…in the changing rooms! We'd be in hysterics. It would happen a lot. You'd see them come in and feeling the rubber on the racks and we'd think, hang on a minute, one of them's going to come. There was a certain age group who didn't really view it as fashion: they viewed it as one step up from the traditional sex industry. We had two distinct groups of clientele, one being the young punks, and the other one older people who thought it was fetish proper. Alan Jones

Heavy-duty discipline.

Tapper Zukie, Jamaican toaster

It was a very heroic time. You could be a hero in your own time. All you had to do was put on the uniform and you were a part of it.
Joe Corré

On one occasion I walked into Sex on a Saturday at about noon and they were all there: Jordan in rubber with beehive, Michael Collins, Alan Jones, Vivienne at the back in a pair of furry ski-boots, leather trousers and a stencilled shirt…all fine and dandy. To the left, fingering the rubber, was your archetypal dirty old man with greasy hair, raincoat and thick, horn-rimmed glasses. Not so fine or dandy. I think he even clutched a brown paper bag that probably contained a *Health & Efficiency* mag or worse. It was not at all difficult to imagine him hanging upside-down from the ceiling in a rubber suit. It dawned on me that some people actually take this shit seriously…and, what's more, do it.
Chris Sullivan

Sex did open a lot of doors for the gays, straights and lesbians. It was very liberated. They're probably the most open people from that period. They really didn't give a fuck because they realized there was nothing to give a fuck about. What did they care if some bloke wanted to wear a rubber mask and wank off in his room? They would just think it was his little bit of subversion, but the bloke didn't see it like that. He saw it as a way to get off and that was all. As long as no one was harmed, it was cool, and who were we to say otherwise?
Marco Pirroni

Reginald Bosanquet, the newsreader, used to come in the shop and we thought, hey, what the hell? Then, one day, we were at Linda's [a dominatrix's] flat in Buckingham Gate near the Houses of Parliament (she was very popular with the politicians – some things don't change). We walked in, but the door was a bit heavy, so we pushed it open to find Reginald hanging on the back of it. Linda picked up this whip and hit him with it, then she said to us, 'Have a go if you want.' So we did. We couldn't talk about this at the time, but he's dead now, so it doesn't matter.
Alan Jones

I used to get given Malcolm and Vivienne's stuff – rubber T-shirts, gay cowboy stuff, all that. I was up in my bedroom putting on this rubber T-shirt – didn't want my relations and people to see. I was living in Brixton and I was the fucking laughing stock wearing all this gear. I put this rubber T-shirt on. It's kind of hot, so I try to get it off. It feels really uncomfortable. I try to get it over my head, but it gets stuck. So I've got this fucking rubber T-shirt wedged around my neck and it's fucking killing me. I'm too embarrassed to call anybody…and I'm dying. I get on the bed and hook the fucking rubber T-shirt over the bedpost. I'm pulling at it, but it's strangling me. I'm hanging from the bed, and then it fucking rips. Vivienne nearly killed me.
Don Letts

Vivienne is very honest about the designing. She sort of nicked everything from bondage-wear magazines. Every designer has a source of inspiration.
Alan Jones

Above: Tits T-shirt from Sex

Above: Debbie Juvenile and Vivienne Westwood

'Oh bondage,
up yours'

Song by Poly Styrene and X-ray Spex

My mother used to have this little green Mini, and when I was about 10 we went on this road trip around the country visiting her suppliers. We went to all these really weird, out of the way places, like this factory where they got their dog collars made, and the guy that made the rubber masks, and the whip-maker, and the guy that sold all the Nazi stuff. We went with Gene Krell, who was drying out at the time. I remember we were in Glasgow in a funny little shop right at the end of this mad estate. This bloke was nuts about Nazis. He had Nazi fucking everything. He had a cabinet that was full of Nazi memorabilia and it was Nazi everything you could think of. He used to make these weird objects. He was also a mad inventor. He made bizarre posters and some theatrical-effect liquid that you could pour over your body and light without it burning your skin. I remember going to this strange country mansion where some bloke had a hobby making all this rubber stuff. This guy was absolutely hilarious – big beard, sitting there in these mad contraptions made of rubber. He was your typical rubber-wearing madman. They have the oddest things, these people – these fucking rubber capes, with these weird pants underneath, with everything cut out, plus a big rubber mask and some hat…like a complete suit. I think prior to that Mum found out about all this stuff through mail-order catalogues but, unlike most people, Mum had to go and visit them all, and she took me and my brother with her. Joe Corré **The bondage suit was based on the straitjacket – how apt.** Nigel Wingrove, founder, *Stains* magazine

All I know is a lot of people
couldn't handle it. Frank Kelly

Apart from the shock value, one must appreciate that Vivienne Westwood, aided and abetted by Malcolm McLaren, started something totally new. Her inspiration was fetish wear, but she took the concept and put it in a place where the fetish designers never thought it would go – on the high street some 25 years later. Doing something absolutely new in clothes design is an impossible task as one has to accommodate, for the most part, two arms, two legs and a torso, and it's all been done before. She, with the bondage boots, the bondage suits, the parachute tops, the T-shirts with the bones on, took style to a place that it had never visited or even dreamt of. The later cardboard cut-out punk look was an aberration that I'm sure she disliked, but at the beginning she did something that few designers this century have achieved. I am convinced that the successful spread of punk *per se* was more to do with the style than the music – as with most British counter-culture. It was the look that attracted a lot of people. That is certainly true for me.
Chris Sullivan

On one occasion there was this banker. He came in the full regalia – bowler hat, the brolley and the pinstripes. Sex was making a rubber outfit for him. The shop had a dressing-room that was really just a rubber curtain. He went in and put on this outfit, which had an inflatable head. He stood very proper and said in his upper-class accent, 'How does it fit? Is it working for me?'
Gene Krell

The Sex crowd – Sue Catwoman, Siouxsie, Jordan, Rotten and Sid – all looked extraordinary. Vivienne and Malcolm also looked extraordinary, and they weren't copying anybody. Not one of those people had a role model. They all just kind of came up with this fantastic thing completely off their own backs, and I loved that. I thought it was absolutely brilliant.
Nils Stevenson

Vivienne knew people were stealing. She didn't care so long as they looked good. She'd even give good-looking kids clothes to get them started – a Sex starter pack, if you like. Gene Krell

The fetish scene had been going on long before Sex, but Vivienne put it all up front. She took all the things that society had ignored and turned its back on, and wanted to deify them, to put them right slap in people's faces.
Ted Polhemus, author of *Street Style*

The whole look was from Vivienne. I never believed that Malcolm had that much say in it. I think time has shown that, and she would never have become the designer she is if she hadn't had the ideas. Malcolm might like to say that it's all him, but it definitely wasn't. She definitely set the look for the Pistols. He might have told her how to answer questions, but she was the one who gave them the image that we all love.
Alan Jones

All I know is I came up from Wales, walked along the Kings Road to Sex and it did my head in – 100 per cent.
Mark McCarthy

Opposite, left to right: Unidentified girl, Alan Jones, Chrissie Hynde, Jordan and Vivienne Westwood

Acme Attractions –
well, they were
the opposition. ■ Nils Stevenson

As Let It Rock gave way to Sex, there was a mismatch of styles, from '50s to S&M. However, within days of the Grundy show at the end of 1976, 430 Kings Road went through its final transformation to become Seditionaries. This time Vivienne Westwood had the opportunity to realize her design ambitions in a single-minded way, as Malcom McLaren was now fully occupied with the Sex Pistol project.

The new interior, designed by Ben Kelly, was much more functional and industrial than before. Large photographs of bombed-out Dresden added to the air of bleakness. It had a very different ambience from Kelly's later work, The Hacienda club in Manchester.

The new clothing range was much more coherent than before. Bondage suits were joined by bondage dresses. Alongside new designs, such as the Destroy distressed muslin shirts, there was now a range of accessories, including armbands embellished with a swastika or an encircled capital A. All these new Seditionaries clothes had their own label with an anarchist A and the words: 'For soldiers, prostitutes, dikes and punks'.

With Seditionaries, Vivienne Westwood's profile was increasing. It was an important stepping-stone to her later design career. Her reputation was moving towards the mainstream, mirroring the popularization of punk in general, with all the consequences that entailed.

There was a definite rivalry between Sex and Acme Attractions. John Krevine had Don Letts pumping out radical dub and the clothes were cheaper, but Sex produced fashion that was art, and it was much more than a clothes store – there ain't no way round that.
Stephen Colegrave

Above, top to bottom: Red trousers with plastic pockets from Sex; Appliqué porno T-shirt from Too Fast to Live Too Young to Die; Blue boots from Seditionaries

Malcolm gets the punk rock thing going and I've got to tell you now that, at first, I was kind of pissed off about the whole thing. In Acme Attractions, I reigned supreme. I had dreadlocks and a leopardskin waistcoat, I smoked my spliffs, and I was THE man. Then punk rock comes along and I was like, hold on a minute, they're stealing my thunder. Jeanette Lee (she was my girlfriend at the time) was really the one who totally embraced the whole phenomenon because until then I guess she was a bit swamped by my black culture which, to an extent, I was pushing in the shop and musically very much so. At first I was reticent about the whole punk vibe, but through Jeanette, and I can't stress this enough…through her interest, I realized that these guys were worth checking out because there was something going on there. And I've got to say, it was through her that I got to meet the main players because she was already into the scene. She went to see the Pistols probably before I did. I think the first gig I saw was at the Nashville.

Anyway, I'd got to know Paul Simonon, Mick Jones, Johnny Rotten, Sid Vicious, so I got in at the high end and realized that there was something going on here. I couldn't just write them off as a bunch of crazy white guys. They were turned on by the dub sounds that I was playing in the shop, so I realized we were turning each other on through our respective cultures. I was into their crazy antics and their publicity tactics, maybe more than the music. They were into the political content of the reggae music, the rhythms, the heavy bass, the ganja. In Jamaica, they placed a lot of emphasis on sloganeering, like Tapper Zukie's phrase 'heavy-duty discipline' that the Clash had stencilled onto their clothing. It was the language of the street – that's all from Jamaica. We spoke in the currency that the punk rockers could relate to.

Don Letts

There was no point in going down the Kings Road.

I couldn't afford it.

Window-shopping is a wind-up. Paul Simonon

The Kings Road in '76 was amazing.
It was like a film set.

Mark Powell, London tailor

I was a buyer for Acme and used to travel all over the country looking for dead stock – brand new stuff that hadn't been sold the first time around. I remember going to some dusty old shop in the East End of London to buy some original drape-coats, only to find that Malcolm had already been there. Then I went to buy a batch of old shirts from some place in Southampton or somewhere, only to discover that Malcolm had again bought a load of them before me. At the time, I didn't realize that these were the shirts they stencilled on and customized. Malcolm always got there first.
Roger Bourton

We couldn't afford bugger all, so we nicked everything. Of course we didn't buy it.
John Egan, hairdresser at Smile

The whole Kings Road and Soul Boy scene just didn't exist anywhere else. You only saw these people down the Kings Road. My mum and dad didn't get it. They kept saying, 'We've never seen anyone else dressed like this.' I'd say, 'Well, there are lots…unfortunately.'
Marco Pirroni

I remember all the Soul Boys at the Lacy Lady in Ilford used to wear those see-through Sex T-shirts, the red trousers with plastic pockets, and plastic sandals. On a Friday you'd sometimes see John Lydon, as well as a few other trendy types, in the club. You'd get all sorts: girls in Red Indian outfits, in see-through nighties or leather; and men in demob suits they'd bought from Johnson's when the Swing revival was going on at Canvey Island. Even Chris Hill [the original disco DJ] did a punk night on a Monday – not a lot of people know that.
Mark Powell

It's difficult to know where it all came from. There was never anything in the fashion magazines or in any of the other magazines that people of that age would read, and there weren't any fashion magazines for men. It sort of came out of the blue.
Marco Pirroni

The Kings Road at the time was like a melting pot of ideas. You bowled down of a Saturday and you'd see fashion from the '50s and '60s, leather, rubber, bondage; you'd hear rock'n'roll, dub, funk, '60s soul. We all felt as if anything could happen and anything could be worn. It pretty much did, and very much was.
Chris Sullivan

There were these twins from Aylesbury. They were on the Kings Road every week. Both were really skinny, had Bowie–Thin White Duke haircuts and wore lurex cardigans, plastic sandals, shorts and make-up. This was on a Saturday afternoon. They were right lads, could have a right tear-up and sold hotdogs to tourists in Trafalgar Square.
Frank Kelly

There was an odd collection of people on the Kings Road: Soul Boys from Canvey Island, people like me, Siouxsie and Severin. To my mum, we all looked the same. We wore the porno T-shirts and leather. It was darker. We were heading towards punk.
Marco Pirroni

Opposite, foreground: Sue Catwoman, with Simon Barker behind her and Marco Pirroni to her left • Right: Kings Road, 1976

The Sex clothes were shocking, but they were art. I know 'cause I've got them on my wall. Marco Pirroni

Above, left: 1950s-style glamour photo tie from Let It Rock • Above, right: Bondage boots from Sex • Opposite, left: Anarchy shirt • Opposite, right: Kensington Market copy of a jacket from Sex

Part of the reason I collect punk clothing is that it's shocking. The main reason is that it's great.
Dan Macmillan, Viscount Ovenden, latterday punk aficionado

I've seen original Sex T-shirts go for a grand.
Barnsley fahion mogul

People stood out in Sex clothing in the same way that a man today stands out in a fine bespoke suit.
Mark Powell

Original Westwood is art. At the time they were first produced, they were controversial, contentious and cutting edge. The same can be said today, but they cost 100 times as much.
Miles English, art director, *GQ* magazine

Vivienne Westwood took the conventional, such as ties, and by attaching '50s glamour cards in plastic on their front, gave the traditional a much-needed twist. No one has done that so well since…but they all try.
Stephen Colegrave

Westwood was copied so much. They say that is the highest form of flattery…I'm not sure whether she would agree.
Roger Bourton

Louise's was truly decadent

Mark Taylor, club promoter

It was a lesbian club. I had a good time there. There was a lot of lesbians and fag hags. Used to get me cock sucked in the bathroom quite a lot. Steve Jones

We all used to go to the more soul-type clubs that were often a bit gay, like the Sombrero in Kensington High Street and Chaguarama's, the club that became the Roxy. Around the beginning of '76, we started noticing these moody types hanging around together in the clubs, looking slightly aloof and rather distant. They stood out because they wore creepers, leather trousers, muslin tops and these T-shirts with pictures of cowboys with their knobs sticking out. These people were to become the driving force behind British punk. My friends and I were halfway down that road, being into Lou Reed, the Velvets and Iggy. Like most impressionable young things, we were rapidly drawn into this world of outrage as an act of one-upmanship. Then we went to Louise's, which was like nothing I'd seen before – a quasi punk/lesbo/gay club that was like something out of the film *Cabaret*. It appeared truly decadent.
Chris Sullivan

When I first went to Louise's, with my friend Yellena, I think it was, I was told it was a lesbian club. We waltzed in, only to see all these men in suits dancing with other men in suits. We thought, 'This isn't lesbian. This is gay.' Then we realized that all the 'men' were women in drag. It was so camp and '60s, like the movie *The Killing of Sister George*. We loved it. Louise was on the door looking ever so glamorous…and French. We started going every week, and then word got around.
Phillip Salon

The other clubs we used to go to late at night were like Louise's…kind of cool and glamorous, yet what punk had turned into wasn't glamorous at all. The floor was sticky with beer, and people were bumping into each other and really kind of out of it. They were not a very sophisticated crowd at all, but that was where we were supposed to be. You had to shift your sensibilities because you knew that this was where you belonged, but it wasn't really where you wanted to be. So we hung out at Louise's and, later, the Speakeasy.
Nils Stevenson

The interesting thing about Louise's is that you had this complete culture clash between the rather traditional-looking, dikey lesbians and the feminine lesbians dancing cheek to cheek. Then you had all these strange punky types entering the picture. The poor woman DJ, who was a friend of Phillip Salon's, had the unfortunate task of trying to balance the music to suit these different groups. On the one hand she played smoochy cheek-to-cheek music for the lesbians, and on the other hand she played the A and B sides of 'Anarchy in the UK' [the Sex Pistols' first record] over and over again because it was the only damn punk record that existed. So you've got this strange mix of things going on. You've got elegant-looking Louise and her friend Francis Bacon and their bottle of champagne. I remember people popping outside and having sex with all the Sex Pistols in a van on one occasion. Louise's closed down shortly after that and became a gentlemen's club, which was a great disappointment.
Ted Polhemus

Louise was a 60-year-old French émigrée who used to sit there with her best friend, Francis Bacon, while all around her were these lunatics bouncing about. It was a laugh. Chris Sullivan

Above: Vive le Rock T-shirt from Sex

Louise's was great when I first went there. You suddenly thought, 'Wow, I've discovered the real underground!' There were people there you could not fucking fathom out at all. I remember standing at the bar the first time I went there and this big, heavy dike came up to me and said, 'Do you see her over there? I'm right in there.' I wasn't freaked out, but I was kind of confused. She was talking just like a guy. Another time I remember seeing a really old queenie bloke who was fucking ancient, like Jabba the Hutt from *Star Wars*. He was surrounded by these boys, and he had to be carried in. He was obviously rich and was paying for everything. This was the real underground; these were the real misfits. It was extremely decadent. It reminded me of Berlin in the '30s. I could never figure out who or what the fuck some of these people were. I'm sure they didn't like it when there was an influx of new blood – these kind of weird youngsters. All of a sudden you had all these women who could've easily passed as blokes, and the very thing they were hiding was openly shoved in their faces. Illustrations of every perversion they could possibly harbour were being worn on our chests in the form of T-shirts. Marco Pirroni

I don't think so much grief was caused to so many people by so few T-shirts before – or since. Nils Stevenson

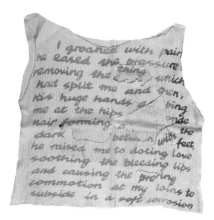

Above: A selection of T-shirts from Sex (left to right) Wet-look; Anarchy in the UK; Handwritten porno

The most controversial
T-shirt, other than the Cambridge Rapist,
was the two cowboys. Gene Krell

Malcolm didn't originate any of those things. He just found them in books by
Tom O'Finland [illustrator of gay culture] that he'd bought along the way.
Gene Krell

I left the shop wearing the infamous cowboy T-shirt and went to meet a friend in
Piccadilly. I was arrested for vagrancy on the grounds that I offended public decency.
They put me in a Black Maria, took me to the police station and charged me. It was
horrible and humiliating.
Alan Jones

Alan Jones was arrested for vagrancy under the laws of offending public decency and
he was fined £15. I actually went to court wearing one of the T-shirts, and Malcolm and
all the early punks were very protective of me. They thought that, being American, if I
was arrested, I might face deportation.
Gene Krell

I was working at the ICA [Institute of Contemporary Arts in central London], where
I instituted the first-ever series on fashion designers. I'd already done a series in '75

about named designers, and I wanted to do a follow-up about up-and-coming
designers. I had my eye on Malcolm McLaren and Vivienne Westwood. I'd never been
in the Sex shop, and it took quite a bit of courage to go there, but eventually I did.
I found Malcolm McLaren, told him I was from the ICA and asked if he and Vivienne
would like to appear in our fashion series. He told me the ICA was a boring,
bourgeois institution and they would never have anything to do with us, but I gave
him my card and I had a phone call from him soon after. He said that they had been
busted for making obscene T-shirts. He proposed a deal whereby Vivienne, Jordan
and some other people would appear at the ICA so long as I agreed to appear as a
character witness at their trial, talking about their major contribution to British fashion.
This sounded cool, so I went along to the trial, but I was of absolutely no use to them.
They lost the trial, if I recall correctly, but of course that was good publicity. It was
probably the most bizarre trial in English legal history. The T-shirt with the two
cowboys on it was produced as evidence. The prosecution alleged that the cowboys'
penises were touching. The defence lawyer leapt up and said, 'No, my lord, they're
not touching.' Somebody went and got a ruler to measure the distance between the
cowboys' dicks. It was all very strange.
Ted Polhemus

Nah,
it's all
played aht,
Bill,
getting too
straight.

Joe the Cowboy

I remember the first thing I bought from that transition period was the Anarchy shirt. I took it home and I didn't know how to wear it. I didn't know whether it should be tucked in or not. I couldn't wear it with creepers – it looked stupid. That was the other thing about Vivienne. You couldn't ever just wear one thing. You had to have everything. It wouldn't look right with anything else. You couldn't wear an Anarchy shirt and jeans; you couldn't wear an Anarchy shirt and pegs.
Marco Pirroni

I loved the mohair jumpers. I lived in mine. I think Vivienne had them knitted up in some old people's home for about three quid a pop. But they cost £20.
Nils Stevenson

I quite liked the bondage trousers. It was said that I was the only person who could set up a whole PA wearing those dumb bondage trousers.
Roadent, aka Steve Connolly, Pistols' and Clash roadie

I just think the bondage trousers were the pinnacle of everything she was doing, with all the zips and straps.
Alan Jones

I thought the bondage trousers were brilliant. Vivienne would walk in wearing what she'd been making at the time. I remember one day she walked in dressed in a white shirt with stencilled writing: 'Be Reasonable – Demand the Impossible'. I always thought there were loads of these shirts, but there was only one, so it was obviously a prototype Anarchy shirt. She wore the bondage trousers, but without the straps on, and I think she may've been wearing the Spiderman boots. I was thinking, 'I don't get this look at all. It's not based on anything I've ever seen.'
Marco Pirroni

I remember Malcolm drawing these bondage trousers when we were in Bell Street. I asked him, 'What are they for?' and he said, 'They're for women.'
Helen Wellington Lloyd

The thing about the bondage trousers was that you couldn't run in them with the straps on, which was murder when you had all the Teds after you.
Frank Kelly

I love the bondage trousers. I've had about 20 pairs made in all different fabrics.
Dan Macmillan

Bernie Rhodes [manager of the Clash] came up with that first situationist T-shirt, the 'I woke up one morning' one. That's where Malcolm got the Sex Pistols' name.
Helen Wellington Lloyd, assistant in Sex and McLaren muse

The first T-shirt I designed was purely about waking up one morning and] trying to determine…which side of the bed you'd been lying on. [On one side of the bed] there would be a list of either 'good' names or 'bad' names and [these could be used to make a comparison]…that ultimately might change popular culture itself. In that list there was a name – the Sex Pistols – which meant to me all sorts of things. It came about by the idea of a pistol, a pin-up, a young thing, a better-looking assassin.
Malcolm McLaren in *Please Kill Me*

The thing that summed the whole scene up for me was that T-shirt they always had in Sex. It said: 'You're going to wake up one morning and find out what side of the bed you've been lying on.' That said it all for me. It drew a line. It said you're either this or you're that.
Steve Walsh

I designed that T-shirt.
Bernie Rhodes, manager, the Clash

Bernie had some of these T-shirts on which was written 'You're going to wake up one morning and *know* what side of the bed you're lying on!' The writing on the shirt also referred to Steve 'Cutie' Jones and his sex pistol (he was a real ladies' man). This was where Malcolm got the name of the band from.
Gene Krell

Opposite: Johnny Thunders wearing a T-shirt from Sex • Above, clockwise from top left: Wet-look T-shirt; Handmade Stalin shirt; Leather jacket from Let It Rock; Parachute top; Marabou punk T-shirt

149

Keep on sniffing, you punks.

**Mark Perry,
SNIFFIN' GLUE,**

issue 1

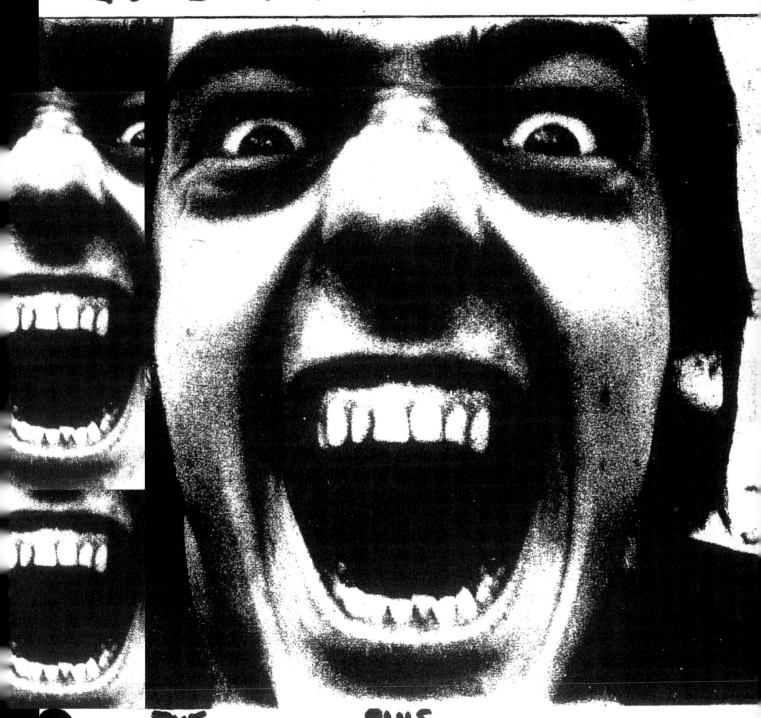

LIVE AND ALBUM REVIEWS.

THE PLUS
SUBWAY SECT + CHELSEA

SNIFFIN' GLUE
became the chosen rag of the blank generation.

John Cooper Clarke, punk poet, in the foreword to *The Essential Punk Accessory*

In an age when guys looked like Open University lecturers and even your uncle wore flares, the Ramones came in like a breath of fresh carbona, inspiring Mark Perry from south London to launch SNIFFIN' GLUE, the first of the fanzines... With its cheapskate house style and semi-literate enthusiasm, it conveyed there was a piss-or-get-off-the-pot urgency about the whole production. John Cooper Clarke in *The Essential Punk Accessory*

After a Ramones gig in early July...I went straight home and typed the first words of my fanzine, *Sniffin' Glue and Other Rock'n'Roll Habits* – a pinched title straight from the Ramones' song 'Now I Wanna Sniff Some Glue'. I thought that if anything summed up the basic approach to the new music it was the lowest form of drug-taking.
Mark Perry in *The Essential Punk Accessory*

I don't know nothing about fanzines. I was too busy getting out of it.
John Egan

There was something about punk that made you have to get involved. You either formed a band or a fanzine. No way could I sing, so it had to be a fanzine. I never really knew what a fanzine was until the Pistols played in Plymouth on the Anarchy tour and someone was selling copies of *Sniffin' Glue*. I thought it was really exciting – it was fantastic. I think it was number seven, it had Gaye Advert on the front. I remember going home and deciding to write my own fanzine. It was called *Stains,* and I started work on it over Christmas 1976.
Nigel Wingrove

Although Alan Jones had introduced me to the Sex Pistols early on, and Bernie Rhodes to the Clash, it was nearly a year before my paper, *Melody Maker,* would publish any of my stories about punk. My editorial board was a group of weak, misogynist men, especially since my mentor, Penny Valentine, had left. It was ironical that it took a fight at the Nashville to get them interested and carry my first article, 'The Rock Revolution', on 28 July 1976. In the meantime, Mark Perry launched *Sniffin'*

Glue, which meant that at last the fans had a way of getting information. Mark played a vital role in those early days. In some ways I was concerned that punk would sell out as the broader press took interest. After all, most white rock'n'roll bands had done just that. Fanzines were the voice of the street, whilst the music press had its own vested interest.
Caroline Coon, journalist

Never had much time for fanzines. I liked drugs.
Nils Stevenson

Mark Perry was very instrumental in getting punk going. Fanzines didn't really exist before *Sniffin' Glue.* He came along and galvanized the scene. He actually put it out there. If it happened today, it would be on the Web. I like Mark a great deal. He actually understood what it was all about immediately.
Alan Jones

For me, punk meant an escape from a very boring job in banking. It gave me a chance to be creative and share my ideas with others who seemed to be on the same wavelength... I thought I could change the world. We were in action; we had the time; we had the vision. It wasn't just punk rock, *Sniffin' Glue*, the Sex Pistols, the Clash...it was art in action.
Mark Perry in *The Essential Punk Accessory*

It was all a bit Dada really, wasn't it? I don't know.
John Egan

ee beer glasses we
alright, that was bad-
nd <u>does</u> happen at many
.It's just stupid, that's
p the violence on punk-
stort the truth!

mething is happening,
ecently played Upstairs
t seems that a member of
up currently rehearsing)
a Disco-kid'cause he was
got branded

"SNIFFIN'GLUE...'is the mag for you,
Mark P's the editor and don't care a
Steve Mick's a writer,one of a glass
And if you don't like the mag you ca
                              it up you arse!"

Also sticking things in various pla
Rick Brown(who's a fool for a banan
Steve Walsh(who's likewise for roll
Jonathan Richman cover).

Special sneers to:Roco(CLASH photo:
the other people I love dearly(you

SOUNDS, NME, MELODY MAKER *and the new* ROCKSTAR *should stick to writing about the established artists.* Leave our music to us.

Sniffin' Glue, issue 5

I hired a Xerox machine. I don't know what possessed me to ring Rank Xerox. This guy on the phone said, yes, they could do it. A few days later one of the biggest lorries I have ever seen in my life arrived in the little street at my mother's house. The photocopier must have weighed half a ton. We set it up in the lounge, hidden behind the sofa, but it took up half the room. It was just insane. Basically I ended up printing all the fanzines for the area, probably more than 24 fanzines. People would have small runs: some 20 copies a day; some 100. They would come with their artwork on single pages. Xerox used to give me reams of paper, so I just kept going.
Nigel Wingrove

It was a very creative time, even though a lot of the fanzines were crap. People were actually trying to do something for themselves. They were actually sitting at home churning out these magazines – maybe only 10 pages of their thoughts and pictures and ideas. They just did it.
Mark Powell

I interviewed everyone who came to Plymouth, from the Pistols to the Damned. Captain Sensible actually stayed at our house. He tried to have sex with my mother, and tried to have sex with my girlfriend, and actually even tried to have sex with me.
Nigel Wingrove

Yeah, fanzines…bloody expensive!
Chris Sullivan

I would go out to the concerts, photograph the bands, process all the shots at art school and then go backstage and do an interview. My first interview was with Cherry Vanilla, who played in Plymouth. Her backing band was called the Police. I remember going backstage and this bloke called Sting came up to me and asked if I wanted to interview him. I said, 'No, thanks,' because no one had ever heard of him or his band.
Nigel Wingrove

We've got to make somethin' real happen here. Most British rock is past it now, but the punk scene isn't. Let's build our own brands up instead of drooling over the NY scene. I'm not putting that scene down, but if we've got something goin' on here, we wanna make it better. We're gonna try to do a bit for the scene, but it's all up to you – the kids (and, of course, the guys who feel young). London punk is great, so let's go!
Sniffin' Glue, issue 1

Fanzines…well, yeah.
Tom Sandor, newsagent

My Xerox machine was great. People forgot that without it there wouldn't have been fanzines. You could create them instantly. Seconds later you would be flogging your fanzine at a gig or a record shop. I'd never seen anything like this before, and I loved it. That was until the inevitable happened. I hadn't really taken much notice of the little counter on the top of the copier. But it seemed that every time you printed a page, it was a penny or something like that. I had actually clocked up an enormous bill that went into thousands of pounds. Then I received this statement and demand for payment through the post. Of course, I'd loved my Xerox so much I used it to its maximum. I'd been knocking all sorts of stuff off and doing loads of silly things. We'd do pranks like cut out people's heads and stick them on pornographic pictures and festoon parts of Plymouth with certain people we didn't like.
   I kept getting these bills for thousands of pounds. Eventually my mother found them and I wrote this grovelling letter to somebody very important at Rank Xerox saying I was only a poor student and how could they do this to me. In the end, the guy who'd leased me the machine was given a court-martial, or whatever they do for giving an expensive piece of equipment to a poor art student. Eventually they took the machine back with no charge. I escaped to London and my mother got the other half of her lounge back.
Nigel Wingrove

Fanzines were amateurish nonsense. Beginning of the end. Lowest common denominator. *Sniffin' Glue* says it all.
Chris Sullivan

Opposite: Shane MacGowan

Malcolm aimed to create the whole Factory vibe with Sex and the crowd around it, and to some extent succeeded. Chris Stein, Blondie

Because of my size and the way I was brought up, the punk era was the most liberating time of my life.
Helen Wellington Lloyd

In those days you could shock people by having short hair and tight trousers.
Clive Langer, songwriter and producer

No one made clothes that would look good on me. Then, when punk came along, I finally found an artistic way to dress. The clothes I wore made me feel as if I belonged to a club. There were only a few of us. You felt privileged; you felt part of something. Suddenly, I had the courage to wear ridiculous things that made me stand out. For the first time I didn't try to merge into the background. I wanted people to look at me with my chains, safety-pins, foxtail and black eyes. For once, being a dwarf didn't matter. I remember going to a club in Earls Court with some gay friends. A guy on the tube was looking at me in amazement because the foxtail was sticking out between my legs like a well...you know, someone's pussy. It was stupid, but it was great.
Helen Wellington Lloyd

Like Warhol, McLaren and Westwood created an arena where the burning youth – strong and vulnerable alike – could run wild...freed from the imposition of adult company and lies. Like Warhol, their very lack of conventional morality...was both liberating and the source of their power. It meant that the emerging movement could not be easily defined, yet, through its childlike aspect, it was particularly vulnerable to perversion, once defined.
Jon Savage, *England's Dreaming*

When I first went to see the Sex Pistols, it was the people that had the biggest effect on me. Characters like Jordan, Sue Catwoman, Phillip Salon and Alan Jones were unlike anyone I'd met before. It was all about the scene. The music was secondary. The scene gave you a place to go and a sense of belonging.
Clive Langer

Living in London in 1976 was like living in Poland. You couldn't buy Perrier water, and spaghetti came in a can.
Robert Elms, broadcaster and journalist

Punk energized a lot of people who were bored out of their brains. There was such electricity in the air that those in the early scene felt completely invincible.
Roger Bourton

We were just 16 and saying no to everything around us. People forget how young we were.
Steve Severin

There was a right load of oddballs hanging round Sex – transvestites, rubber fiends, a dominatrix, arty types, posh bods, thieves, ragamuffins, builders, an undertaker, young kids. It was Malcolm's little zoo. I know because I was there.
Frank Kelly

Louise's was our Factory in a way, I guess. Maybe Malcolm did kind of take the Factory as a blueprint. Certainly he was always ringing me or Simon Barker [leader of the Bromley contingent of punks] to galvanize us into some sort of action, such as going on the Grundy show.
Steve Severin

The rest of the scene was straighter than the Sex lot. Some of them were bending the gender, as it were. I guess that's what happens when you listen to a lot of David Bowie.
Chris Sullivan

I think there's a strong parallel to be made between the Factory and Sex, and everybody was certainly very aware of it. Malcolm was trying to manipulate everybody to create a scene. I believe he thought, 'There is this kind of creativity in London. Let's get all these people together and see what happens.' I don't think he had a grand design and it wasn't altruistic. It was all to perpetuate the myth of the Pistols and whatever he was doing personally.
Steve Severin

There was a right good scene going on before the Pistols, which I thought was better. We had a band called the Killjoys with a saxophone player and two girl backing singers. I wore a rubber coat and winkle-pickers, and I sat on the stage doing torch songs. After a while we found ourselves on the same bill as the punk bands, but the audiences wanted punk and nothing else. I think punk was a major interruption. It just got in the way.
Kevin Rowland, Dexy's Midnight Runners

Left, clockwise from top left: Alan Jones, Lynda Ashby and Jordan • Above, right: Sue Catwoman • Opposite, top, left to right: Sid Vicious, Nils Stevenson and Lynda Ashby • Opposite, bottom, clockwise from lower left: Siouxsie, Debbie Juvenile, Phillip Salon, Simon Barker (with arms crossed), Steve Severin (with legs in the air), Steve Berlin (with hand on head), Sue Catwoman, Sharon (in cap) and Lynda Ashby

I think Malcolm and Vivienne started off the whole punk thing in this country
because they couldn't dance.

Helen Robinson, designer

There was no information to be had. There were no style magazines and no Internet. You really had to scrabble around and it was all word of mouth, so Malcolm's shop just became a focal point. You'd walk up the Kings Road on a Saturday afternoon, and you'd bump into people that you'd seen at a club or an early Pistols' gig and you'd have some common ground. If you saw someone who dressed remotely like yourself, you remembered them. I think Sid talked to me at about the tenth Pistols' gig I'd been to. We checked each other out and eventually he said something, and we grunted at each other. As usual, people who are into the same things slowly pen together.
Steve Severin

The scene before had been predominantly funky. Now it was the time for the rock'n'rollers to have their day.
Mark Powell

When I first met Siouxsie, she never went anywhere except gay clubs, like J Arthur's and Chaguarama's, which became the Roxy. Lynda Ashby or another one of the Bromley contingent dragged us down to Louise's. Where else could we go?
Steve Severin

In early 1976 a style emerged that was a departure from the '50s look and a little more extreme, with the drainpipes, dyed hair, mohairs, multiple earrings and winkle-pickers. At the end of the Kings Road the Sex lot (who were mainly from the more arty side of the fence) were not content with a merely retro appearance. They started taking a leaf out of the Lou Reed and Velvet Underground school of style and began to wear things that were not only darker but, at times, really rather odd. Soon the drainpipes were ditched in favour of bondage and leather trousers, and the winkle-pickers were replaced by creepers and Sex boots. Eventually the look became known as 'punk', even though the term did not yet exist and was universally hated once it did.
Chris Sullivan

Siouxsie and I and all the rest of the Bromley contingent had gained a lot of respect because we'd been right at the heart of the scene and the whole thing just sort of grew by itself. As soon as they gave us somewhere to go, everybody came and gravitated around one or two places. It was like it had been brewing for years. It started at Louise's and Crackers, and then obviously all the Pistols' gigs in the early days. Chaguarama's was the next place, and by that point the scene was really starting to grow. Then we started meeting all the boys from the Lacy Lady [in Ilford]. There were probably only about 800 to 1,000 people involved in the whole scene, but it seemed like thousands.
Steve Severin

I was wearing the Anarchy shirt with its swastika armband and everything to the premiere of *A Chorus Line* at the Theatre Royal in Drury Lane. I was with five friends and we were four rows from the front. The theatre manager saw me and delayed the curtain. He came down, pointed at me and said, 'There is no way you are going to be watching this performance wearing that shirt when I fought in the war. This is the Theatre Royal, Drury Lane. Get out.' I stood up and we had this five-minute argument in front of everyone. I said, 'I'm not taking this. I can wear what I like, free country, blah blah blah. I'll turn it round so the actual swastika bit doesn't show. Will that be good enough?' 'Yes, I suppose so, because we can't hold the show up any longer.' I sat through the performance knowing that everyone in the entire place hated me. Even my friends were furious because they were always saying I'd get them into trouble.
Alan Jones

I realized punk was catching on when normal punters in the Kings Road stopped gawping at us. I knew then the rot would set in.
Frank Kelly

No one wore the swastika as a political statement. It was an attempt to shock, just like the gay T-shirts. In retrospect, it was really stupid, but we were all so young. I never wore one, but I knew many who did, and half of them didn't even realize its significance. Shock was the order of the day, and wrong as it may now seem, it did just that.
Nils Stevenson

I never agreed with the swastika, perhaps because I was fully aware of the significance of it. I didn't think it at all amusing.
Chris Sullivan

Below, left to right: Phillip Salon; Lynda Ashby and Sharon (in cap); Debbie Juvenile, Billy Idol, Siouxsie and Peter Fenton (of the Banshees) • Opposite, clockwise from top left: Vivienne Westwood, Johnny Rotten and Jordan at the Snax Deluxe Hotel in Paris • Opposite, inset: Helen Wellington Lloyd

I think we are being taken for a ride. Lord Shawcross, director of EMI Records

The Sex Pistols are a group with a bit of guts for younger people to identify with…a group that their parents actually won't tolerate. We haven't had a band like that since the Stones and the Who. It's not just the parents who need a little shaking, it's the music business itself. Us middle-aged executives are the ones who will 'not understand' the new wave that will follow in the wake of the Sex Pistols. I think that's why a lot of people won't sign them. They've taken it all too personally. It's a gut-level excitement to which 16- to 18-year-olds can relate. Nick Mobbs, A & R executive, EMI

The first line I wrote was 'I am an Antichrist'. And I couldn't think of a damn thing to rhyme with it. 'Anarchist' fitted just nicely. Johnny Rotten in *The Filth and the Fury*

When I first heard 'Anarchy in the UK' I thought it sounded like old man Steptoe wailing over a dodgy Black Sabbath riff. Captain Sensible, bass player, the Damned

So we got the single out and it was selling – nothing miraculous, but it was out there. All the way through, there was never any hint of trouble from the people we were dealing with – Nick Mobbs, the press people, whoever. They'd even had us photographed in the same stairwell as the Beatles, for Christ's sake. That was their idea. They genuinely believed they were looking at the next Beatles. Then somebody at the top level got cold feet, and the decision took everyone by surprise. I mean, we heard all the rumbles about a shareholders' meeting, but when did anything ever get decided at a shareholders' meeting? There was a connection between EMI and Thames TV, and obviously the incident when the band swore on TV, front pages in the press – was very embarrassing for them, but right up to the last, there was no clue that anything would go wrong. John 'Boogie' Tiberi, Sex Pistols' tour manager 1977-79

The first time the Pistols performed this number ('Anarchy in the UK') the audience surged in front of the stage, ripping at each other's jackets and T-shirts, throwing themselves at each other and bouncing off again – a seething, gleeful mass of bodies forming a trampoline of human flesh. It was obvious that if ever there was to be a single, then this should be it. But it was difficult to imagine how the band could capture all that excitement on vinyl. They have done it, though. The single is an epitome of their sound, at the band's most furious, venomous best. The song is a threat, a malediction. In the last bar Johnny Rotten (19), with the feel of an urban desperado, yells 'D-E-S-T-R-O-Y!' Caroline Coon, *Melody Maker,* 18 October 1976

Go on, you've got 10 seconds left. Say something outrageous. Bill Grundy, TV interviewer

You dirty fucking rotter. Steve Jones

Opposite: Stills from the notorious Grundy show • Above, left and centre, front row: Johnny Rotten, Steve Jones, Glen Matlock, Paul Cook and Bill Grundy; back row: Simon Barker, Steve Severin, Lynda Ashby and Siouxsie • Above, right: Bill Grundy

I was so angry and disgusted with this filth that I took a swing at the TV set with my boot. It blew up and I was knocked backwards. James Holmes, lorry driver, describing his reaction to the Bill Grundy interview

Queen and Freddie Mercury cancelled their appearance on *Today*, so the programme came to me looking for someone else. I suggested trying the Sex Pistols, who'd just signed to EMI. I never liked the Sex Pistols' music, but I always knew they were going to be monster. Eric Hall, agent

We were rehearsing at Harlesden. Malcolm came down and said we'd got an interview on the *Today* programme. Queen were meant to do it but they blew out, so they needed a last-minute replacement. The publicist Eric Hall, who used to work at EMI, got us the programme. We jumped into a car to go to the studio. We were knocking back all the free drink in the Green Room. We didn't know what it was all about. Grundy interviewed us unrehearsed. We didn't even know the programme was live. At the beginning of the interview Grundy was being really sarcastic. 'This band has been given £40,000 by EMI and they can't even play,' he said. 'Look at the state of them. And we've got them on later.' It pissed us off. Paul Cook, drummer, the Sex Pistols

Malcolm called us up and asked us to come down to LWT – me, Siouxsie, Simon Barker. So we went down and there's the Green Room with all the free drink. We're all broke, don't forget, so we take full advantage. Then there's the show. Grundy was horrible, really taking the piss out of us and of course the band reacted with a few swear words, nothing that bad, and anyway, we thought it would be edited. Nobody had any idea it was going out live, except Grundy, and he then asked us to say something outrageous. And we did. Steve Severin

I saw the Grundy show while I was having my tea. I thought, 'Oh, that's a bit warm.' Paul Durden, former roadie, now scriptwriter

A pop group shocked millions of viewers last night with the filthiest language heard on British television. The Sex Pistols, leaders of the new 'punk rock' cult, hurled a string of obscenities at interviewer Bill Grundy on Thames TV's family teatime programme *Today*. The *Sun*, 2 December 1976

We got into the car afterwards and shot off back to the rehearsal. To be honest, I didn't think anything of it. We went out that night and got drunk like we usually did. We were going on our first tour the next day with this big American band the Heartbreakers, plus the Clash and the Damned. We thought the Grundy thing wasn't that bad – a bit of swearing, but so what? Of course, we didn't know it was going out live. Paul Cook

We arrived at night and were picked up in a limo. We were taken to some hotel in Bayswater and then went for burgers at The Great American Disaster or something. I thought that was funny. In the morning,

Jerry Nolan [of the Heartbreakers] bought all the newspapers, and the Sex Pistols were on every god-damned front page. There was uproar. Jerry threw the papers on the bed screaming, 'Look at this shit, man. I knew it was a bad idea. I fucking knew it. It's all fucking Leee's fault.' Walter Lure, guitarist, the Heartbreakers

Jerry Nolan, who was a vampire and never slept, came into my room with all these newspapers. Every headline said things like: 'The Sex Pistols – the Day the Air Turned Blue'. According to Jerry Nolan, it was all my fault. He said, 'Look what you've gotten us into.' I just thought, 'Oh, my God, here we go again.'
Leee Childers, ex-manager, the Stooges and the Heartbreakers

Nothing was different until the next day, when it was on all the front pages. We were still in bed at 1.00 p.m., so we missed all the early papers banging on the door. The *Evening Standard* was there, though, shouting: 'Wake up, where are you?' We ran down Oxford Street to our offices and they were all running after us. People recognized us and were pointing at us in the street. All hell had broken loose. Malcolm did his best to control the situation. After that we had security guards and bouncers because the press wanted to get any story that was going. Paul Cook

When we left the studio, Malcolm was shitting himself. Then the next day, once he'd seen the press coverage, it was all his big idea. Glen Matlock

I seem to remember I was back at my mum's by then. Malcolm was on the phone and was fucking hysterical. He just lost it completely, as he often does. He was bonkers. He said, 'It's all over. It's finished.' Nils Stevenson

I knew the Bill Grundy show was going to create a huge scandal. I genuinely believed it would be history in the making, and in many regards it was, because that night was the real beginning – from the media's and from the general public's point of view – of what became known as punk rock.
Malcolm McLaren in *Please Kill Me*

I was frankly appalled [by the Grundy incident] because if you took any four or five lads off the street...made them feel important, filled them full of beer, put them on television and said, 'Say something outrageous,' they'd say something outrageous. I rather suspect that – as a middle-class individual of 38 – if they did the same to me, I'd do the same. So for those people then to wring their hands in horror and say, 'This is outrageous,' is just bare-faced hypocrisy... I was really outraged by that.
John Peel, Radio One DJ, in *The Sex Pistols: The Inside Story*

After Grundy, it was a media circus. It was great in one sense, that we were a household name, but it was kinda the start of the downfall of the band because it just pushed us way too fast. It was too much too soon. Steve Jones

Judge in 'murder' pardon shocker

By ARNOT McWHINNIE

A JUDGE made an astonishing attack yesterday on the way a man convicted of murder was given a royal pardon.

He told a jury: "You may well have come to the clear conclusion that he was rightly convicted."

The man at the centre of the storm is 48-year-old Patrick Meehan, who was freed from jail in May after serving nearly seven years.

The judge, Lord Robertson, said: "There is no legal justification whatsoever for saying that Meehan was wrongly convicted."

He went on to suggest that Meehan's conviction for killing elderly Mrs.

Meehan yesterday

Rachel Ross still stood, despite the pardon.

The judge spoke out at the end of a second trial over the same murder.

This time, 33-year-old Ian Waddell was in the dock. He was a prosecution witness when Meehan got a life sentence in 1969.

Yesterday, the jury acquitted Waddell of murder—and also cleared him of giving false evidence at Meehan's trial.

During the judge's summing up, Meehan stormed angrily from the public gallery at Edinburgh High Court.

He said outside: "I might as well tear up my royal pardon. It's a worthless piece of paper. It seems I am still convicted."

The judge said of the pardon: "In the ordinary use of language, if you pardon someone you pardon them for something they have done—not for something they haven't done.

"It certainly doesn't quash the conviction."

THE GROUP IN THE BIG TV RUMPUS

Johnny Rotten, leader of the Sex Pistols, opens a can of beer. Last night their language made TV viewers froth.

When the air turned blue..

INTERVIEWER Bill Grundy introduced the Sex Pistols to viewers with the comment: "Words actually fail me about the next guests on tonight's show."

The group sang a number —and the amazing interview got under way.

GRUNDY: I am told you have received £40,000 from a record company. Doesn't that seem to be slightly opposed to an anti-materialistic way of life.

PISTOL: The more the merrier.

GRUNDY: Really.

PISTOL: Yea, yea.

GRUNDY: Tell me more then.

PISTOL: F——ing spent it, didn't we.

GRUNDY: You are serious?

PISTOL: Mmmm.

GRUNDY: Beethoven, Mozart, Bach?

PISTOL: They're wonderful people.

GRUNDY: Are they?

PISTOL: Yes they really turn us on. They do.

GRUNDY: Suppose they turn other people on?
PISTOL (in a whisper): That's just their tough s——.
GRUNDY: It's what?
PISTOL: Nothing—a rude word. Next question.
GRUNDY: No, no. What was the rude word?
PISTOL: S——.
GRUNDY: Was it really? Good heavens. What about you girls behind? Are you married or just enjoying yourself?
GIRL: I've always wanted to meet you.
GRUNDY: Did you really? We'll meet afterwards, shall me?
PISTOL: You dirty old man. You dirty old man.
GRUNDY: Go on, you've got a long time yet. You've got another five seconds. Say something outrageous.
PISTOL: You dirty sod. You dirty bastard.
GRUNDY: Go on. Again.
PISTOL: You dirty f——er.
GRUNDY: What?
PISTOL: What a f——ing rotter.
GRUNDY: Well, that's it for tonight . . . I'll be seeing you soon. I hope I'm not seeing YOU again. Goodnight.

THE FILTH AND THE FURY!

A POP group shocked millions of viewers last night with the filthiest language heard on British television.

The Sex Pistols, leaders of the new "punk rock" cult, hurled a string of four-letter obscenities at interviewer Bill Grundy on Thames TV's family teatime programme "Today."

The Thames switchboard was flooded with protests.

Nearly 200 angry viewers telephoned the Mirror. One man was so furious that he kicked in the screen of his £380 colour TV.

Grundy was immediately carpeted by his boss and will apologise in tonight's programme.

Shocker

A Thames spokesman said: "Because the programme was live, we could not foresee the language which would be used. We apologise to all viewers."

The show, screened at peak children's viewing time, turned into a shocker when Grundy asked about £40,000 that the Sex Pistols received

By STUART GREIG, MICHAEL McCARTHY and JOHN PEACOCK

from their record company.

One member of the group said: "F——ing spent it, didn't we?"

Then when Grundy asked about people who preferred Beethoven, Mozart and Bach, another Sex Pistol remarked: "That's just their tough s——."

Later Grundy told the group: "Say something outrageous."

A punk rocker replied: "You dirty sod. You dirty bastard."

"Go on. Again," said Grundy.

"You dirty f——er."

"What?"

Uproar as viewers jam phones

"What a f——ing rotter."

As the Thames switchboard became jammed, viewers rang the Mirror to voice their complaints.

Lorry driver James Holmes, 47, was outraged that his eight-year-old son Lee heard the swearing . . . and kicked in the screen of his TV.

"It blew up and I was knocked backwards," he said. "But I was so angry and disgusted with this filth that I took a swing with my boot.

"I can swear as well as anyone, but I don't want this sort of muck coming into my home at teatime."

Mr. Holmes, of Beechfield Walk, Waltham Abbey, Essex, added: "I am not a violent person, but I would like to have got hold of Grundy.

"He should be sacked for encouraging this sort of disgusting behaviour."

WHO ARE THESE PUNKS? PAGE

WHO ARE THESE PUNKS?

By RUSSELL MILLER

THEY wear torn and ragged clothes held together with safety pins.

They are boorish, ill-mannered, foul-mouthed, dirty, obnoxious and arrogant. They like to be disliked.

They use names like Johnny Rotten, Dave Havoc, Sid Vicious, Rat Scabies and Dee Generate. They are the teenage punks of the Punk Rock bands, nervously hailed in some quarters as perhaps the most exciting development in rock music for a decade.

Punk rock is the aggressive, fast and loud music of kids with cheap guitars and more enthusiasm than talent. It grew, they say, out of the boredom and frustration of being on the dole.

A few months ago, no one had heard of it. Today, three punk rock records are in the charts and one band, the Sex Pistols, have signed a £40,000 contract with EMI.

Tomorrow, the three leading punk bands—Sex Pistols, Clash and The Damned—begin a nationwide tour.

"It is very likely there will be violence at some of the gigs," says tour organiser Malcolm McClaren, "because it is violent music.

"We don't necessarily think violence is a bad thing because you have to destroy to create."

McClaren, 28, is the owner of a Chelsea boutique called Sex which specialises in punk gear — ripped T-shirts, dresses made from plastic rubbish bags, moth-eaten sweaters and "Cambridge rapist" leather masks.

Anarchy

The essence of punk is anarchy and outrage. So the bands and their followers dress and behave in a manner calculated to shock or disgust—like wearing safety pins through their ears, noses or even their cheeks.

"We even try to outrage each other," says Rat Scabies, 19-year-old drummer of The Damned.

"At a gig in France we were drunk out of our heads all the time, urinating on the floor and out of the hotel windows. It was incredible."

Incredible, yes, but no more so than the sudden rise of punk music. Dozens of bands turned up to play at the first Punk Rock Festival held in London in September. The event ended with fist fights, chaos and a girl losing an eye when she caught a flying glass full in the face.

Banned

Since then, punk rock groups have been banned from most London clubs —but the music industry has decided the punk bandwagon is one it cannot afford to miss.

"As a record company we are very much involved in what is new and exciting and so it was natural we should sign the group in the forefront of the movement," Paul Watts, manager of EMI's pop division, explained.

"It is true they may not be very proficient musically, but we don't think that is a major consideration. What is important is that they generate excitement."

Some punk rock bands are so terrible that entire audiences have walked out.

At High Wycombe last month The Damned found themselves without an audience after Captain Sensible, the inaptly named bass guitarist, abused the small crowd.

"I gave them a verbal-ling because they didn't seem to be enjoying it," he said. "I can't under-stand it. We're the greatest."

Captain Sensible, like most punks, was on the dole before he joined a band. Unemployment and a deep sense of disenchantment created the climate for punk rock.

It was a feeling of being deserted by their heroes—the pop superstars with private jets and country mansions — which led to kids making their own music.

Punks claim they are a social movement. "Kids want something that can change their whole way of life," said Malcolm McClaren.

"It is the biggest thing to happen in years and no one can stop it now.

"People don't like it because they feel threatened by it—it is like having a bucket of cold water thrown in their faces."

ROTTEN: Johnny the Sex Pistols' leader.

Chef (REGD) square-shaped soups satisfy like a good soup should.

And we'll give you 6p off to prove it to your family!

Delicious Chef Box Soups not only taste but feel good. And at 6p off any two varieties, they're even better value than they are normally.

Cut out this coupon now, and tonight you can sample one of the many ways Chef have of satisfying your family's appetites.

6p | EXPIRY DATE 11th Dec. 1976 | 6p

6P OFF

CONDITIONS OF OFFER
To the Consumer: This coupon, worth 6p, is valid towards the retail purchase of any two boxes of Chef Box Soup on presentation to your Grocer. It must not be used towards the purchase of any other products as this would constitute a breach of the terms of this offer. Only one coupon will be accepted against each such retail purchase of two Chef Box Soups.

To the Dealer: This coupon will only be redeemed if received by Crosse & Blackwell Limited, Coupon Redemption Centre, Cox Lane, Chessington, Surrey and provided (a) it has been accepted by you in a normal retail sale to the Consumer, as part payment for any two Chef Box Soups, and (b) you have reasonable proof of your purchase which may be called for by Crosse & Blackwell Limited.

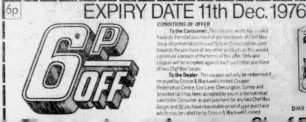

Chef SOUP Minestrone

DMR 2

THE RAGGED REBEL

THE LATEST and youngest—punk rock band played their first professional gig in North London last night.

Called Eater, their average age is just 15.

... from Caterham, Surrey. Unfortunately his voice has not yet broken so he sounds slightly incongruous when he is talking about his commitment to punk.

"Some bands might get accepted," he piped, "but WE will never be acceptable."

His mum, Mrs Helen ...

... seen the band play I can see what they are trying to do," she said.

"I think it is great really. You should see him walking around—he looks like an old ragbag. It's so funny."

"Unfortunately, we are having a bit of trouble with his school right now because he has ...

That was it. One four-letter word done everything.

Paul Cook

You have to understand the times as well. For me the worst bit was all the violence and the paranoia, the heaviness of it all. Looking back on it…you can look through rose-tinted glasses – I think people do a bit about punk. But it wasn't a very enjoyable experience at the time, I must admit. People can always gloss over the colourful, mad things. Paul Cook The next day we got a phone call from Glitterbest [the Pistols' management company] asking us to come in for a press conference. We got on the bus in Chiswick, where we lived at the time. This bird I used to see was on the bus. It was one of those days when you sort of say hello. Instead she gave me such a dirty look. Then I realized it was because of the Bill Grundy show. While we'd gone out and got hammered, everything had totally changed. There was this small thing called pub rock. There wasn't even a name for it. Then, all of a sudden, these lemons in the club were going, 'You're a fucking punk.' The word punk was invented by the music press, who seized on it to headline a big article that autumn. Now it was all over the country. Glen Matlock The Sex Pistols, leaders of a whole new cult called 'punk rock', [are] set to be as big as mods and rockers were in the 1960s. Lionel Morton, *Nationwide*, December 1976

Published by Glitterbest Ltd. 40 Dryden Chambers, 119 Oxford St. London W.1.

Further copies from Glitterbest

Printed by:- **zigzag** (WE AIN'T PROUD) LTD. 0734-583958

Put it this way, I was staying in a hotel room that had hot and cold water. It was luxury.

Paul Simonon

Above: The Anarchy tour bus, with Mick Jones, Johnny Rotten, Billy Rath, Paul Simonon and Joe Strummer in foreground, from left

We were all really excited.
We were all young lads and this was our first big tour. Paul Cook

The tour came along and that looked really promising 'cause it looked real high profile. We were all thrilled that Johnny Thunders and the Heartbreakers were coming over.
Nils Stevenson

Malcolm called me from England. He said, 'Do you want to tour with my band the Sex Pistols?' At the time I'd never heard of them, but I said I'd call him back. I called Johnny Thunders and asked him if he wanted to tour England with some band called the Sex Pistols. Of course, Johnny had never heard of this band either, but he did remember Malcolm. He said, 'He was that weird guy who managed the Dolls for a few months and made us dress like Russians.' Then he thought for a moment and said, 'It should be fun. It's a trip to England. Let's go.' So we did.
Leee Childers

Mick [Jones, of the Clash] was really excited about them coming over and playing 'cause of the Johnny Thunders and New York Dolls stuff. I didn't know anything about them. Culturally and musically our attitude was completely different to the American punk thing, which was generally more arty.
Paul Simonon

Malcolm bought the plane tickets and we arrived on the night of the Grundy show. They met us at the airport. Nils was in one of those big, fluffy Vivienne Westwood sweaters and had this little pixie haircut. I thought he was Malcolm's assistant, so I said, 'Hello, you must be Sophie.' That went over really well with Nils. The airport people kept us there forever because Malcolm had done nothing about any kind of work permit. We thought we were probably going to be sent back again. Jerry Nolan was blaming me, of course. Malcolm got around the authorities somehow and got us into the country. I'm sure he'd have had a much harder time just a few days later.
Leee Childers

Amazing response from the national press: the story's on every front page and news bulletin. We're no longer enigmatic freaks – we're suddenly despised 'punks'.
Nils Stevenson, *Vacant: A Diary of the Punk Years*

We were suddenly about to tour Britain with this band that were on every front page in the country.
Leee Childers

I was late for the coach. I'll never forget that. It was really humiliating. They'd had to wait for me for hours. The night before I'd gone back to Finchley to my mum's house with some Teddy girl who was really horny. My mum was away, so I shagged this girl all night, and the next day I just couldn't get myself out of bed. I turned up really, really late. The big coach was there with the Clash on it and everyone was waiting. Malcolm was done up in this brand new coat he'd got for the tour – black fur with a silver fleck. He hit the roof when he saw me. I thought, 'This is a bit of a boring way to start a tour.'
Nils Stevenson

Driving off, we felt like the cat's whiskers in our brand new togs. (Of course, much later we discovered that Malcolm had charged us a lot for all these clothes from his shop.)
Glen Matlock in *I Was a Teenage Sex Pistol*

Nils had rung to say that Norwich – the first date on the first-ever punk tour of Britain – had been cancelled.
Leee Childers

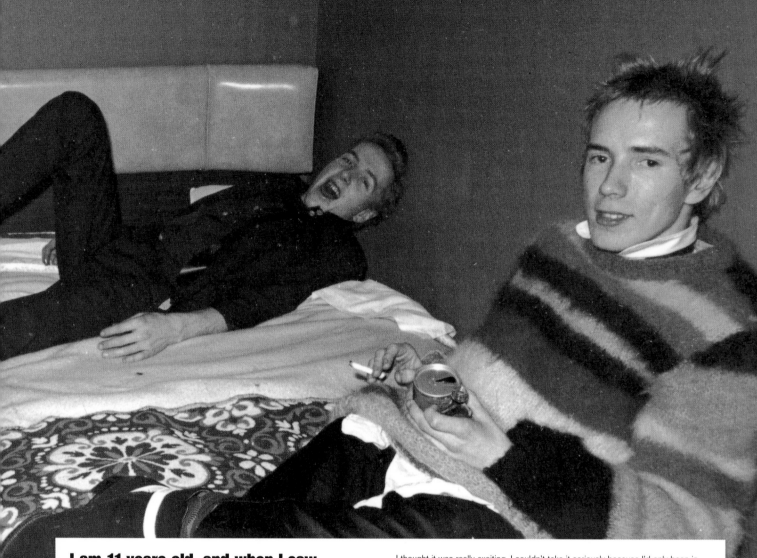

I am 11 years old, and when I saw those people in the 'Mirror' with safety-pins through their nostrils it made me sick. If I saw them, I'd tell them how dangerous it is and how stupid it looks.

Julie Hynes of Mansfield, Notts, in the *Daily Mirror*, December 1976

I had this poster for the Anarchy tour, and as the tour progressed, I'd cross each date out. When things were re-arranged, I'd put the new date in, but then I'd have to cross that out more often than not. There had originally been 19 dates, but by the end there were something like 23 cancelled and five played – more cancellations than the original tour. It was quite a laugh.
Roadent

I thought it was really exciting. I couldn't take it seriously because I'd only been in the group for a short while, so for me it was a new adventure.
Paul Simonon

The Clash sort of looked up to the Pistols on the tour, but the Pistols were arrogant bastards who didn't give a shit about anyone. Thunders was amusing because he thought he was better than everyone else and simply couldn't be bothered.
Roadent

We hadn't toured before, so we didn't know any different.
Steve Jones

It was a great idea, the Anarchy tour: all the main groups of the moment. And in a way it was even better that most dates were cancelled.
Chris Sullivan

From the moment we got on the the coach and the four bands were there, there seemed to be some friction between Malcolm and Jake Riviera [manager of the Damned].
Leee Childers

We were told we had to audition for some fucking council. All of us, especially Johnny and Jerry, thought, 'Fuck this shit.' Walter Lure

The band were asked to audition at one joint in Derby, and they could only play if the local councillors approved of what they were doing. Malcolm quite rightly said, 'Fuck off.' I'm not sure if this is true now or not, but the Damned tried to team up with the Clash to do the tour without the Pistols. (I've heard that Jack Riviera claims it isn't true.)
Nils Stevenson

These people insisted on a special performance at 3 p.m. 'behind locked doors'. Malcolm sent the sound and lighting crews to set up and all the preparations were made. At 3.15 Nils called up to say the venue was all ready, but it was swarming with reporters. Ten minutes later he called again, saying they were all waiting and asking where we were. Malcolm then took the band into his room, locked the door and had a very secret meeting. Twenty minutes later, they all emerged. 'Get all your stuff together,' he said. 'We're leaving. We're not going to encourage censorship. If we perform for these idiots, we'll end up doing matinees for every council in the country.' It wasn't until we were all aboard the coach that Malcolm told us and the driver that we were going to Leeds.
Ray Stevenson, Anarchy tour photographer

My boys – the Heartbreakers – wouldn't audition for some jumped-up council, not in a million years.
Leee Childers

The Committee have decided that, in fairness to the public of Derby, the group known as the Sex Pistols will not perform here tonight. But we are quite agreeable that the three other groups that have been booked will go on.
Derby Council's official statement, 4 p.m., 4 December 1976

When the coach finally rolled out, there was another farce…the Damned had been left behind. They'd been sacked from the tour that afternoon after their road manager had helpfully suggested that they could play the gig 'since the civic ban doesn't actually apply to us', which didn't go down well with either Malcolm or Bernie [Rhodes]. I remember taking Brian James [lead guitarist of the Damned] back to London, where the Damned played the Hope and Anchor the following night to get some money in…and to tell the rest of the punk world they'd been fired.
John Shearlaw

That night I went to have a drink with the Damned and ended up on their tour bus, going back to their hotel with them. While we were staying in expensive five-star places, they were in some bed and breakfast. 'Wouldn't you rather be with us?' I said. 'We would, we would,' they all said…
Glen Matlock

We wouldn't go against the grain. We were in it together. So we went along with the Sex Pistols and the Clash, and the Damned went back to playing in dreary pubs in north London. The rest, as they say, is history. The Damned were all very nice boys, though.
Leee Childers

Jake came from a pub rock background and had no time for Malcolm, who he saw as little more than a jumped-up schmutter merchant, with no understanding of the music business. Malcolm thought of Jake as a real pleb – the Bill Brown of rock'n'roll, he called him – nothing but darts, public bars and pints of bitter.
Glen Matlock, *I Was a Teenage Sex Pistol*

When Malcolm McLaren put the Anarchy tour together, he and Bernie Rhodes needed to bring in some better known bands like us [the Damned] and the Heartbreakers. After all, the Pistols had really only played the odd art college, and the Clash hardly at all. Of course, the Grundy show changed all that and Malcolm suddenly realized they didn't need us. He tried to push us into supporting the other bands rather than giving us equal billing. We told him where to go and left the tour. We didn't agree or care about politics – we just wanted to play our music. It was only rock'n'roll.
Brian James, guitarist, the Damned

The Clash were on the Anarchy tour, and so were the Damned. But the Damned got thrown off after a couple of gigs because they were such sissies. The drummer and the guitarist, Captain Sensible, they were tough kids, but the others were a bunch of poofs. They wanted to ride in their own bus. The Pistols were a little afraid of us too, but they tried hard not to show it.
Jerry Nolan of the Heartbreakers in *Please Kill Me*

Malcolm really controlled the Sex Pistols. He wouldn't allow them to talk to any of the other bands. They had to wait until he went to bed to do so.
Brian James

Opposite: Joe Strummer and Johnny Rotten • Above, left to right: Captain Sensible and Dave Vanian of the Damned; Johnny Thunders; Joe Strummer and Paul Simonon

175

Top, left to right: Keith Paul, the Heartbreakers' sound man, Jo Faul, Johnny Thunders, Ray Stevenson, Nils Stevenson, Walter Lure and Paul Cook • Bottom, from left: Nils Stevenson, Debbie Juvenile and Tracey O'Keefe (on the bed), Paul Simonon and Keith Paul (wrestling)

People started pairing off. We caught Glen and Mick playing 'Let It Be' in their room. I suppose someone had to. Paul Simonon

The first job I ever did for Malcolm was a gig up in the north of England, somewhere so dismal and forgettable I've actually forgotten where, to get the Heartbreakers some money. They'd been brought over for the Anarchy tour and it had all but collapsed. They were back in London with no money and nothing to do. For Malcolm it was like: 'Just get them up there and do the gig. Get them out of the way.' Their connection went back to New York in 1975, but Malcolm wasn't interested this time.
John 'Boogie' Tiberi

People used to get out of my way, but now they barge me off the pavement. Malcolm is fuelling the animosity between Teds and punks – there are running battles in the Kings Road, and Chelsea football hooligans smash the windows of the shop [Sex] on Saturdays. The 'Anarchy in the UK' tour is on the road to nowhere. All but three gigs out of 19 scheduled are cancelled after the Grundy incident. Malcolm has pushed himself into the limelight and is now conducting interviews on behalf of the group. He's in his element, feigning outrage about the way the Sex Pistols are being persecuted.
Nils Stevenson, *Vacant: A Diary of the Punk Years*

It was all whispers and rumours, a crazy day in a solid and not very interesting English town. The music press were trying to keep out of the way of the mainstream newspaper reporters, who were behaving just the way you'd expect in a spoof movie – all notebooks in the face and size 12s in the door. But we weren't exactly a united front in opposition. Some music press journalists passed the Bernard Rhodes/Clash and Malcolm McLaren political correctness test and got allowed on the coach.
John Shearlaw

On the Anarchy tour, we were followed across the country, from gig to gig [by both press and fans]. We had to turn up to show willingness to play, presumably so that we'd get paid, although it looked a pound to a penny they weren't gonna let us play. We were banned in this town and that town: it wasn't really about us playing any more.
Steve Jones

The Sex Pistols were absurd anarchist theatre on the four dates they actually managed to appear – Leeds,

Manchester, Caerphilly, Plymouth. I was travelling with the camera and we shot the Labour councillors at Derby announcing the ban on the gig there in real trade union style: 'The Committee have decided that in fairness to the public of Derby, the Sex Pistols will not perform here tonight.' They'd been banned in the University of East Anglia too. The student response there was early 1970s direct action: they staged a sit-in. Once the Pistols got to play, finally, at Leeds, there was this huge pent-up volume of gob [spit] because everyone by that time had read about spitting at punk groups. There were these volleys of spit and the band were just leaning into it, letting it go over them. John looked fantastic with all this snot and gob all over his hair.
Julien Temple, film director

I loved it [the Anarchy tour]. I fucking loved it. It was like, 'Finally, I've arrived. Let the circus begin.'
Steve Jones in *The Filth and the Fury*

Initially there was a real feeling of bonhomie brought on by an us against the world situation. Bonds were even formed with the Clash, who we had regarded as second-rate. Sleeping in proper beds after the stinking rehearsal studio in Denmark Street was marvellous – we were all drinking a lot and taking tons of speed. But after a while it got very tedious. The hotel rooms started feeling very claustrophobic and people began to argue. Then the girls – Debbie, Tracey and Jo Faul – started turning up from Sex, but that only made everyone more competitive, and the situation became even more volatile. Glen appeared to be happier with the Clash. Rotten was not amused.
Nils Stevenson

As the tour went on, the whole party broke up into factions. Mick Jones was my mate. We hung out together, roomed together and had a laugh together on the coach.
Glen Matlock, *I Was a Teenage Sex Pistol*

We waited around a lot, drank a lot of beer, and ate a lot of sandwiches. But when we did play, it was like whoa!
Walter Lure

Punk rock…to many people is a bigger threat to our way of life than Russian communism or hyper-inflation.
Brian Trueman in *The Punk Rock Issue*, TV documentary, January 1977

Right: Johnny Thunders on stage

177

I was told that the Pistols and the whole Anarchy tour were coming to Caerphilly. I said, 'Don't be ridiculous.' Chris Sullivan

My memory of the tour is boredom. We spent most of our time hanging around hotels waiting. Gig after gig was cancelled. We had no idea what was happening. We just sat around hoping there would be somewhere we would be allowed to play.
Glen Matlock

We'd heard that a couple of shows had gone on and then suddenly we heard that the Anarchy tour was coming to Caerphilly of all places, just 15 miles from where I lived at the time: it was an omen. We thought, this won't happen – no chance. Then I switched on the TV and there was this almighty fuss. I belted down to the phone box (no one had a phone indoors at that time, not in Merthyr Tydfil anyway), and called my mate Jonathan (who did have a phone as his dad was an undertaker). I gave my other mate a knock on his door, slung on the studded leather jacket and trousers, plus the jackboots, and left. There was no time to waste.
Chris Sullivan

The places we stayed in were besieged by journalists and photographers, so we spent endless hours in a room with the Pistols eating sandwiches and drinking beer.
Paul Simonon

In the foyer of the Dragonara Hotel, Leeds, a TV reporter asked if I was anything to do with the group. He said he'd been waiting for an hour and wanted to talk to Mr McLaren or the Sex Pistols. I told him it was unlikely, but I would tell 'Mr McLaren' that he was here. I asked if I was also to tell 'Mr McLaren' that he would like some swearing for his TV show. The TV reporter smiled at me.
Ray Stevenson

Other journalists got barred, thrown off or threatened. And in the middle of it all, Julie Burchill sat there taking it all in, in complete silence, possibly hating every minute of her first-ever tour.
John Shearlaw

Basically, on that Anarchy tour, the Heartbreakers just blew *everybody* away. They were a great rock'n'roll band. They had their roots in good old solid rhythm'n'blues. While the rest of the bands were still getting their act together, the Heartbreakers would just step on stage and kick ass. When you've got a great bass player, a Johnny Thunders on guitar and Jerry Nolan on drums, what you have is great rock'n'roll, and there ain't no way round that. The audiences, of course, went crazy.
Leee Childers

On the Anarchy tour the heartbreakers really were a good time rock'n'roll band. Everybody appreciated that. Some of their subject matter was a little controversial of course, such as 'Chinese Rocks'. In fact Johnny Thunders wanted to change the name of the band to the Junkies. The Pistols weren't like the Heartbreakers at all. They were difficult and were there to bury rock'n'roll, yet they were part of the same movement. It was very confusing. After the tour and towards the end of their stay in England people were just going along to see if Johnny Thunders would keel over and die on stage in front of them. That was second wave punk.
Nils Stevenson

I remember we played at Manchester and a load of people turned up to see the Pistols 'cause they had lots of media attention. Unfortunately, we did a really good show and the Pistols didn't…but that's the way it goes.
Paul Simonon

My mates and I had been travelling back and forth between Wales and London for a few years, and had caught the Pistols and the Clash at the 100 Club, plus a few other one-offs at places like El Paradiso. We were quite surprisingly on the pulse in our own rather curious way. When we heard that the Anarchy tour was coming so close to home, it really got us going. We got a few cars together to drive to the venues, but when we arrived, it was awful. There were coppers everywhere, hating us and treating us like child murderers, and all we'd done was try to watch a bloody group. Or, as my mate Damian said, we were almost 'arrested for attempting to listen to a popular music combo'. It really was absurd.
Chris Sullivan

In Caerphilly the band was surrounded by religious maniacs trying to stop the show. It was great. I remember Steve Strange [from the New Romantic band Visage] was in the audience with loads of mad bods. He turned up the next night fucking miles away in some car park outside a club we were supposed to play. I knew then that we had something, though I wasn't sure what it was.
Glen Matlock

The venue was the old Caerphilly Cinema. There was a car park on a hill opposite the cinema, which was packed with cars belonging to the Bible-bashers who were trying to stop us going in. As a result, we had to park a long way off, and suffered a gauntlet of hymn-singing as we made our way to the door. Inside it was lovely and warm; outside it was drizzly and really cold. The first band, as I remember, were the Clash who, up until that moment, I'd never been that keen on, but they just blew the whole place to bits. Then came the Heartbreakers, and they just rocked us and everyone else to pieces. The Heartbreakers were a hard act to follow, but the Pistols disappointed us a little bit, as we'd seen them play better before, but the whole show was fantastic. My mate, Mark McCarthy, was literally stunned, shunted and showered. I don't think he ever recovered. On the way out, most of the God squad had departed, only to be replaced by gangs of Grebos [wannabe Hell's Angels] and a definite absence of rozzers. As a result we had the usual fight or two, which got way out of hand. We had to make a driving 'dive in the car' getaway as we fought these hairy twats, which was par for the course in Wales. I think going in to the do was worse, though.
Chris Sullivan

The Clash were the first band to start taking punters away from the Pistols. It began at the 100 Club, and became obvious when people started painting their shirts, adopting the Clash style, so to speak. The band had made a big impression. They were very accessible.
Roadent

The Welsh audience were the most outrageous-looking people we'd ever seen.
Nils Stevenson

Do you remember when some people used to fake putting a safety pin through their nose or their cheek? Well, a lot of these Welsh punks had done it for real – their noses were all sort of green and scabby. It was horrible.
Leee Childers

Opposite, clockwise from top left: Welsh fan with Johnny Thunders; Paul Cook and Mick Jones; Johnny Rotten (far right) and Paul Cook (second left) with unidentified friends; Johnny Rotten with fan; Joe Strummer and Paul Simonon (on the table), unknown fan (sitting); Welsh fan with Paul Cook; Debbie Juvenile; Local 'character'

The Pistols played a second night in Plymouth and there was hardly anybody there. They had an entourage at the front selling the programmes. I think I bought mine from Sue Catwoman. She and the others seemed a lot more sophisticated than the provincial punks. We were all trying our best,

jeans or trousers set you apart from everybody else. Most of those early punks wore basketball boots or trainers, and drainpipes and jackets with short hair spiked up a bit. The look was very naive really.

Nigel Wingrove

The highlight of Plymouth was the partying back at the hotel after the show…people thrown in the swimming pool, smashing up rooms, all that lark.
Glen Matlock

When it was all finished, we went back to London.
Paul Cook

We were back in London, it was Christmas and we were all fucking skint.

Ray Stevenson

Above, left to right: Unidentified man with Johnny Thunders; Debbie Juvenile, Tracey O'Keefe and Mick Jones; Johnny Thunders and Jerry Nolan • Opposite, top: Johnny Rotten with a roadie • Opposite, bottom, left to right: Glen Matlock, Johnny Rotten, Malcolm McLaren, Paul Cook and Steve Jones

I remember '76 – I had my first punk Christmas. Steve Walsh

Caroline Coon had a Christmas party at her house and pretty much everybody got called. We were all there and she fed us all, so you couldn't really fault the way she treated us. It was Christmas and I was feeling a little sad and nostalgic.
Leee Childers

Caroline Coon's Christmas party? Can't remember anything about it.
Paul Simonon

We were down on the very bottom floor of the house, me and the Heartbreakers. They were flaming up the Christmas pudding, which meant nothing to me 'cause we don't do that in Kentucky. I could hear a Jim Reeves' Christmas album playing, which made me kind of sad, so I went into this little room where it was on the stereo. There was this little guy sitting there crying. I sat down on the chair opposite him and I started crying too. When the record ended, I said, 'Wow, that was really great. I'm from Kentucky and that was really my kind of Christmas music. Hi, my name's Leee.' He said, 'My name's Sid,' and I thought, 'Oh, my God, I'm in the room with Sid Vicious.' That's the first time we ever met.
Leee Childers

Caroline Coon and John Ingham [a journalist at that time] had a Christmas do round at their house. It was a great big house somewhere in Earls Court, with four storeys. They had invited all these urchins and punks round for Christmas. It was really Dickensian – they had literally invited these urchins off the street. It soon degenerated, with alcohol and drugs. About halfway through the day all the people from New York arrived. The Heartbreakers came with their manager, Leee Childers, and their roadie Keith. That was the minute that heroin turned up on the scene because the New York contingent brought smack with them in a big way.
    It was a fascinating day because Malcolm McLaren was there. I remember sitting next to him at the Christmas dinner itself and he had a glass of champagne. He said it was his favourite drink. It was vintage champagne; it wasn't some shit. Malcolm was intriguing, but also his timing was great. Everything was just waiting to happen. People like Malcolm pick up on ideas and just spark things off. He was a kind of '60s person. He hadn't really done much in the '60s, so he was disaffected. It always seemed to me, from the first time I met him, that he wasn't part of the main crowd. He was always looking to do something else. I thought, this guy knows how to run things. It was like a scene out of a movie.
Steve Walsh

Left: Malcolm McLaren • Opposite: Caroline Coon

The Sex Pistols are featured in the Christmas issue of *NME* under the headline 'Sex Pistols, this week's episode'. More of the band's dates being cancelled are detailed, and rocker Pat Travers issues a challenge to the band. Travers has challenged the Pistols to a battle of the bands anytime, anywhere. They will even go as far as to feature their bassist playing with just two bass strings and their drummer playing on a three-piece kit. They bragged that even with that handicap they could outplay the Sex Pistols.
George Gimarc, *Punk Diary 1970-1979*

By the end of the day the whole house was wrecked. Steve Jones was doing Rod Stewart impersonations with a standard lamp that had a live wire coming out of the top. He was pretending it was a mike and singing along to Faces' songs. These nice, well-intentioned middle-class journalists had invited all these punks and ruffians round, so they couldn't be surprised when their home was wrecked and they all fucked off.
Steve Walsh

Everybody was exhausted from the Anarchy tour. I wanted to have a traditional Christmas. Fortunately, Jonh Ingham was house-sitting a huge house just off Ladbroke Grove. I did turkey, Christmas pudding and all the trimmings. It was open house: everybody from all the main bands came. It was perfect until the Americans arrived. They were pigs in leather jackets and boots. They kicked their way into the house. They had no manners, no sense of respect. The family atmosphere was destroyed. Things were stolen, ripped off and they all rang America and ran up a £400 phone bill. Several people were ill; later I found out it was because of heroin. The Americans were a negative influence on the young Brits. They were older and very middle class. They could afford to be destructive, jaded and nihilistic because they could always go back to their safe, middle-class families if anything went wrong. Of course, the British kids were susceptible to their influence, even though their outlook was much more positive, and drugs were originally dismissed as being too hippie. They were bound to change, and not for the better.
Caroline Coon

Punk changed out of all recognition *during the course of 1977. Although the Grundy TV episode had thrust the form into popular consciousness, punk was essentially mute for most of the nation. Only the Damned and the Pistols had actually managed to release a record by the beginning of '77; the Buzzcocks did so by the end of January. Touring with the Heartbreakers had been a formative but ultimately frustrating experience for the Clash and the Sex Pistols. As most of the dates were cancelled by cautious town councils, the interest inspired in the country's youth by sensational media coverage was unsatisfied: potential fans remained in the dark. This was about to change. As for all movements, popularization is often a greater challenge than establishment. The punk phenomenon was no exception.*

In January 1977 all this was very much in the future. The Anarchy tour was over, but Leee Childers had stayed in London with his band, the Heartbreakers, forging a very important link between London and New York. Although he saw great potential in London, at this point his band was virtually starving. Fortunately, Andrew Czezowski had just persuaded the owners of Chaguarama's, a predominantly gay discotheque frequented by aficionados of Vivienne Westwood's shop, Sex, to let him re-open the bankrupt nightclub as a permanent punk venue.

The Roxy, as it became, lasted just 100 days, but it gave many early bands a real alternative to the tired pub circuit, and a chance for their fans to find a home. It also, unfortunately, provided Sid Vicious with the opportunity to invent the pogo. On the other hand, it allowed Nils Stevenson to establish Siouxsie and the Banshees. In the first days of the Roxy the Clash made the biggest impression musically, Generation X followed hot on their heels, and Subway Sect became the most popular among the scene's innovators.

By the end of January, Glen Matlock had played his last gig with the Pistols and Sid Vicious had achieved his ambition of joining the band. The final element of Malcolm McLaren's new Bay City Rollers was in place, but that ever so subtle chemistry was gone. The 100 days of the Roxy were to have a lasting impact. Strange alliances were formed and precedents were set. Members of the New York fraternity, such as Cherry Vanilla, the Ramones and Patti Paladin, appeared on the same bill as British bands. Wayne County seemed a permanent fixture, as did the Heartbreakers, who started a marathon recording session that seemed to last until the summer. The Roxy also gave many new and talented female artistes a chance to be seen. For the first time, girls such as Gaye Advert, Ari Upp, Poly Styrene and Siouxsie were considered serious players in their own right.

The most interesting alliance was created by Don Letts, the DJ at the Roxy. Unperturbed by the lack of punk records available at the time, he introduced reggae and dub to the scene. These had previously been exclusive to the sound systems of London's West Indian communities and small bands of devotees left over from the skinhead boom. There were similarities between the anti-establishment ethic of punks and Rastafarian culture. Both groups were generally viewed as outsiders, and both employed contentious sloganeering as a means of promotion. Don's legacy was to build a vibrant reggae scene beyond its ethnic roots, which would be celebrated in Bob Marley's 'Punky Reggae Party'. Patti Smith, not known for her reggae roots, went so far as to invite Tapper Zukie and Don Letts to join her on stage at her Hammersmith performance. Wonders would never cease.

For the nation as a whole, however, the Sex Pistols remained synonymous with punk. Having been signed by record mogul Richard Branson, the band had encouragement and support.

They also had Malcolm McLaren's brilliant ability to attract publicity, as demonstrated by his plan to subvert the Queen's Silver Jubilee celebrations. The Sex Pistols' performance on the River Thames, the record signings outside Buckingham Palace, the banning of 'God Save the Queen' and the trial of the record shop owner who had the affront to display Never Mind the Bollocks in his shop window gave the Pistols and the UK scene a public profile beyond anything achieved by punk's US counterpart. The movement's mythical status had grown way beyond its musical capability, which led many to believe that it would extinguish sooner rather than later.

Towards the end of 1977, McLaren had decided that only a full-blown Hollywood movie could do justice to the attitude of the Sex Pistols. In a stroke of eccentric genius, he persuaded Russ Meyer, legendary director of big-bosomed blockbusters such as Super Vixens, to direct Who Killed Bambi? After battling with Equity to allow him to import suitably large-chested actresses to appear in the movie alongside the Pistols, Meyer returned home without actually shooting any film. McLaren would have to wait until the demise of the band to resume his film project. It would be called The Great Rock'n'Roll Swindle. Nobody knew it at the time, but 1977 was to be the last year the Sex Pistols played live in the UK. Many have said that it was McLaren's constant thirst for sensation that killed the band's very promising future. Fans would soon be spoilt for choice, however, as hundreds of bands burst onto the scene. There were many truly individual voices, such as Ian Dury, who had a long pedigree with Kilburn & the High Roads, the eerie monotone of Poly Styrene, the obvious sex appeal of Billy Idol in Generation X, and the novelty of Dee Generate, a 14-year-old schoolboy by day and a performer with Eater by night. Punk even had its own poet, Mancunian John Cooper Clarke, while the Ramones remained the epitome of punk, with their two-minute tracks and incomprehensible image – half punk, half heavy metal.

Of course there were several bands, such as the Stranglers and the Jam, who weren't punk at all, but played in the same venues and benefited from the movement's growing popularity. By the summer of '77, many records displayed all the hallmarks of the so-called 'new sound' and found their way into every kid's bedroom. At last punk had found its voice. 'White Riot' by the Clash soon became an anthem across the nation. The Roxy expired and was replaced by the Vortex. But by now London was losing its exclusive hold on the scene. The provinces were in on the act, the elitism of the early fans was now under threat, and punks were becoming just another tribe, like Teds or hippies. The movement was losing its innovative edge, just as many were discovering it for the first time.

For many people, the death of Elvis in August was a turning-point. When Danny Baker announced his death on the stage of the Vortex, he was shouted down. Something had changed. The new fans were less interested in pushing musical or cultural boundaries, and more interested in pogoing and spitting in a speed-induced frenzy, before returning home to change into their everyday clothes. Anarchy was becoming a badge of conformity rather than an alternative way of living.

The essence of '77 is captured in The Punk Rock Movie shot by Don Letts, whose film-making career started when a Vogue employee gave him a Super 8 camera at the Roxy. Watching this film 25 years later, it is surprising how young, sweaty and extremely unsophisticated everyone looks. At the same time, there is no denying the raw excitement and attitude that propelled punk through a year of huge expansion and change. Its record sales might have been only a fraction of the next year's, but for the original fans, 1977 was the best, the worst and probably the end of the scene as they knew it. For the rest of the country, in the words of the Carpenters, 'It Had Only Just Begun'.

God save the Queen...

I put in 100 days.
It was like being on tour without even moving.
Andrew Czezowski, founder of the Roxy Club

There was a tremendous sense of urgency by the end of '76. Towards the end of the Anarchy tour and within months of the Pistols becoming notorious the Roxy opened and a whole bunch of people were able to achieve their 15 minutes of fame by catering to this new audience.
Nils Stevenson, Sex Pistols' tour manager, 1976

I was the accountant for Sex and Acme Attractions. It was about October or November. Gene October of the band Chelsea had written the song 'Walking the Streets of London'. He knew the people who owned Chaguarama's and he got a booking for my band, Generation X. We had set the date for December, but in the meanwhile the band came to me and said they didn't want Gene to be their singer. Billy Idol wanted to be the singer and not the guitarist. I called up Chaguarama's, which had gone into receivership, and said I was still happy to do the deal. Although I wasn't a friend of the management and Gene wasn't playing in Generation X, I agreed to hire the place off them,

even though it was right in the middle of winter. I was up all night pissed and smoking, but I hired the old Chags, which was now the Roxy.
Andrew Czezowski

While we were on the Arnarchy tour, Andrew Czezowski opened the Roxy in Neal Street, Covent Garden. The do-it-yourself ethic is taking off, and even though the club is pretty unglamorous, it's always busy providing gigs for all the new groups. It's become a regular hang-out since everything closes down so fucking early, including radio and TV, which are crap anyway.
Nils Stevenson

Just before Christmas I bumped into Malcolm at the Ship pub in Wardour Street. Leee Childers, the manager of the Heartbreakers, was with him. They owed loads and there wasn't any money. They couldn't get back to America. They didn't even have anywhere to live. I said, 'I can't do anything for you, but do you want a date at the Roxy?' By then the

Heartbreakers had had a lot of press coverage, but they couldn't play anywhere and Malcolm wouldn't let the Pistols play anywhere. So I said, 'Phone me next week and I'll get you the date and Generation X can support you.'
Andrew Czezowski

It opened with Generation X because Malcolm wouldn't let the Pistols play there, presumably for fear that the band would appear less important if they shared the stage with their bastard offspring at a small club that was run by someone who used to work for him.
Nils Stevenson

Club owner René Albert has accepted the offer of a three-month contract to let Andy Czezowski and his two partners, Ralph Jedaschek and Barry Jones, run his club, renamed the Roxy. The canopy that marks the small doorway on Neal Street [Covent Garden] has instantly become the place to hang out and heckle passers-by.
George Gimarc, Punk Diary 1970-1979

No one directed us.
We couldn't have got away with it anywhere else.

Gaye Advert in *Vacant: A Diary of the Punk Years*

The Roxy wouldn't have started if it hadn't been for a friend of mine, Barry, who hocked his guitar to put on the first nights in the club. We didn't have any money and the £30 he got made the difference; otherwise it would all have been off. I think he did get his guitar back eventually. At the time, none of us were working, even though we had great ambition.
Andrew Czezowski

We were really broke, then, thank God, Andy asked us to play the Roxy. We started playing on our own, but still weren't making nearly enough money. I remember the boys would be allowed one treat a day. Johnny would always get a tube of Smarties, Jerry Nolan would get a

Granny Smith apple. I don't remember what Walter got… They were allowed one treat a day and that went on for a long time.
Leee Childers, ex-manager, the Stooges and the Heartbreakers

Don Letts was DJ. His brother Des worked behind the bar. He was part of the security. We had no idea what security meant, but the fact that we were five years older than the ones queuing to get in seemed to be enough. We didn't really have any trouble because the punk kids just enjoyed each other's company, which was what it was all about. Anybody else just didn't have the balls to go in there.
Andrew Czezowski

The audience was so young. I remember seeing the Heartbreakers looking in amazement at the 14-year-olds . I'm sure they felt as if they were playing at a youth club.
Chris Sullivan, author

A lot of the kids used to turn up at the Roxy straight from school. They were younger than people remember, just teenagers. Kids were queuing up to buy their Damned tickets with their school caps on. The whole Roxy thing was accidental. This wave came along and it picked me up and helped me with the promotion of bands. Of course, I let the Police play there and they didn't do too badly. They were probably the most successful band to come out of the Roxy.
Andrew Czezowski

Above left: Gaye Advert at the Roxy

I used to go to the Roxy and bug Don Letts to see what records he was playing. I was 14, I think.
Andrew Weatherall, international DJ

There was usually a small queue into Neal Street. Then you'd get past Andy, who'd do the door himself, and you'd be in the upstairs bar, tiny, like a little corridor… Everyone would pack in shoulder to shoulder in this little space, holding their cans of beer.
Gaye Advert in *Vacant: A Diary of the Punk Years*

The bands from outside London played really well at the Roxy, but looked like shit. The London bands looked good but didn't play so well, though their attitude was great.
Don Letts, film-maker and former DJ

The Roxy was the place to be, but the bands were terrible. I never saw a single decent outfit at the Roxy because you had awful bands emerging there, like the Police and the Cortinas.
Steve Walsh, guitarist, the Flowers of Romance

I came down [to the Roxy] with Jimmy Page to check out the Damned. I was impressed… I thought they were good, especially Rat Scabies, the drummer. He's really got it.
Robert Plant of Led Zeppelin, *New Musical Express*, 20 January 1977

A lot of bands came through the Roxy: Slaughter and the Dogs, X-ray Spex, Siouxsie and the Banshees, Wayne County. The Buzzcocks were always one of my favourite bands. They were a little different to the rest of them. And, of course, the Jam…many

people thought they were uncool. Three months ago it wasn't cool to say you liked the Damned. Now the black sheep of the New Wave are the Jam. It makes me puke. That kind of bullshit is just as vacuous as peace signs and half-hour guitar solos.
Tony Parsons, *New Musical Express*, January 1977

A lot of music press used to come down in their Doc Martins. They were never on the scene before, but suddenly there were more and more, and they loved all the shit bands like the Jam – you know, good old rock'n'roll, man. Then after the good press came all the wankers – hippies last week, punks today – then it was fucked, the whole thing. All of my lot started going to the Speakeasy, as did the bands who played the Roxy.-
Frank Kelly, Sex Pistols aficionado

For the most part, the Roxy crowd were less concerned with the more (to my mind) glamorous fashion statements that we had been keen to express than they were with adopting a cheap, stereotypical punk look. In effect, the Roxy denied our elitist Kings Road roots and made it easy to be part of an egalitarian movement. It wasn't only the look that was cruder: so was the music made by the newer bands at the Roxy. The famous claim that anyone could be a Sex Pistol was patently untrue – the Pistols were too fucking good, having rehearsed and honed their craft in all the shit-holes around the country for some considerable time, and the chemistry within the group was magical. However, many of the bands that played the Roxy lived (and died) by that ethic. You got the rank amateurism that Malcolm claims to love as the music got faster. Performances were more frenetic and the style more crude. After a while, the Roxy became the place for all the people who'd read and believed all the rubbish about 'punk' in the *NME*.
Nils Stevenson

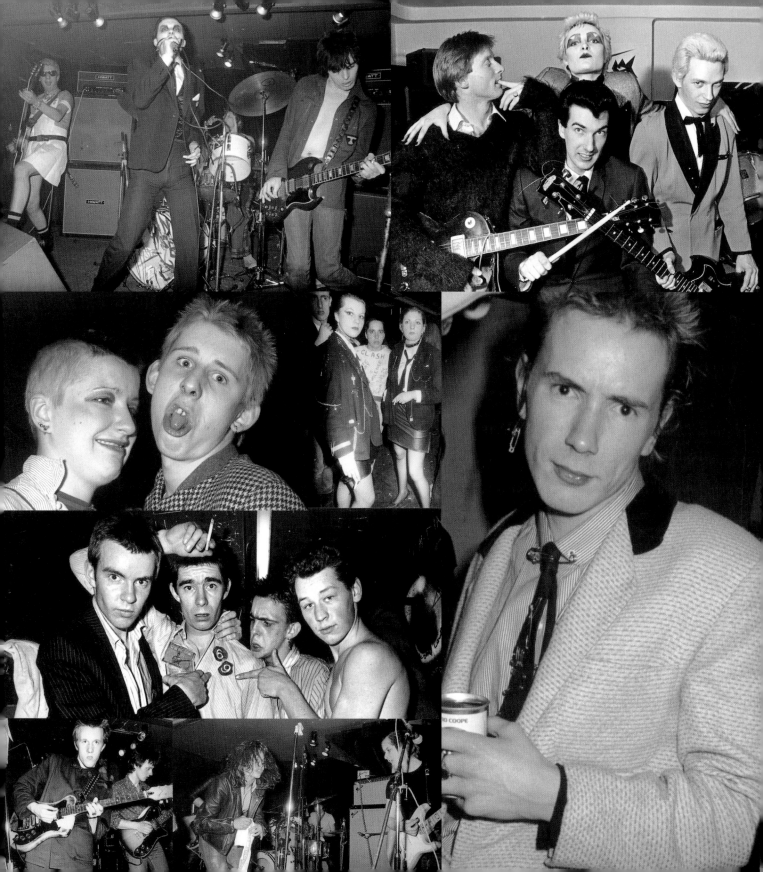

You have to destroy the previous generation to invent your own. Andrew Czezowski

The Stranglers were playing one Friday night when things went mad. They had just come off tour and were beginning to get a bit more professional than the rest of the bands. Their road manager had the tour money in his briefcase. It was about midnight and we had just finished the gig. Everybody had gone home. It took several hours to pack everything up. We had about £500 in takings and the band had about £600 of tour money. Four guys came in through the door saying they were the police drug squad and asked us to put our hands up. I thought, 'Hang on a minute, they don't look like police.' I said, 'Can I see your warrant card?' They started saying fucking this and fucking that. I said, 'You're not policemen.' They locked us in the cupboard, took all the money and left. When we finally escaped, we went to the police station and told them we'd been robbed. The police just couldn't be bothered at all. I suspect that the guys who robbed us really were policemen and that they were in with the crooks who used to hang around the club on Friday nights, and had done ever since it was Chaguarama's.
Andrew Czezowski

The impetus might have fizzled out had it not been for the Roxy keeping it going and allowing new bands to develop as pure punk bands rather than appearing as supports for naff pub rock acts. They would have risked being assimilated into the main-stream, which might have dissipated the energy.
Nils Stevenson

The Roxy had nothing more or less than all good clubs. It allowed similar-minded kids to get together, to try to achieve something by their sheer raw energy. They made themselves stand out from everything that was normal, and they triggered off other like-minded teenagers. Although punk had great impact, it was the attitude more than the music. Personally, I thought the Jam, the Buzzcocks, and the Pistols were good. Although the Clash were never favourites of mine, they actually made a huge impact. As for the rest, you can almost count the good bands on the fingers of one hand. The most important thing is that punk was young and against the previous generation. I think it's marvellous to destroy the last generation's culture and build your own.
Andrew Czezowski

Andy Czezowski had agreed to pay the ridiculously high figure of £25,000 a year to lease the Roxy. It was simply impossible to make enough to cover this, and the inevitable happened. Somehow keeping everything going for 100 days, the owners finally closed in on him and had him physically thrown out of the front door. Those 100 days were essential to the development of punk.
Stephen Colegrave

I just got sucked into the Roxy for 100 days. I was working six days a week to put punk bands on, which was just madness. I never made any money, but that wasn't why I did it. It was the bands. I loved the bands… On the last night we had Siouxsie and the Banshees at an all-girl night. Don Letts, my DJ, was given a film camera by an admirer. He managed to capture on film the magic that was going on.
Andrew Czezowski

The whole punk thing had grown in popularity, just as a trendy pair of trousers would. Unfortunately, it attracted the types of bloke who wore really boring trousers.
Brenda Lamb, punk trendsetter

The Roxy, for all its failings, remains the quintessential punk venue, even to this day. Stephen Colegrave

Opposite, clockwise from top left: The Damned (Captain Sensible, Dave Vanian and Brian James); Peter Fenton, Siouxsie and Steve Severin of the Banshees, plus unidentified drummer; Johnny Rotten; Ari Upp and Viv Albertine of the Slits; Mark Powell (left) in Alternative TV; Sham 69; Shane MacGowan of the Nipple Erectors and unidentified woman; Assorted punters

There aren't any punk records to play, so what's Don Letts going to do?

Don Letts

I was in the Roxy from the day it opened. Andrew Czezowski gave me the job of DJ because of my background at Acme Attractions, but there weren't any punk records to play, so I kept on pumping reggae. I did make some concessions to my white friends. I'd been to see the New York Dolls, so I tried to slip in a few of their records. But it's funny: when the punks started releasing records, I couldn't stand them. I didn't like the Damned and the Clash's first singles. So I'd leave all that punk shit out and keep playing the reggae. The punks liked it. It was a cultural exchange. When I was DJ-ing (we're talking back in the days when you had one deck and two spliffs), the gap between the records was crucial. People came up to me and asked me for requests. I'd say, 'Fuck off. Why do you want to hear something you know already when you can hear something new?' It was a different type of DJ-ing. I didn't make no concessions, no requests – just one deck. That was Don Letts' DJ-ing.

Don Letts

The funny thing was that people asked me what type of music I played at the Roxy. There were no recordings of punk music back then. There might be a bit of garage rock from America, a little bit of Ramones, perhaps some Dolls. But Don's interest was basically reggae and he rightly has the reputation for bringing punk and reggae together as partners. Of course, it changed a bit as more and more records came out.
Andrew Czezowski

They tell me I'm responsible for the punk–reggae link. I guess I did introduce those people who were out-of-towners and on the fringe to a side they would not necessarily have heard. But people like Paul Simonon, Joe Strummer and Johnny Rotten were already there. When the Pistols took to the stage, they wiped the slate clean. It was cultural year zero. I always got a kind of vibe with John and, through mutual respect, we became really close. I used to take him to reggae clubs, like the Four Aces. Many times he'd be the only white man in the house. All the guys in the club were a bit stand-offish, but they respected him because he was anti-establishment. Basically we were outsiders, rebels, and we aligned ourselves. Who else were the punks going to align themselves with in London? They weren't going to align themselves with the soul boys. All this pop stuff wasn't rude enough for us, but the punks we could relate to.
Don Letts

A lot of people had been into dub as a result of the whole skinhead thing. Don via Acme just strengthened our love of it. It was the saving grace of the Roxy.
Chris Sullivan

Above: Don Letts

I got to make serious reggae connections because all of a sudden I'm Don Letts the film-maker and the DJ from the Roxy.

Don Letts

For me the biggest musical influence in punk was Don Letts, the DJ at the Roxy. He played the best dub. His music was just the best. Punk and dub are two extremes. That's why we loved them both. On the one hand you've got a slowed-down, spiritual sort of dub, and on the other you've got your neurotic, wired-up punk. One was fuelled with ganja, the other with sulphate. But, if you think about it, it was good for everyone's health.
Steve Walsh

When I first got the job at the Roxy, all my mates in Brixton laughed at me going to work with these stupid fucking punk rockers. But two weeks later they were begging me for jobs. The punks liked a bit of weed with their dub, but couldn't roll their own spliffs, so my brethren would sit in Forest Hill rolling up spliffs. We'd sell them over the bar. So in the end the Roxy was run by me and four other rasta guys, with Andrew Czezowski

sitting in the office. I remember some guy going up to the bar and saying, 'Give me two beers and a spliff.' That's cultural exchange in motion, isn't it?
Don Letts

My favourite time at the Roxy was when the bands had finished playing. I'd go downstairs and Don Letts would switch on the dub. Then we would all just smoke and listen to the best music ever. In terms of music, dub was revolutionary. Punk music wasn't actually revolutionary, and after a while it all just sounded the same – very unsophisticated. You see, I'd grown up listening to jazz, punk and a bit of soul, and also Lou Reed and the Velvet Underground. Although bands like the Velvets were raw, there was sophistication in there. They owed much to the European art tradition. Now it was all changing. Those of us who were drawn to

the innovation of early punk were now having to put up with people walking around and spitting on us.
Steve Walsh

Even before the Roxy, I had some good connections. When I worked at Acme Attractions, I really got into the punk thing. My favourite clothes were bondage trousers. Bob Marley used to come into the shop and I sold him weed. The bastard even tried to pull my girlfriend, Jeanette. I'd go round his place and he used to take the piss out of my trousers. He said I looked like a fucking mountaineer. I said, 'This is the new look. This is punk rock.' And he replied, 'What, them nasty people I've read about in the Daily Mirror?' 'No, Bob,' I said, 'that's the tabloid version of them. They've got something going on here. They're not crazy bald heads. They're my mates.' 'Get the fuck out of here,' was his reply. 'You'll see,' I said. Two months later Bob released 'Punky Reggae Party'. Of course, by then he'd been in London a while and he'd got to know the vibe. He'd been speaking to various journalists and other people and realized there was something in this punk rock after all.
Don Letts

I'd heard the reggae records before Don played them from the sound systems in Hackney, but to the young white kids into punk at the time, it was something totally new. Seeing young white kids getting into reggae gave the Roxy a vibe all of its own. Don was never a sound system DJ. He was playing anything and everything. It was

like a house party in a club. I was one of only three or four black kids down at the Roxy. I loved music. I loved reggae and ska. But I wanted something outside Hackney. I never actually fitted into the stereotype that was expected of black people.
Dennis Morris, photographer and record industry figure

Shabeens were where all the action was in London because the Jamaicans insisted on their right to party. They'd open up their own place or, even though the law was not on their side, they would seize a place and open it up like a squat and throw house parties that went on all night. You paid maybe 10 bob to get in and you'd have your Red Stripe and your Nutriment and your Lucozade, major icons. That's where the punks and the young Boy George would go, especially down to Weasel's Shabeen, that's where everybody went. All the punks and the Rastas would gather together.
Viv Goldman, features editor, *Sounds* magazine

Dub was a refuge, a bit of sanity and rhythm after all the shit bands.
Mark McCarthy, Clash fan

I managed to keep the dub thing going for the punks even after the Roxy. The Clash, especially, used to take me out on the road on their tours. I took this sound across the length and breadth of England. I had my own spots, like when the Clash played at the Music Machine.
Don Letts

NATTY
CULTURAL
DREAD

Dub became the unofficial soundtrack for the era. Miles English, art editor, *GQ* magazine

Big Youth – Manley Buchanan – was an absolute monstrous influence. Robert Elms, broadcaster and journalist Big Youth was like a cartoon superhero character. He had a real sense of music. I was fortunate enough to meet him, and the place came alive just by his presence. He was an amazing person. He had a ruby and a diamond on his teeth, which inspired people like Mick Hucknall from Simply Red to do the same. Dennis Morris **Big Youth did that album** *Dreadlocks Dread.* **Before them it was all skinhead stuff, like 'The Israelites' by Desmond Dekker. Big Youth had a different attitude. They were more political, whereas 'The Israelites' and the Rude Boy stuff was more gangsterish and individual.** Paul Simonon, bass player, the Clash 'Screaming Target' by Big Youth was always my favourite. I've got to be honest – I've bought it more than once in my life. That record is almost like the essence of why that period was so magnetic. We were all crazy about that track. Viv Goldman **King Tubby was probably one of the most influential Jamaican producers. People recorded a song and took it to Tubby for him to mix or re-mix. He would always do a dub version. He had this special way of playing with sounds and echoes. When you were in a club and his mixes were playing, they sounded fantastic, with all the echoes and loops. He influenced the re-mixes we know now. Most bands have a re-mix and a dub version, so he has been very instrumental.** Dennis Morris

Johnny Rotten was instrumental in bringing reggae to the forefront. Dennis Morris

John did a Radio 1 show with John Peel. He had been asked to bring along his favourite records. All the records he brought, except for one, were reggae, and they really were the best. As he was such a strong figurehead for all the punks, they thought reggae was really cool and what they had to be listening to.
Dennis Morris

I met King Tubby. I went to his house with Kate Simons and I remember he was very charming and soft-spoken, completely the opposite of Big Youth or Tapper Zukie, who were full of brag and flamboyance. He was sort of graceful, a low-key and laid-back individual. I remember he had this filing cupboard…he pulled open the bottom drawer, gets out this crown and puts it on his head for the pictures, bless him, entering into the showman role. He was obviously a very thoughtful, deep and creative sort of guy, and it was really disgusting the way he met his end. It makes one reflect with sadness on how Jamaica eats its young.
Viv Goldman

Lee Perry played at the club I ran – the Wag. It took me two hours to get him on stage via coercion with all sorts of artificial stimulants. Then, when he finally did go on, he played the same song 15 times in a row: 'Dis is me new singal, y'know' – much to the bewilderment of both his band and the audience.
Chris Sullivan

When Johnny played reggae on the radio, it had a big effect. The radio stations wouldn't play it. You never heard Big Youth on the radio. It was an underground thing.
Paul Simonon

Reggae was very much represented by Rastas. They were called Black Heart Men in Jamaica, and they were regarded as the dregs, the untouchables, much as the punks were here. There was that very pivotal time when Bob Marley and Lee Perry were around and Bob was staying at Basing Street Studios, which was just up the road from me and we used to hang out a lot at that period. We would say to him, 'There's a lot of parallels [between reggae and punk] – the protesting, the inequities of society and the injustices of the system. Bob just said, 'See all those people with a safety-pin stuck through their ears? I like to see a man who can suffer pain without crying.'
Viv Goldman

Tapper Zukie was one of the Jamaican musicians who was hanging out in New York. He hooked up with Patti Smith and worked with her on an album. It was put out on her label and started the influence of reggae on the punks in New York, which then filtered outside. He came to England to see Patti, and that's how he brought his music to London. He was totally respected in his community back in Jamaica. Whatever money he was making from his music, he pumped back into his

community, so he was very respected and protected. Although he was an educated guy, he brought that whole gunman connection with him.
Dennis Morris

When Patti Smith was playing at the Hammersmith Odeon, we'd become close. I invited Tapper Zukie to the gig and we were standing in the wings watching Patti Smith play. Then she came into the wings, grabbed me and pulled me onto the stage. There I was on stage at the Hammersmith Odeon and it was full up. What the fuck could I do? I started to pretend to play guitar. I bluffed it, put dark glasses on and grabbed Tapper Zukie. I pulled him onto the stage and gave him my guitar. He couldn't play guitar, so he bluffed too. Then Patti Smith gave me the microphone. I picked it up and broke into my heaviest Jamaican accent. Funnily enough, they ended up having to drag us off stage because we'd hijacked the concert.
Don Letts

U-Roy had this voice. When his record came on, the room would literally shake just from his voice. It was unique.
Dennis Morris

Sly Dunbar and Robbie Shakespeare were the dub rhythm kings. Nobody could touch them. Disco dub was so brilliant it was excruciating. They are gods.
Chris Sullivan

Bob Marley was never really connected to the punk scene because he had his own thing going. He didn't disrespect punk, but he really had a different position. He represented the black youth of England and, more importantly, the black youth of Jamaica. In a sense, if you look at Rasta philosophy, there were parallels with what was happening in England. It was as if Rastas were Jamaican punks. They were totally against the system in the same way that the punks were in England. But Bob was not just against the system. He didn't want to burn things down in destruction – he wanted to know what was going to flower from it. Whether he came across a young black or white person, he always urged them to have a revolutionary consciousness. Unfortunately, not enough punks really had that consciousness. That's what killed punk, especially after 1977. Too many punks only wanted to get pissed out of their heads. The smart ones were the ones that wanted to do something with punk and get something else, and not just see it as a fashion thing. Time was running out for them, even then.
Dennis Morris

Opposite, clockwise from top left: King Tubby; Lee 'Scratch' Perry; Sly and Robbie, top Jamaican rhythm section; Tapper Zukie

spiral scratch

Additional artwork from the collection of Howard Devoto: silkscreen print - Phil Diggle 1977-78; colour photos - Electric Circus, Manchester, 10th November 1976, by Linder Sterling. Mute Mail Order available from 429 Harrow Road, London W10 4RE. Send S.A.E. or phone 24 hour credit card hotline +44 (0) 181 964 0029 or fax +44 (0) 181 964 3722. www.mute.com

DATE 3 JAN '76	72 GARTSIDE ST MANCHESTER M3 3EL ENGLAND	INDIGO SOUND STUDIOS HAPPY 16-TRACKING	
NO.			
CLIENT			
TITLE BUZZCOCKS			
PRODUCER			
MATRIX TAPE NO. ORG 001	TEL: 061-834 7001		
ITEM			TIME
SIDE 1 A BREAKDOWN		1-55	5'05"
B TIMES UP			
SIDE 2 A BOREDOM			5'06
B FRIENDS.			

Once again we had to find our own way.

Howard Devoto, vocalist, the Buzzcocks

The second gig at the Lesser Free Trade Hall [in Manchester] marked the end of my promoting career. We'd sold all the tickets, and this time, unlike the first gig, the Buzzcocks had indeed been ready. We couldn't book the hall after that. The whole thing was growing...

and growing. Journalists had come up from London to see us. We'd only done one gig and already we were being reviewed in the music press. My life had turned round. I was fully engaged with something I really cared about. My mind was just full of Rotten and McLaren and the psycho-dynamics of it all. But once the London lot trooped off again, there was a sense of 'What do we do now?' For the first gig we'd only written 'Breakdown' from the songs that eventually appeared on the 'Spiral Scratch' EP, so obviously we had to think about new material. 'Anarchy in the UK' [the Sex Pistols' first

single] was out on EMI, and 'New Rose' [the Damned's first single] was out on Stiff Records, so we knew what we were supposed to do. But you didn't just put out a single... already you kind of knew you had to have a picture sleeve. Stiff was a definite reference point – I remember phoning them to try and get some advice, but not getting very far. Once again we had to find our own way, scraping together the money for a few hours in a studio with a 16-track, and then finding the money for a first pressing, wondering if we'd even sell 1,000 copies.
Howard Devoto

Above and opposite: Collage of images from the 'Spiral Scratch' EP by the Buzzcocks

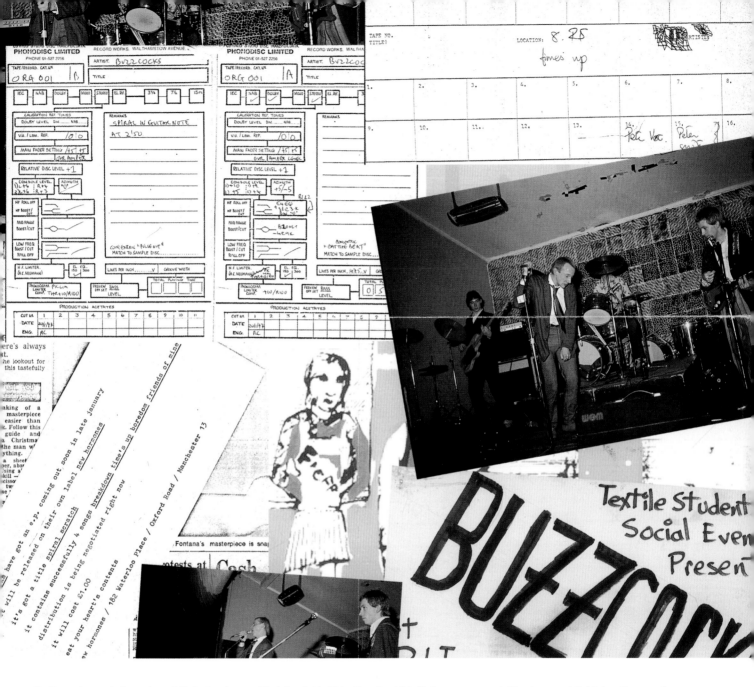

The Buzzcocks were fucking underrated. Maybe they chose the wrong name, but they definitely should have been bigger. Why weren't the Buzzcocks as big as Oasis?
Keith Levene, guitarist, the Clash

October 1976 was the Buzzcocks' moment…when they did what anyone else could have done, but no one else but the Sex Pistols did…fix the present, open a door to the past, and let the pent-up energies of the forbidden and the forgotten sweep them…and whoever might hear them, into the no-future. In October Howard Devoto [vocals] Steve

Diggle [bass], John Maher [drums] and Pete Shelley [Stanway guitar] went into the local Indigo Sound studio and, for under £100-worth of mike time, cut their songs. Released in February 1977, the EP 'Spiral Scratch' was only the third UK punk disc to be issued… It was the first independent, do-it-yourself…UK punk record. More than that, it was definitive. With no sheen of notoriety, celebrity, scandal or glamour, 'Spiral Scratch' redefined punk as ordinary conversation – funnier than usual, sharper, a sting in every side. Conversation you had to rise to, but a conversation anyone could join. 'Boredom' ('I'm living in this

movie,' Devoto snapped, 'but it doesn't move me') was an instant anthem, or rather a fragment of an album floating away to be caught by its listeners.
Greil Marcus, journalist, in the press notes for the 'Spiral Scratch' EP, re-released in 2000

This is a special release…financed by…friends… 'Breakdown' took three takes because…the band had to warm up. The other three tracks are first takes and…Pete Shelley dubbed an extra guitar on each track… Total recording time was about half an hour.
Original Buzzcocks' press release, January 1977

As girls, we were being accepted for the first time. All the huge dinosaur bands, like the Who, Queen and so on, wouldn't give you a look in. They just saw us as sex objects. Now you could get involved, front a band or take photographs. It was up to you.
Erica Echenberg, photographer

I loved the Slits with unqualified love. I thought they were wonderful because they had it all. Their performances were totally unpredictable. Ari Upp [singer with the Slits] was unpredictable in real life. She attacked Paul Cook at the Roxy one night. For absolutely no reason she just went up and started attacking him. You just never knew what she was going to do next. She was psychotic, but this volatility made her really attractive. Although you didn't want to get involved in any way, it was fun to watch at a distance.
Nils Stevenson

I thought the Slits were really great. They were completely narky and had no rules. It was girls on stage with guitars. The only time we'd seen that before was with the American group the Runaways. The Slits were a million miles better. They were fantastic.
Paul Simonon

Slits – fantastic! They all started at the wrong time doing different songs – superb. They were the bridge between punk and reggae.
Chris Sullivan

I loved the Slits. They were genuine. It was Ari I loved. I still have a crush on her. They were the real article, really amateur. They were the worst of the worst. They were so bad it was appalling. That's what you loved about them.
Gene Krell, punk clothing entrepreneur

Ari stabbed my dad in the eye with a pen.
Chris Duffy, bass player, Bazooka Joe

I liked the Slits. They played so badly, you couldn't make out what the fuck they were doing.
Marco Pirroni, guitarist, Siouxsie and the Banshees

Girls could be boys and boys could be girls. Erica Echenberg

Their performances were completely unpredictable, but lots of fun. You didn't know what they were going to do next. That seemed to be the essence of it. That's what the Pistols and the Banshees were like in the beginning. The Slits took it to the next stage, when it was complete and utter chaos. Funnily enough, they did great songs, and their lyrics were amongst the best. 'New Town' and 'Typical Girls' have fabulous lyrics. Their voices are great, and Dennis Bovell did a great job with the production. I think the production is phenomenal. It took them a long time, but the material was good, even if they didn't play it very well to begin with. When they got it right, it was great.
Nils Stevenson

The Clash made a point of wanting the Slits to be their support at the time. They wanted to see them break through. I just did an interview with Ari. We talked at length about those days. She still says that, despite help and support from people such as the Clash, it was incredibly hard. I remember when the Slits' album came out with them naked and coated in mud on the cover. I was working for *Melody Maker* at the time. I took it to Richard Williams and said, 'We've got to write about this. We must make a big splash.' He gagged and said, 'Take it away from me. How can they do that? They look so revolting and so fat.' This wasn't true. They were just normal-looking girls – if anything, they were on the slim side, but it showed you the prejudice there was then.
Viv Goldman

I ended up managing the Slits. I say manage, but actually I gave them a load of money and then hung on for dear life because they were unreal. It's unfair the way they've been written out of the big picture. I'd like to redress it. Look at all the things they did – the content of their music, the politics, the bad girl thing. And were they pretty? Courtney Love, Madonna and all the others, they have to give the Slits maximum respect.
Don Letts

My little master plan was to turn Siouxsie into the female equivalent of Johnny Rotten. I secreted her and Steve Severin into the Pistols' studio while we were on the Anarchy tour. She had the face – the female Johnny Rotten. Nils Stevenson **I just remember a young woman parading around in front of the stage dressed like a character from an arty porno novel. When it came to fetishes, her get-up certainly covered the waterfront: dominatrix make-up, fishnets, heels, black plastic lingerie, swastika armband and breasts pushed out and up by a mail-order sex catalogue bra. She got the attention I assume she craved, but only from press photographers. The punk inner circle were too concerned with their cool – and the rest of us too English – to say a word.** Glen Matlock, bass player, the Sex Pistols It was fun at the beginning. In 1976 we were the most hated people on the planet – we thought that was great. Siouxsie, the *Daily Mail*, 20 January 2001

There were very few sexy women in punk. **For me, Blondie, Siouxsie and Gaye Advert were the only ones that were OK.**

Nigel Wingrove, founder, *Stains* fanzine

Blondie got a lot of flak for being popular. I think that's rubbish. They were pop with a slab of irony and a lot of twist, even though their roots were in New York punk.
Stephen Colegrave

Blondie were like a '60s pop band and yet even they were hailed as a punk band. What did it all mean?
Nils Stevenson

People were afraid of Debbie, the media people were sort of scared of her and very wary in the beginning.
Chris Stein, guitarist with Blondie

[Debbie] Harry wasn't trying to look exactly like Marilyn – and she wasn't aiming to die sad and on drugs. She left her roots dark; she wore fetishistic, ripped, and androgynous clothes. She was angry, confrontational, bristling with attitude. She was a punk. Yes, she was being ironic, she was deconstructing an image, she was striking a pose. But it's more than that: she wasn't just reacting to something received; she was actively creating.
Cathy Che, *Deborah Harry: Platinum Blonde*

I liked Blondie from the first time I saw them. The word at CBGB's was that they sucked. They couldn't play their instruments and they were unmusical. But when I saw them, Debbie was dressed in a military outfit with a huge poster of a Japanese monster. She did the first song really well, but she couldn't move because the stage of the old CBGB's was minute. (This was before they moved it to the back.) During 'Rip It All to Shreds', she ripped up the big poster of the monster. I thought that was great. It was a real acknowledgement that she was wearing a costume, that she was on stage and putting on a show. To me it's important that a band is aware that they are here to entertain me, not just to play their music. If they were there just to play their music, I would leave.
Viv Goldman

We liked the Shangri-Las probably before it was fashionable to like them, but I guess that was the whole punk thing. I genuinely liked a lot of that stuff. I mean personally I was influenced very heavily by movie music and film scores, John Barry and Nina Roder and all that stuff. That's what I was paying the most attention to when I was a kid growing up, more than the bebop stuff.
Chris Stein

Debbie and Chris Stein worked for *Punk Magazine,* so we always saw them. Originally, they were not a very good band, but everyone liked Chris and Debbie so much that they supported them. Then, one day, you walked in and they were actually good.
Legs McNeil, writer on *Punk Magazine*

Poly Styrene was my favourite. Roberta Bayley, photographer

My favourite British band was X-ray Spex with Poly Styrene. They were wonderful. Their manager, Falcon, was one of the nicest people in the business. He's still around.
Hilly Kristal, owner of CBGB's

I loved Poly Styrene. She was fantastic – one of the greats. Actually, I asked Malcolm and his spokesman why they didn't use Poly Styrene for Bow Wow Wow. They just felt she had no sex appeal. But I thought she was wonderful. I just loved her.
Gene Krell

X-ray Spex weren't just another stereotypical punk group. Their songs were full of irony about fakery and commodified culture.
Nils Stevenson

Poly Styrene was brilliant. It was interesting that after punk both she and Lora Logic [former member of X-ray Spex] went off into extreme religion.
Viv Goldman

I never really liked Patti Smith. I thought the first album was OK, but it was a bit wimpy. She was a bit of a hippie. I didn't know what she was going on about anyway. The whole poetry thing kind of left me cold.
Marco Pirroni

At one point Patti Smith's album *Horses* was all you could get hold of. It was huge in the pre-punk era. Nobody should denigrate or under-estimate the importance of Patti Smith.
Chris Sullivan

All the females are jealous of Cherry Vanilla, especially all the dike Patti Smith fans. They sit there passing their bitchy comments in her direction but she don't care a shit. She's great – a bird that's honest. I can't help admiring her, and that's something from me 'cause I normally can't stand women rockers. Don't fucking go [to] see her and start with all that 'not relevant to the scene' crap. She's in it for the fun, so that's why you watch her – for fun. She sold her whole apartment to visit London. So don't forget it – dig her!
Sniffin' Glue, issue 8, March 1977

Lydia Lunch was a star. I mean, Teenage Jesus and the Jerks – what a great name for a band!
Chris Sullivan

I…waited for Joey Ramone to come home from England. Before he went, I said, 'What do you have to go to England for? Don't go to England. England sucks. I had never been to England. Or anywhere else… When Joey came back, you could see in his eyes that something had happened. Joey kept saying, 'Legs, you wouldn't believe it! You wouldn't believe it. They love it.'
Legs McNeil

We usually wear out our audiences before we wear out ourselves… Our set consists of 17 songs and takes 30 minutes to perform. Last month the same set lasted 37 minutes…and we're getting faster every day.
Johnny Ramone, *New Musical Express*, May 1977

Get out here quick.
It's a gold mine. Leee Childers

I liked the Heartbreakers from the first time I heard them. They were weird because they were the first professional punk band. They were good. They could actually play. We were amazed at how tight they were. They started at the same time and ended at the same time and they had their own distinctive style… They wore these weird leather jackets with white or red lapels. We suddenly thought leather jackets looked really cool. They became a really easy uniform to wear.
Marco Pirroni

We had to come over to London. It was where it was all happening. We didn't make any money, but hey – what's new?
Leee Childers

We were in a hotel in Leeds and me, Gerry and Richard were just sitting there waiting for the sound-check. There was a knock on the door so we opened it and a guy said, 'The manager says you are not to make so much noise.' Then there's another knock on the door and a guy says

he's from the SAS and the building is surrounded and that we're not allowed to leave the room. I'm thinking, 'This is a movie.' The guy pulled a gun and told us to stay inside. Walter arrived and the guy asked him to come in. I said, 'I tried to tell you.' We were in the room for two hours until finally Gerry said. 'Look, man, we got a sound-check.' The guy went out and then came back in again and said, 'Don't tell anyone I was here. Don't tell the police because I'm in the Secret Service. You're allowed to go now.' Gerry later said that the guy wasn't for real, so we called the police and told them the whole story. They had to come to the show because they thought this guy was going to turn up with his gun. They fingerprinted the whole room. Johnny wasn't there because he was driving up in his own car. Three weeks later the police called us and said they'd arrested the guy trying to rob a car and that the gun was a replica.
Gail Higgins Smith, Heartbreakers' tour manager

The Heartbreakers played the Roxy many times. It was the Roxy that convinced me that the London punk scene

was going to be big. I called Wayne County and Cherry Vanilla. I said, 'Pack your bags. Get over here quick. It's a gold mine.' They weren't ever going to get a record deal in America. They came to England and they both got record deals almost immediately.
Leee Childers

The decision to come to London was all very quick. Malcolm had called David Johansen [singer with the New York Dolls] for the Dolls to do the Anarchy tour, and David had just turned him down flat. Then Malcolm called Leee [Childers] and the rest is history. I remember the first time I saw the Sex Pistols. It was in the reception of a hotel, some shit-hole in the Bayswater Road. They came into the lobby like kids at a school dance. The boys were on one side and the girls on the other. Everyone was asking how we were and checking out what everyone was wearing. Little did I know they were in awe of Johnny [Thunders]. John [Lydon] was just going, 'Got any dope, man?' But John and Johnny hit it off after a while.
Walter Lure, guitarist, the Heartbreakers

Opposite, clockwise from top left: Joey and Johnny Ramone with Seymour Stein, unidentified man, Mrs Stein and Dee Dee Ramone; the Heartbreakers (Billy Rath, Walter Lure, Jerry Nolan and Johnny Thunders); Walter Lure; Jayne County • Above: The Ramones

211

The Ramones created the sound of punk. Marco Pirroni

We weren't real happy with the English punks, you know. I was living with the Ramones at St Mark's Place, where Joey and Dee Dee lived. I remember sitting with Joey one night, listening to 'White Riot' by the Clash and we looked at each other and went, 'Hmmm…' The Ramones were a little bit pissed off, and then the Sex Pistols album came out and it was great. They kind of stole everything, and it was good. It was a great record. So that was like the last insult. I mean, copy us and then do it one step better, so we were all kind of pissed.
Legs McNeil

The Ramones had got it together before us and developed in parallel to us…although the Pistols had all

at Dingwall's, we really didn't feel we had that much in common. We considered them more of a comedy band. I always reckoned the reason all those other bands copied the Ramones was because they couldn't afford that much rehearsal time, so they had to hurry through their set and finish it before they got slung out of their rehearsal rooms.
Glen Matlock, *I Was a Teenage Sex Pistol*

We thought of the British scene as basically friendly competition. We were happy that there was a scene, but of course we wanted to be the best. It was exciting to be part of a scene and that's pretty much what we thought of it.

Dee Dee hated the British scene. He thought you were ripping him off.
Jayne County, singer, actress and DJ

The Ramones were just brilliant. They really did invent their own punk style and they gave punk its speed. The Pistols and the Clash weren't particularly fast to start with. It was the Ramones who took everything one step further and simplified it even more. Apart from that, they wrote great songs. Their first three albums are just brilliant.
Marco Pirroni

The Ramones aren't punk – they're the Ramones.

When we returned to London, Nancy Spungen turned up.
Walter Lure

When we returned to London after the Anarchy tour, Nancy Spungen turned up at our flat in Pimlico. She used to follow us about in New York. She was local. She loved the Dolls and the Heartbreakers. She was a pig, but she was friendly. Johnny [Thunders] and Jerry [Nolan] loved her because she lent them money to buy drugs. She made her money from dancing naked in a bar in the middle of the afternoon. Jerry would pawn his guitars, and Nancy would give him the money to get them out. When we went to England, Jerry told her that when she had enough money to get his guitar, she could come and stay with us in London. Lo and behold, a month later she showed up at the front door of the flat. She'd got Jerry's guitar and some money for drugs. We gave her some

money to go away and kicked her out. Johnny and Jerry treated her pretty shitty. I know she was making money doing whatever she used to do. We used to run into her at clubs. Jerry and Johnny would do drugs with her, but they wouldn't let her stay in the flat. I don't know who introduced her to Sid. We used to run into them at the Speakeasy all the time. She developed an English accent. It was a marriage made in heaven.
Walter Lure

When Track records went bust we had to pay this little kid to climb up the drainpipe of their office and get us our 24-track tapes back. It was a nightmare.
Leee Childers

Track Records went bust, and I guess we should have known all along. At the time they were paying for the flats and they put the tour together. We had a bus, and they gave us spending money every now and then. If we

wanted to buy clothes, I'd go to Sex and sign their name and I guess they paid. We finished our album before they went bust. It seemed to take forever because we all fucked up. Speedy Keen was doing the engineering mix in a little studio off Wardour Street. It took another six months.
Walter Lure

Working with the Heartbreakers was…well, interesting. I had to ban all the drug dealers from coming round and I'd always ban the wrong people. Sometimes I'd have to stand next to the stage with a bucket ready for Johnny to throw up in. But there are always unusual habits that come with creative people…it goes with the territory.
Leee Childers

We did get a reputation for drug-taking, but then we did do a lot of drugs.
Walter Lure

Above, left to right: Lynda Clark, Leee Childers, Nancy Spungen, Sid Vicious, Dee Dee Ramone

New York 3 – London 2

Above: Johnny Thunders, Nils Stevenson and Leee Childers

One thing I want to put straight is that a lot of the people in London at the time didn't realize that they were directly influenced by the New York scene…the punk thing is more New York than London. They were the rebel version of what every type of music was.

Gail Higgins Smith

What gave British punk its edge, in one way, over New York was its youth and exuberance – and that, along with the media, is what killed it. The New York scene was allowed to grow, whereas in Britain, where it was hailed as the next big thing, a bandwagon was hastily erected and all kinds of people got on board carrying their misdirected perceptions of it with them. As a result, it suffered from the folly of youth, ostracized the innovators and never achieved what the New York scene had done musically. It was a case of too much too soon, the usual British ailment. Maybe this was the fault of the press. I'm sure if the Sex Pistols had been left alone, they would have become even bigger than they were, and I'm also sure that if the Velvet Underground were in the UK, they would never even have been allowed to play live or make an album. It's bad enough now, but imagine in 1967 the outrage the Velvets would have caused in the UK – singing about heroin and sado-masochism. Compare the two scenes: New York, which began it all, produced music that was far better, as it was allowed to gestate. Proof of this is that one can still listen to 80 per cent of the American produce. The British scene, on the other hand, provoked a bigger reaction,

was better at the start than the New York scene in terms of style, yet was far sillier at the end. Looking back, I'd say if it was a match, the Americans won – but it was close. Then again, Britain had reggae....
Chris Sullivan

We hated reggae. I'd go over to Joey's house and listen to Lou Reed and Herman's Hermits. I hated the PIL album.
Legs McNeil

To us, reggae was like pop music – it was old, it was like Eric Clapton's 'I Shot the Sheriff'.
John Holmstrom, editor, *Punk Magazine*

Maybe if the Yanks could have got hold of good dub, then they would have liked it…but then again, they don't like soul or funk. It's a lot more segregated.
Mark McCarthy

Everything was fuelled by amphetamines.

Chris Sullivan

Perhaps they used to spit at everybody because amphetamine sulphate produces a large amount of saliva. Chris Duffy

It was very bad sulphate. It would give you a headache and a nosebleed. Not very clever at all. Steve Walsh

I don't remember having any coke at that time because it was £5 for a gram of sulphate and £60 for a gram of coke. None of us wanted to do marijuana. We were all kicking back against the hippie dope thing. It was all adrenaline driven until the Americans – Johnny Thunders and all those bands – came on board, and then came heroin. Chris Duffy

Maybe our scene wasn't as intense because there wasn't nearly so much speed as in New York. Amphetamine wasn't as popular as in England. There was more cocaine about than Quaaludes [downers]. Bob Gruen, photographer

I didn't have any heroin. I was on amphetamines. Alan Jones, assistant in Sex, 1975-7

He [Steve Jones] had a prescription for them [speed pills] from an infamous doctor in Harley Street. They were meant to be for his weight, but I'm not sure that I believe that. I thought maybe he'd convinced Malcolm that he was overweight – which he wasn't. Malcolm had this real thing about us looking the part, so Malcolm sprang for the script. And Steve got the free speed he was after. Glen Matlock, I Was a Teenage Sex Pistol

They [the Drug Squad] searched my bag – nothing. [They went through my] ashtrays [and found] nothing but [cigarette] stubs… [Then they looked in] my briefcase, with its tour itineraries and road maps, [and discovered] a pretty little art deco tin brimful of white powder – my sulphate stash. A look of triumph. 'What's this, then?' I took the initiative. These guys had been acting like clowns… 'Don't you know anything?' I said, scornfully. 'Haven't you the faintest clue about music? Don't you know about playing live? Do you realize how hot it gets under the stage-lights?'…[They] closed the tin [of what they thought was talcum powder] and put it back in the case. Johnny Green, roadie, A Riot of Our Own

Speed was the big drug in New York before heroin. I loved it. I would still do it if I could. The most successful people in the back room of Max's Kansas City [a legendary New York club] would never have considered themselves speed freaks, but there was a lot of speed energy. People were up all the time, very active, and could be a little mean, like getting angry with whips in Warhol films. There was some heroin, but nothing like you saw later. Jim Fourrat, nightclub owner

Of course, in those days, sulphate was the drug of choice.

It got you on the road. Clive Langer, songwriter and producer

I did some mad things on drugs. I didn't put it down to drugs at the time. I just thought I was trying to get the Banshees' careers together for them. One night, after I was really pissed off with their performance, I wanted to scare them and stir them about a bit. I used to have a huge Granada, a ridiculous car. I'd parked in one of those multistorey car parks. I drove out of the car park like a madman, hitting the walls on either side. The band were shitting themselves as I smashed the car on the walls. I knocked all the chrome off, but barely dented the car. I could never do that again in a million years. They still put up with me for six years. Nils Stevenson

I didn't take drugs, but everyone else did. It was just routine. I went to see the Ramones at the Round House [in north London]. I'd never bought drugs before. I bought a gram of speed but, never having used it before, I didn't know how much to take. I took a bit and nothing happened, so I took a bit more, and then a bit more. An hour later it hit me and I didn't sleep for two days. We went to see a mate to get some 'fatherly advice' (in other words, some downers). I knew he'd be up because he was always taking speed. We stayed jabbering away for hours. We were sitting on the floor with Steve and Sid, who were passing round this syringe of speed, so I took a shot. Sid was saying, 'Don't tell Malcolm,' because Malcolm had told him he had to stop taking drugs or he was out of the band. The next three days I felt pathetic. I started feeling really ill, so I went to the doctor and found I'd caught Sid's hepatitis. I should have bottled it – it'd be worth a few quid now. That was really the first and last time for me – some drug induction! Andrew Czezowski

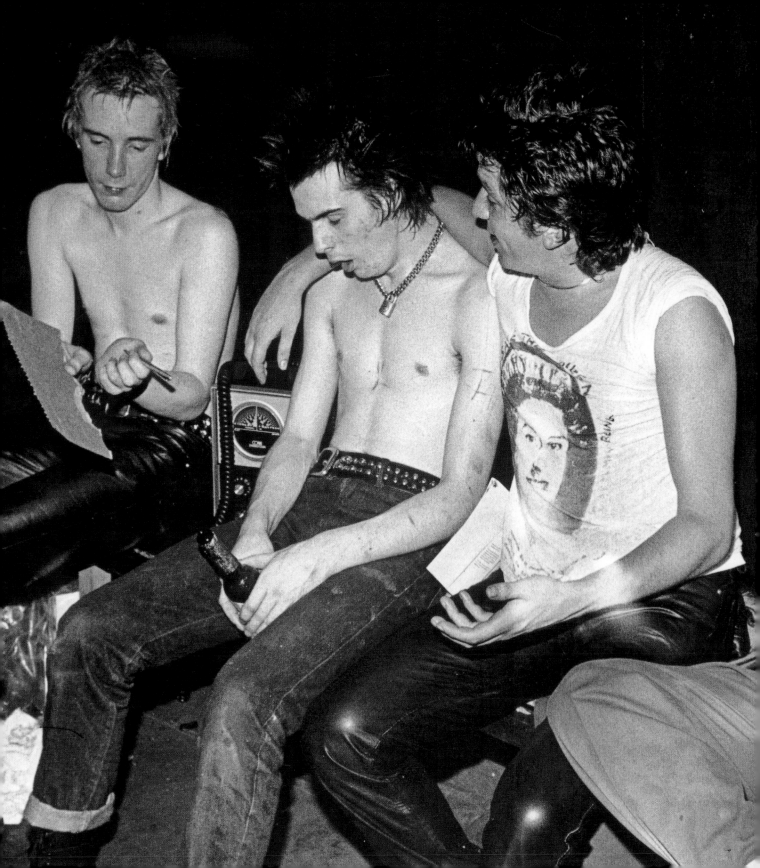

It all became very tough; it all became heroin; it all became very dark. Nils Stevenson

Years later Johnny Thunders came to my flat. He sat on the couch and took his shoes and socks off so he could search for a vein in his foot to inject himself. Then I went into the kitchen and found his German manager drunk, flat out on the floor with his face in the cat's food dish. He was meant to be the manager. I expected him to behave like a manager, but he was worse than the rest.
Helen Wellington Lloyd, assistant in Sex and McLaren muse

When I first knew Johnny Thunders, he wasn't even taking drugs. He was just always crazy. When I lived with him, he started taking downers a lot. Then, when I came to the UK and toured with the Heartbreakers, he'd started doing heroin. The tour was like it was because Johnny was on drugs. There were times when I would love Johnny and times when I would rather kill him. They would drive into the city where they were playing a gig and, before the bus had even stopped, they would be running off to find drugs. They would show up from scoring just two minutes before showtime.
Gail Higgins Smith

Throughout '77 everything went downhill. I just got more and more into speed. I was living in a squat and I was in a bad way. Heroin started coming in, and everyone was jacking up. Then a drug dealer thought I'd ripped him off. He was 6 ft 5 in, Irish, bisexual and angry, so I put all my possessions in a bag and left. The next day, this bloke turned up looking for me.
Steve Walsh

A lot of people from New York came to London to be part of the scene. They were older than us, not just in age, but also in attitude. They brought over serious drugs, like heroin, we'd never seen before. It started on the Anarchy tour. Until then we thought heroin was a female character in a 19th-century romantic novel.
Chris Sullivan

I hate to say it, but it was the New York crowd who first infiltrated heroin into the English youth music scene at that time. It's a horrifying thought, but that's probably how it happened.
Gail Higgins Smith

Sid moved from speed to heroin pretty quickly. It took him over. He became very irrational. There was trouble with him everywhere we went.
Paul Cook, drummer, the Sex Pistols

I went to New York with the Banshees. I went on Concorde; they went economy. My drug dealer was waiting in the airport terminal for me because it took three and a half hours to get there and I couldn't do without smack for longer than that. It was all mad. Everybody was mad, but we came out of a mad tradition. It's not like that any more.
Nils Stevenson

The Heartbreakers brought heroin with them. Heroin is an all-encumbering drug. Once you get into it, it's like a kind of plague and you can't get out of it. It changed the music. Heroin took energy out of it because heroin takes everything out of everything.
Marco Pirroni

I was the first guy to turn Johnny Rotten on to heroin, the first guy to shoot him up. I'm not proud of that. I didn't like the feeling I got from it and I changed my mind about turning people on to drugs. I didn't do it any more after that. Nancy, who I introduced to Sid, was the first to turn Sid on. One time I shot Sid up backwards, pointing the needle *down* the vein rather than up. He didn't know you could do that. It scared the shit out of him, but he didn't want to say nothing.
Jerry Nolan, drummer, the New York Dolls and the Heartbreakers

Opposite, left to right: Johnny Rotten, Sid Vicious, Steve Jones and Paul Cook

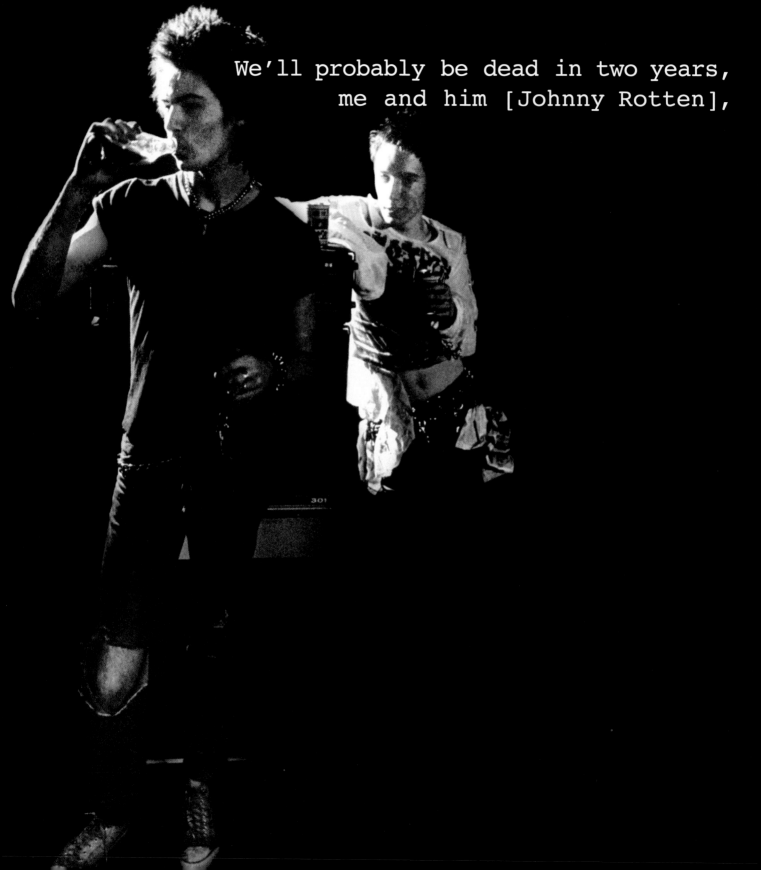

We'll probably be dead in two years,
me and him [Johnny Rotten],

but we're going to try anyway because somebody has to do it. Sid Vicious, Ksan Radio interview, 1 April 1978

The Sex Pistols must be considering getting rid of bassist Glen Matlock. Sid Vicious is not even an official Sex Pistol yet he still does a Transatlantic phone interview with Los Angeles disc jockey Rodney Bingenheimer, where he describes meeting a girl who 'licks toilet bowls'. Sid was referring to Nancy Spungen, who had recently arrived in the UK on the heels of the Heartbreakers. It's unclear whether Sid is in the band or not. He was 'auditioning' for the band last Friday, but Glen hasn't been let go. Sid thinks he's in, but is he?
George Gimarc, *Punk Diary 1970-1979*

When I get so annoyed over something, I need an enemy,
somebody who's done something to me
so I can take it out on them and beat them to pulp.
And I always find I'm sitting in a room with a load
of friends and I can't do anything to them,
so I just go upstairs and smash a glass and cut myself.
Then I feel better.
Sid Vicious, *New Musical Express*, 2 February 1978

Vicious was kind of John's mate, I suppose, who John knew from art college. John always thought that me, Steve and me were mates, so he wanted to bring his mate in. John and Glen fell out in a very big way you know, and in the end one of them had to go. The problem was probably to do with Glen going to grammar school or something.
Paul Cook

I'd had enough. I just didn't want to do the punk thing any more. The other reason was that Malcolm didn't want me in the band because it became quite obvious that me and John had a problem. EMI knew what was going on and said they'd take me as a songwriter, that I could earn a shit-load of money. I didn't say yes right away, but you know, I was getting a total headache from the band, and I wasn't getting backed up from Steve and Paul, so I decided to go.
Glen Matlock

It was good when Glen went as he was always fucking moaning – about this, about that, about fucking everything.
Steve Jones, guitarist, the Sex Pistols

Another thing, Malcolm was starting to believe that he was the puppet master, and I didn't want that. I was quoted as saying, 'It's like being in the Monkees,' but I didn't want to be in the Monkees. That band was put together to cash in on the British invasion, you know. We started the bloody thing, in Britain anyway. No, when I left the band, we divvied up and there was only three grand rather than 50 grand in the kitty. I got stitched.
Glen Matlock

Malcolm McLaren sends a telegram on 26 February to all the music papers announcing that Glen is indeed out of the band because 'he went on too long about Paul McCartney'. He said Sid's credentials were that 'he gave Nick Kent [*NME* journalist] what he deserved many months ago' – in other words, a slap.
Chris Sullivan

Sid Vicious used to come down to Acme Attractions all the time. He called himself John Beverley and said, 'Everybody keeps beating me up.' I'd say, 'Sid, look at this jacket. It was Elvis's jacket. Do you want it?' 'Yeah, I'll have it,' he'd say. Really it was Keith Bloom's jacket, gold and blue lamé. I'd bought it off some geezer who had come to sell clothes. I wore it for a week and then sold it to Sid. He loved it.
Don Letts

He was a funny mixture of character. I know it's a real cliché, but he was supposed to be a bit hard, but he wasn't. Everyone used to say, 'Oh, he was a big pussycat.' But he got more messed up when he joined the Pistols.
Steve Walsh

When he got into the band, he had to live up to his hard image, so he was always getting into shit situations. He was a real pain in the arse.
Don Letts

Sid fucking Vicious…what a wanker.
Frank Kelly

He always had great attitude. Sid started the pogo. When we used to play our small gigs, it was so crowded, he just used to jump up and down and bash everybody about. We used to go mad. The only way he could dance was jumping up and down.
Paul Cook

I hated the pogo. Being a dwarf, it was really frightening. I thought they would fall on me. After a while I thought, fuck it, and would walk through the crowd and grab their legs and – bang! – pull them apart and walk through. They didn't know what the fucking hell was going on.
Helen Wellington Lloyd

Above and opposite: Sid Vicious

When Sid joined,
it did spoil
    the chemistry
        of the band—
    we just didn't know it
at the time. Steve Jones

Sid and I used to hang out at a squat in Davis Road, and then we moved to one in Elgin Avenue. The whole band went there. He didn't get out much. He wrote a few songs. We had one guitar but junkies broke in and stole it. The whole thing was really squatsville. The funny thing that struck me about him was that we both liked Rupert Bear books and Tin-Tin when we were kids.
Steve Walsh

When I looked at the documentary *The Filth and the Fury* from the distance of time, I realized that Sid was the icon for the whole movement. It made me feel even worse about his death because I thought, if only we'd known that he was the one who was going to take it that far.
Alan Jones

Once I went back to his house in Dalston where his mum lived. They lived in this massive big tower block from which you could see these twinkling lights over Hackney Marshes. His mum had obviously been a junkie and a beatnik. She was one of those types who took him off to Ibiza when he was seven on the back of a motorbike. The flat was as clean as a new pin, a really well-kept council flat, as was normal in east London. There were all these records that he'd had since he was a kid or early teens. There were so many Bowie records. He had all the Bowie bootlegs and everything that Bowie had ever done – even records like 'London Boys'. They were all in those protective vinyl covers, like people in the '70s used to keep their record collections in. Everything was neatly annotated and labelled. I said, 'Fuck, look at all these Bowie records.' I really liked 'London Boys'. As it was the original Decca single, I said, 'This must be worth a fucking mint,' and he said, 'It's fucking shit.' You know, he was trying to make out he didn't really like it or anything. I just thought it was funny the way people did it then, especially him. He just tried to write out his past. It was definitely a defect in his personality, down to some insecurity or something.
Steve Walsh

I could have slept with Sid. There was one day when Sid said to me, 'I think you've got a really big knob,' and I replied, 'Well, there's only one way to find out.' He said, 'OK then, let's do it.' To be honest with you, I couldn't do it because he was a friend and I didn't do anything because I didn't want to upset him, but I always remember it.
Alan Jones

When Johnny and Malcolm first talked about Sid joining the Pistols, Steve and I weren't up for it in the beginning, to be truthful. We'd just got to a point where we'd done all the work learning to play and just got the songs together. We thought, fucking hell. He couldn't play bass at the time, but he was a great face – he looked great.
Paul Cook

Sid really looked the part, but couldn't play, and now we could.
Steve Jones

The whole reason he got hooked on heroin was because of his mother's boyfriend. He was no good.
Alan Jones

Johnny and Sid weren't that close. I wouldn't say they were great bosom buddies, but they knew each other. Although I was quite suspicious about the idea of Sid joining the band, I thought, here we go. But, to be fair, when Sid first joined the band, he was really up for it. He was determined to learn bass and fit in, and he did, which was surprising. In fact, when Sid joined, it turned out to be one of my favourite times in the band. I got quite close to him at the time. He worked hard because he wanted to be in the band. It all slotted into position; he looked great as well. The band now felt complete, at least in looks anyway.
Paul Cook

I never saw them when Vicious was involved…fuck, no. I had my pride.
Frank Kelly

Although John got Sid into the band, they started falling out straight away. Sid wouldn't calm down. He said, 'I'm gonna take this all the way. I want to go mad.'
Paul Cook

This cowboy [in an American diner] recognized Sid…invited him to join him at the table and eat with his family… I heard the cowboy say, 'Oh, you're Vicious. Can you do this?' I looked over just in time to see the cowboy putting a cigarette out on his own hand… Sid hit his (own) hand with a knife and it made a small cut in the skin…blood started seeping out, slowly working its way down until it reached the plate of eggs. But Sid didn't care. He was hungry and just kept gobbling them up. The more Sid ate, the more horrified the cowboy became, until he completely freaked out…gathered up his family and started running for the door.
Bob Gruen

By this time, John was quite serious about the band. I think eventually he saw Sid come along, who was totally interested in causing chaos. That's why they started to fall out. Of course, Sid got involved in drugs and then he was totally off the wall.
Paul Cook

John has never admitted that he did not get on with Sid at all. I'm sorry to say they never liked each other. He always saw Sid as a threat. He can argue otherwise until he's blue in the face, but it won't make any difference.
Alan Jones

The drugs started pretty much straight away – I think because he met Nancy virtually as soon as he joined the band. He'd been in a band with my mate Steve Walsh, and they always used to take speed. He said the only time he ever 'shot it up' was with that lot, and he ended up getting hepatitis. Pretty quickly he got into heroin. He became very irrational. Everywhere you'd go there'd be trouble with him. You could walk down the road and end up in a big fight

because that's the way he was. We kept his girlfriend, Nancy, at arm's length. We didn't want her around. John really hated her. She came over with the Heartbreakers because she heard this thing was going on with punk and wanted to get involved. God, did she get involved.
Paul Cook

Nancy was revolting. I just thought, 'Oh, stupid fucker. What's Sid gone and done that for?' I felt angry with him more than anything else. He was so stupid.
Steve Walsh

Even Jerry Nolan wanted to get rid of Nancy… Too much for Jerry Nolan? I mean, *come on*.
Nils Stevenson

You couldn't shake her. Nancy was a fucking pain in the arse. I think our scene was probably the first scene where guys and girls hung out as friends, equally. Even so, Nancy was a whine. I mean, it was hard to like her. We used to sit up and make jokes about her. She'd always come over to my apartment. She wanted to 'cop' and she'd just keep bugging me until I said yes.
Elliot Kidd of the Demons in *Please Kill Me*

Sid was such a strong person. The one thing I really want to believe in all of this was that he really did love Nancy. I hope that's true. I'd hate to think that he didn't have anything.
Alan Jones

I've never told anybody before, but before Sid and Nancy went to America a weird thing happened. I had to get permission from Sid to use this image in my punk rock movie. I remember them coming to the office to sign a release. He had this fucking long knife and was playing around with Nancy with the knife. He was just sticking her gently with it. At first she liked it, then she said, 'It hurts, it hurts,' and a week later…boom, boom. I ain't saying shit, but that's what I saw.
Don Letts

People liked him, but he tried to rule it out. In the end he was quite a sad character because of everything that had happened to him. That's how I felt after I heard that he'd killed his girlfriend and then killed himself.
Steve Walsh

224

Sid had the iconic punk look.
As much as I loved the others, Sid, on image alone, is what all punk rests on. Alan Jones

Punk would have been only 200 people if it hadn't been for the media.

Punk always needed the Bill Grundy show. If the tabloids hadn't reacted the way they did, punk would have fizzled out almost immediately. It's very easy to look down one's nose at the kids from Aberdeen or from Walsall. The only way those kids' lives could have been touched by this phenomenon was through the media. The media was rightly condemned for its stereotyping, but people forget that punk was a rag-bag of different styles, people and attitudes. The media very quickly managed to weld this into one image. I believe that the world needed punk and therefore it needed more than 200 kids doing their own thing at the wrong end of the Kings Road. Nothing would have happened if it hadn't been for the media. Ted Polhemus, author of *Street Style*

The Grundy thing at the time just attracted a lot of grief and a lot of lemons – yes, grief and lemons.
Chris Sullivan

I remember when punk first came to Plymouth. Nothing happens in Plymouth. Bowie and the Ziggy Stardust tour had petered out and nothing was happening in fashion. It was really dull. In August the Sex Pistols were going to play in Plymouth. When I first heard they were coming, I didn't know who they were. Out of interest, I went to see them play, but they didn't turn up. However, during the course of the summer, there were little bits and pieces appearing in the *NME* about the band beating up members of the audience. By September there was much more coverage. It felt exciting – something that was for my generation, not us trying to pick up on what the older generation was doing. It felt unique to us.
Nigel Wingrove

People's was the punk club of Norwich. There was one in every city; then, when punk was dead, there was one in every town. In a suitably perverse way, punk was proclaimed dead as it was spreading further afield to the more obscure provinces. The quicker it died, the more alive it was. It brought life to the countryside and market towns. We rural types were slower to latch onto it.
George McKay, professor of counter-culture, University of Central Lancashire

It didn't just attract lemons, of course. There were a lot of quite exceptional exceptions. A lot of really amazing people started off in the punk milieu and went on to make the country a lot more interesting.
Chris Sullivan

Every Sunday, we'd head off to the Pogo – a gogo club in Kirkcaldy. I would sneak out of the house with my punk gear in a bag. An enlightened parent drove us to our destination, while we changed in the back. I had purloined a blue boiler

suit, which I'd laid out on my bedroom floor before dripping neat bleach onto it. It looked fine, but smelt terrible, and my mother was always puzzled by the large white stain which had appeared on my bedroom carpet.
Ian Rankin in *British Greats*

I had an epiphany, before I even knew there was such a thing, at a gig in April 1977 at St Andrew's Hall, Norwich. I was 16 years old, and that was the gig when I knew I was a punk. In the pre-punk days we'd sit on the wooden floor in the dark and watch bands like Hawkwind and Gentle Giant, only standing up for the encore. Dr Feelgood were the only band I can remember who had any energy in the entire pre-punk music desert. But here's my epiphany, my moment of being. It's a gig by a band called the Stranglers, on their first national tour. The place is two-thirds empty and St Andrew's Hall is too big to disguise the scale of emptiness. It affects the crowd; we're miles away from the stage. Pockets of youth sit around, some incongruous in Soul Boy bags or Bowie-style hair. Us Norfolk lot don't yet know what we're supposed to do with punk. Maybe we're here to find out.
Professor George McKay

To many people, punk was the most amazing thing ever. It was the universal liberator.
Stephen Colegrave

Suddenly there's a band on stage [London], conjured out of the dark, violent, clattery drums and out-of-tune guitar. You can just about hear the singer above everything else. One hundred and fifty curved spines straighten as the crowd pays swift attention. It's been shocked and scared. Equally speedily, it's over. Then we see the vocalist standing at the front of the stage. He has blond spikes turned green by the lights, square shades that don't fit, and a tattered, whitish shirt with daubed images hanging from a wasted frame. He's holding the mike like it's an

enemy, cajoling the audience, sneering at us: 'Come on Norwich, ain't you heard? Things have *changed*. This is punk rock. We don't play to hippies sitting on the fucking floor. Get up off your fucking arses now. Stand up and get down the fucking front. What's up? Are you scared, me old carrot crunchers?'
Professor George McKay

Johnny Rotten was a real snob. I don't think he cared for anybody outside London, and not many within. A lot of people thought it was part of the act…but I assure you it wasn't. He was totally sincere. He dislikes almost everyone, and, unlike a lot of people, is not scared to show it.
Nils Stevenson

I'm pulled up like I'm on a dog lead, running towards the stage, kicking past people on the floor, sprinting towards this green energy, wanting it right now. There's power there, electricity. As I run, I think everyone else is running too. How could anyone ignore the sound, the vibrancy, the defiance you've been waiting for when it shoves itself down your throat out of nowhere? Yet there can't be more than 20 or 30 others acting like me. We form a thin, unruly line at the front of the stage, near a pissed-off bouncer who somehow knows his job's changed forever. There are acres of empty wooden floor behind us as the rest have moved even further back. Close up I see the singer has snot running out of his nose.
Professor George McKay

The whole scene was great before it was named punk, then it became a magnet for loads of 'Erberts. It attracted lots of hippies. They'd get their hair cut, badly, and turn up in their brand new T-shirts that they'd just ripped up and put back together with their mum's safety pins. It was so bloody silly, it was almost satirical. They've all probably got really responsible jobs now.
Chris Sullivan

As with every fad, it could not stay stuck at the wrong end of the Kings Road forever. It had to reach the provinces and then change – it was inevitable. Stephen Colegrave

We're the punks in the provinces now, jumping like we're celebrating freedom, gulping the music down, being new, dancing our difference. The support band to the Stranglers is called London: the big city's come to Norfolk to wake us up. They give me an extraordinary punk moment I didn't even know I was waiting for. They touch something – a dissatisfaction, a desire – in small groups of people all over the country. I'm ecstatic. I've found myself, after all these lost years in England.
Professor George McKay

Some people didn't half talk a load of old shite about the whole affair. It was a fad, a fashion, nothing more – mods, rockers, skinheads, punks, soul boys, New Romantics, the same old, same old… Some people have made a career out of analysing the whole thing. It tickles me.
Chris Sullivan

Liverpool was very influenced by London. We saw all the bands at Eric's [club]. They might be playing in London on a Saturday and we'd get them on a Sunday night. The Clash were there early on. It was only the Sex Pistols who were hard to see, and we were really keen to see them after the Bill Grundy thing. When they played the secret tour, we knew where they were playing, so we'd shoot down to Middlesbrough or wherever to catch the gigs. In some ways, we had more exposure to the actual bands than the punks in London. When we saw people like the Clash, we could get close to them, talk to them afterwards, even have a jam. It was really healthy up there.
Clive Langer

There were 300 or 400 folk running about the place in London thinking they were the kings of punk rock, which they were. But what about us? What about Edinburgh?
Dempsey, punk fan

I was the only punk in my year on my foundation course in Plymouth. There were a couple of punks in other years. Then I started going out with this girl who wanted to become a punk as well. She was only beginning to be a punk. She'd put some red dye in her hair and invested in some latex plastic trousers. Her mother said, 'We've never had a punk in the family before.' Just like we were aliens from outer space.
Nigel Wingrove

For a while it's singles, not albums. You have to stand, not sit. You want to feel, not listen. I don't realize all this at first. When I do, I take the punk line, the line of speed and newness. I hate the Jam, but I love their album title: *This Is the Modern World*. It is, and I'm glad to be in it. You're on the cusp of something. Everything's new. We clear out our wardrobes and record collections. There's an arrogance with this attitude, and that suits me. I'm only young after all.
Professor George McKay

I remember going into my local pub with my girlfriend, who had blackened her eyes and back-combed her hair. The landlady said she wasn't going to serve me or that strumpet with me. This was punk in Plymouth.
Nigel Wingrove

The first punk shop in Scotland opened up. It was called Arizona State and was in Dunfermline, believe it or not. I bought a pair of Clash trousers. They were £22.50, an outrageous price. I also bought a big fishnet mohair jumper that was black on one side and red on the other. I went camping for the weekend. When I came back, my mother put it in the bin, thinking it had rips in it, not knowing that I'd saved up money to buy the thing. I couldn't complain about it because she would have killed me if she'd known how much I'd fucking spent.
Dempsey

As well as writing my fanzine, *Stains*, I tried to manage a punk band. They were called Mascara. It was a disaster because they thought the way to be punk was to smash up their dressing-room at the Metro. I then discovered that managers have to pick up the pieces afterwards.
Nigel Wingrove

I wore the colours of punk, had that brightness of hair and the ragged clothes. I bought cotton shirts at jumble sales, dyed them green, red and yellow, then stencilled and sprayed them with words and images. I found white trousers on a back shelf in a faded menswear shop and dyed them a range of colours, dipped them in and out of buckets over a month or two. My wardrobe also included old men's coats and jackets, all too big, with rolled-up cuffs, a tinted snot-rag or thick scarf hanging from a pocket. I had boots, all sorts of boots, big black things that made you walk funny. Bits of army surplus rubbed

shoulders with shiny dance gear from a previous era, baggy jumpers handed down from big sisters, stripes and patterns, tight and loose. Hair was peroxide with roots showing, or phoney blue-black. And I was an understated punk.
Professor George McKay

The whole punk thing was great in that it brought a lot of people out of themselves.
Chris Sullivan

Those of us who were into punk used to get together outside the Virgin record store in Plymouth. There was a wall which was a sort of gathering place. There were some pubs there that focused on our music and fashion. It was young and exciting. You felt part of something.
Nigel Wingrove

I had a white cotton shirt which I spray-painted with thick, vertical black lines, and the word 'Bars' across the front. I hated it when people asked what it meant.
Professor George McKay

I remember we came up to London for the weekend and had to meet those we were staying with in a pub in Covent Garden. Of course, because of the Roxy no pub would let us in: they had signs saying 'No punks'. We didn't even look that extreme, just leather trousers and biker's jackets. So we couldn't find our friends, had nowhere to sleep and had to go all the way back to Wales.
Mark McCarthy

Before we saw the Pistols we thought we were really fashionable. When we saw them we just thought, 'Fuck, we're nowhere'. But in those days you could shock people by having short hair and tight trousers.
Clive Langer

I always wore a dog-collar when I walked down the street. It seemed just as normal as putting on my socks. I hennaed my hair because it was difficult to get Crazy Colour, which had just come out. We'd mess around with food dye, but it was always a disaster because as soon as it began to rain, it started running down your face. The main thing for us was to stand out a mile. People knew exactly what you were – a punk, one unapologetic punk.
Nigel Wingrove

INJURED AMIN 'FLEES UGANDA'

By NICHOLAS DAVIES
Foreign Editor

PRESIDENT Idi Amin has fled from Uganda after being wounded in an assassination attempt, it was claimed last night.

Two of his bodyguards were killed when gunmen ambushed Amin's car near Entebbe airport on Saturday, it was reported from neighbouring Kenya.

And last night he was believed to be in hiding receiving medical treatment in a "friendly" African country—possibly Nigeria.

The reports were impossible to confirm last night, as the

GONE TO EARTH: Amin

Ugandan authorities ordered a strict blackout on news of the president.

They refused to accept calls inquiring about Amin, and Uganda Radio—Amin's mouthpiece—ignored reports of the attack.

But Ugandan refugees in Nairobi said the attack was the work of rebels determined to rid the country of a bloody tyrant.

What is certain is that military activity was suddenly stepped up yesterday.

Troops in armoured cars moved in to control key areas of the capital and the provinces, and roadblocks were thrown up around Kampala and Entebbe.

Survived

Amin, 52 next month, has survived at least a dozen attempts on his life since he seized power in a bloodless coup six years ago.

The latest came last year, when three grenades were hurled at him as he left a police passing-out parade.

But the bid failed. Amin survived, although his driver, bodyguard and the would-be assassin all died in the blast.

He has always said he is not afraid to die. He claims he is in direct communication with God, who has told him exactly when he will die — so he knows he is safe until then.

PUNK ROCK ROTTEN RAZORED

By STUART GREIG

PUNK rock star Johnny Rotten's face has been slashed in a savage razor attack.

The lead singer of the controversial Sex Pistols group was ambushed by a gang outside a London pub.

Later, 20-year-old Rotten was taken to hospital where stitches were put in his wounds. Two people with him were also injured.

Last night there were fears that the attack was part of a backlash against the Pistols and other punk rock groups.

The Pistols and Rotten, their lead singer, are seen as possible targets because of their anti-royal record, "God Save the Queen." It describes the Queen as a moron.

Ambushed

The attack on Rotten—real name John Lydon—was the second aimed at the group within days.

Last week an art director working with the Sex Pistols was beaten up in a street and left unconscious with a broken nose and a broken leg. His four attackers escaped.

Rotten was ambushed in the car park of the Pegasus pub in Highbury. With him were recording studio manager Bill Price and record producer Chris Thomas.

Bill Price said last night: "We were probably marked down for attack when Johnny Rotten was recognised in the pub.

"The gang cut his face and his arm, but didn't manage to do any serious damage.

"Chris also had his face cut and I got a deep cut in my arm.

too popular because of the record about the Queen."

A spokesman for Virgin Records, who issued the controversial "Queen" disc, said: "It looks as though punk rockers are in for a hard time.

"The attackers were not teenage thugs, but men in their thirties.

"It seems they were aiming for Johnny's face to try to disfigure him. We are worried that this could be the start of a wave of attacks on the group and other punk rockers.

"A lot of people were upset at the record about the Queen, and that could be part of the problem.

"Johnny is a target because he is the king of the punk rockers—the figurehead.

"We're going to have to take special care to protect him."

A Scotland Yard spokesman said last night: "We are investigating this apparently unprovoked attack."

VICTIM: Punk rock star Rotten.

END OF THE WORLD!

But it's all a TV hoax

By JILL PALMER

THOUSANDS of viewers were terrified last night by a chilling TV programme which suggested that the world was doomed.

Switchboards of the Mirror and ITV companies throughout the country were jammed with panic calls.

Viewers wanted to be assured that the documentary - style programme's claim about a new ice-age was false.

One angry viewer who phoned the Mirror, George Forde, of Peterborough, said:

"The people who put

collaborating to set up a colony of scientists on Mars.

But the whole thing was a huge hoax. A joke that misfired.

The only clue that the Anglia TV programme, Alternative 3, was make-believe came right at the end.

The date on which the film was made was flashed on the screen: April 1.

One angry viewer who phoned the Mirror, George Forde, of Peterborough, said:

The programme had reported an escape plan by Americans and Russians,

out this programme must be sick in the head."

"Why show an April Fool's joke in the middle of June with no explanation that it was all a hoax.

"I have never seen anything so irresponsible in my life."

Young mother Jane Jones, from Andover, Hants, said: "There are lots of UFO sightings around this part of the country and when I saw this programme I was really frightened.

"I had no idea it wasn't

true. Nothing was said to indicate it was a joke."

A spokesman for the watchdog Independent Broadcasting Authority said the programme had been passed by them.

"We thought people were more sophisticated," he said.

An Anglia TV spokesman said: "This was put out as a thought provoking programme.

"Everything was based on what could happen. We do not consider we were irresponsible in putting it out."

Anglia's switchboard was jammed for more than two hours after the programme ended.

People didn't like it, and that means grief. Frank Kelly

I got attacked in Shepherd's Bush. I was just walking down the road with my girlfriend after visiting my parents. We were going to get the bus back up to the West End when I saw these rockabilly types staring at me. They were looking at my creepers saying, 'What the fuck are you wearing them for?' I said, 'Cos I fucking like them. What's your problem?' They walked off in a hump. About 10 minutes down the road they were still there, and all of a sudden I was attacked from behind.
Paul Cook

It was at the time of the punk and Ted wars. The punks and Teds would meet on the Kings Road. Obviously, as manager of the Heartbreakers, I was officially a punk, as of course was Joe Strummer [of the Clash]. However, both of us went through a phase of dressing like Teds. We started wearing our hair in quiffs. We thought it was really cool-looking. One night we went together to the Music Machine [a club in Camden Town] to see the Boomtown Rats. The place was packed with all these punks. They were saying really rotten things to us and bumping us. Joe and I thought it was hilarious. I managed the Heartbreakers and he was the lead singer of the Clash, and these punks were bumping us because we were dressed like Teddy boys. So we left. As we were walking up Camden High Road to get a minicab, Joe and I hatched this plan. We called a music journalist and told him that a gang of punks had jumped on us and beaten us up because we were dressed up in Teddy boy gear. We gave our names as Joe Strummer and Leee Childers. That week all the music press had the story about how these two major punks were beaten up by their own kind because they were dressed in the wrong clothes. It never happened. This is the first time anyone has known. Joe Strummer may get angry with me. (Sorry Joe.)
Leee Childers

When I got all punked up, people actually crossed the road to avoid me. Things became more violent when we started wearing leather jackets. The local Hell's Angels and greasers really disapproved. They were grown men and we were really young wimps. Getting chased around Plymouth by drunken motorbike guys became a major factor in our lives. Then there were the Marines. They had the IQ of a small brick, but they wanted our punk blood.
Nigel Wingrove

The kids around Clapham were a problem. I used to wear the clothes my mother gave me – there wasn't any option. I remember when I was only about seven having to wear some transparent thing with zips. The other kids used to give me hell, saying, 'Look at you, you little poof.'
Joe Corré, son of Vivienne Westwood and Malcolm McLaren

The whole punk/Ted conflict was exacerbated, yet again, by the media. The Teds, loyal *Sun* readers to the last, read the newspaper and believed that attacking anyone resembling a punk was the thing to do, so they 'd come down to the Kings Road by the busload. They weren't kids, they were men, some as old as 40 and your average

punk was about 16. I personally hadn't been down the Kings Road for a few months; the whole affair was a bit stale. I then popped down one summer Saturday in 1977 and stumbled on a war. There were running battles in the street and riots in Sloane Square tube station. I remember all these Sloanie women screaming and running for their lives having just exited Peter Jones [department store], and a Ted dying after being thrown on the track. One thing to remember – it wasn't gentle fisticuffs, it was cut-throats at dawn with hammers to match…and all because of clothing.
Chris Sullivan

I think those of us who were in at the beginning did get tired of being in the front line when anything happened. People were starting to threaten us with violence, and I just didn't feel comfortable any more.
Alan Jones

The arty college punks forgot that if you sing about anarchy, sometimes someone will do it to you, and sometimes with violence.
Mark Powell

Looking back, I suppose we were very provocative. I remember the time when Jordan and I got on a crowded tube. She'd just got the part in *Jubilee* with David Jarman. She was talking about her movie career, and then we started talking about sex. Everyone in the whole carriage was totally appalled by our conversation, but we didn't care. We just did it on purpose. We had to do it.
Alan Jones

Above: Teddy boys and police invade the Kings Road in 1977

It was pre-AIDS and post-Pill. It was like the permissiveness of the '60s. Everybody was fucking everybody. If I told you the people I shagged then, you wouldn't believe me. I fucked everybody. It wasn't a big deal. Girls would come over to see Steve [Jones] at Denmark Street. If Steve wasn't there and there wasn't anything on telly then, while we were waiting for Steve, we'd you know what…it was ridiculous.
Nils Stevenson

One of the reasons we went to all the punk gigs wasn't anything to do with the music, but because all the women had their tits out and were wearing suspenders. I used to think how could they say no when they were dressed like that. So I'd hang out next to the toilets or, hopefully, in the toilets. Still didn't have much luck.
Chris Sullivan

When I came over from New York, I thought everyone was gorgeous. I was like a kid in a candy shop. The high point for me was the sex and the rock'n'roll, and the low point was the drugs.
Gail Higgins Smith

I was living in Denmark Street, which was only five blocks away from the Roxy. If I felt like a shag, I'd go down there. I can't remember any of the bands, or even if the Banshees were on, because I was in the toilets shagging some bird, or two birds.
Nils Stevenson

A lot of punks were gay.
Andrew Czezowski

I must admit that the great punk sexual revolution passed me by. But then I was young, skint and Welsh – not the best recipe for pulling in London.
Chris Sullivan

I remember an S&M woman, who used to live in Pimlico. I often went to her place. She used to service MPs. She had a baseball bat and would put it up her arse and shit on a glass coffee table. Everyone used to hang around there. She had all the drugs.
Steve Walsh

I had the major hots for Siouxsie. It couldn't be love because that wasn't on in that scene. You couldn't show affection. You were in denial about affection. It could only be sex.
Nils Stevenson

Left: Sexually emancipated revellers • Opposite: Cherry Vanilla and pipe

SEX

was as casual as a handshake. It was ridiculous. Nils Stevenson

I was having sex with millions of people at Louise's. I was dragging people into the toilets like there was no tomorrow. Sex was really good fun. We did what we wanted, we wore what we wanted and took no prisoners. The '70s were the last decade we could do literally anything we wanted to sexually without ever worrying. We had the lot – warts, gonorrhoea and syphilis. It didn't matter. You just went to the clinic and got it sorted out. I'd recognize so many people in the clinic – it was a sort of social centre. It was brilliant. Alan Jones

'White Riot'.

Single by the Clash

I'd auditioned for London SS, which didn't go that well, and I thought that was the end of it…until I met Mick Jones in Portobello. I was having a hard time at the art college because I wanted to do life drawing, but nobody wanted to teach it, so I expressed my enthusiasm for the arts by getting involved with music. Mick said, 'Come round to my penthouse,' which was a council block, and we proceeded to go over these chord shapes. That was a disaster 'cause Mick didn't have the patience and I'd never touched an instrument in my life. We decided it was a waste of time for both of us and that we should get hold of a bass 'cause it's only got four strings and I could learn parrot fashion, which is pretty much what I did in the beginning. Then I met Keith Levene, who was a friend of Mick's, and we got pally and suddenly it was me and Mick and Keith rehearsing together. Then I had this brainwave. Why don't I save time by putting stickers on the fret of the guitar? 'cause Mick'd say, 'This bit goes from F and then to C and then G and all you need to do is get one hand pumping away and put your fingers on these bits.' With the stickers I knew exactly where to put my fingers, and to this day Mick calls it the Paul Simonon school of music, which even Don Letts has joined 'cause he used to write the notes on his keyboards when he was in Big Audio Dynamite.
Paul Simonon

The Clash were all nice guys – really down to earth.
Jock Scott, stand-up poet

I couldn't work out why Mick wanted me in his band. His best mate Tony was a bass player, so why did he need me? Basically, what happened was that Bernie said to Mick, 'You need a new group – get one together with Paul.' This all came about because Bernie had worked a lot with the Pistols. It was Bernie who got Rotten in the Pistols, even though they weren't sure about it because Steve Jones was the singer at the time. Bernie had got

involved with the T-shirts and all the early Pistols' stuff, but fell out with Malcolm and went about trying to get his own group together, which involved me and Mick initially.
Paul Simonon

I used to see Strummer a lot in the 101ers. He was great, but the band were like pub rock.
Clive Langer

We were looking for a singer, and we'd spent what felt like a few years, but was probably months, at Riverside Studios. Wally Nightingale, who used to be in the Pistols' original line-up, knew somebody who knew somebody who had access to the space. We would rehearse there with this guy called Billy Watts. We saw Joe playing in the 101ers and thought he'd be perfect for our group 'cause our singer didn't cut it and left. Bernie approached Joe and said, 'Do you want to join this group? You've got 48 hours to make up your mind.' A couple of hours later Bernie said to Joe, 'Forget the 48 hours. I want a decision now.' This would be '75 going on to '76.
Paul Simonon

I remember when Paul Simonon met the Ramones at the Roundhouse. Johnny asked him, 'What do you do? Are you in a band?' Paul said, 'Well, we just rehearse. We call ourselves the Clash but we're not good enough.' Johnny said, 'Wait till you see us – we stink, we're lousy, we can't play. Just get out there and do it.' And they did within a few weeks.
Danny Fields, ex-manager, the Ramones

We first played under the name the Clash at the Mucky Duck in Sheffield with the Pistols. That was with Keith Levene in the group as well. That was my first time on stage. Fortunately, I knew basically how to play the songs, but I never learnt how to tune the guitar. So in the middle of a set Mick used to have to come over and tune it for me. I remember we actually got a review that said we were rubbish and '…can you believe it, the guitarist has to go over and tune the bass player's guitar' but it didn't bother me. It was interesting 'cause I think quite a few hip characters picked up on the grapevine what the Pistols had been doing and went to check them out. Of course, we went on tour as the support group, and for us it started from there. It was our first show. I'd been playing for about six months.
Paul Simonon

I suppose the way to explain the difference between the Sex Pistols with McLaren and the Clash with Bernie Rhodes is by that old joke about the two bulls sitting at the top of a hill looking at a herd of young, nubile cows. The younger bull says, 'Hey, come on, let's run down and shag us a few cows!' The older and more experienced bull looks at him sideways and says in a slightly superior tone, 'I've a better idea. Let's walk down and shag them all.' The Clash eventually shagged more cows – metaphorically speaking.
Chris Sullivan

I'd never met anybody like Bernie before, and haven't since. I really liked his aggressive attitude and sort of found him a challenge. I used to go up to his house a lot when the group was moving along, and we'd talk about albums and artwork and posters and all sorts of stuff, so I got on well with Bernie. He'd say, 'What do you think about South Africa?' Or, 'What would you do if you had £100?' Unfortunately, the drummers that arrived for the try-outs were subjected to this as well and they didn't know whether they were joining a group or a political party. Bernie was just sounding everybody out on where they stood and what they wanted from a group. It was always a bit more than being in a band.
Paul Simonon

Up until now I thought everything was the cat's knackers and every group was great. I used to go to all the concerts…that's all I did, until somehow I stopped believing in it all. I just couldn't face it. I suppose the main influences are Mott the Hoople, the Kinks, the Stones, but I just stopped believing. Now, what's out there [points out the window] that's my influence.
Mick Jones of the Clash in *Sniffin' Glue*, 28 September 1976

I suppose our influence was early '60s mods, but the skinhead thing in the late '60s was an important element too. There was a lot of attention to detail, like when you put your braces on, you had the clips at the back together, not separated, 'cause then you'd look like a farmer. All these little things were important, a hangover from the mod thing, so with that on board, as well as the Jamaican Rude Boy two-tone suit, it was always to do with trying to look sharp. This was difficult when you depended on second-hand clothes.
Paul Simonon

I remember the drummer Terry Chimes, he was a good drummer and a great bricklayer, but all he talked about was bricklaying. We'd be backstage and talking about girls and drugs, sort of real rock'n'roll and he'd be talking about building a fucking wall.
Walter Lure

If all we've achieved is someone wanting my autograph, then we've gone wrong.
Joe Strummer, Clash guitarist and singer, in *Rock Confidential*

Look! The situation's far too serious for enjoyment.

Joe Strummer in *Sniffin' Glue*, 28 September 1976

With all those elements in the Clash, it was great, brilliant. We don't have groups like that any more. Groups try to be like *they* were, but fall short, by a fucking long chalk. They were the real thing, man. Jock Scott **There were always two camps in London. The Sex Pistols were about Chelsea and Soho. The Clash, who were a slightly more earnest bunch, were about Notting Hill – a more west London kind of thing. They were more rootsy and much more politically motivated. They actually believed there was a redeeming social side to life, whereas the Sex Pistols were hedonistic and didn't give a fuck about anything, which I always thought was the right attitude.** Steve Walsh The Sex Pistols and their following always had an air of decadence about them, whereas the Clash were the complete opposite. Which quality is the most important depends on your point of view. Stephen Colegrave **They're the most important group in the world at the moment. I believe in them completely. All I said about them in the past is crap. With this single 'White Riot', they've proved that they have been working. Nothing but hard work could produce a sound like they've got. I can't wait to get the album.** Mark Perry, *Sniffin' Glue*, issue 8, March 1977 When I heard the first Clash single 'White Riot' I went on about it for almost two months. It sounded angry and I thought it was called 'Quite Right', so I was gesticulating and being angry and singing, 'Quite right, quite right, quite right an all', and do you know what? Quite right too. Dempsey **We had a guy, Mickey Foot, who was essentially a sound man. There was a lot of suggestions from Mick and Bernie, but me and Joe didn't really have a clue. I remember some technician said to Joe that we needed to have separation, and Joe said he didn't like the sound of separation and he didn't want it 'cause me and Joe were just into banging the songs out. The Pistols were produced by Chris Thomas, who made them sound really good, but maybe he lost something in the production. Our sound was really quite raw and bare.** Paul Simonon The Clash were great to watch, not listen to. Helen Wellington Lloyd **I'd rather play to an audience and them not enjoy it, if we were doing what we thought was honest.** Joe Strummer in *Sniffin' Glue*, issue 3½, 28 September 1976 The Clash were very earnest politically from the first album onwards. *White Riot*, *Police and Thieves*, *Combat Rock*, *Sandinista*, etc. were all politically motivated. That is maybe why they were so good live – they really believed in what they said and were committed. Chris Sullivan **They had a whole lot of commitment. They were good, really good. I was with them when *Sniffin' Glue* interviewed them. It was funny because Mick Jones and Joe Strummer were mumbling on about politics, and in the middle of it Paul Simonon goes, 'Does anyone want a ginger biscuit?' Mark Perry didn't put that in his article. I thought 'ginger biscuit' was the most relevant comment for the article, never mind anarchy, chaos and bloody politics. They were bloody earnest, the Clash.** Steve Walsh The Clash weren't irreverent enough for me. I liked them, the music was fine, but I needed irreverence, not politics. Nils Stevenson **I spent a lot of time with Joe and the band through that period, and they were all as sound as a pound those boys in that group. I think they had some unnecessary stick for what they actually achieved. Joe's the same age as me and from a slightly different background, but I always thought he was a gem. You know, he did care about the social angle and the fans and what was actually happening at the time. Sound as a fucking pound.** Jock Scott At the time of the Anarchy tour I couldn't stand the music, but they were great guys. Later on, when they got a better drummer, they got more professional. They were great guys. I loved Paul, Mick and the rest of the gang, and Joe. Joe was the one who actually spouted the communist propaganda or whatever. On the bus he'd go through this political agenda. I really don't think he took it seriously, but I think he might have been trying to convince himself. Walter Lure **There was a method with Bernie. He did fire them up and inflame situations, even though some were unintentional, but in the end he sort of claimed it was all intentional. It doesn't matter: he was one of these catalysts. The Bernie I met back then was a major buzz…one of the intellectuals that gave the movement depth, just as Malcolm and Vivienne did.** Don Letts The Clash album is like a mirror. It reflects all the shit. It shows us the truth. To me it is the most important album ever released. It's as if I'm looking at my life in a film. A story of life in London. Playing in and out of the flats. A school that didn't even know what an O-level was. A job that sat me behind a desk and nicked my brain. All that shit is no longer in the dark. The Clash tells the truth. Mark Perry, *Sniffin' Glue*, issue 8, March 1977 **I was surprised that it went to number 12 straight away, considering we sort of banged it out over a couple of weekends, but then again, we'd had like a year and a half of getting those songs together. I remember me and Joe walking up the street thinking, 'What are we worried about now that we've got an income?' Before that we were just financially boracic [skint].** Paul Simonon Michael Jones – well, you know if he hadn't been there, with all that guitar stuff, it would have sounded radically different. I love his guitar playing, you know. I always like to hear a nice guitar player, whether it's John McLaughlin or fuckin' Chet Atkins. I thought Mick Jones was extraordinarily good and very deliberate…he stole all the best licks and gave them a lovely sound. Paul Simon too is always bang on the money; he knows exactly what's going on. Jock Scott **I made all the Clash videos. I feel honoured to be associated with them. Our lives have become interconnected for so many reasons that it actually goes beyond words. I would say that I worked in the shadow of the Clash and have been inspired by them. I was lucky enough to be close to them.** Don Letts The reggae thing was really before punk and it was the only music that had anything to say. I used to spend a lot of time with Bernie and we both had an interest in reggae. It was talking about things you understood, like politics with a small 'p', social situations – it was real. Bernie kept saying, 'Joe, you should write about things that affect you,' which is exactly what Jamaican music had going for it. It was rebel music: they wouldn't play it on the radio stations unless it was like a Culture Club cover of 'Everything I Own'. You couldn't hear Big Youth on the radio at all – it was a totally underground thing. It was an influence that eventually came through in the Clash because I grew up in Brixton and Ladbroke Grove. I was living with this music, just as Rotten did in Finsbury Park. Paul Simonon **They called me Don Letts DJ, and because of that the Clash used to take me out on the road on their tours DJ'ing. I took this dub reggae sound across the length and breadth of England.** Don Letts I thought the Clash were great. There were three bands I really loved: the Sex Pistols, the Clash [and] Subway Sect. I really adored Subway Sect. They were sort of in the Clash/Bernie Rhodes stable. I still think that first Clash tour they did on their own was one I kind of followed around…down to Hastings and up to St Albans. They were a great band. There was that fantastic moment when I went down with all the Ealing lot, Graham Ball and all them guys, down to Hastings. We all had on brothel-creepers and winkle-pickers and tight jeans and leather jackets. The police stopped us because they thought we'd come down to beat up the local punks, who had school uniforms and safety-pins. We were like, 'We are the punks.' Robert Elms **I followed the Clash all over. To me, coming from Wales with all the unemployment and everything, the Clash gave me something I could identify with. At first I was too young to see any political relevance in punk, but later I saw what they were all talking about when I had to find a job. The other thing was that they always had Don Letts playing the records, and we had always loved black music, especially reggae, which was a very working-class thing. The Clash had the whole package and I think they really changed a lot of people's outlook regarding politics and race. These were really big issues then, and are today. The difference is that today nobody cares.** Mark McCarthy

Captain wore a nurse's uniform, Dave drove around in a hearse and Rat set his drum kit on fire. Erica Echenberg

I was in London SS, but I fell out with the rest of the band when they auditioned Rat Scabies and didn't pick him, even though he demolished the drum kit. I thought he was great. He played like Keith Moon, but was nuttier. So Dave and I formed the Damned. Rat cleaned toilets for a living with Ray at the Fairfield Halls in Croydon. Ray became Captain Sensible. Rat arranged for Ray to audition with a tall guy with spiky hair. The tall guy didn't show up. When we met him again later he was calling himself Sid Vicious.
Brian James, guitarist, the Damned

The Damned was one of the very first punk bands I heard. It was great to be able to hear covers of Iggy and the Stooges' 'No Fun' and 'Raw Power' live on stage. Their own stuff was pretty good too.
Nigel Wingrove

I went downstairs at the Hope and Anchor and fell in love with Brian James. He became my boyfriend for the next 10 years. It wasn't just Brian; the rest of the band were unlike anyone I'd met before. I had never met someone called Rat, and certainly not with a real rat hanging from his earlobe. It was a band of real individuals. That's probably why it didn't last very long. Dave was quite Goth, Captain was cartoon, Brian a rocker and Rat was like Keith Moon. Of course, it all changed when Stiff Records took them on. Their marketing was much slicker and the gigs bigger.
Erica Echenberg

This guy from Caterham comes in while we're rehearsing and, fuck me, he's got scabies: he's itching all over, sitting behind the drum kit. I remember Bernie putting newspapers on all the seats, paranoid he'd catch something. That night, when we rehearsed with this guy, who was then Chris Miller, this rat just came out and stood in the middle of the studio. Somebody dropped a brick on the rat and killed it, and we started calling Chris Miller Rat Scabies because he had scabies and we killed the rat. Three weeks later we're in the Portobello Road and, fuck me, Chris Miller comes walking towards us and he's wearing a black T-shirt with a rat on the front and the words Rat Scabies.
Tony James, bass guitarist, Generation X

The Damned weren't as political as the Clash, or as fashion-conscious as the Sex Pistols, but they were great fun, especially live. The Damned fans were quite different – a mix of gothic and T-Rex-type people like Dave, serious guitar people like Brian, and boiler girls, who were any old girls who wanted to get dressed up in ripped clothes and who fancied Rat and Captain. In fact, Rat and Captain used to play a game based on who could sleep with the ugliest boiler girl. But the band was very innovative. They were on record, TV and touring America before either the Clash or the Pistols. It was difficult to keep the group together when Rat left. Brian was never really a punk. He had far wider ambitions, whereas the rest of the band didn't take themselves very seriously. So in 1978 they split up and Brian moved into heavy rock.
Erica Echenberg

Above: The Damned (Dave Vanian, Captain Sensible, Brian James and Rat Scabies) • Opposite: The Buzzcocks (Steve Diggle, Pete Shelley, Howard Devoto and John Maher)

Peter Shelley of the Buzzcocks was so fucking funny with that Woolworth's guitar and those green tights. Nils Stevenson

To be honest, we loved them. The Buzzcocks weren't stereotypical angry punks. Peter Shelley looked like an awful retarded prick. He looked mad, but you just loved him. His lyrics were so funny. All of it was brilliant. They produced great three-minute singles. I wish I understood how they got their label together.
Nils Stevenson

I liked the Buzzcocks. When they managed to put out their single [the 'Spiral Scratch' EP] in 1976, I thought that was amazing.
Marco Pironi

I didn't think much of the Buzzcocks. I didn't get it.
Gene Krell

The Buzzcocks were great when Howard Devoto was in the band. They were really good when he was singing.
Paul Simonon

Even though Howard Devoto always struck me as being a wired guy, I must admit to being shocked when I heard that he'd left the Buzzcocks. It seemed to me that Devoto

needed some form of expression. With the release of their EP 'Spiral Scratch' and [the resultant] interest from a couple of major record companies, the Buzzcocks have got the chance to break into bigger things, which means bigger audiences, and bigger responses.
Sniffin' Glue, issue 5, November 1976

The day we wrote 'Boredom', Howard was working a night shift at the tie factory, and during the night he'd written these words. I looked at these words and before he went to bed, I wrote the music. We got reviewed on our first concert, and I even got a name check. As soon as the magazine came out, I rushed out and bought three copies of it: instant stardom. I was thrilled because it was actually about doing things and entering the mystique of being written about. There was no turning back then…
Pete Shelley in *England's Dreaming*

At the time Malcolm McLaren was really excited about the way punk was taking a hold in Manchester. He felt his message was working. After all Howard [Devoto] and Pete [Shelley] had simply walked up at a gig and

offered to put the Pistols on. He was also shrewd enough to notice that Pete Shelley was taking money at the door at the first concert, because the Buzzcocks still weren't complete, and then actually playing in the support band at the next gig a month later. That was proof for him that DIY punk was working somewhere other than London. Then the Buzzcocks took it one stage further and became the first band to get a punk single out completely independently, simply by borrowing a few hundred quid. 'Spiral Scratch' was a really important release because it sold direct simply by word of mouth. It proved to people like Geoff Travis at Rough Trade that there was a future for real independent record labels.
John Shearlaw

For me that first burst of energy started to die out after the Pistols' released 'God Save the Queen'. That felt pretty incredible, but things were moving on. My life turned round when I got involved. I'm sure hundreds of thousands of people felt that things had opened up to them. There was a change of all kinds of guards.
Howard Devoto

What was exciting about Subway Sect was their total lack of interest in anything at all.

Marco Pirroni

I don't know if anyone else liked them. I know my friend Debbie and I liked them. We were probably their only fans, but they didn't give a shit. They were totally passive. They had a complete apathy about everything they were doing. For example, when they supported the Clash, the guitarist broke a string. When someone in a band breaks a string, you either swap guitars or you change the string as quickly as you can to get the gig under way again. But they didn't bother. They just stood there, and Vic Godard laid down on the stage until Mick Jones [of the Clash] rushed on and changed the string for them. He knew that if he hadn't done it, they would have stood there all night. They just didn't care what anyone thought.
Marco Pirroni

Subway Sect perform a very subdued set [at the 100 Club] but Malcolm thinks they are a better bet than Siouxsie.
Nils Stevenson

Subway Sect – I really liked them.
Paul Simonon

This band are real punks. Vic Godard still wants to dribble when he's 25. Their music is very simple, usually using just two or three chords, but the strength of the band's personality as a whole makes up for their lack of expertise. They deserve more gigs, more chances to show how much they're worth. Rumour has it that a small record company called Warm are interested in 'em. A band like this needs to be heard. They're an example to every kid who wants to do something positive.
Sniffin' Glue, Christmas special, December 1976

Vic Godard started doing that lounge music just so he could have a lie-down on stage.
Chris Sullivan

I thought I wasn't going to like going on stage, but when you get up there it's just like you're one of the audience. When we play I always take the attitude that we're just practising in front of a load of people. So it seems to me we do exactly the same when we're practising as when we play live. There's only one difference – when we practise and we do something wrong we stop, but when we play live and we do something wrong we just carry on.
Vic Godard, *Sniffin' Glue*, issue 5, November 1976

They were not huge.
John Baker, record mogul

I interviewed the Subway Sect for my fanzine when they came to Plymouth. They said no one had ever interviewed them before, so I did and they were very pleased.
Nigel Wingrove

They were great. I think Vic Godard must have been on heroin before anyone else.
Alan Jones

Billy Idol, who was to be the guitarist in the Banshees, has now left Chelsea and formed Generation X.

Nils Stevenson

Generation X may well be the punk rock group that many people have been waiting for. [Their] songs [have] lyrics about change and revolution, but with melodies cute enough for 'boy meets girl'.
Tony Parsons, *New Musical Express*, 27 January 1977

We made three singles: 'Your Generation' was the first one. The great thing was we did a stint at the Marquee Club, where we played every Thursday for four weeks. The first single came out then and went in the Top 40, which was a big deal in those days. Went on *Top of the Pops*. It was a dream to be on that because proper groups went on *Top of the Pops*. We never had this problem about going on television, we so wanted to be stars. After *Top of the Pops*, we did 'Ready, Steady, Go'. We worked with Phil Weyman, the legendary producer who produced all the Sweet hits. We wanted him because he produced 'Ballroom Blitz'. He did our first few records. Martin Rush produced the others, which we recorded in two days. It seemed a long time. It takes two days just to do bass and drums now. How times have changed.
Tony James

Billy Idol's voice constantly surprises me with its flexibility and range. Thrashing around stage during songs, his face [goes] into contortions befitting of a generation's crooner… Both guitarists play with [a] confidence that must reflect [their] pride in the material. I don't usually bother with lyrics but [those] that I've caught, to songs like 'Listen', 'Above Love', 'Youth' and, already a classic, 'Ready Steady Go', can't be dismissed with a routine adjective… Some people look upon Generation X as [the] black sheep because they're the 'pop group' of the lot…however, when the detractors write a 'Youth', I'll listen to them.
Sniffin' Glue, issue 12, Aug–Sep 1977

Generation X, who signed with Chrysalis four weeks ago, have their debut 45 'Your Generation' released today. The single is destined to be a theme song for the New Wave movement in its stance of 'trying to forget your generation…your generation don't mean a thing to me'.
George Gimarc, *Punk Diary 1970-1979*

Generation X were never taken that seriously mainly because Billy is too bloody good-looking.
Chris Sullivan

This ['Your Generation' single] is dreadful garbage. It doesn't do anything for me, and the Ramones do this sort of thing much better… [If you] hear it first thing in the morning, you'll want to go straight back to bed. It's hideously recorded.
Elton John, *Sounds* magazine, 1 September 1977

Above left: Tony James and Billy Idol • Above right: John Towe

Generation X were one of my favourite bands. Their single 'Ready, Steady, Go' was amazing.

Jayne County

Generation X really came out of Chelsea, and when we were working with Chelsea, Billy and I were never happy with Gene October as the singer. We were doing a gig at the Nashville, and for the encore Billy and I planned to come back on and do a song that we'd written called 'Prove It'. Billy would sing, but we hadn't told Gene about it – pretty horrible when I look back. So we came on and we did the encore with Billy singing, and we decided that Billy should be the singer from then on. In those days Billy had the side parting and didn't have spiky hair. We chose Andrew Czezowski to be the manager of the band, but we had to find a guitarist as we had a gig booked for three or four weeks later. After literally years of not finding one with London SS, it seemed an impossible task, yet that very weekend Billy went out to a party at Fulham Arts Club and there was a little band playing in the youth club next door. Billy went out and took a look, then phoned me up all excited and said, 'I think I've found this bloke who could be the guitarist.' This bloke had long hair, he played brilliant and he was like 17. After he auditioned, we went, 'You're the bloke,' even though he was like a kid, 'cos we were in our 20s. He became the guitarist and we cut his hair short, which he hated, but the gig just seemed to work. So we became Generation X, after a paperback book that I'd found at Billy's house one day when we were round there. On the front it had Generation X in the very typeface that we used, and it was a book about mods and rockers in the '60s, so it seemed to be the right thing. This all happened in the space of a few weeks.
Tony James

We were the outsiders of punk.

Hugh Cornwell, guitarist and singer with the Stranglers, *Daily Mail*, 20 January 2001

I thought the Stranglers were brilliant, but then again, I suppose they weren't from punk origins. They were more like a rock band that turned, which is curious in itself. They were happening at the same time, but they weren't really punk.
Chris Duffy

They were quite good. I saw them live a few times. They had a few songs I liked, but they weren't part of the main scene of punk.
Walter Lure

The Stranglers were one of the first bands on the scene. I didn't really take to them the same way I did to the Pistols.
Nigel Wingrove

The Stranglers should have been called the Misfits – we were the outsiders of punk. I was bemused by the whole phenomenon then, and have no desire to be burdened with the label now. Unlike some other bands that emerged at the time, we did not have overnight success…we were older than the other punk bands, more melodic, and we had a keyboard, which was very uncool. But our first record coincided with punk and it was convenient to lump us in with that. When our audiences became more aggressive and started throwing things at us, we responded by becoming belligerent.
Hugh Cornwell, *Daily Mail*, 20 January 2001

The group consists of a very straight-looking drummer, who keeps a very sound beat throughout, an organist, who looks like he's just come home from Woodstock (real hippy-looking), a bass player who looks like a Ramone (leather, jeans, rubber) and a singer/guitarist who just looks scruffy. Together they add up to one of the most original groups I've seen on the pub circuit.
Sniffin' Glue, issue 2, August 1976

The Stranglers are always lumped in with the rest of the punk thing but to me they were just a straight pub rock band. The drummer could easily have been in the Eagles, they had a hippie keyboard player, Jean-Jacques Burnel, who looked like a New York punk but was not as interesting as his name implies, and a singer who looked as if he was old enough to know better. I thought they were fine. A lot of bands got lumped in with the whole punk bit, but bands like the Jam and the Stranglers were absolutely nothing to do with it, which is nothing to be ashamed of.
Stephen Colegrave

Above: Jean-Jacques Burnel, bass player and vocalist with the Stranglers

What do I have in common with those New Wave apostles, *les* Pistols? Well, class. Johnny Rotten's a Catholic too, isn't he?
John Cooper Clarke

He was like the most literate rapper ever seen.
John Shearlaw

Linda Stirling [a former girlfriend of Howard Devoto of the Buzzcocks, now an artist] was the first punk I ever saw. She had the bin-liner dress, the black lipstick and the safety-pin earring, and that was in 1975, before the Sex Pistols had played in Manchester. I was at the first gig, which would have had to be the size of Shea Stadium to hold everybody who said they were there, but I definitely was. The Pistols invented the whole package – the clobber, the attitude, the rules. It was just a dress code with me first off; definitely no cheesecloth shirts or flares. It was serendipitous: I looked like a punk already, so why not do the same thing with my own poetry?
John Cooper Clarke

I remember someone with a very long memory, and a great cross-cultural appreciation, calling John Cooper Clarke the New Wave's answer to George Formby [the 1930s music hall entertainer], and they were nearly right. They share a knowing madness peculiar to their time.
John Shearlaw

High energy was the buzzword; everything was speeded up. I took what poetry I had and speeded up the delivery. It was very rough to begin with. The reaction I got was the same as a lot of the bands, noise coming at you. But you're a poet; you can't turn the amp up and put your head down. You're on your jack. One person parroting is always going to struggle. Things got better once I'd been in the *NME*: the writers were on my side, and after that people would listen rather than throw bottles. I would have given up if they hadn't. I'm not a commando, yet there I was playing places you wouldn't want to find a poet. I was bottled off the stage early on, but that was in Glasgow and I was playing with Be Bop Deluxe [pre-punk pub rockers]. Once I started playing with punk bands, there was no problem.
John Cooper Clarke

Seeing this gaunt, suited figure taking the stage at punk gigs was unforgettable. He'd be dying of stage fright, on his own, and still rattling off machine-gun stanzas like he was making them up every time he drew breath. John Cooper Clarke defined the very British background everyone in punk shared, whether they realized it or not.
John Shearlaw

'Beazley Street' is a sort of evergreen, I suppose, which made it onto the education syllabus. Some guy even got an MA at Oxford on that work. I can look back on poems like 'I Married a Monster from Outer Space' and see how they were right for the time, and how they were interpreted. That one touched on racism in a way, which got me onto the Rock Against Racism circuit, I suppose.
John Cooper Clarke

I took what poetry I had,
then speeded up the delivery.
People thought I was a nutter.

John Cooper Clarke

Punk's poet laureate, John Cooper Clarke, used to be a mortuary attendant, and while his wasted looks and dress sense are an integral part of the Clarke experience, he will be remembered for the nasal whine of his street-smart poetry when he himself is pushing up daisies. Clarke first penetrated the public consciousness with the punk explosion of 1976. The fact that he survived as the warm-up man for the Buzzcocks and the Fall without being ripped to bloody rags is testimony to the power of his words. Johnny showed a generation that poetry could be rebellious while sharing the same concerns and speaking the same language as the man in the street.
Paul Dale, journalist and John Cooper Clarke fan

Up until punk, I was working in the light entertainment arena, getting myself booked into clubs and trying to find a poetry audience. But what was a poetry audience? Is there such a thing? My material was old movies, adverts, tabloidese, sex magazines, the more disposable aspects of daily life. It's all been said before, but it was about finding the universal in the particular. What punk brought to my poetry was velocity, a chance for it to be disseminated so much faster.
John Cooper Clarke

John Cooper Clarke would have stood out in any generation; he's still writing and performing now, and his observation is brilliant and unexpected.
John Shearlaw, music journalist

the rip-off riff's authentic ring
a singer who can't really sing
can only mean one fucking thing
punk rock revival
John Cooper Clarke, 'Punk Rock Revival', 2000

One minute we were awkward, slightly nerdy adolescents,
the next we were hometown heroes with a surfeit of 'in-depth' sociological journalistic features on us.

Andy Blade, singer with Eater, in *A Diary of the Punk Years*

Eater were the youngest group around. They were still at school. Dee Generate, their drummer, was only 14 at the time. Leee Childers took Eater under his wing.
Nils Stevenson

In the evening we'd be driven around London with the Clash, gate-crashing posh music business parties, meeting our pop star heroes, whilst discussing Punk's relevance, taking speed and getting off with girls, many (and, in some cases, many, many) years older than ourselves. The next morning we'd be back at school, throwing paper aeroplanes at Teacher. It was a brilliant double life.
Andy Blade, *A Diary of the Punk Years*

Eater were funny live. When I saw them at the Roxy, Andy Blade was chopping this huge pig's head up on stage with a big hatchet. There was blood all over the Roxy. It was mad. Andy was going completely mental, singing these crazy songs of his about being outside of things. Naturally, Leee fancied him like fuck. Even now, I can't say I really liked their records.
Nils Stevenson

I like it when old grannies laugh at me on the tube and we spit on 'em. We know what's happening in the world; they don't.
Dee Generate, drummer with Eater *Sniffin' Glue*, issue 6, January 1977

If we did get on *Top of the Pops*, it wouldn't be degrading. It means our record's selling well, which means…we're getting the message over.
Andy Blade, *Sniffin' Glue*, issue 6, January 1977

I used to laugh myself silly when I saw Eater in London. They were kids, and didn't do anything for me musically.
Walter Lure

Since the Pistols/Grundy thing exploded all over the nationals, Eater have had a lot of…publicity…as 'the band that's going to take over the Sex Pistols' audience'.
Sniffin' Glue, issue 6, January 1977

Eater were the last straw, the one that broke the camel's back, the salt in the wound, the nail in the bleedin' coffin. No more had to be said.
Frank Kelly

Above: Dee Generate of Eater

Ian Dury wasn't a punk act

by any stretch of the imagination, but he was a big influence on a lot of them. Gene Krell

I first saw Ian Dury front Kilburn and the High Roads at the Warwick Castle pub in Shepherds Bush in 1974. The DJ Charlie Gillett was singing their praises in *Let It Rock* magazine, and he was right on the button. There were very few characters like Ian Dury around. He had all the 'greaser' moves, he looked hard and he certainly knew his rock'n'roll. He'd always chuck in a few classics because that's what pub bands did. But there was a much harder, more confrontational edge to him, and the band's own stuff was funny, sarcastic…and somehow very new to us. We carried on the pilgrimage until Kilburn and the High Roads went their separate ways. But it was still a year in the wilderness before Dury got the Stiff make-over he needed and deserved… he was a great originator in everything from names to attitude to musical heritage.
John Shearlaw

The Kilburns were a complete exception to the general run of so-called pub bands. They had a range of unclassifiable music and strange lyrics, rebellious vignettes and sentimental fantasies from Ian Dury's teenage years. Both John Rotten and Madness came to see him and were obviously inspired by Ian's whole thing, which was to take the person he was and make it larger than life. I thought the Kilburns were completely original and unique.
Charlie Gillett, writer and broadcaster

When a lot of people who liked the energy and initial idea of punk found that it had all gone a bit daft, we all went onto Ian Dury. Both he and Deaf School were the only bands in '77 that were doing anything interesting.
Mark McCarthy

Ian Dury and Kilburn and the High Roads certainly influenced us, Madness, as well as the Pistols. Lydon on stage was pure Dury. The thing about him was that he was so English, so Dickensian, a real artful dodger, which is what Lydon would have loved to have been. He also took the music a step further away from the same old boring rock'n'roll riffs into funk music hall and beyond.
Suggs, singer with Madness

Dury comes on later with his carrier bags and Cockney bonhomie, throws millions of button badges out, in different colours, each with a word and an ampersand: sex &/drugs &/rock &/ roll &… all the musicians come on at the end for an extended encore of 'Sex & Drugs & Rock & Roll', during which the power breaks down and the crowd keeps the chorus going for what seems like forever.
Professor George McKay

Opposite and above: Ian Dury (second left) and the Blockheads

It's not a punk rock version
of the National Anthem,
but the boys' own genuine tribute
to the Queen. Malcolm McLaren in *The Filth and the Fury*

Malcolm was honest in one respect in that he said he had no control over us. And he didn't. [We had] a bloody good punch-up, in a limo, before a signing… It was a good fight too – 'No, you're the biggest cunt.' 'No, you're the worst cunt.' 'No, you're the cunt.' There was only one cunt I wanted to smack and that was Malcolm… Then the door opened, and we had to do the [A & M] signing.
Johnny Rotten in *The Filth and the Fury*

At the time we thought it was glamorous and newsworthy but, looking back, it seems crazy. They were just four scruffy blokes getting out of a car outside Buckingham Palace, then signing up [for A & M] before we all got moved on by the police. It was nothing really, but because it was the Pistols, it was the picture every newspaper wanted.
Richard Young, paparazzo photographer

This is a unique business opportunity to be linked with a new force in rock music which is spearheaded by this group. I believe the Sex Pistols will effect some major changes in rock music and we at A & M are excited by them, their music, and to have entered into a worldwide recording agreement.
Derek Green, managing director, A & M, March 1977

The company will not be releasing any product from the group [the Sex Pistols] and has no further association with them.
Derek Green's spokesperson, just one week later

I'm shellshocked. Four weeks ago I flew to Los Angeles to meet Herb Alpert and Gerry Moss, who head up A & M, and a week ago we signed up. They knew what they were getting. Managing director Derek Green even said that he wasn't offended by the group's behaviour and that he thought they were fresh and exciting. Then I got a telex from them, saying it was all over.
Malcolm McLaren in *The Filth and the Fury*

When we got to A & M Records, total bedlam broke out. The secretaries were terrified. Sid's foot was bleeding, I had a black eye and Malcolm was running around…then we got in a car and went to the studio where we were recording 'God Save the Queen'. It was just a totally mad day. The next day we woke up and Malcolm said, 'Well, A & M have fired you.'
Paul Cook

After the initial shock of getting fired by A & M, there was never any feeling that the band wouldn't get another deal.

The songs were there, and the interest was there. The idea was to keep all these record companies salivating until Malcolm got the deal he wanted with a really big company, which had to be either Polydor or Warner Brothers. We were talking to them all; big ideas were being put forward. The whole Hollywood idea had already taken seed with Malcolm – the band starring in a movie about themselves… The danger really was the stagnation, the Greater London Council ban on our gigs, the odd bit of trouble Sid was getting into.
John 'Boogie' Tiberi, Sex Pistols' tour manager, 1977-9

The Sex Pistols are like some contagious disease – untouchable. I keep walking in and out of offices being given cheques. You know, take the money and don't come back. What are you supposed to think about that? When I'm older and people ask me what I used to do for a living, I shall have to say, 'I went in and out of doors, getting paid for it.' It's crazy.
Malcolm McLaren in *The Filth and the Fury*

They've given up through fear and business pressure. They've kicked us in the teeth. We mean what we say. A record company is there to market records – not dictate terms.
Johnny Rotten in *The Filth and the Fury*

The Vortex kicked in and it was fantastic for me because I put the Banshees on.

Nils Stevenson

I was expelled from college three times, but I kept going back. We went to London for an evening lecture on design. I sneaked out of it, with a girl from college, and went to the Vortex. As Plymouth punks, we were intimidated by the London scene. We felt like yokels. The London punks were wearing all the gear; we were too poor. Nigel Wingrove **Up the pub at six, out three hours later, legless and ready to take on the Vortex. In the door, down the stairs, into the bar, then…anything can happen and it often does… We have fun, much to the disgust of the posers, who occasionally spare a cool, superior glance at the giggling huddle falling over and going 'Waaayyy!' at every familiar face. 'Look at them, [they're] not as cool as us, their hair's getting a bit long, too clean to be real punks.'** Sniffin' Glue, issue 12, Aug–Sep 1977 The Banshees had developed a following by playing the Roxy so much. This guy Dave Wood, of March Artists at CBS, had also booked them around the country. By the time the Vortex opened I had found my feet and knew how it was working. Nils Stevenson **The Vortex expanded to become London's first 24-hour punk venue and, as such, filled the gap left by the closure of the Roxy. It featured recorded music during the day, live bands at night and a record shop. The pre-publicity billed it has being 'What Carnaby Street was to mods…Hanway Street is to punks,' and in the main that was true.** Stephen Colegrave The Vortex, which opened with the Buzzcocks, the Fall and John Cooper Clarke, held a lot more people than the Roxy. It had a legal capacity of 600, but you could cram in many more punters than that. It became our [the Banshees'] staple source of income. Nils Stevenson **The opening night of the Vortex Sham 69 played on the roof followed by a camera crew. That's just how sad the whole thing had become.** Frank Kelly The Vortex was set up by Terry Draper and John Miller. They were seriously hard men. But we came away from there with good money because we got a percentage of the gate. It really felt like a second home. I knew how to work the punk system. The Banshees had got used to playing on a stage. They had learnt their craft. They had watched lots of films that Don Letts had shot at the Roxy, and learnt how to improve their act. I really felt that I was managing a professional band. Nils Stevenson **I took Tina Brown [later editor of *Vanity Fair*] to the Vortex. The Heartbreakers were playing there. It was the punk showcase. We went with Dan Loggins, whose brother, [singer] Kenny Loggins, was a client of mine. Dan was the A & R man at CBS. He said, 'Shall I sign the Clash?' I said, 'Yeah, why not? Sign anything. You're fucking desperate.' I was only 18 and stupid. But it was great to have a free drink. The Vortex didn't last very long. The record companies vacuumed it up and then said 'Fuck off'.** Alan Jones I remember gonorrhoea spreading from one end of the Vortex Club to the other. Ted Polhemus **It was a red-letter day. Danny Baker [journalist and later DJ] strode on to the Vortex stage and announced that Elvis was dead. The audience cheered. Baker panicked and started claiming that he wouldn't have been there if it hadn't been for 'the King'. A barrage of glasses was hurled at him and he dashed from the stage. He was very upset.** Nils Stevenson Everybody at the Vortex that night thought that the death of Elvis was funny. To me it only served to illustrate how much this rabble really did not understand. Chris Sullivan **[People] flung glasses and gobbed at Danny Baker when he tried to explain that you shouldn't cheer when a geezer snuffs it…[he said] Elvis went through worse shit 20 years ago than you ever did. Whatever he did with his last 15 years, Elvis was the bloke who started it all. Anyway, soon the jeers turned into cheers and a girl with a face about as attractive as a bus accident, who'd flung a glass at Dan, wanted to kiss him.** Sniffin' Glue, issue 12, Aug–Sep 1977 Punk was similar to Elvis in 1956. It had an attitude that said, 'Fuck you, if you don't like it – this is our music.' After all, Malcolm's big thing was rock'n'roll. It wasn't that different to Jerry Lee Lewis – just a different interpretation of the same old thing. Punk was another facet of rock'n'roll. It wasn't any different from seeing Elvis Presley 20 years earlier. It was just a difference in degree and dress code. I think rock'n'roll started dying the day punk died. A lot of people say punk started dying around the time of Elvis Presley's death. It was appropriate somehow. Paul Durden, former roadie, now scriptwriter

MON. DEC. 12TH

MENACE

SKUNKS

BACKLASH

Pic by Erica Echenberg

TUE. DEC. 13TH

ER

RAPED

MEMBERS

DICK ENVY

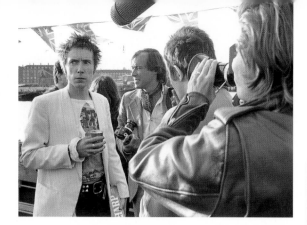

Above, top to bottom: Johnny Rotten; Richard Branson; Malcolm McLaren and Richard Branson

Vivienne Westwood was drunk and pissing over the side of the boat. That was the end for me. Alan Jones

Malcolm had all these weird ideas such as 'God Save the Queen' and doing the boat on the Thames for the Jubilee. These ideas were very special. They were very dramatic at the time. Perhaps more so than they appear now.
Joe Corré

Virgin arranged an 'alternative' celebration for the Queen's Silver Jubilee with a boat trip down the River Thames. My brother and I weren't invited, thank God, since the boat was boarded by the police and a lot of people were arrested. Paul Cook told me Malcolm and Vivienne were thrilled by the experience of being incarcerated, whereas for him and Steve Jones it wouldn't have been exactly a novel experience.
Nils Stevenson

When we went down the Thames on a boat for the Jubilee, the record people were there. All hell broke loose with the police. Malcolm got arrested. That was funny.
Paul Cook

It was awful. We were having a great time, drinking, smoking, food, everything. The next thing we knew, the police were following us. We had to stop. Someone had kicked the French photographer down. He got a bit

paranoid. These people [the Sex Pistols] loved being photographed, they loved to be in magazines, but they'd probably had too much to drink or too many drugs. They got a bit bolshie, so they kicked this Frenchman down the stairs.
Helen Wellington Lloyd

Six police boats…were pulling up next to the party boat and demanding it pull over to the nearest pier. The band then asked for requests and launched into a venomous version of Iggy Pop's 'No Fun'. The band played on while the boat was boarded and finally the power to [the] amplification was pulled. At the pier the River Police were joined by the Metropolitan Police, who then, in a very rough and surly manner, cleared the boat. Cameras were smashed, party-goers were pummelled and punched, and dragged away to the waiting police vans.
George Gimarc, Punk Diary 1970-1979

For me the whole thing ended with the boat party. I just couldn't stand it. I mean, I loved going on the boat. It was great to see everybody. Vivienne was drunk and pissing over the side of the boat. My one enduring image is of Vivienne in her anarchy shirt. She's holding on to the side-rail and literally pissing over the boat into the

Thames. Then we were surrounded. People started getting beaten up. I thought, 'That's the end. I'm not doing this any more.' I'd already had one brush with the law, not that I really cared about that. I decided this was the right end to the story. I just withdrew slightly and moved on. That was that.
Alan Jones

The psychos were taking over and the camp element were abandoning ship. Alan Jones, who was one of the most interesting dressers, was one of the first to drift away. It really wasn't his scene any more.
Nils Stevenson

The police were actually not far away anyway. I remember docking. Talk about a come-down. It had all been great. The Pistols were playing. There was a buzz, and then the night became so desolate. Vivienne started something and then the coppers dragged her off. Malcolm came to her assistance, but he was terrified, completely terrified. I wasn't arrested. A few of us got a cab home. I didn't know where Malcolm and Vivienne ended up – I wasn't going to the police station to find out. I was going home.
Helen Wellington Lloyd

Opposite, left to right: Kenny Morris, drummer with the Banshees, Vivienne Westwood, Malcolm McLaren and unidentified friend • Above: Guests arriving for the Jubilee boat party • Overleaf: Johnny Rotten • Page 253: The Sex Pistols (Sid Vicious, Johnny Rotten, Paul Cook and Steve Jones)

253

You don't write a song like 'God Save the Queen' because you hate the English race.
You do it because you love them and you're fed up with them being mistreated.

Johnny Rotten in *The Filth and the Fury*

One week after signing to A & M the Sex Pistols were sacked. They copped £75,000 for doing absolutely nothing. After being dismissed by the company, they celebrated in their offices in Oxford Street by swigging lager and chucking lager at an NBC crew who were hanging around. Twenty thousand copies of 'No Feelings' – the first A & M single – are sitting in some boring pressing plant doing nothing. The Sex Pistols have got one copy – a white label – and it is brilliant, from the 'God Save the Queen' intro to the 'No Future For Me/You' ending.
Sniffin' Glue, issue 8, March 1977

The Sex Pistols' current record, 'God Save the Queen', is at number one in the Capital Hit Line. But the IBA [Independent Broadcasting Authority], which administers the Broadcasting Act, has advised us that, particularly at this time, this record is likely to cause offence to a number of our listeners and have asked us not to play it in our normal programming.
Capital Radio announcement, June 1977

The Independent Broadcasting Authority has issued a statement to all UK radio stations saying that, in their opinion, the record was in breach of section 4:1:A of the IBA Act. This covers material that 'offends good taste or decency, or is likely to encourage or incite to crime, or

lead to disorder, or to be offensive to public feeling'. The BBC, as well as BRMB, Piccadilly, Clyde and Capital Radio, all refuse even to play a paid advertisement for the single. Robin Nash, producer for *Top of the Pops*, declared: 'It is quite unsuitable for an entertainment show like *Top of the Pops*'. It will be interesting to see what happens when the Sex Pistols release their debut album at the end of the month.
George Gimarc, *Punk Diary 1970-1979*

'God Save the Queen' was pretty unique. Britain abolishing the number one for the Sex Pistols was like their knighthood. But after that, the forces unleashed against them and within them meant the band was going to die a slow death unless it was knocked on the head.
Julien Temple, director, *The Filth and the Fury*

It alienated the entire country. If they'd hung us at Traitor's Gate, it would have been applauded by 56 million. 'God Save the Queen' was the alternative National Anthem. But it was never number one. There was no number one that week. Whatever we were saying and doing hit a nerve, a raw nerve.
Johnny Rotten in *The Filth and the Fury*

I really don't think what the band was singing about [the Queen] was that outrageous. They weren't saying 'Let's

kill her' or 'Let's fuck her'. They were pretty much pointing out what the truth was.
Steve Jones

We released 'God Save the Queen' in Jubilee week. When it was banned, that was even bigger news than Grundy. I think that was the pinnacle of our success. It all went downhill after that.
Paul Cook

For all the successes of the Jubilee cruise, things didn't work out so well afterwards. The single was banned, although the BBC didn't actually have charge of the charts at the time. In W.H. Smith's [a leading record retailer in the UK] they got people pulling off all those little stick-on plastic letters that made up the name of the record – so you'd get a blank where we were supposed to be. Meanwhile, Richard Branson [founder of Virgin Records] persuaded John [Rotten] to do *Top of the Pops*. It was Branson's way of getting out of his one-hit label thing, moving Virgin on as a record label. We filmed 'God Save the Queen' with Mike Mansfield and it was terrible, in the same way that *Top of the Pops* is terrible. It was a difficult time for all of us, trying to record the album, with John getting attacked in the street.
John 'Boogie' Tiberi

Malcolm wanted me to get the Sex Pistols out of his way, so we went to Berlin.

McLaren was on the verge of getting a record deal with Virgin, on his terms, so the pressure was on me to take them [the Sex Pistols] away and out of his hair. I started by making suggestions, with the emphasis on having a **good time.** Paris was out because they'd been there. Berlin was the strongest contender because Bowie had lived there, and he was a big **hero** of the band, especially John and Sid, so it was settled there and then.

I'd spoken to a rich German woman I'd met called Nora Springer [Johnny Rotten's future wife, although they didn't meet on this trip] to find out where Bowie had stayed in Berlin. She thought it was the **Kempinski,** which was the best hotel in Berlin, so off we went. Sophie [from the management company] arrived at the airport next morning with Sid, who had a brand new British Visitor's Passport. I was introduced for the first time to Sid's luggage: a dirty pink canvas bag that contained no socks, no **underwear,** a dirty pair of jeans, a top or two, an original Seditionaries' Anarchy shirt and a pair of brothel creepers. Steve and Paul arrived together at Heathrow. John had to make his own way. By later standards, they were well behaved.

I left London with a huge wad of cash and five return tickets. I kept the band outside in the cars while I booked in at the hotel, which was a work of **diplomacy,** but they liked the look of the cash. We could all relax at last. We had successfully escaped the tedium of London.

The day we arrived we had a slap-up meal in the hotel restaurant. It was grand. Sid ordered a steak and everybody copied him. When it arrived, it was covered in a sauce that pissed Sid off, so he sent it back. It returned with the sauce cleaned off. Sid didn't like that either. He was very **fussy** about his food, but everybody else enjoyed theirs. The bill was huge, so from then on, it was sandwiches only from room service.

I gave the band a daily allowance for them to eat out. When they got back to London, they tried to buy some breakfast at the airport. **John paid** with a pocketful of deutschmarks: he hadn't spent a single pfennig throughout the whole trip.

On the first evening in Berlin, we went out to a club, a **transvestite** club run by someone called Romy Haag, appropriately enough. John thought these were the best sort of clubs, and that 'these' people knew how to **enjoy** themselves. Nora had given me the name of the club, the one that Bowie apparently went to every night. The drinks were green and very expensive. There was no sign of Bowie. And nobody had heard of the Sex Pistols.

I hired a Beetle and took the boys for a tour of the **Berlin Wall.** Sid's British Visitor's Passport would not get him through Checkpoint Charlie. I didn't want to leave him behind, so we went around to the little viewing points, climbed up and looked over. It was desolate – there wasn't any graffiti in those days. We were quite **hypnotized** by the sense of looking back in time. I filmed the band on 16 mm, in black and white, outside the checkpoint, thinking it was something we could use for our film compilation.

Paul was getting impatient and Steve thought it was time for lunch. We watched a Bruce Lee film near a **bombed-out** church while eating *wurst* and mashed potato with toothpicks. Steve liked the food, and then went **whoring.**

We visited the club again (we went there every night). Paul wanted to go home early, as he didn't want to spend any more money. He was pissed, so I had to give him a lift in the car. Unfortunately, when I turned off the main street to park outside the hotel, I forgot it was a one-way street. We were hit by a V2 driven by an ex-**Luftwaffe** pilot, who took off the front of the Beetle. We both needed a stiff drink. When the police arrived at our hotel room, we offered them one too.

It had come as some surprise to find this city and its **decadent** lifestyle. The nightclubs were full of kids who'd travelled hundreds of miles to party for the weekend, very different to Britain. We were quite envious. We were aware that we were going to have to go home soon. Back to the **pathetic** scene of London – the speed, the smell of Watney's Red Barrel and the punk poverty.

Despite the wad of cash, money soon became a problem in Berlin. I telegraphed Sophie at Glitterbest [the Pistols' management company] asking for **more funds.** Upstairs, everybody but John was hungry. I found him in his room watching East German television. 'This place is really good. There are so many different channels on the TV, and most of them are **Communist,**' he told me. 'I want to come back here one day. I'm going to write a song about it.' He'd already started putting down the lyrics to 'Holidays in the Sun' on a fag packet or something before we left.

Berlin was a world away from a country where we couldn't play, and couldn't even walk down the street. All the band's **optimism and ideals** were finally freed up. I felt we really had started the ball rolling for the film, the next stage. I was shooting the band outside the Berlin Wall, in black and white on 16 mm, and it was looking great.

Because no money was sent from England (Malcolm had put a block on any further funds), I decided to **quit** while we still had some left, and to fly back to England the next day. We spent one last night out on the town. It was very **tempting** to do a runner, but I thought that the authorities would probably have caught up with us at the airport. We signed for A & M straight after getting back from Berlin.
John 'Boogie' Tiberi

Berlin was depressing. It was horrible. # I didn't like it. Steve Jones

There was no sign of Bowie in Berlin
and nobody had heard of the Sex Pistols.

John 'Boogie' Tiberi

ACHTUNG
Sie verlassen jetzt
West-Berlin

ACHTUNG
Sie verlassen jetzt
West-Berlin

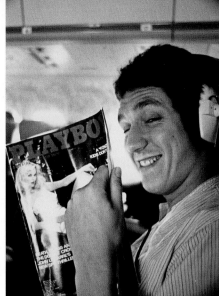

The tour manager had worked with Abba.

John 'Boogie' Tiberi

We had to get out of London and away from the round of press, promotion and aggravation that was dogging the band. We'd hooked up with a very nice agent in Sweden, who was completely 'on message'; he responded to our situation perfectly. We were back to basics – small clubs that virtually any band starting out could have played – and it was great. We travelled around in a Mercedes bus, with all the gear bunged in the back, and had a fucking great time. The tour manager had worked with Abba, while the audiences were always kids – young people out for a good time – which is what we needed. Steve and Paul, even when they weren't playing, which of course they hadn't been, were so fucking professional. Every day they would practise, practise, practise. No matter what else was happening, they were the real pros. They just loved playing. The whole Swedish experience, then a couple of gigs in Holland afterwards helped point the way to the Spots tour.
John 'Boogie' Tiberi

We flew to the next gig. Since they hadn't been expecting me there wasn't much room on this little plane. I had to sit on Johnny Rotten's lap while it took off. He didn't stop complaining. He kept saying: 'Oh, you're a fat bastard – get off me!' He was a moany git anyway. This time it was obvious he didn't want me there. The whole thing about Sweden was getting away from all the trouble they'd had. They really did need the break. Then it nearly all finished there. After a while, Sid Vicious found his way up front and proceeded to fly the plane…
Alf Martin, editor, *Record Mirror*

I filmed nearly the whole Stockholm gig as part of the ongoing film concept. It meant organizing the cameras locally, then giving them Virgin's number in London, so we didn't have to pay on the spot. We did it on the second of the two nights. It was the biggest production number we'd done up until then, with two cameras. The whole idea was to capture this event from the historical perspective. You can look back with hindsight and see it was the right thing to do, but there was a strong imperative, even then, to get it while we could. It was extraordinary, and the footage really worked. We edited back in London, working with Julien Temple, who'd come up with the idea of filming off the monitor to complete *Number One* (a Sex Pistols documentary). We were able to project footage from Stockholm at gigs as a

valid film of the band in action, a real demonstration of their power. Without it there would have been no record because there simply were no gigs in the UK… Julien filmed later gigs at Penzance on the Spots tour and Huddersfield, and, together with the Stockholm footage, they form an incredible picture of the Sex Pistols in action, a chance for history to judge them at their best.
John 'Boogie' Tiberi

The only time the whole thing really became a drag was when Malcolm sent the Pistols over to Holland and Scandinavia. He thought Sid was getting into smack because he didn't have enough to do, but if you're trying to keep someone away from smack, you don't send them to Holland. So we all used to take turns in staying up all night with Sid just to try and keep it away from him, and he still found it. You'd be a nervous wreck afterwards. John started to take himself too seriously, I think. While he was just 'out there' having a laugh because he didn't

believe it could all be true or he didn't think anybody was listening to this ranting madman, that was fine. But then he started believing it and you see that now: he's just boorish and he's got a horribly inflated opinion of his own importance. The others were getting pissed off with John's attitude and Sid doing smack, so the whole thing just started turning in on itself – everyone was going round the bend. Mind you, it was good getting a phone call from the *Sun* saying we were banned from Finland. We phoned up the Finnish embassy at three in the morning to ask if this was true. We thought we'd get a secretary or something but we actually got the ambassador. That was funny. I thought Finland was important.
Roadent, aka Steve Connolly, Pistols' and Clash roadie

Everything was neat on the tour until the final confrontation in Stockholm, which was nothing to do with the gigs really. The local equivalent of the Hell's Angels (I've forgotten their actual name, but these are older guys, bikers, and

really quite menacing) were outside picking fights. They were aware that something was going on, but didn't understand it, and were getting into violence instead. I had to get the band away and out of there. It was the *only* time on tour with the Sex Pistols that we had the actual full-on police escort – accelerators pushed to the floor, all the blue lights flashing, the shouting and the crowd…now that was fantastic!
John 'Boogie' Tiberi

Basically the Sex Pistols were being banned everywhere in the UK, so were forced to leave the country. I found out they were in Sweden, and I was on a bloody train for nine hours before I even got near to where they were playing. It was a sort of social club attached to a factory; the audience seemed to be the sons and daughters of those who worked there. These were real young kids, and the atmosphere was more like you'd get at a weekly social…
Alf Martin

Above, top: A Pistols' audience in Scandinavia • Above, lower: Roadies setting up the stage for a Pistols' gig

259

ELVIS PRESLEY IS DEAD

THE IDOL: Pop king Elvis Presley as his millions of fans throughout the world knew him.

ELVIS PRESLEY, the unchallenged king of Rock n' Roll, is dead.

And the 42-year-old superstar who had millions of adoring fans throughout the world, was alone when the end came yesterday.

He collapsed yesterday afternoon in the sprawling mansion in Memphis, Tennessee, that he had turned into a fortress against the world.

Elvis was found by his road manager. He gave him the kiss

From
ANTHONY DELANO
in New York

of life, but could not revive him. Elvis was then rushed to hospital, with his bodyguards following the ambulance

There, they broke down in tears as doctors pronounced him dead. Later, a hospital spokesman said the rock king may have had a heart attack.

But it was an open secret that Elvis — a recluse hiding inside his palatial home for months — was using drugs, including heroin.

The star who never smoked or drank had been ill for months.

But for years before that, liver trouble and increasing weight problems had led to fewer and fewer stage appearances.

In fact, the once slim and handsome singer who made untold millions with over 20 years of record hits like Hound Dog, Heartbreak Hotel and B'ue Suede Shoes had become immensely fat.

He also had to live with the memories of a broken marriage.

While doing his army service in West Germany, he met and fell in love with the colonel's beautiful daughter, raven-haired Priscilla Beaulieu.

They married in 1967 and had a daughter, Lisa, whom he idolised. But then in 1973, Priscilla left him.

After that, Elvis's problems started growing.

By 1975, it became clear that something was badly wrong.

He had to cancel a Las Vegas appearance for a stay in hospital, and for the first time fans noticed how flabby he had become.

Elvis insisted it just looked that way because he was wearing a bullet-proof vest. It emerged that he had a morbid fear of being shot while performing.

Health

After that, however, his deteriorating health made him stay in seclusion for longer and longer periods, broken by several stays in hospital.

Last night, after hearing the news of his death, Priscilla immedi-

THE ROCK WORLD MOURNS..

THE pop world was in mourning for the king of rock last night.

Disc jockeys on Radio Luxembourg and Capital Radio played Elvis records all night as a mark of respect.

Radio Luxembourg also cancelled all its advertisements for the night.

The Daily Mirror switchboard was swamped with calls from Elvis fans — many of them sobbing girls.

By JACK LEWIS

records, books and posters.

"The roots of pop music have been taken away. He was the man who started it all."

Members of the British

Cheshire, changed his name last year. His home was a shrine to Elvis.

He said: "He was like a god to me. He will live forever in my memory."

Louis Coutteiene, the chief of Elvis's record company, RCA, said in

Elvis was dead before he died,

*and his gut was so big
it cast a shadow over rock'n'roll
in the last few years.
Our music is what's important now.*

Johnny Rotten, *Melody Maker*, 18 August 1977

Above: Elvis performing in Las Vegas

The Spots tour was the peak of punk for me and most of my friends. Nigel Wingrove

The Spots tour was quite a laugh. I remember things like Julien Temple falling through the ceiling of a club down in Cornwall, right in front of the stage: that was good. I don't think people thought or analysed too much at that time. They just sort of ran head first into the whole thing, and that was part of the fun of it.
Roadent

Just getting something on the road was a major achievement, and this was only meant to be the start of a tour running well into the following year. The UK, the States, followed by Europe again – all the dates were in place to do Scandinavia, and maybe even Russia after America. Steve and Paul were just loving being back on the road again; that's what they'd been born to do. All that practice, practice, practice… Now they were exactly where they wanted to be. It was pretty grim trying to keep the tour going but I had to believe it was the start of something because so many things were against us.
John 'Boogie' Tiberi

In the early stages of punk, there were so few of us it was quite dangerous. Then it all exploded. When the Sex Pistols played the first time in Plymouth, there were virtually no punks there. By the time they came back on the Spots tour, the whole thing had been transformed. Punk had become so popular that there were hundreds of punks. It all happened within the space of about 10 months.
Nigel Wingrove

The Sex Pistols were finding it difficult to play live because of the huge publicity. Virgin therefore set up the Spots tour which stood for 'Sex Pistols on Tour Secretly'. This tour made occasional appearances around the country, but required carefull orchestration to ensure that although officially secret, enough of the right fans turned up for each gig. This requirement made a mockery of Virgin's assertion that these concerts had to be held clandestinely, and if word leaked out, they would be canceled. For those lucky enough to catch the tour, they probably heard the Sex Pistols at they very best – musically at least.
Stephen Colegrave

When we started to assemble the footage for *The Filth and the Fury* the Spots tour was very important because that's when everything really kicked in. It was all coming together. It actually began life as the Never Mind the Bans tour. The Pistols hadn't played live in the UK for six months. All the problems associated with the Anarchy tour were still there, the local councils still saying no. Of the dates they did play, the best film was shot in Penzance. It's powerful stuff, proving just how far the Pistols had come. They'd gone away with this reputation, forged in front of relatively small audiences, and now they were back with people being turned away at the door.
Julien Temple, film director

The Spots tour was more sophisticated than the Anarchy tour. The energy was different, and it was more of a show. The aggression and everything that was punk was still there, but it was changing. It's a bit corny, but you could feel there was a change, a real shift.
Nigel Wingrove

Above left and right: Sid Vicious, Steve Jones and Johnny Rotten • Opposite: Johnny Rotten squeezing his spots • Inset: Steve Jones and Paul Cook on the tour bus

We were top drawer. Paul Cook

The Sex Pistols pop up again at the Winter Gardens in Penzance… Strangely enough, this is one of the few gigs on the secret tour where the secret is too well kept.
George Gimarc, *Punk Diary 1970-1979*

Around that time we did another tour of England. It had to be secret. Everyone from all over the world wanted to know what this big phenomenon was that was happening in England. The press came from America and all over the world to do interviews, to see what the latest thing was. So the only way we could tour, without hassle, was to tour secretly.
Paul Cook

And I did some top shagging on that tour. I was the top boy when it came down to it.
Steve Jones

Punk had really broken on a nationwide scale. There were bands coming out of the closet all over the place, but there were three top ones [the Pistols, the Damned and the Clash]. We were top drawer. To tell you the truth, we hated most of the other bands. We had nothing to do with them. All those third-rate bands like Chelsea were just jumping on the bandwagon.
Paul Cook

On the face of it, the tour is looked on as a short, shambolic outing which contributed to the Sex Pistols' early demise. But it was a crucial stage in their history. So many of their internal dramas were being played out on stage: Sid's terrific insecurity as a live performer, John's control over the audience, and over Sid, Paul and Steve's quantum leaps into the really powerful musician

category. It had all happened over that six months away, when things had moved on in the UK punk scene…
John Shearlaw

I went along to photograph the live gig at Brunel University, and when the band hit the stage, the whole place erupted. There was a lot of violence from the audience, and it seemed to be entirely directed towards the band.
Dennis Morris

It [the gig at Brunel] was a fiasco. We were in that big hall, which was jam-packed, nobody really knew why anybody was there, least of all us. I was very confused by the sheer popularity of it. I thought, 'This is horrible, it shouldn't be like this.' I'd seen us as a small, clubby band. We were way ahead of ourselves. We didn't know how to get past the first 20 rows.
Johnny Rotten in *England's Dreaming*

It's almost impossible to think of any other group who've created so much impact with so few live performances. The opening the Sex Pistols had created was being filled so quickly by other bands who were signing deals and building bloody great tours, and here the Stranglers, among others, spring to mind. 'Punk' in inverted commas was a huge live draw, and it was starting to sell records. Meanwhile, the prime movers in the movement were being marginalized and excluded. The Sex Pistols were backed into a corner – they really were taking on the United Kingdom and being all but destroyed in the fight. It shouldn't be forgotten that those seven or eight gigs were the last they played in the UK until they re-formed in 1996, when virtually a whole generation were ready to turn out to see the Pistols live.
John Shearlaw

Opposite, far left: Johnny Rotten on tour in Scandinavia • Near left: A Scandinavian audience • Right: Johnny Rotten's self-customized shirt and a backstage pass

265

I picked up a Super 8 camera and that was the birth of the Don Letts that the world came to know. Don Letts

I kick myself for not filming or photographing, or doing as much as I could. Don was conscientious. Someone gave him a camera in the Roxy and he decided to learn how to use it. When he was a DJ, he had nothing else to do, and he was the one who ended up with the footage. Andrew Czezowski **When my white mates around me were picking up guitars, I thought, I've got to get involved in this shit. The DJ-ing was great, but I wanted more. Caroline Barker [fashion editor for** *Vogue* **at the time] picked up that I wanted to do something. For whatever reason, she gave me a Super 8 camera. Then, I had to learn how to film for myself. It was mainly at the Roxy that I started to film the punk rock groups.** Don Letts Without Don, we would have lost forever the energy, rawness and attitude of the early days of punk, before it was sanitized by *The Great Rock'n'Roll Swindle* or sold out with tired punks on the Kings Road. *The Punk Rock Movie* captures a vibrant musical scene on the brink of selling out…just before the real early scene moved on. Nigel Wingrove **I learnt punk tactics. I picked up the Super 8 camera, and did the DIY thing by filming the bands at the Roxy. The next thing the press was saying, Don Letts, DJ at the Roxy, is making a movie. I thought, that's a good idea, that's punk rock. And that became** *The Punk Rock Movie***, which ran at the ICA for six weeks with queues around the fucking block.** Don Letts Don Letts' *Punk Rock Movie* is his first film and he's moved on a hell of a lot since then. That does not detract, however, from the fact that he shot an essential document of the time. He caught the Sex Pistols at the Screen on the Green backstage with Generation X, the Slits, Wayne County, Siouxsie and the Banshees, the Clash on the White Riot tour, footage of the informal gatherings at his flat in Forest Hill after the Roxy. The most important part of it was that Don, unlike many, could get closer to all the main players than anyone else as he was one of them, but in his own way, he was totally aloof from it. Chris Sullivan

Who Killed Bambi?
with Russ Meyer and the Sex Pistols – fucking ridiculous. Joe Corré

The Sex Pistols are preparing to enter the movie world. A film is being planned and the script is supposedly finished. However, the details are a highly guarded secret. It is known that Russ Meyer [of *Supervixens* fame] is being brought in to shoot the piece.
George Gimarc, *Punk Diary 1970-1979*

The idea of showing the Sex Pistols on film was there from a very early stage, partly in response to not being able to play anywhere, partly as a sort of public information thing. *Number One* started with me cobbling together all the bits of TV I could find – the Grundy show, *So It Goes*, the funniest bunch of stuff. Already I had a strong instinct towards documentation. But how were we supposed to edit? And where was the money coming from? Once we'd grabbed the concept of doing it ourselves, it was down to a back room in the Moving Picture Company in Soho, where someone had said, give us a grand and you can get on with it. Before that, we'd been playing around; somehow we had a print of *Quatermass*. I cut *No Future* (later retitled *God Save the Queen*) to *Quatermass*. Later we bought an English Tourist Board film and used their images. That was the guerrilla bit about it – we never had any fucking cameras. We'd do interviews with TV crews, but only if they gave us a copy of their film, meaning we were able to build up a collection of mad stuff. *Number One* was ready for the second gig at Screen on the Green. After that, it was meant to be played at colleges, student's unions… If the band couldn't play, we could show the film instead – show audiences what was going on, what they were missing…
John 'Boogie' Tiberi

I was at the National Film Training School in Hertfordshire when I first came across the Sex Pistols. They were rehearsing in a warehouse in Rotherhithe, and I was wandering around the docks, when I overheard a Small Faces song coming out of the window. Instead of 'I want you to know that I love you baby' they were singing 'I hate you', which made me laugh. It was the sort of song I wanted for a student film I was doing, so I went in. I saw this band, who were unlike any other group on Earth at

the time. I was intrigued and wanted to document their progress. Eventually, I had a key cut for the NFTS camera room so I could 'borrow' the school's cameras at night to film their gigs. I was also one of the early owners of a video machine, when it was £15 for a two-hour tape. I used to tape round the clock, which meant I had a lot of weird bits of footage to use.
Julien Temple

After the black and white filming in Berlin, which aimed to start the ball rolling for a movie about the group, we came down to the really meaningful bit for me. OK, I was naive! What kind of movie, and what kind of director? Here was this amazing opportunity, and we're talking about something like *Carry On the Sex Pistols* – you know, Sid James as Johnny Rotten's dad. There were so many different views. *Performance* was an influence; that was a film that really got London, and that was one way we wanted to go. We also knew all Russ Meyer's films going back to the 1960s, and somehow we clicked on that. When enquiries were made in the States, we found out that Russ Meyer was thought of as a real cowboy – nobody in Hollywood actually liked or respected him. Having him to direct the movie was stretching the whole concept right out – a really valid idea at the time. We were ready to push the boundaries of the way we saw ourselves – really 'expanding the window'. It was a very focused project, using Glitterbest's own money, and the industry was really up for a Sex Pistols film…
John 'Boogie' Tiberi

I was assistant director to Russ Meyer, and part of my job was to take him to the punk clubs and hang-outs, which he was having to learn about. He was amazed. He couldn't believe there weren't any big breasts. He was complaining, 'None of these punk chicks have got any fucking tits…'
Julien Temple

There was a great script, and a great title, *Anarchy in the UK*. Malcolm McLaren was trying to change everything, scribbling notes in the margins, trying to get revisions done on the script. He was playing out all his worst scenarios in a film script. We hadn't even

started filming and he was breaking up the band in his margin notes…
John 'Boogie' Tiberi

Every generation of hip young writers and presenters discovers Russ Meyer and reassesses his career. The late 1960s underground press celebrated him as a subversive, based on *Faster Pussycat, Kill, Kill, Kill*; the early '70s student press reckoned he'd destroyed the myth of Hollywood in *Beyond the Valley of the Dolls*. More recently, presenters like Jonathan Ross in the UK have celebrated Meyer's deliberate non-PCness and brought him back into the limelight. But at the time, especially in the summer of 1977, it seemed that the Sex Pistols were just too raw and too threatening for him to take on. Malcolm McLaren kept releasing 'stories' about the movie, but the real meat and potatoes coverage that summer was about the band – the boat trip, the gigs abroad, the council bans in the UK. The music press desperately wanted the Sex Pistols to be a real band, playing real gigs; the '100 Club with big tits' ideas that McLaren, along with screenwriter Roger Ebert, was coming up with would have ruined their credibility. The idea of the Pistols disappearing into a film studio like Elvis Presley was strongly dismissed by the music press, and since Virgin Records had nothing to do with the film, they were pushing for the Pistols to be a 'real' band as well. Anyway, by the end of August the Pistols were back on the road, Russ Meyer had gone home, and it was back to rock'n'roll business as usual…
John Shearlaw

I think one of the funniest things they tried to do was make the film *Who Killed Bambi*? Russ Meyer was going to direct it. Steve Jones and Malcolm went and spent some time with him in America. It was going to be a semi-porno funny film featuring the Sex Pistols. Some local person from their record company at the time in France had agreed to put all this money into the movie. They contacted Russ, started the movie and contracted Russ to direct it. Then the main person at the record company in America found out. He stopped it because he thought it was a lunatic idea.
Joe Corré

Opposite: Russ Meyer on the set of *Beyond the Valley of the Dolls*

Russ said her breasts were properly contoured. Joe Corré

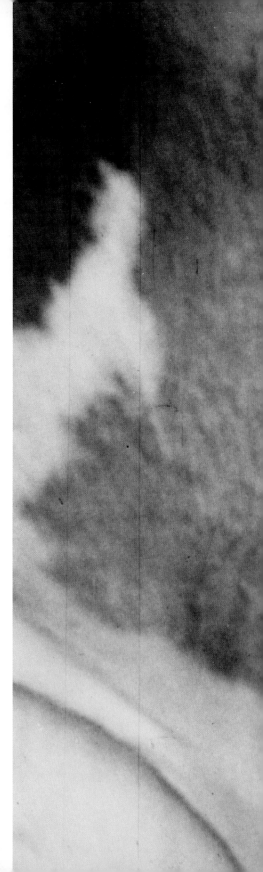

I was in the Vortex when Malcolm introduced me to Russ Meyer. He wanted to make a film which became *The Great Rock'n'Roll Swindle* but at this time was called *Who Killed Bambi?* His game plan was to persuade Russ Meyer to direct. Somehow or other, I ended up buying drinks for Malcolm and Russ, which to this day completely pisses me off because I barely had enough left over for my taxi fare home. Russ Meyer was on the look-out for female punks with big bosoms. He was gravely disappointed by the fact that most female punks, Jordan and my first wife, Lynne, excepted, didn't really have much in the chest department. I think this, combined with the fact that Malcolm is such a fucking impossible person, probably scuppered the deal. But it's a pity they didn't do it because the idea of Russ Meyer working with the Sex Pistols would have been pretty fantastic.
Ted Polhemus

They were about to start filming. They'd got all the sets ready. Malcolm got a call to say that the company was pulling the money out. Russ said, 'Are you firing me from the job?' Malcolm said, 'Look, mate, we'll try to find the money from somewhere else. We've got a bit of a problem because they've pulled the rug out from under us.' But Russ just said, 'You wanna fire me, you wanna fire me?' So Malcolm said, 'All right, then, if that's what you want, I'm fucking firing you!' Then Russ said, 'Well, you must fire me in front of my men.' He stood up on the table saying, 'Right everybody, gather around…come on, fire me.' Malcolm just said, 'All right, Russ, you're fired. Fuck off.'
Joe Corré

God Save the Queen!
The final draft of a script for a Sex Pistols movie
Scene One:
EXT. – WAPPING – day

The four SEX PISTOLS in a parody of the FOUR MUSKETEERS are portrayed marching, arms linked, to CAMERA. They are established as being on a TREADMILL (or four independent, similar treadmills). In the background, displayed proudly, is a huge UNION JACK painted, billboard-size, on a brick wall. The effect: similar in concept to the corny WWII Andrews Sisters Hollywood propaganda films.

In CLOSE-UPS, each SEX PISTOL has pertinent statements to make to the camera.
STEVE JONES: We don't make music – we make noise.
PAUL COOK: We're so pretty vacant and we don't care.

SID VICIOUS: We like noise – it's our choice.
JOHNNY ROTTEN: People think we never get anywhere, but we prove them wrong.

STEVE JONES: Passion ends in fashion.
PAUL COOK: Never mind the ballocks [sic]!
JOHNNY ROTTEN: You got a problem – and the problem is you!

During these close-ups the beat of the TITLE SONG has been insistently ESTABLISHING itself beneath the dialogue. Now the VOCAL begins as well:

CUT TO:
TITLES (Roll Up)
MUSIC: The SEX PISTOLS singing 'ANARCHY IN THE UK'
Script extract from *God Save the Queen*, Matrixbest, 22 August 1977

Russ Meyer wanted all these American girls with big tits to be in the movie. He had to explain to Equity that he was unable to find British girls with the right breasts. One of the funniest stories was when Russ was in a union meeting explaining why they needed a particular girl from America. The only reason he could come up with was that her breasts were properly contoured and stuck out properly, rather than sagging down. In the end, in total frustration, he stood on the table and said, 'Do you know what? You can't make a movie in this country. You can't even make cars in this country, and you've got no women.' Apparently this carpenter at the back said, 'What do you mean we can't make cars in this country?' Russ said, 'What have you got? A Triumph Dolomite?' And that was it. He fucked off.
Joe Corré

The Sex Pistols' proposed movie *Who Killed Bambi?*, under the direction of American Russ Meyer, had been cancelled in pre-production when one of the financial backers quit as costs began to skyrocket. Intended to be a low budget affair, expenses climbed to one million dollars. There have already been several weeks of preparation to begin shooting the project at Bray Studios, but now Meyer has returned to Los Angeles and the sets are being dismantled. The proposed film was to have a reported love scene pairing Marianne Faithfull to Johnny Rotten.
George Gimarc, *Punk Diary 1970-1979*

I hated that film right from the start.
Johnny Rotten in *England's Dreaming*

Opposite: Kitten Navidad, a favourite Russ Meyer 'actress'

We moved into a squat in Lots Road, in the far reaches of Chelsea. It was romantic, with candlelight, wooden boxes and a mattress on the floor… We mixed a lot with the punks, and I took that energy and ran it through my own circuits, waiting to see what would happen. It was punk nerve that fed, like direct current, right into the rage of 'Broken English' (album). Sid Vicious and I shared the same drug dealer, and I was once actually cast as Ma Vicious, Sid's mum, in Russ Meyer's Sex Pistols film. I can imagine what a deluge of new hate mail that would have brought on:

'You dirty little bitch…'

Marianne Faithfull, singer

Opposite and above right: Russ Meyer and some of his hand-picked 'actresses' • Above left: Marianne Faithfull

Deaf School was fed up with the complacency of long-haired rock bands.

Clive Langer, songwriter and producer

Roxy Music influenced us. Being from art college, we were more of an art college band. We thought we were really fashionable and up to date until we went to see the Pistols at the Nashville. It was only half full, but when we saw them we just thought, 'Fuck, we're nowhere.' Here was something really new happening.
Clive Langer

Deaf School had begun before the Pistols and were quite a draw between '75 and '77 – in fact, probably Britain's hippest band for a while. The lead singer, Steve Allen (aka Enrico Cadillac Junior), was decked out crooner mode, all pencil moustache and greased back hair; co-singer Betty Bright stepped right out of a '50s glamour mag, with her Swanky Modes dresses and Cleopatra haircut; Clive Langer, the guitarist, would not have looked out of place in a Nicholas Ray movie; and the magnificently coiffeured Reverend Max Ripple sported a kilt and full tartan bondage. The band almost cracked it before and after punk. They were a big name for those

who felt that punk lacked class, which they possessed in wagon loads. The UK was just not ready for them.
Chris Sullivan

After we saw Kilburn and the High Roads, we realized that playing an instrument properly was not the most important criterion for creating a successful band. This influenced the way we started. We picked people that were interesting, like our drummer – we picked the best painter at college because he had the right look. If someone looked good at college, they were likely to end up in the band. We started off with about 14 or 15 people in the band, but eventually had to get it down to seven or eight. So there was that new ethic that you didn't have to be a musician. You could just be interesting on stage.
Clive Langer

We played with a real mishmash of bands. The Stranglers usually supported us, and lot of other up-and-coming bands. The mixture didn't help. We went

out of fashion for a while. As a live band, we were popular, but the music press didn't take us seriously. Our Roxy influences weren't popular. If we'd turned up after punk, we would have done better. We were too early. After all, later you had hundreds of Roxy Music types with bands like Split Enz and everyone doing well. Many of the people who came to see us live and were our real fans went on to become quite famous, like the Crucial Three, one of whom later went on to join the Teardrop Explodes. I wish we'd stuck to our guns and ridden the wave. But it was too frustrating at the time. I didn't feel that all the people in Deaf School understood what was going on. I felt a bit alone in what I wanted to do.
Clive Langer

I was so taken by Deaf School that I married the singer. Clive Langer, the guitarist, went on to produce all of Madness's records.
Suggs

Above: Deaf School (Humphrey Ocean, Betty Bright and Steve Allen) • Opposite: The Undertones (Feargal Sharkey third left)

Northern Ireland's answer to the Ramones.

John Shearlaw

The Undertones were a sublime pop band who guaranteed their place in the hall of fame with 'Teenage Kicks' alone. The DJ John Peel really has to take most of the credit for that. He played the first pressing to death, and it went from there to *Top of the Pops* before they'd really signed with anybody. The single was a one-off deal with a Belfast independent [Good Vibrations], which they later told me was their only option. They'd come up in a hard school, playing covers in Derry clubs, and encoring with Gary Glitter's 'Rock'n'Roll', but the punk explosion had propelled them into writing their own stuff – most of which was rejected by the new independents on the mainland. I know Stiff and Chiswick turned them down, and the bigger labels weren't interested until they'd had a hit. The upside was that they had loads of brilliant material when they did strike a deal. *The Undertones* [the first album, released in early 1979] was a tremendous debut. It seemed like they'd arrived fully formed – Northern Ireland's answer to the Ramones.
John Shearlaw

On a night when one of the world's top bands, Ireland's favourite sons Thin Lizzy, were packing them in at Ulster Hall [in Belfast], it was no mean feat that a bevy of local talent could draw 500 to Queen's University across the far side of town for a night of raw rock'n'roll debauchery. Stars of the evening were the Undertones, the rough and ready outsiders from Derry... It was their first performance in the capital and, with titles like 'Teenage Kicks' and 'True Confessions', how could it be bad? This was real rock'n'roll, inducing images of deserted bus shelters, bottles of wine, and fish and chips.
Gavin Martin, *New Musical Express*, 8 July 1978

There was a freshness and an unfakeable enthusiasm about what they were doing. They seemed almost the youngest of the new bands coming through, yet at the same time there was a hint of life experience that went beyond what they were expressing.
John Shearlaw

*The vision is
to create modern music.
If, indeed, we are not
going to reach the
future – someone better
bring the future.*

David Thomas, singer with Père Ubu, *Search & Destroy*, issue 6, 1978

Père Ubu were one of the first bands to use the
synthesizer with full force. This, and a strong melodic
bass, gave their music an industrial edge, which wasn't
surprising, seeing as they came from the arse end of
Cleveland, Ohio.
Stephen Colegrave

Père Ubu recently played CBGB's. The audience was
fairly normal-looking – what some regulars might call
New York University/Long Island types. This doesn't
upset Ubu – they look pretty normal themselves. They
can move around fairly easily without being noticed.
Fewer problems. They look like pretty regular working
people, and they all were regular working people until a
few weeks ago. Most of them worked at record stores or
factories – that's what most musicians do in Cleveland.
Ubu quit their jobs for the latest East Coast tour.
Char Latanne, music journalist, *Search & Destroy*, issue 6, 1978

We understood the relation of sound to vision. You'd
go by the steel mills and there was this very powerful
electrical feeling, combined with a particular sound in
the air, that conjured up a whole set of visions with it.
The original idea was to make sound stimulate the
imagination; we always saw what we did in very visual
terms. In the end we almost transposed the guitar and
bass functions. We were aware of this.
David Thomas in *England's Dreaming*

The spring's big tour was the first visit by Père Ubu,
whose thorough grasp of technology and mature
aesthetic was a revelation to the teenage group who
supported them.
Jon Savage, *England's Dreaming*

I didn't get Père Ubu at all. I always felt one needed to
have a degree to get their drift, and I didn't have one.
Chris Sullivan

Left: David Thomas of Père Ubu

They were like a B movie
come to riot. Steve Severin, bass player, Siouxsie and the Banshees

The Cramps are the kind of people you couldn't fail to look at twice were they to pass you on the street. Three guys whose taste in clothes runs to fake leopardskin and leatherette, and one gal with a more sedate dress sense and a cemetery stare. One way to describe the Cramps' corporate visual appeal would be to say if Darts [1950s R&B band] were members of the zombie mafia instead of candy-suited goody-goodies, this is what they would look like. I can't see Bournemouth pavilion rushing to book the Cramps. The Darts reference goes yet further. Cramps' music is also rooted in the '50s, though not in R&B so much as its illegitimate white offering, rockabilly.

Paul Rambali, *NME*, 10 June 1978

I loved the Cramps. I was into them right from the beginning. They had such great style and they were funny as well. They knew there was loads going on and they took it to the extreme. Taking it to the extreme is always important.

Steve Severin

They sounded and looked like a cartoon, but they were actually like that. At first I thought their sleazy rockabilly image just required a lot of dedication, then I realized they were for real, which is a lot more scary.

Bill Dunn, senior editor, *Esquire* magazine

There were something like a quarter of a million advance orders for Never Mind the Bollocks. John Shearlaw

We got in through the back door in 1977. We weren't the real thing. But the revolution was upon us and you had to pick sides. I thought, well I'm certainly not going to go with the Genesis mob – I'll go with something I actually agree with. And although in the initial stages I didn't really get off on the Sex Pistols' music, the attitude was so compelling I had to side with that lot. I was into serious music. I didn't even listen to rock music…

I never listened to Led Zeppelin or anyone like that. In fact, to me, the Sex Pistols' sound was very much an extension of that. However, it was the verbalizing that went round it that really struck me. But then I really *did* get into the Sex Pistols, and my favourite album for a whole year was *Never Mind the Bollocks*. It was so heavy.
Sting in *Punk: The Illustrated History of a Music Revolution*

There was a bootleg cassette going round, and we even got as far as reviewing it. Our source – not a million miles from Virgin Records themselves – claimed the album was going to be called *Another Load of Bollocks from the Sex Pistols*, which was close, and that it was going to be banned from all the big record shop chains like Smiths and Woolworths, which actually turned out to be true.
John Shearlaw

The Sex Pistols changed my life in 1977 and in 1996. They are gods. Rock'n'roll should always be this great. This was *Never Mind the Bollocks* note for note. It's still beautiful. If you don't get it now, you would never have got it then. Britpop? More like Shitpop. You're welcome to your mediocrity. This band are our alternative royal family. God save the Sex Pistols.'
Alan McGee, founder of Creation Records

I thought it sounded great. I still do. Me and Steve would go in and do the guitar and drum parts, which is pretty unorthodox, it's usually bass and drums, but we knew the songs so well that we could do without the bass. We got them done quickly. Chris Thomas was professional; he seemed to know how we wanted to sound.
Paul Cook

Everything at that time was about trying to get the film funded, to get shooting started. With the sets built at Bray, money had been spent. People had been hired. There wasn't as much concentration on the album as there should have been…like it wasn't the priority, the film was. We weren't in a normal rock'n'roll situation here. But Virgin were going ahead with all their marketing and their release date, and I gave them a track listing and a running order. Then 'Submission' got added on, and Virgin got what they wanted – *Never Mind the Bollocks* at number one in its first week of release…
John 'Boogie' Tiberi

Christopher Seale, a Nottingham shopkeeper, was taken to court for displaying a 9 x 6 ft copy of the album sleeve in his window, violating the 1989 Indecent Advertising Act. Defending the case was John Mortimer QC [writer of *Rumpole of the Bailey*] who brought in Professor Kingsley, head of English studies at Nottingham University, who told the court that the word 'bollocks' had been in use for almost 1,000 years. It was an Anglo-Saxon word for a small ball and had been employed in veterinary manuals, literature and bibles ever since. It had also been applied to describe clergymen who spoke, what was fondly referred to, as nonsense. The defence went on to suggest that the furore and resulting court case were not directed at the use of the actual word, but at the band in question. The cover was ruled to be 'decent', setting a legal precedent, and thousands of shopkeepers were now able to display the said cover without fear of prosecution. Marvellous!
Chris Sullivan

There had been so much anticipation it wasn't surprising that *Bollocks* went straight in at number one, but already it was like, what's the next surprise? There's so much potential here, what happens next? This was just an album, basically the history of the Sex Pistols up to that point. And pink and yellow posters up and down the country in all the Virgin shops seemed to be diluting the impact rather than strengthening it.
John Shearlaw

They spent a lot of time arsing around, changing track orders and stuff like that, so it came out late. But it stood head and shoulders above anything else. It captured that feeling of anarchy, that twisted up inside feeling, when you just want to walk out and pop someone. It was stunning stuff. But then it became part of that old machine.
Roadent

There were something like a quarter of a million advance orders for *Never Mind the Bollocks*, which was big news at the time for an industry that was still dominated by soft rock and ballad singers; it proved to the sceptics that something had really changed, something new had arrived. I think it was actually Sir Cliff Richard who got 'knocked off the top', as they still say. But the world didn't change overnight. A week later it was business as normal, when *Bollocks* dropped off the top slot.
John Shearlaw

Never Mind the Bollocks was fantastic. There's not a bad track on it. I still play it.
Jayne County

They smashed the shop all to pieces. Joe Corré

I used to really like it in my mother's shop. Once, I walked back from school to the shop. When I arrived, there were builders everywhere. They'd smashed the shop all to pieces. There was nothing left. They were re-doing the whole thing. They were changing from Sex to Seditionaries. As I entered the smashed-up shop, I thought that everything, my whole world, had gone. The builders took pity on me. One of them telephoned my mum and said, 'I've got this little kid who's in tears. Is he anything to do with you?'
Joe Corré

When my old man saw me in Seditionaries' clothing for the first time he said to me, ''Bout time you got yourself a straitjacket. I didn't think you'd have to pay for it, though.' Typical.
Chris Sullivan

Seditionaries came along when it all became a big business. It became a lot more professional: the stuff

was really well made. You had the full look and, to be fair, it wasn't at all punk as the general public perceived it at the time. There was the parachute shirts, with the ring in the centre and the straps over the shoulders, which, with the bondage trousers and the parachute boots that looked like orthopaedic footwear, was a really smart look – one that's stood the test of time and hasn't dated one iota. Seditionaries sold a very deliberate and well thought-out look that really had none of the haphazard scruffiness that punk was known for at the time. It was fantastic.
Mark Powell, London tailor

Seditionaries followed straight on the heels of Sex and took the whole concept that Vivienne Westwood had created a step further. She created a totally new style genre, one that was not gleaned from the past, that was absolutely new. This was a major achievement.
Chris Sullivan

Malcolm did not do it all: [Vivienne] was the creative one. Yes, she took some of Malcolm's ideas, but she made them happen. She was the one to graft, to craft and make them work…I think she had a big effect on him, but I don't think he had any wish to give her credit.
Bella Freud, designer, in *Vivienne Westwood: A Fashionable Life*

I thought Vivienne Westwood at Seditionaries was at last bringing out into the open the sado-masochist and bondage fantasies which had previously been hidden away in male magazines on the top shelf. She brought them onto the streets and stopped them being a secret male preserve. This prevented them from being detrimental and disparaging of women. Punk women were reclaiming this look for themselves and saying, 'We are in charge. We are going to wear this look and we're going to control it.' So punk women redefined the face of women for the future.
Caroline Coon, journalist

Opposite, clockwise from left: 1976 parachute top from Sex; 1977 net shirt from Seditionaries; 1977 sleeveless shirt from Seditionaries

281

Malcolm and Vivienne's transformation of Paradise Garage into all the following shops was revolutionary.

Roger Bourton, clothing supplier to the film industry

After 1977, the T-shirts became vehicles for more calculated outrage and, as such, lost potency. At the end of that year, McLaren ordered a number from a gay sex shop in San Francisco, which included the Mickey and Minnie design, and another depicting a cartoon scene of gay men fist-fucking under the exhortation, 'Fuck Yr. Mother, And Run Away Punk!' Meanwhile, a gay orgy entitled 'Prick Up Your Ears' contains a quote from Joe Orton's diaries: 'I'm from the gutter so don't you forget it because I won't', and the death of Nancy Spungen was commemorated with a rush-released shirt displaying Sid Vicious clutching roses under the words: 'She's dead. I'm Alive. I'm Yours'.
Paul Gorman, *The Look*

The clever thing about Seditionaries was that, as with Sex, they had a real iconic staff. They weren't just shop

assistants – they were stars. Jordan was maybe the main figure of the punk movement bar none. Her attendance at a function was priceless in the hip stakes. Tracey was not only beautiful but eminently stylish, and Michael Collins was the camp and slightly wicked ne'er do well. All in all, they provided the shop with an undeniable atmosphere. It was like entering a completely different world with its own cast of characters, its own rules and its own language.
Chris Sullivan

On other T-shirts the commodification of childhood was explored: Mickey and Minnie Mouse were shown enthusiastically enjoying sexual congress, while a startled Snow White engaged in an orgy with the seven dwarfs.
Paul Gorman, *The Look*

For some years, Vivienne determinedly distanced herself from this transformation in which she and McLaren had played a crucial role. Her denial of punk's importance rests on three facts: a fundamental failure to grasp the influence, importance and power of the movement she helped unleash; a bitter battle with Malcolm, which led her to dissociate herself for many years from the fruits of their labour; and a sea-change in her attitude towards her career. She was disillusioned that punk had not turned out to be the social revolution McLaren had led her to believe it would be – just an opportunist craze that had turned violent. She no longer wished to challenge the establishment but to join it, and her punk credentials did not sit happily with this new ambition.
Jane Mulvagh, *Vivienne Westwood: A Fashionable Life*

Above: T-shirts from Sex, 1978 and 1979 • Opposite, from top left: Parachute top and jacket from Sex, 1976; Marabou top from Let It Rock, 1974; Dickens T-shirt from Seditionaries, 1979; Mohair jumper from Sex, 1976

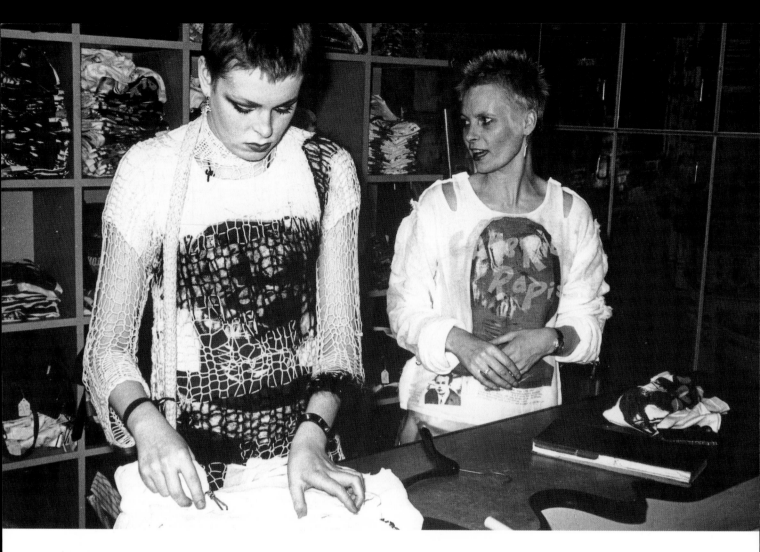

Vivienne's worst days are better than most people's best days.

Gene Krell

Vivienne is probably the kindest, most moral person I've ever met in my life. I was addicted to drugs and had a terrible drinking problem. Everyone had given up on me, except for Vivienne. She locked me in her house and I managed to get free. She chased me down the street in her bondage pants.
Gene Krell

My mother's never been interested in money. She's a perfectionist. She wants to make the best trousers she can make. She doesn't care if people buy them or not, but they do, and that's why she's always been independent. She will never be part of a huge corporate fashion empire.
Joe Corré

She was extraordinary because if people didn't have enough money for the clothes and she thought they looked good in them, she'd often just give them away.

She was very charitable. World's End was a working-class neighbourhood. There were lots of meths drinkers who didn't know where their next meal was coming from. Any time they came to the shop, she always helped them out with a meal. Punk did not believe in materialism or the trappings of pop stardom. It was about anarchy with a sense of real morality. Vivienne was responsible for that. She is the founding mother of punk. That's the way history should view her.
Gene Krell

Years later I had an exhibition of Malcolm and Vivienne's clothes. I went on at Malcolm and Vivienne for months to persuade each of them to get involved. Eventually I was successful, but neither realized the other was coming. Vivienne didn't arrive until 9 o'clock. By then the evening had been going on for hours. We'd filmed Malcolm, who'd laid claim to designing everything. She just stood

there and said, 'I'm not coming in while he's talking.' Malcolm didn't even acknowledge her presence. He just kept waffling on about, 'I designed this, I designed that.' Eventually she agreed to come in if we found her a brandy. She stood there for about half an hour with a double brandy listening to him. Then she walked over to him and said, 'Actually, Malcolm, I designed that. You didn't design that.' He totally blanked her and just carried on. She kept coming back at him. Eventually he began to soften, saying, 'Oh, did you? I don't remember that.' It was so ridiculous. Eventually they managed to find mutual terms on certain things and they talked for about an hour. They hadn't seen each other for years. It was typical, Malcolm laying claim to absolutely everything, and Vivienne hanging on his coat-tails, not being able to find a voice, but finding a voice through him. Of course, she's found her voice now. She's an incredibly talented woman.
Roger Bourton

Malcolm McLaren gave voice to a generation and knew how to tap into culture in the most resourceful way. Gene Krell

Malcolm is brilliant, but he needs a good collaborator. He was the ideas man and liberator for Vivienne (and many others) who realized those ideas. His talent is getting things wrong, but getting the best out of people. left to his own devices, his work never succeeds. He has had two great collaborators in his life – first Vivienne, then me.
Nils Stevenson

Malcolm was like a rooster strutting his stuff and peeking about. He loved shiny things, anything alternative. He didn't just talk about it, he did it, finished it and then got bored. Malcolm was actually tone-deaf, but that didn't matter. He was always trying different types of music and styles, whether it was punk or hip-hop or double Dutch. He was so ahead of his time. I love Malcolm.
Helen Wellington Lloyd

When I first heard the Sex Pistols, I knew Malcolm had tapped into something that had real substance. Their music was very powerful and had real muscle. With the Sex Pistols, he created something that was very Warholian in its philosophy. Malcolm shook us all out of our complacency. He knew how to show us that we had enough balls and ability to get up there and do it. I don't think it's possible to overestimate the contribution punks made.
Gene Krell

Malcolm needed to be surrounded by people who could actually make his dreams a reality. He was great at coming up with ideas, but it was always Vivienne who would embellish them and say, 'Look, let's do it like this because this is much better.' He would ride with her suggestions, but Malcolm was always 10 steps ahead, coming up with more and more ideas. He was unstoppable.
Roger Bourton

Punk is a whole legacy that's never left Malcolm. He will always be there in everybody's mind because nobody wants to let go of that punk rock thing. Malcolm wants to forget about it and move on to new things, but he can't get away from it. He's like Sean Connery – even 20 years after his last Bond film, he's still being called James Bond on the street.
Joe Corré

Malcolm's great talent is to catch the ball and go the whole nine yards and turn a very bad situation to his own ends.
Gene Krell

The kids really loved it, even the young ones.

Bill Wright, promoter at Ivanhoe's

I know Paul Cook thought the Sex Pistols played one of
their best gigs as a benefit for the Children of Firemen and
One-Parent Families in Huddersfield.
Nils Stevenson

One night, while seeing some of my bands audition at
Wakefield, I got a call from the Sex Pistols' agent: 'How d'ya
like a date on the Sex Pistols?' I said, 'Yeah, great.' I thought
he was joking to start with. Like everybody wanted them,
but you couldn't for love or money. If you'd offered them 10
grand it would have made no difference. All they wanted
was the right situation and the right club. Then he said,
'They fancy doing Christmas Day. How about it?' I couldn't
believe it, but that was the Pistols, that was the way they
went about things. It was decided that Ivanhoe's should be
the venue and the cost a mere £600…a pittance for them.
Virgin, their record company at the time, wanted to make
it a really special occasion. Between us we decided to do
an afternoon show for the underprivileged kids of the area
and then a show for the regular fans on the night. Can
you imagine it, the Pistols playing to five-, four-, even
three-year-olds…unbelievable, but it happened.
    So it comes to Christmas morning and there I was, shrugging
my shoulders, sublimely accepting that no one would turn up.
But I was wrong; they did, all 500 of them. A gigantic cake was
laid on, a splodgy one full of cream, and a few other goodies,
like a sweet mountain. Anyway, the kids got stuck into the
goodies, their faces a delight to see. Then, just before the
Pistols were due to go on, Johnny came out and went up to
the giant Christmas cake. He got this huge knife and cut an
enormous chunk out of the cake. He passed this piece to a
little girl who tried, but failed, to take a bite out of it. So he
took one instead, then some more and more. Then they all
joined in. He finished up by jumping into the cake and they
all splodged him. They did that performance and the kids
really loved it, even the really young ones. At the end of the
night a bloke representing the Pistols came up for the £600
cheque. I wrote it out, signed it and from that day to this,
they've never cashed the cheque, just never did. I don't know
whether they lit a cigar with it or threw it out of the plane.
But what they did immediately from there was to fly over to
America and we all know what happened there…
    So it ended…the gig of the century had made good all
the losses I'd made in the previous three months promoting
up-and-coming punk bands. Those were the days.
Bill Wright

Opposite and above: Sid Vicious, Nancy Spungen and children at Ivanhoe's, Huddersfield, Christmas 1977

There's no doubt that 1978 *was the most successful year for punk in commercial terms. By the end of the year bands were competing for chart space with the likes of Abba, Elton John, Rod Stewart and the Electric Light Orchestra. Big record companies with big marketing budgets had assimilated the anti-establishment and enlisted its support in the battle for record sales. However, the most famous punk band in the world – the Sex Pistols – started the year with one last madcap tour, as Malcolm McLaren made a bid to conquer the United States.*

Before the year was even a month old, the Sex Pistols had played their last gig. The musical finale was a chaotic rendition of 'No Fun' at the Winterland Ballroom in San Francisco. Appropriately, Johnny Rotten, alone at the microphone, shouted in frustration, 'Ever get the feeling that you've been cheated?' The break-up of the band was officially announced in New York two days later. By this time Sid Vicious was in hospital in Queens, New York, recovering from a methadone overdose. Steve Jones and Paul Cook were on their way to film and record with the Great Train Robber Ronnie Biggs, yet another McLaren ruse designed to attract publicity. John Lydon found himself alone in New York City with $30 in his pocket and a future that was uncertain to say the least.

Back in the UK, punk was no longer just three bands and 200 fans. It was now a popular and musically vibrant movement, with an eclectic mix of bands beginning to develop styles that would soon grow into New Wave, electro, and two-tone, and further bolster record company sales. Punk was firmly in the

public domain, there to be seen by millions every week on Top of the Pops. Of course, the original scene had moved on. Vivienne Westwood had sold the rights of her designs to the owners of Boy and chosen to take on the fashion world almost under its own terms. No self-respecting art student or hipster would be seen dead amongst the pogoing and spitting fans at a UK Subs or Sham 69 gig. They'd rather be dancing to the likes of Kraftwerk and the Monochrome Set in the post-punk Billy's club or, later, the Blitz.

It was in 1978 that Billy's started its infamous Bowie nights, the result of a small band of former Sex customers and Pistols followers having become dejected by the squalor of punk and returning to their roots. By some quirk of fate, they found themselves congregating at Billy's after the last night of David Bowie's week of concerts at Earls Court. David Claridge, a friend of Andrew Czezowski, spotted a gap in the market, having put two and two together, and began the Bowie nights at Billy's that were to provide the foundations for the movement that became annoyingly known as New Romantic.

The music scene in 1978 had something for everybody. The Undertones had their own take on the Ramones' fast punk formula, and 'Teenage Kicks' keeps its freshness more than 20 years later. The Gang of Four out-Clashed the Clash when it came to political attitude, and the Fall's lyrics were so obscurely profound that they are still a mystery today. Joy Division was building up its monotone take on the world, and XTC were making plans to be New Wave. Although much of this music bore little resemblance to the Buzzcocks or Sex

Pistols in 1976, it could not have happened without them, for it was they who sowed the seeds of what was once insurrection and was now conformity.

The Clash remained one of the most important bands, and in many ways was even more important now that the Sex Pistols had disintegrated. Their second album, Thanks for Giving Us Enough Rope, was also distributed in America by their record company, CBS, and started to build them a transatlantic following prior to their US tour the next year. Meanwhile, the Damned were finding it difficult to sustain their act and played a farewell gig at the Rainbow in north London. However, Siouxsie and the Banshees' persistence finally paid off, and even their manager, Nils Stevenson, agreed that they should sign to a major label, Polydor. They celebrated with a successful Top 10 single, 'Hong Kong Garden'.

Already in every record shop on vinyl, punk was now becoming public on film. Derek Jarman produced his own fittingly anarchic and sensationalist view of punk in Jubilee, with plenty of unscary violence, unerotic sex and an uninteresting storyline. A virtually unknown and distressingly naked Toyah Willcox was joined by a varied collection of more familiar faces, including Jenny Runacre, Wayne County, Adam Ant and Gene October. While well-heeled audiences were reliving the madness of punk in Jubilee at the Gate Cinema in Notting Hill, Malcolm McLaren was furiously rewriting history and re-creating the old Nashville on film. Viewed out of context, the resulting Great Rock'n'Roll Swindle is a likeable if offbeat film: as a historical record, it makes Goebbels look honest; as a comedy, it makes the Carry

Ons seem sophisticated; and as far as performance is concerned, it redefined the term wooden. Some of the most anarchic moments, such as the simulated rape of Paul Cook by Sting in the back of a Cadillac, did not, unfortunately, make it past the cutting-room floor. However, it was still worth watching just for the Sid Vicious rendition of 'My Way' on stage, replete with gun and tuxedo.

Despite the celluloid, as 1978 drew to a close, fact became stranger than fiction. All four members of the Sex Pistols went from Dada to Surrealism. It was strange enough when Steve Jones and Paul Cook swapped angry cowboys for a Rio beach party with Ronnie Biggs. It was even stranger when John Lydon was hailed as an anti-colonial hero by the Rasta community in Jamaica and helped Richard Branson sign up the best reggae artists for his new Front Line label. However, tragedy took over when Sid Vicious woke up from a drugged sleep to find Nancy quiet for once and for ever. Conspiracy theories abounded. The New York police were eager to accept the facts at face value, and Sid genuinely could not remember what had occurred that fateful October evening. For the general public, this was vindication at last that punk really was a dark force, and for posterity it was the first step towards the creation of a myth. The movement had gone virtually as far as it could in 1978. Now it had only to be polished, re-packaged and ruined for future generations, courtesy of the establishment.

While many were just becoming aware of the whole scene, others were already trying to forget it. Punk was now overground and in the hands of the powers that be.

Paul Anka, who wrote 'My Way', said his favourite version of it was by Sid Vicious.

Nils Stevenson, Sex Pistols' tour manager, 1976

Right: Still from *The Great Rock'n'Roll Swindle*, showing Sid Vicious performing 'My Way'

I was worried about getting killed in the States, really worried.

Paul Cook, drummer, the Sex Pistols

We were meant to start the US tour in New York, but it was cancelled because our visas were turned down. We couldn't get over there to start the tour, so we ended up starting in Atlanta. Warner Brothers had signed us to their label. There were all these ex-Vietnam security guys in combat jackets. Warner Brothers were terrified there was going to be trouble. I was worried about being killed, really worried. We had police standing on the side of the stage. It was horrible, with all the guns. It was totally out of control. Things deteriorated gig by gig.
Paul Cook

We were all ready to go. We were in a photo booth getting the pictures for the visas…and lo and behold, the visa applications were turned down. It wouldn't have mattered if the tour had been cancelled, as there really wasn't a lot at stake. Nobody had heard of the band in the States, so there was no risk at all in going. But Warner Brothers had done their deal. The record [*Never Mind the Bollocks*] was in the shops. It was entirely down to them. Getting the visa decisions reversed just showed the power of big business. Money was put down – a kind of bail bond to guarantee good behaviour, but Warner's made damn sure nobody got arrested.
John 'Boogie' Tiberi, Sex Pistols' tour manager, 1977-9

Malcolm didn't want to take the ordinary route and play in front of the critics, who'd compare them to everyone else. He wanted the Pistols to be a phenomenon. So they just played in clubs in towns across the southern circuit, where only the local inhabitants would come to see them. The strategy worked pretty well because it created havoc. People came out to see this band that was being nasty and obnoxious, and they reacted as nastily and obnoxiously as they could.
Bob Gruen, photographer

The Pistols in the USA was fundamentally a great idea. Personally, I thought things would start working properly again as soon as we got on the road. We'd start happening as a group and respond to the occasion. The reason that didn't happen again can only come down to John being ignored… Malcolm's agenda was to avoid the East Coast; he had this thing, again going back to 1975, about the taste-makers there. He simply felt they hadn't picked up on the Sex Pistols, and they hadn't taken enough notice when they should have.
John 'Boogie' Tiberi

I was following the Sex Pistols in the press, thinking this is trouble. They interfered with our Ramones' agenda all over the place, not rightly or wrongly. They were just diverting attention and energy from what we were doing.
Danny Fields, ex-manager, the Ramones

I never understood why they were so popular with the American press, especially as the press in the States weren't nearly as interested in music as they were in England. Until then, the only people who had written about the Pistols were *Roxy* and *Creem* magazines, and they'd said good things about them. Most of the press didn't cover rock'n'roll. That's why I was amazed when I went to the opening Sex Pistols' show in Atlanta and the national press were there: the *Los Angeles Times*, *The New York Times* and *Rolling Stone*. I couldn't work out what attracted the media to them. The New York Dolls didn't get that kind of coverage, yet the Dolls were a great band that everybody loved. Perhaps it was the name. The first time I saw the band's name in the paper I remember saying to David Johansen [lead singer of the Dolls], 'How are they going to say that name on the radio? How are they going to play their songs?' You couldn't say the words 'Sex Pistols' in public. To me it was shocking – it wasn't really something you wanted to say out loud, especially here in pure America. Now you

have bands with horrible names like the Butthole Surfers, and people take them for granted.
Bob Gruen

Back then 'Sex Pistols' was an outrageously shocking name.
Gene Krell, punk clothing entrepreneur

I hated the American tour. It was very fucking depressing being out there. It was weird having all them security guards, but then again, there was some good-looking birds around, which was pretty much all I was interested in at that point. I'd given up trying to keep the band together, so I spent most of my time trying to get laid…there was a lot of tarts about. I was the top man!
Steve Jones, guitarist, the Sex Pistols

I was in Los Angeles, staying at the Tropicana and hanging out with the Ramones and Alice Cooper, when the Sex Pistols landed in Atlanta. It was really bizarre because as the Pistols made their way across America and the hysteria was broadcast on the news every night, kids in Los Angeles, and I imagine the rest of the country, were suddenly transforming themselves with safety-pins, spiked haircuts and ugliness.
Legs McNeil

Walter Cronkite at CBS News was the most important of the national broadcasters. He did a story about the imminent arrival of the Sex Pistols, those bad boys who vomit at airports, start riots and bleed. There were TV crews from New York all over Memphis for their concert.
Danny Fields

The Sex Pistols were at the sound check when the *Variety 77* television show presented them on national TV for the first time. Alan King and Telly Savalas made a point of announcing their appearance every five minutes:

'Coming up soon, the sensational Sex Pistols.' Sophie, Malcolm's assistant, arrived from London for the rest of the tour and was overheard saying, 'I don't want to go on tour with this poxy band.' She enjoyed the show that evening, as did everybody.
John Holmstrom, editor, *Punk Magazine*

They were just another new band. They were practically unknown in America. Their songs were very underground and their album had no commercial potential; nobody was going to play it on the radio. But I went to see the opening show. Afterwards, in the parking lot at the back, I was saying goodbye to Malcolm as the bus was getting ready to leave. I said, 'I know you boys are going to have a good time in America. It's too bad I can't come with you.' Malcolm said, 'We can only take 12 people. There's the band, the bodyguards, Sophie and me, and the driver.' He counted and realized, 'That's only 11, Bob. Why don't you come?' Joe Stevens [a friend and photographer] said, 'Wait, Malcolm, I'll go,' but Malcolm said, 'Sorry, Joe. Bob asked first.' I ran back to the hotel, checked out and jumped on the bus to Memphis.
Bob Gruen

There were great moments out on the road. I was happy with the whole idea of cracking America by making a stir in the heartlands rather than taking the accepted routes. And it underlined for me so many of the things that were great about the Sex Pistols. It was just so cool to walk into a place – a truck stop, a burger joint in Idaho – with these guys. They were so natural – stylish, cool, different. What I'm looking for is some sort of recognition of that honesty. These kids were saying 'Express yourself,' and they represented that as a normal, healthy expression for kids of their age. Right to the end, that was their strength.
John 'Boogie' Tiberi

It's unbelievable that a rock group that played no more than 100 performances (less than 50 according to guitarist Steve Jones), and existed for [only] 27 months, could become so internationally disliked as the Sex Pistols.
John Holmstrom

We did a lot of TV. We were being quite difficult with the television and the press. They always wanted to ask the same old questions. We felt we were justifying ourselves all the time. They'd ask us stupid questions, real tabloid stuff, like, 'Why do you call yourselves punks?' We just got fed up with it in the end.
Paul Cook

To me, the Sex Pistols were political radicals. It was in their lyrics; it was in the posture of the band. But it's dangerous when you move from the music section of the newspapers onto the front pages. Unless you're powerful enough, like the Beatles, you're in trouble. No one should ever want to be on the front page.
Danny Fields

Above: Steve Jones prepares for another night out with his sex pistol

PISTOLS SHOCK USA.

Melody Maker, 14 January 1978

Travelling with the band was a real contrast compared to just seeing their concerts. Their shows were complete chaos, but the bus was actually mellow. Mostly we drank beer, passed joints and listened to dub reggae music. But then the bus would pull up, the doors would snap open, and there would be three television cameras pointing up from the bottom of the stairs. The fans would be gathered around and the madness would start.

Bob Gruen

We had everything about us: we had the look; we had the music. We were getting really good. Now that Sid had joined the band, I think that, musically as well, we had a great band.

Paul Cook

They knew their music. They could play it, although Sid was never much of a musician. People don't realize it's not Sid on the album and it's not Sid on his own solo record. On stage he was an actor. At the end of the shows it was such chaos that Johnny said, 'Have you felt like you've been cheated?' They hadn't been cheated because they were a really good band. But it was always more about chaos and 'situation'.

Bob Gruen

What they did, in terms of music, was radical, which no one really appreciated. They were famous for the wrong reasons.

Danny Fields

The audiences were stunned, confused, angry and amused. Malcolm liked to rile up the audience. Johnny Rotten was like the guy in the circus that you were supposed to throw the ball at and dunk in the water. Basically, Johnny just yelled insults all night and people threw things back. They were different to any other band. It was the first time somebody had come out on stage and thoroughly insulted the audience instead of trying to please them. The Pistols were shocked by the intensity of the violence in America, and I think they were scared by it. In Texas, a guy came into the dressing-room and pulled his coat back to show them he had a gun in his waistband. He said, 'I just want you boys to know, if there's any trouble, I'm on your side.' These were kids from England who had never seen a policeman with a gun.

Bob Gruen

I think Malcolm was really shit-scared of what was going on, but loved every minute of it. He knew he was getting them into trouble. When they went on the American tour and were playing a gig in Texas, he told Johnny to go out and tell the audience that 'All cowboys are faggots'. It all ended in a mad fight. Sid bashed some bloke with his bass guitar. There was blood all over the place. That was typical of Malcolm.

Joe Corré, son of Vivienne Westwood and Malcolm McLaren

Opposite: The Sex Pistols in the USA

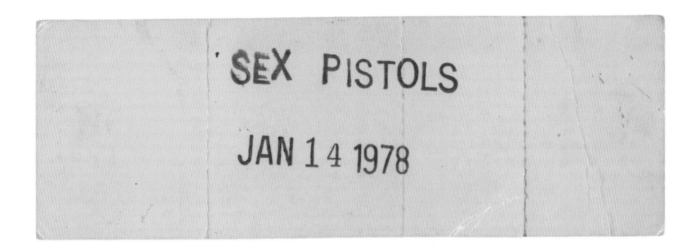

They were throwing pigs' noses and rats at us.
Paul Cook

We wanted to see how horrible it was. We wanted to see real cowboys – not rhinestone imitations. I got this weird call. It was like totally FBI, saying, 'You're leaving on a plane tomorrow. Don't ask any questions. You're going to San Antonio [Texas]. We're fixing your tickets, first class. We're paying for it. This is your assignment. John [Holmstrom of *Punk Magazine*] was already there, when I showed up at Randy's Rodeo. It was one of the most intense shows – the one where Sid hit a guy over the head with the bass. Roberta Bayley, photographer **The Sex Pistols arrive in San Antonio to play at Randy's Rodeo, their largest American date so far, holding about 2000 people. The band is beginning to fray at the edges. Paul and Steve hang together, Sid is off with groupies and drugs, and Johnny is disgusted with everyone. Johnny has been working on some new songs, one of which is called 'Religion'. It's intense, perhaps too intense for Steve and Paul, who aren't sure about taking on that heavy a problem.** George Gimarc, *Punk Diary 1970-1979* There was a pile of beer cans several feet deep. People had been throwing them at the stage. It was incredible. Many of them were full when they threw them. I think Sid took a full one. Sid hit someone. The lights went down and there was a weird murmur in the club. You didn't know if there would be an incident where the entire audience would go up and kill them or not. This was San Antonio. They were all weird macho fucking cowboys. John Holmstrom **We played at all these mad cowboy places down south. It was madness. They'd seen all the publicity. They were throwing anything they could at us – pigs' noses, beer cans, rats. It was really awful.** Paul Cook It was pretty scary. It's more scary now thinking about it than it was at the time. We'd never been anywhere like America. Shit like getting rats thrown at us and guns being waved about doesn't happen in England. Looking back on it, there's some right nutters in America. We were lucky we didn't get shot. Steve Jones **After the sound check, where the Sex Pistols rehearsed their latest tune, they went to the TV bar and mixed with the local clientele – mostly cops and hookers. In a corner of the bar, Paul, Steve and Malcolm discussed the problems they were having with Rotten.** John Holmstrom She is only the second girl who ever hit me. One time, at a Ramones' gig, this girl

Above and opposite: A ticket for the Pistols' concert in San Francisco came up to me and said, 'Are you Sid Vicious?' When I said I was, she hit me. Only I didn't know it was a girl. She looked just like a guy, so I stomped her. Sid Vicious, *Dallas Morning News*, 10 January 1978 **For 10 days on the road with the band I slept in my clothes. Beer and stuff was spilt on them but it didn't matter. I was still probably one of the cleaner people on the bus. Before we got to LA, Sid was actually beginning to smell really bad. He was so drunk all the time, he was walking around like a baby. I told the roadies, 'You really must wash this guy, not just for me, but for the rest of us.' I persuaded two of the roadies to fill up a tub full of water in his hotel room. I made them both take his clothes off and physically lift him up and put him in the tub. He just let it happen. He was like a cuddly little baby. They washed him off. I thought, thank God, because I couldn't take him any more.** Bob Gruen We waded through 300 religious demonstrators handing out leaflets. Cain's Ballroom [in] Tulsa, Oklahoma, [is an] authentic '50s-style country and western beer hall. [Pictures of country singer] Roy Acuff, Gene Vincent, Elvis and many others are framed and hung against the wall, each larger than life and ensconced with his own candle. You can believe that the crowd – redneck hippies, cowboys and a few Indians – did not come to praise; they came to take the dare. Would the Sex Pistols get them off? Of the 800 attending, half left during the performance. The ones who stayed stood staring, awestruck – [there was] no pogoing. Annette Weatherman, *Search and Destroy*, issue 5, 1978 **Me and Steve used to go off all the time, with anyone who would take us, to all the local night spots. We just wanted to escape from the madness, but we ended up in even stranger situations.** Paul Cook Being at the Sex Pistols' concert [in San Antonio] was the most frightening thing in my life. Roberta Bayley **Sid went to some girl's house with the bodyguard. He started playing with the bodyguard's knife and asked if it was sharp. The guy said, 'Yeah.' Sid asked, 'How sharp?'…'Razor sharp,' he replied. Sid cut his own arm. The cut was about two or three inches long and half an inch deep. Blood was spurting out. The bodyguard took him to hospital and, for whatever reason, the hospital wouldn't even treat him. I don't know what he said or what he did, but they didn't even sew him up. They just sent him back out without even a Band-Aid. Sid had this big open wound on his arm for days. I realized nobody was going to do anything about it, and I didn't want to see it get infected, so I washed it out, taped it up with butterfly stitching and put a bandage on him.** Bob Gruen

The security, the people on the tour, the bodyguards, everyone hated Malcolm and they did everything to break up the band.

John Holmstrom

It all got fucked up. The air of paranoia around the band was terrible. We had people following us all over the place – the American press, the English press, guys filming us. Malcolm was paranoid. He thought the CIA were after us. We always thought someone was going to get arrested.
Paul Cook

Of course, the places we played were where all the worst nutters lived. It wasn't like major cities. San Antonio is bad now, but it was really weird back then. The idea was to play in places where nobody else played. It was all for the sake of publicity. Everything was for publicity's sake with Malcolm. He was doing what a good manager would do, but didn't really care about what we felt.
Steve Jones

Our benefactor, Tom Forcade, who founded *High Times*, was credited with breaking up the Sex Pistols. He paid John [Holmstrom] and me to go on the trip. There were rumours that the FBI were watching the Sex Pistols. They thought Tom Forcade was the FBI, so they were calling him FBI at the time, but he probably wasn't. After all, Noel Monk, who was the road manager of the Sex Pistols, had had a run-in with Tom a few years earlier. The rumour that Forcade was FBI was started by Allen Ginsberg [the Beat poet] for some reason. He later denied it, but rumours tend to go on. Tom was such a pain in the ass that people wanted to believe something bad about him. What he really wanted was to take over the Sex Pistols from Malcolm McLaren and manage them because he thought they were the future.
Roberta Bayley

When Holmstrom called me from the road and told me to meet him in San Francisco for the last show of the tour, I had no interest in going. But John told me it was my job,

that I was [the] resident punk and I had to show up, it would be good for the story he was writing. Also, Tom Forcade was making a movie, and had given us a lot of money and I owed it to Tom and him to show up. So I picked up the receptionist from *Playboy* magazine and we drove up to San Francisco.
Legs McNeil

One night on the tour, I'd loosened my pants while sleeping. I rolled over and actually broke my zipper. I came out of my room and Johnny was sitting there with like 40 safety-pins on his jacket. I said, 'Look pal, I know this is part of your costume, but would you give me three of them?' I spent the rest of the tour with safety-pins in my flies.
Bob Gruen

Malcolm's strategy for the Pistols was the theory of chaos. It was out of control and it had nothing to do with this phenomenon of terror that was coming over from England.
Gene Krell

They put safety-pins in the Queen's nose [on the poster promoting their album] and they would vomit and curse and say it's the end of the world.
Danny Fields in *Please Kill Me*

I had a pair of boots I'd got much earlier, the same time as I bought a pair from Johnny Thunders. They were good, heavy American motorcycle boots with a steel toe. Sid loved my boots. I fell asleep on the bus and left my boots sitting on the floor next to me. Sid picked them up and started walking around in them. I heard from Joe Stevens later that Sid took a knife and held it to my throat while I was sleeping. He turned to them all and said, 'If I killed him, I could keep his boots.' Nobody said anything; they just watched. He didn't really mean it because he

didn't stab me. When I woke up he was wearing my boots, and he just said, 'I like your boots. Do you mind if I wear them for a bit? You can wear mine if you like.'
Bob Gruen

The Pistols sucked at Winterland [Ballroom, San Francisco]. The show was awful, but it didn't seem to matter. Everyone was just thrilled to be in the presence of the Sex Pistols.
Legs McNeil

The Sex Pistols close their first US tour with a show at the Winterland in San Francisco. It's their second biggest show ever, in front of over 4,000 fans…local punk acts the Nuns and the Avengers opened the show. Just before the band came on, the 25-minute film *Number One* was shown. It's [a] pastiche of news clips and interviews that serves as a propaganda piece to stir the audience up. When the band finally hits the stage, the crowd goes wild.
George Gimarc, *Punk Diary 1970-1979*

Every time the Pistols interacted with anybody in America, something went wrong and just caused more trouble. Malcolm was playing up to it. He wanted risks and trouble, but didn't seem to know how to deal with it. However, one way he tried to eliminate too much trouble was to make sure we never stayed in the hotel we'd booked because everyone would know we'd be there. He'd find some other motel, some cheap place down the road. He'd hide the bus round the corner and get us rooms. The last time we went to San Francisco we were booked into the Morocco, but Malcolm wanted to stay in some hidden, out-of-the-way place. I said, 'I'm not really in the band. I'll see you later at the Morocco. There's a big bath tub waiting for me.' That's where I ended up.
Bob Gruen

IT WAS SCARY.
That was one of the main reasons why we split up.
Paul Cook

Sid wore his best bare chest; all freshly cut and scratched. Tying off his left arm was eight inches of foul bandage. Sid did not care that his Johnny Thunderesque bows and pirouettes – his absurd attempts to style Thunders' sneer – made him look juvenile and the copycat – *he doesn't care*.
Annette Weatherman, *Search and Destroy*, issue 5, 1978

Annie Leibovitz, the *Rolling Stone* photographer, paraded through the dressing-room and began setting up all her equipment in the bathroom at the end. She said, 'Ah, excuse me…Johnny, could we get you in here for a shot with Sid?' 'Fuck him,' Johnny said. 'Why should I have to go over to that bastard. Tell the wanker to come over here!' 'Ah, Sid, do you think you could join Johnny on the couch so I can get a shot of the two [of you]?' Sid said, 'Fuck off!'
Legs McNeil

We had a big showdown in San Francisco. We found Sid on some girl's floor. He'd taken an overdose and was half-dead. I just thought, 'Fucking hell, this is too much.' We were meant to go straight off on a tour of Sweden and Europe. I thought there was no way we could do that. We weren't in the right state of mind. Sid was off on one of his benders. We decided we'd had enough.

Paul Cook

It was a bloody mess by the time we got to San Francisco…which was never meant to be the end of the tour. There were gigs set up in Finland for the following year. Overnight, the band broke up, and everything had to be cancelled. John had disappeared. He was meant to be staying in this poxy motel. I had to go and find him, and he wasn't there. Sid had gone off after the gig with a bunch of rich American kids, who were into drugs and had too much money for their own good. I got this phone call from them in the middle of the night: 'Boogie, come over, Sid is dead.' I got there and Sid was just turning blue on the bed. None of them were together enough to do anything. I rang [rock promoter] Bill Graham and we got Sid out to Marin County, where he knew this alternative doctor who would be able to do something with acupuncture.
John 'Boogie' Tiberi

By the time we'd done San Francisco, I'd had enough – *had enough*, mate. John wanted to carry on, but I'd had enough. I said to John, 'That's it. I've had enough,' and fucked off to Brazil.
Steve Jones

We had a big showdown meeting with John in the hotel. We said it was all over. But John wanted to carry on and get rid of Malcolm. This was his idea and, in retrospect, it was quite a good one. But there was just no way we could carry on.
Paul Cook

I went back for Sid the next day, and there he was sitting up in bed in pyjamas and a dressing-gown, looking like he'd just graduated from college, looking like punk had never happened. That alternative doctor had some powerful 'juju' going there! But, at the same time, Sid was pleading, 'Get me out of here!' We flew to New York the same day on the red eye, travelling first class as the record company was still paying. When we arrived, Sid didn't wake up. I still don't know what he'd taken on the flight – though it must have been a prescription drug of some sort. He was out cold. The stewardess said the only thing to do was to make him colder still, so there we both were literally throwing ice cubes at Sid. Meanwhile, the curtains had gone back, and the economy passengers at the back were filing past looking at us. Then, for the second time on the tour, we had sirens blaring and the full police

escort, taking Sid through Manhattan, up to the Jamaica Hospital.
John 'Boogie' Tiberi

McLaren accused Rotten of turning into Rod Stewart. Rotten accused McLaren of trying to turn him into Rod Stewart. Paul Cook and Steve Jones used their tickets to go to Rio…Johnny Rotten flew to New York.
John Holmstrom

I am sick of working with the Sex Pistols.
Johnny Rotten, *New York Post*, 18 January 1978

I walked in [to CBGB's] and Johnny Rotten was there. He had flown in from San Francisco. He said, 'Did you hear the news?' I said, 'What news?' He showed me his T-shirt that said 'I survived the Sex Pistols' tour!' Johnny had written on his shirt, 'But the band didn't!'
Bob Gruen in *Please Kill Me*

I thought we would probably split up for a couple of months and maybe get back together after it had calmed down. But it wasn't to be.
Paul Cook

The management is bored with managing a successful rock'n'roll band. The group is bored with being a successful rock'n'roll band. Burning venues and destroying record companies is more creative than making it.
Malcom McLaren's press statement, 19 January 1978 (withdrawn two hours later)

After the Sex Pistols' tour, I had no interest in doing *Punk Magazine*. It just felt like this phoney media thing. Punk wasn't ours any more. It had become everything we hated. It seemed like it had become everything we had started the magazine to rage against.
Legs McNeil

My only regret is that we did not keep the Pistols going another year. I don't think Malcolm realized how good the music was. We'd really only done one album – *Swindle* was just a film soundtrack. I would have loved to have done another album. We had an idea to do another album with Sid before he died. He was going to be the singer. He could have been a great front man.
Paul Cook

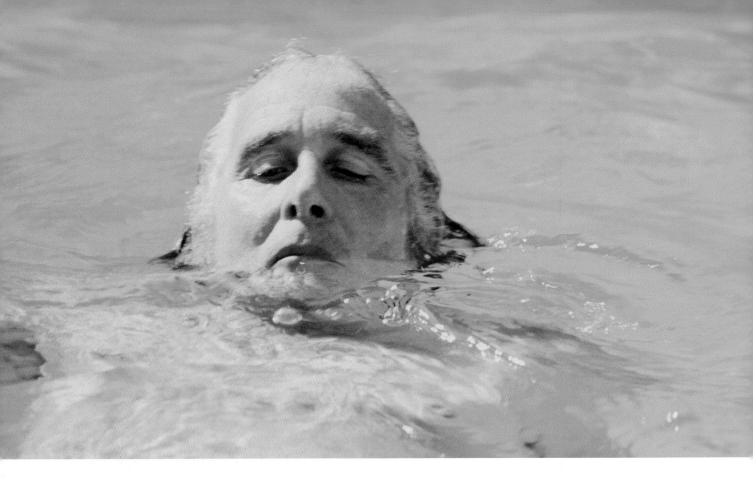

So Steve and me flew to Rio. Paul Cook

Above: Train robber Ronnie Biggs

Visiting Ronnie Biggs [the escaped train robber] was my idea, even before we left for America in December 1977. There had been a story in the papers about Biggs being tracked down in Brazil, and it seemed like a good plan to meet up with him. I got the number from John Blake, the journalist. We made the contact, but didn't really get much further. Then, once everything started to go wrong in America, the whole Ronnie Biggs idea came back into play again.
John 'Boogie' Tiberi

We ended up going to Rio. That was Malcolm's idea. We didn't want to go back home anyway – to go back to London and face the music. As far as the band was concerned, it was all over in San Francisco.
Paul Cook

Well, we went down to Rio and got hooked up with Ronnie Biggs and tried to put everything behind us.
Steve Jones

I just couldn't see how going to a police state to see a failed bank robber had anything to do with us. What was the connection? Malcolm had the nerve to tell me that's what the Pistols are all about, and I had to tell him, 'Ducky, I am what the Pistols are all about. You are not required any more.'
Johnny Rotten in *The Filth and the Fury*

Malcolm got a film deal to do a story around the band. We never really wanted to make a film. We were sort of railroaded into doing it.
Paul Cook

Right: Steve Jones and Ronnie Biggs

305

All I did was cash in on the fact that I'm good-looking and girls like me.

Sid Vicious in *The Filth and the Fury*

It's a pity in a way – all these rich kids becoming punks. I find that revolting. It's like an army now…a faction, chic. I'm not chic. I could never be chic. I was in it from its inception.
Sid Vicious in *The Filth and the Fury*

A vital part of the puzzle in making *The Filth and the Fury* [released in 2000] was giving Sid Vicious a voice. Then, in amongst the old footage in the vaults, we uncovered an interview Julien [Temple, director of *The Great Rock'n'Roll Swindle*] had done with Sid in Hyde Park [London] the year before his death. Julien wanted each of the band members to have an identity. When we saw that interview, we knew Sid would be able to have a voice too, which was very important. What's wonderful about the footage is that Sid is so surprisingly articulate and reflective, and so *funny*. Everybody just thinks he was a schmuck, but he had a razor-sharp wit.
Amanda Temple, film producer

All I did was cash in on the fact that I'm good-looking and I have a good figure and girls like me. What do they want? A fucking angel in flares and an anorak? 'Cause if they want that, that ain't me, baby.
Sid Vicious in *The Filth and the Fury*

Sid was never really angry. For him, things would always go wrong. He'd start off doing something not too serious and would fuck up…really fuck up. He was fragile and really just a kid.
John 'Boogie' Tiberi

Who needs the fucking UK? It's a load of fucking shit. So we were left doing nothing. I was just sitting there…we didn't even fucking rehearse, nobody wanted to fucking rehearse or do anything. So like, y'know, it's a logical conclusion, d'you know what I mean? Boredom. And like, I'm that way inclined. So what do I turn to?
Sid Vicious in *The Filth and the Fury*

He was eating a hot dog. I went to take a picture and Sid said, 'Wait a second.' He took more mustard and ketchup. He smeared it on the hot dog…and then on his face to make the picture. He knew exactly what he was doing.
Bob Gruen

The Swindle was becoming more and more Malcolm's story, and I still had Sid to take care of. We shot 'My Way' in Paris, in the same theatre where Johnny Halliday and Edith Piaf had played. Back in London we shot 'C'mon Everybody' in the streets around Paddington and he was brilliant. We did some great stuff with Sid, even if dealing with him on a daily basis was becoming a nightmare. You went to his place, got him up, took him to wherever…but there was a certain point beyond which you did not go, where you left the door firmly closed. I couldn't influence what he was doing beyond that point.
John 'Boogie' Tiberi

The Sex Pistols were over and Sid was in limbo, but the normal rock'n'roll things were still going on – record releases, video shoots for the film which none of us thought was ever going to happen, interviews… He might have been smacked up and depressed, but to the record company, the press and the management he was still working… He even managed a gig in Camden as the Vicious White Kids with Glen Matlock.

Nobody really wanted to do the Sid and Nancy story. In the end it was our no-nonsense Scottish deputy editor on *Record Mirror* who drew the short straw. She'd witnessed the worst side of the Bay City Rollers with Tam Paton [their former manager] in the mid-1970s and claimed she wasn't easily shocked. She got through the words bit OK. It was only when Sid and Nancy repaired to the bathroom for the pictures that she decided to make her excuses and leave.
John Shearlaw, music journalist

It got to the stage with Nancy where we were thinking, 'The only way we'll get rid of Nancy is if we personally grass her up to the police.' Which of course we couldn't do, even if it was being thought about. Imagine what the headlines would have been: 'Sex Pistols' management inform on drug dealer!' It just shows what a fucked-up bunch of idealists we really were.
John 'Boogie' Tiberi

And, like, the others just didn't understand. They thought, you know, oh you, you can handle it man. But…dope sickness isn't like that. It's not something you can just blow away. It's the worst sickness you can ever imagine. You can't get comfortable…you're boiling hot and you pour with sweat. And your nose dribbles and, and…and all of a sudden you get the colds and the sweat turns to fucking ice on you…you put a jumper on and then you're boiling hot again…you take it off, and then you get cold again… you just can't win…you lie down and that's not comfortable. You sit up, that's not comfortable. It drives you insane.
Sid Vicious in *The Filth and the Fury*

In a lot of ways the work was unaffected. We were shooting 'C'mon Everybody' on a tiny budget, just me and Julien [Temple], and Sid's belief, his confidence, was tremendous. We must have done about 12 separate takes before we got one scene, and he hit his camera mark every single fucking time. He was amazing that day.
John 'Boogie' Tiberi

Almost as soon as he got off the plane back to London, Sid Vicious gave an interview to me for the *NME*; it was simultaneously filmed for Lech Kowalski's documentary *DOA*. As he lay on a bed in his West London mews cottage, with Nancy Spungen next to him, Sid's vocal chords were so destroyed by a combination of drug abuse and sickness that his voice really did sound much of the time like a death rattle – as though this was some wonderful stroke of deeply ironic McLaren-like symbolism. In hindsight, the interview reads chillingly. In particular, Nancy Spungen's request for Sid to be poured only a small brandy: 'Sid's not supposed to drink. Otherwise he'll die.'
Chris Salewicz and Adrian Boot, *Punk: The Illustrated History of a Music Revolution*

There came a point where I couldn't do anything with Sid. By the end of the summer, it was beyond a working relationship. I remember the last conversation, saying goodbye, before he went to join Nancy in New York. He must have seen the nightmare he was flying into. I wasn't really surprised to hear that Nancy had died. Even before he left, my thinking was, 'This is such a fucking waste.' I was thinking of what we'd achieved that year, and all the great stuff he'd done despite it all.
John 'Boogie' Tiberi

Babylon, your Queendom is burning.

Peter Tosh, reggae musician

I went with Johnny Rotten to Jamaica. Don Letts [film-maker and former DJ] was there and Kate Simons [photographer] flew in. The Kingston Sheraton became our second home. It was a happy time. The guys over there loved Johnny because the 'God Save the Queen' single convinced them that he was a major anti-colonial type. They were always saying, 'Chant down Babylon, chant down Buckingham Palace.' As Peter Tosh used to say, 'Babylon, your Queendom is burning.' Rotten had major cred, and they all adored him. They brought him to smoke the chalice which, as a woman, I was never allowed to do. I probably couldn't have handled it anyway to be honest. Viv Goldman, features editor, *Sounds* magazine

I was supposed to go with the Pistols to America, but in the back of my mind I thought, if someone's going to get shot it's going to be me. I knew it would all go wrong. When John came back, he was in a real state. Basically, Richard Branson and Virgin knew he was under pressure and thought the trip to Jamaica would do him good. Richard was keen to get involved in reggae, so as I knew Jamaica well and John was keen on reggae, the idea was for the three of us to go and sign up bands for Branson's new Front Line label. Dennis Morris, photographer and record industry figure **Kate Simons took a picture of John and me on the beach in Jamaica. That was funny. We had that guy Boogie [John Tiberi] hanging around trying to film us.** Viv Goldman

Above: Johnny Rotten in Trench Town, Jamaica • Opposite, top: Johnny Rotten with helper • Bottom: Johnny Rotten tackles the 'chalice'

John was more or less formulating Public Image Ltd while he was in Jamaica. If you listen to _Public Image,_ their debut album, it was basically dub with snatches of vocals every now and then, like a Tubby mix. While we were in Jamaica we went to quite a few dances, and these helped him realize that this sound could work, but in a rock way.

Dennis Morris

I worked in Jamaica and did the PR for Bob Marley. Virgin came to meet us in this weird car, like some sort of carriage, and we were given those nice suites by the pool in what was then the Kingston Sheraton, which was like our HQ. It was the time when reggae was getting hot and Richard Branson had charged John with some sort of A & R type vibe. It used to be such an incredible scene at that hotel. It had like a galaxy of stars – more stars than there were in heaven would be there drinking these fruit punches and concoctions from the bar. That was the big scene, the uptown scene, then not far down the road was Tommy Cowan [Bob Marley's manager]. That was an incredible scene because there would be Big Youth, maybe Peter Tosh, U Roy… There's that famous story about how they got all the money across from Africa. There was some businessman, from Nigeria, I think, arriving with a suitcase. He throws it open and it's crammed full of cash. Maybe it isn't true – I wasn't present, but it's still a good story. That was an incredible scene at the Sheraton Hotel, with worlds colliding. It was like a little island of international luxury, while just down the road, where the guys came from, people didn't necessarily have their own toilet.

Viv Goldman

They took me to Jamaica – why, I don't know. I'd never been there. I was from London.

Don Letts, film-maker and former DJ

When we hit Kingston, we came off the plane, went through customs and immigration, and came into the terminal, which was crowded with fans. 'God Save the Queen' had made John a real anti-colonial hero, but we had no idea it had filtered back to Jamaica. So within days of arriving, we were hanging out with U-Roy and Prince Far I [big reggae stars]. We were walking around Trench Town and everyone welcomed us. They put John to the test with the chalice. He passed easily. They loved him. It was great for him. He could relax for the first time in ages. He was also doing something positive. He would say to Richard, 'You should sign Far I,' and he'd say, 'Sure.' Then Far I would come down to the Sheraton and we'd go to the studio, he'd play a track and Richard would sign him. What was unique about Richard was that he'd do the deal there and then. He'd literally say, 'Come to the hotel tomorrow,' and the cash would be there. The band would arrive the next day and he'd open a suitcase and give them cash – £5,000 or £10,000, or whatever he'd agreed – and they'd give him a tape. This was refreshing for Jamaican artists because usually, when they arrived in England to sign a contract, the record company would renege on the amount of cash. For the first time there was a man coming to them with a suitcase full of money and they were really happy.

Dennis Morris

There was a real connection between punk and reggae. Reggae was very much identified with Rastafarians, who were called Black Heart Men in Jamaica. Rastas were regarded as the dregs – as untouchables – the same as punks were. It was a pivotal time. Before we went on the Jamaican trip, we had all been together with Bob Marley in London. Bob was staying at Basin Street Studios, which was just up the road from me. We used to hang out a lot at that period. It wasn't just me – Don Letts, Neil Spencer [former editor of _NME_] and doubtless other people were bending Bob's ear too. At first he was down on punks, calling them unclean. We would tell him there were many parallels between punk and reggae. Both were protesting about the inequities of society and the injustices of the system. In the end Bob said, 'See all those people with a safety-pin stuck through their ears? I like to see a man who can suffer pain without crying.' That's when he came round and recorded his single 'Punky Reggae Party' to sum up the connection.

Viv Goldman

Richard Branson knew exactly what he was doing. People like U-Roy took Virgin Records to another level of success. The Sex Pistols might have made Virgin Records, but the reggae kept it going afterwards.

Dennis Morris

Everybody jumped on the bandwagon but none of them understood it. Paul Cook

It wasn't about spitting or pogoing or looking like an idiot. It was about playing good rock'n'roll, looking good and spreading your seed.
Tony James, bass player, Generation X

Punk was not a movement to perpetuate itself. It was a movement which had to hate itself. It had to make itself violent by its own ethos – to fuck itself up.
Paul Durden, former roadie, now scriptwriter

As punk became mainstream, it lost the naive enthusiasm that drove it. It didn't happen overnight, but there was definitely a shift. As the violence got more stupid and pointless, many of the original punks moved off.
Nigel Wingrove, founder, *Stains* fanzine

Punk ended up being not quite what I would have hoped it would be. I always hoped for something a bit more intelligent.
Steve Walsh, guitarist, the Flowers of Romance

We [Bazooka Joe] supported Sham 69. The audience were awful – full of skinheads. There was this horrible punk in a jumpsuit he'd bought at Laurence Corner [an army surplus store] who kept gobbing at me. I really wanted to whack him. Then he started leaning over me, trying to play my bass. It was at that moment I felt punk could go either way. By that time, the audiences had got really violent – they would get on stage and start a fight. Everything had got harder and meaner; it had changed.
Chris Duffy, former bass player, Bazooka Joe

For me, by late '77, the whole punk thing wasn't cool. As far as I was concerned, it was finished. But for people who were there at the start, this was the period when they became commercially successful, when they got something out of it. Bands like the UK Subs and Sham 69 really milked it. They were really two-dimensional punks, about as uncool as you could get.
Mark Powell, Soho tailor

What you did get was all these old rock'n'rollers taking their trousers in. People with long hair and all sorts of horrible badges. What it never was was hippie. It was never kind of pub rock, which it became.
Robert Elms, broadcaster and journalist

The whole punk thing had slowly descended into an abyss, one that was, in part, frequented by really horrible, stupid, bland people, those who'd read all the adverse tabloid publicity and actually believed it. Now they were 'behaving as punks' – conforming to the *Sun* newspaper's scathing viewpoint. They pierced their noses with safety-pins, they were smelly, they spat, spilt their beer, they swore (very loudly), they were uncouth and belligerent, they were uncultured and, most unforgivably, they were very dull. For many, it was the ideal excuse for the yob to be in vogue. Now their basic lack of education and supreme ignorance could be a help rather than a hindrance. Their total lack of manners and personal hygiene could go unnoticed. And they could sniff as much glue as they desired without damaging their brain. The perfect illustration of this was that many of these Johnny-come-ridiculously-late punks became skinheads and joined the National Front. These very same people would have worn flares two years earlier. For them it was just a fashion, another trend. It was not a mentality or an attitude. For the initial punk movers and shakers it was about doing what you wanted, like forming a band, designing clothes, starting a magazine. Spitting in clubs and swearing loudly were abhorrent to us.
Chris Sullivan, author

By '78 I'd lost interest. I was in a band, we were doing our own thing and the way punk went had no relevance to me.
Suggs, singer with Madness

The attitude wasn't about conforming – it was about people doing it for themselves, whether collectively or individually. It wasn't about doing what you read in the paper.
Paul Simonon, bass player, the Clash

Above: Punk fans in 1979 • Opposite, clockwise from top: Charlie Harper and the UK Subs in concert; Islington punks; Fashion victim; Jimmy Pursey of Sham 69

We felt we were playing second fiddle to Malcolm and Vivienne.

Helen Robinson, designer

Above: Boy in the Kings Road

When we opened Boy, the people who went to Acme would walk in and ask where the peg trousers were. We said we didn't do them any more, so they walked out. They couldn't handle it. We were stupid. We should have kept the Acme name and we would've made a lot of money. As far as we were concerned, being creative and doing something new was more important than making money. That's why we haven't got any money now.
Helen Robinson

Boy was the offspring of Acme Attractions. It was owned by the same people, namely John Krevine and Steph Raynor, working with the designer Helen Robinson. They had moved from the basement of the Antiquarius Market in the Kings Road to a shopfront just down the road. Unfortunately, they dropped the retro aspect and went gung-ho into the punk thing just as all the groovy types were becoming disenchanted with punk and moving back into a more '50s style. Others were getting into Kraftwerk [the German electro band] and reacting to the scruffy, chaotic uniformity that had become punk with a dose of Germanic order. The only thing I bought there was a pair of peg trousers that were old Acme stock that served me rather well for the next few years. The punk thing was now totally laboured and hackneyed, which is the fate of every aspect of popular culture that is based on sensation. The old adage that the candle that burns twice as bright lasts half as long seems to fit this particular bill.
Chris Sullivan

I thought that Malcolm and Vivienne got all the credit for everything in that period, and Steph and I were quite angry about it. A lot of the people that were part of the scene were in fact clothed by us – Acme Attractions. Only the few with money wore Sex or Seditionaries – the rest couldn't afford it. Everybody bought the T-shirts but the rest was overpriced. The original bondage trousers were made of blackout material from the war, the cheapest material you could buy, but they were brilliant. I just wish I'd done them. With Acme we would have to work our arses off all week just to stock the shop for Saturday, as it would all go, whereas you'd see the same stuff in Sex for weeks. We clothed most of the people on the scene but Malcolm and Vivienne got all the credit. When we went to Boy, Steph and John Krevine just argued continually. Steph had put a lot of money into the shop and Krevine wanted him to put in another £80,000, but Steph refused. We only lasted six months. Then John Krevine bought all of Vivienne's designs and released them under the Boy name, which I would never have done, as I'm a designer myself. It all ended quite badly.
Helen Robinson

To give them their due, Helen and Steph Raynor did clothe a generation of movers and groovers, first of all with Acme, and then Boy, although all the stuff they did at Boy was rubbish, apart from the Seditionaries stuff they licensed. But that wasn't Helen or Steph. That was John Krevine trying to cash in. Then, of course, they opened up a shop in Covent Garden, PX, which used to sell all that slightly space-age, padded shoulder stuff which was all the rage at Billy's, the club that spawned the Blitz.
Chris Sullivan

Andrew Czezowski offered us a shop in James Street, which became PX. The shop was a reflection of our dissatisfaction with punk. Punk was blown out of all proportion, and we didn't want to be part of it any more. It was stupid and horrible. Malcolm and Vivienne's thing worked because it was sex – people walking round with their bits hanging out – and the media loved it. Malcolm was very good at what he did, and nothing else mattered. Everybody had to worship at the shrine of Malcolm and Vivienne. We should have carried on with Acme Attractions. John Krevine did try and form the band Chelsea, with Gene October, Billy Idol and Tony James, but they didn't have the same impact as the Sex Pistols.
Helen Robinson

Boy soon became a tourist shop. We used to sit in the Chelsea Potter and watch all the American tourists buying punk T-shirts to take back home to their kids. Boy tried to cash in and fucked it.
Frank Kelly, Sex Pistols' aficionado

When we did PX, we again used to sell out of everything. With that shop we clothed another new generation – the people who went to Billy's and the Blitz. The Blitz was just down the road in Covent Garden and we used to go there after work. We knew Brendan, the manager. Steve Strange [later of Visage] was working for us in PX at the time, and I introduced him to the Blitz. We also knew the bloke who started Billy's – David Claridge [the man behind the GMTV character Roland Rat]. They'd recently had a Bowie night, so I asked Brendan if we could do something on a Tuesday. I stupidly mentioned it to Steve Strange, and the next thing I knew he'd gone behind our back and was doing a night there. I asked him about it and he said, 'Don't worry. I'll let you in for free.'
Helen Robinson

Above: Shop window detail from Boy

The uglier you were, **the more true to the spirit of punk you were.** Daniela Soave, music journalist

[*Jubilee* is] the first 'official' punk movie. 'Rule Britannia', as mimed by Jordan, should have them pogoing in the aisles.
David Pirie, *Time Out*, February 1978

Derek Jarman was a very respected film-maker, and we really had to look at *Jubilee* [released in February 1978] as very much a rival project, but not one that would stop our film [*The Great Rock'n'Roll Swindle*] from going ahead.
Jeremy Thomas, film producer

If you weren't on the guest list for the Pistols' boat trip, the only alternative was the stilted celebrations of the Queen's actual Silver Jubilee at dodgy street parties all over the country – fold-up tables, miles of bunting and Union Jack hats, and every lamppost bedecked with bog paper. It was surreal and unforgettable, like a broad daylight New Year's Eve party, with tea and Ribena for refreshments. It could only happen in England. Derek Jarman's take was to go right back to the first Queen Elizabeth and bring her into the present, as a way of showing how bizarre and disintegrated the country had become, that things like the Jubilee celebrations could still be going on in the middle of a punk revolution. He also came up with the idea of crazed girl punks running riot, which was

amusing for a while. The whole thing, unfortunately, had a truly duff soundtrack.
John Shearlaw

The enduring image was of a naked, fat and rather frightening Toyah Willcox, who wasn't really an actor, but hadn't yet been moulded into the face of the New Romantic pop star. She must cringe to look at that now. And that Jordan woman doing 'Rule Britannia'! It almost seemed to throw back at you that thing about the early days of punk, like the uglier you were, the better the punk you were, which may have been Derek Jarman's intention.
Daniela Soave

Derek Jarman and Malcolm McLaren went back a long way. Unfortunately, *Jubilee* was a badly acted, over-arty and gratuitously violent pile of rubbish. Jarman had been part of the early Let It Rock crew, and the film bears all the hallmarks of that early art college crowd. The whole punk scenario had moved on by '78, and the film was a nonsensical marriage between the present-day punk reality and its far more arty past. Apart from all that, Toyah Wilcox was in it, which really says it all. As a testament to the era, Don Letts' *Punk Rock Movie* was and still is infinitely more relevant.
Chris Sullivan

Opposite: Jordan in the film *Jubilee* • Above: Stills from *Jubilee*

Sid Sods Off.

Banner title for Sid Vicious's last gig in the UK at London's Electric Ballroom

He was leaving to live in what he imagined was decadent rock'n'roll heaven in New York. By the end of September he was playing the part of vocalist in a set of mostly covers at Max's Kansas City, part of the Idols, with Arthur Kane, Jerry Nolan [of the New York Dolls] and Steve Dior. (Nolan had thoughtfully introduced Sid to his methadone clinic: medical staff there had been astonished by the extent of Sid's addiction.) Chris Salewicz and Adrian Boot, *Punk: The Illustrated History of a Music Revolution*

Above and opposite: Sid Vicious with Mick Jones and the Heartbreakers on stage at Max's Kansas City

Porn Pop art show – **distasteful and unartistic.**

Daily Mirror, 19 October 1976

When Throbbing Gristle supported us at the ICA, me, Joe and Bernie were walking through Soho and saw all these bits of film in the gutter, so we thought we could use them stuck on our shirts under these little plastic pouches. At the time there'd been a big fuss about Throbbing Gristle showing this pornogaphic film with their show, and the police were stopping people and searching them, thinking they would smuggle the film in. As we turned up with all these bits of film in our pockets, the Old Bill searched us and found them. They thought we were smuggling the pornographic film into the ICA, so they almost stopped us going in – and we were playing. We told the police that we intended to use the bits of film, but they didn't understand, and why should they? They were coppers. The film was probably out-takes from some *Carry On* film.
Paul Simonon

We went to see Throbbing Gristle at an old school in the Harrow Road, and they played this 1930s medical film of an actual castration. Then they built these fires with some weird shit in them, and then they made this bloody horrendous, cacophonous racket that was so loud it made your ears hurt. It was delightful.
Chris Sullivan

320

Above: Throbbing Gristle (Chris Carter, Cosi Fanni Tutti, Peter Christopherson and Genesis P. Orridge)

It was more to do with living
in a late capitalist society.

Andy Gill, guitarist, Gang of Four, in *England's Dreaming*

Unlike other punkish bands in the movement, Gang of Four rely more on sparse sounds, heavy bass and rhythm.
George Gimarc, *Punk Diary 1970-1979*

They were an interesting band. They were named after the Gang of Four in China. They had a more cerebral approach to their music. This band actually had a profound sociological message. Their lyrics were much more complex and meaningful than the Sex Pistols. Compared to them, the Sex Pistols were just like some guys on the sidewalk saying 'screw work'. That was about as profound as they ever got.
Gene Krell

Gang of Four – the students loved 'em.
Nils Stevenson

No, I never really had it with the Gang of Four – bunch of miserable northerners walking round indoors with their overcoats and Doc Martens on. Take your bloody coats off! No, manically depressive sixth form common-room music.
Robert Elms

There was terrible violence. [There were] pitched battles between students and British Movement members on the university campus. We could see the struggle between the Socialist Workers' Party and the BM capturing the straying youth. We were sympathetic to the SWP. We had done some benefits, but we didn't make our own approach in those broad political terms. It was more to do with living in a late capitalist society; we were also very concerned about the spectre of Thatcherism, and what it was going to do to the people in this country.
Andy Gill in *England's Dreaming*

Above: The Gang of Four (John King, Andy Gill, Hugo Barnum and Dave Allen)

Joy Division were once Warsaw, a punk group with literary pretensions.
Paul Morley, *New Musical Express*, 3 June 1978

Their record attempts to communicate in an almost tangible way all the
abstraction of [the] Buzzcocks' 'Spiral Scratch'. It is called 'An Ideal for
Living' and is on the Enigma label. It proclaims on the sleeve: 'This is not
a concept EP, it is an enigma.' Despite all this, the record is structurally
good, though soundwise poor, a reason [why] it may not be widely released.
They're a dry, doomy group who depend promisingly on the possibilities
of repetition, sudden stripping away, with deceptive dynamics, whilst they
use sound in a more orthodox hard-rock manner.
Paul Morley, *New Musical Express*, 3 June 1978

I went to their first gig at the Hope and Anchor [in London]. We used to
make up our minds at the last moment whether to invest 60p in going
downstairs, or stay drinking in the bar. It was one of those nights, when
the 60p was probably better spent on beer. Joy Division were depressingly
monotone. They weren't angry, just pissed off in that northern posey way.
It didn't help that Ian Curtis sang so flat.
Stephen Colegrave, author

They were given the punk label because they were around at the same time.
But 'New Dawn Fades' isn't really punk, is it? It's just a beautiful song.
Bill Dunn, senior editor, *Esquire* magazine

Above: Joy Division (Stephen Morris, Peter Hook, Ian Curtis and Bernard Albrecht)

The Fall?
Sorry,
don't get it.
But maybe
I'm stupid…
or just honest. Chris Sullivan

I always liked the Fall, their music and their attitude, notwithstanding my one and only run-in with Mark E. Smith, which was comical more than anything. We'd been booked to play Huddersfield Polytechnic as second on the bill to Sham 69. We drove up there in a beaten-up old Bedford van, nearly dying from the exhaust fumes coming through the back. We were knackered when we arrived…and we walked straight into a row. Mark [Smith] was strutting around like a major rock star, very obnoxious and very, very pissed. Basically his attitude was: 'We're the Fall. We're the local boys. We're the stars up here. We should be second on the bill,' even though we had been booked to be support. The altercation was only stopped when Jimmy Pursey [leader of Sham 69] stepped in to say that he would open the show. The Fall did get to be support, and we got to headline, so honour was satisfied. It was amazing really how many characters in punk were just so much like the old rock'n'rollers the punk movement was meant to be sweeping away. There was protest in the lyrics, but underneath, not very far underneath, it was 'I wanna be a rock star.'
Christos Yianni, musician, the Doll

We've never been signed up [to a record label]. It's a big help. We're independent and that's how we want it… We use a public phone box for getting gigs. It's great [and] works right to our advantage. People can't get in touch with you unless you want them to.
Mark E. Smith, singer with the Fall, *New Musical Express*, 19 March 1978

The Fall's name supposedly came from the Camus novel *La Chute* – a bit more intellectual than Sham 69.
Stephen Colegrave

They made no attempt to sound like punks, which perversely made them even more punk in my book. Mark E. Smith wore his work clothes and couldn't afford a spiky haircut. I liked the fact that he never adequately explained anything either, which just added to the sense of mystery. Fall songs stay with you long after you've grown out of the Sex Pistols. And he keeps moving, too, incorporating new sounds and styles into the Fall, which is very punk indeed.
Bill Dunn

The Fall played with us a couple of times. I always liked Mark E. Smith. He was a character – and still is – but I never got on with the music.
Steve Severin, bass player, Siouxsie and the Banshees

Right: Mark E. Smithi

Pete Perrett
of the Only Ones
was a genius.
Christos Yianni

The song 'Another Girl, Another Planet' gets my vote for
having a great opening line about flirting with death. The
Only Ones were quite poppy really, hardly punk at all, but
Pete was from Camberwell [in south London] so that was
all right. And he married Squeeze's bass player's sister.
Their early stuff had a reputation for carrying hidden drug
references. The Only Ones were OK.
Christos Yianni

Like American bands such as Talking Heads and
Television, the Only Ones are trying for something
genuinely new and individualistic, taking a stand against
the burgeoning encyclopedia of rock clichés that has
clogged up the airwaves from the early '60s onwards.
In addition, these bands are also blessed with a taut,
corporate professionalism that their punk rivals so often
lack. There is a compelling self-confidence behind the
Only Ones' vision, which attracted me from the outset,
[starting] with Peter Perrett's haunting songs and
brazenly unorthodox singing, and stretching through
[to] the resolve and unity of the players themselves.
Nick Kent, *New Musical Express*, 13 May 1978

My uncle, Gerald Thomas, sent the original script back with a note saying, **'I found this in the toilet – where it belongs!'** Jeremy Thomas

The whole film project was about pushing back boundaries. We weren't going to be the fucking Jam, or the fucking Police, playing gigs and building an audience, doing the same fucking things that the Pistols had been against from the beginning. However badly it went wrong, the original idea was a valid one, a fantastically exciting one, a totally different way of looking at things. Seeing the first sets built at Bray Studios was amazing – we'd actually created the Nashville. The early visuals were fantastic.
John 'Boogie' Tiberi

I was involved, right from the beginning, from the earliest script written by [comedy writer] Johnny Speight, which was basically 'Big Tits Meet the Sex Pistols'. I sent that to my uncle, Gerald Thomas, who'd done so much to create the *Carry On* series of films. He eventually sent it back with a note attached. 'I found this script in the toilet – where it belongs!' Then there was the Russ Meyer version, which involved the great director in a search all over Europe for the perfect pair of huge, cantilevered tits, which he never did find. After that I became very close to Julien [Temple], who was fighting to get the film finished. *The Swindle* was a rollercoaster that lasted three years – a rollercoaster that I'd been warned off by my peers, even though it was one of the most exciting and challenging things around at the time. The Pistols were stuck with this reputation for badness, which was hugely out of proportion to what they actually were, and a lot of people didn't want to touch them.
Jeremy Thomas

Malcolm [McLaren] was never keen to have an unknown director do things, and he constantly let me know that. Half of the time he threatened to sack me and bring in some TV director.
Julien Temple, film director

The whole saga of *The Swindle/Who Killed Bambi*? was like a running soap opera, before soap operas, or even pop movies, were really tabloid newspaper stories. Every week there was a new twist or rumour. A new source of funding was found – where did the money really come from? There were rumours that some crazy out-of-work actor or forgotten star had been brought in to play Johnny Rotten's mother or Sue Catwoman's lesbian lover or something equally unlikely. The names themselves were great: cheesy TV funny woman Irene Handl, who earned a reputation on set for talking dirtier than

Steve Jones; Marianne Faithfull, still struggling with her heroin addiction, who was cast as Sid's mum; then, in what seemed like a masterstroke, porn queen Mary Millington was cast to seduce Steve Jones in one scene. What was amazing was that hardly any of this made the papers, Ronnie Biggs in Rio being the only exception. By today's standards there were *Big Brother*-style scandals nearly every week during the whole three years it took to finish *The Swindle*, yet there was hardly a juicy word in the press.
John Shearlaw

Malcolm's method of dealing with everything that was happening was to change the script, and he was only stopped by the entry of the Official Receivers. Once Russ Meyer had departed, Julien was the only person in a position to get the film finished, and he had the vision to stick with that. Glitterbest was collapsing, and a lot of our dreams with it, and we were all looking at things we could do, which is why a recently redundant Sex Pistols' tour manager (i.e. me) ended up becoming stills photographer for the movie.
John 'Boogie' Tiberi

I really made that film. I was learning to be the devil in that picture, but I failed to pull it off. The film's a great shame, like Fairy Snow against bleach. Mild…
Malcolm McLaren, *Time Out,* issue 526, 1980

Above and opposite: Stills from *The Great Rock'n'Roll Swindle*

Sting had to act out raping Paul Cook in the back of a Cadillac. Julien Temple

The film should be retitled *Sex Pistols: Castrated*…no subversion, no excitement and no bollocks. A victory to the music industry and to the legal system, the opposite of what Glitterbest and the Sex Pistols were all about.
Jamie Reid, graphic designer, *Time Out,* issue 526, 1980

There were many original scenes missing in the final version, mostly because of legal problems. The Grundy interview had to go, as did an interview with the head of EMI. There was also a scene with a gay group called the Blow Waves (one of them was Sting actually – he was 'raping' Paul Cook in the back of some Cadillac).
Julien Temple

I'm sure there was one side of Malcolm which never wanted to complete the film. It was the last, living, breathing part of this thing he had created, and it was almost as if he needed to keep it going. The Sex Pistols had split up, but the film had taken over and he wanted that to go on.
Jeremy Thomas

It was aimed against the mafia – the alternative mafia who run the British Film Institute, and what is

supposed to be hip, left, liberal, smug London. I hope they don't like it. I don't think they will. I think they'll think it's a pile of shit.
Julien Temple

Certainly the only punk rock movie worth anybody's serious attention, and, more excitingly…the finest British rock film since Laurence Harvey and Cliff Richard did the *Expresso Bongo* in 1959.
Stephen Woolley, film producer, *Time Out,* issue 526, 1980

I wish *The Swindle* had been made in a more industrial way. It was totally chaotic, and not at all conducive to getting what you intended – partly because of money, partly because of the general anarchy, and partly because of the pressure of events and how the group reacted to them. We weren't shooting the film from A to Z in two months – I mean we had maybe 90 camera assistants over the three years. The Sex Pistols were that kind of group anyway. Their whole approach to the world was fragmented. They wanted to see it splinter in front of their faces.
Julien Temple

The Rock'n'Roll Swindle was like a *Carry On* film – a bad one. When I went to see it in Edinburgh, in one of those old-fashioned cinemas, this local hard man was playing up in the balcony above us, acting the goat, and the cunt fell off right into the stalls. It were magic. The film was shite.
Dempsey, punk fan

I was a bit pissed off with *The Swindle* because Malcolm did try to rewrite history. It was making out that he manufactured us. Fact is, we had a band before he came along.
Paul Cook

Rock'n'Roll Swindle? Yeah, especially if you paid to go see it.
Frank Kelly

Rock'n'Roll Swindle…a really atrocious film.
Brenda Lamb, punk trendsetter

I thought it was crap.
Roadent, aka Steve Connolly, Sex Pistols' and Clash roadie

Above and opposite: Stills from *The Great Rock'n'Roll Swindle*

Talking Heads,

New York's New Wave band-without-an-image, projects feelings of compulsive elation and warped normality.

Search & Destroy, issue 5, 1978

Talking Heads were the clever side of New Wave. Their music was more intellectual. David Byrne was arty but good. I felt much more at home with their music, more comfortable than with Sid Vicious behind our backs. In that second wave of music we needed the Americans.
Clive Langer, songwriter and producer

I liked the Velvet Underground and stuff like that. Then I started liking songs more again, things that I [could] sing. Whereas those other things were interesting to hear, they weren't things I could walk down the street and sing.
David Byrne, *Search & Destroy*, issue 5, 1978

The Talking Heads were at the beginning of punk before British punk started. I think the British movement swept over them and they were in danger of being forgotten. But, like Blondie and other American bands, they re-invented themselves and came back again.
Clive Langer

Talking Heads '77 was Andy Warhol's favourite album of the year, and Eno was another fan.
John Shearlaw

I don't think that the [record company] people…can quite figure us out. They hear some reports that we're a punk band, and then they hear other things that imply we're a regular radio-type rock'n'roll band, and they just don't know what to think. They get confused. I don't care too much for the whole mechanism of promoting yourself, the promotional apparatus that surrounds rock groups. I really feel it requires a lot of thought; I want to re-think the whole idea, figure out the least objectionable way that we can be presented…so as not to turn people off.
David Byrne, *Search & Destroy*, issue 5, 1978

I loved the Talking Heads. They were very danceable, like a garagey, danceable rock band. They were lots of fun.
Hilly Kristal, owner, CBGB's

Above: Talking Heads (Jerry Harrison, Tina Weymouth, Chris Franks and David Byrne) • Opposite: Alan Vega

Alan Vega and Suicide – sort of punky Soft Cell. Frank Kelly

I thought Suicide were extraordinary. Here was a group using technology to play rock'n'roll. When I look back at it, Mick Jones was very visionary to get them over to play with the Clash. I didn't understand it as much as I do today, and Suicide was the number one influence on Zigue Zigue Sputnik, who were a T-Rexed version of Suicide with a drummer. Some of our best tunes and ideas were nicked from Suicide – they were terrific. I thought they were incredibly innovative.
Tony James

I always liked Alan Vega, but the music wasn't really my forte. Suicide used to be put on here in New York as the final band because they would empty the room really quick. Peter would always put them on late at all the Max's shows, and sure enough people would run out of the room. They weren't what I liked, but I appreciated what they were doing.
Jayne County, singer, actress and DJ

Loved Alan Vega and Suicide. I saw them support the Clash at the Music Machine. I went to see them, not the Clash, and I thought the Clash's audience would try to bottle them, which would be interesting. They did and Alan just didn't blink. I thought, 'This is

brilliant!' I just loved the mixture – electronic and space. A lot of their stuff is really beautiful, very minimal. You can trace it back; it seems very sort of New York and '72 or '75. They inspired a lot of people.
Steve Severin

Suicide were huge in 1977/78, but they'd been around for years, since the early days of CBGB's. It took that long for people to get their heads round what they were up to. They were so late '70s New York. They ruled the gaff – they were New York.
Chris Sullivan

Mick Jones got Suicide to come and support us. There was only two them, and it was quite interesting to see how they coped with the Clash audience. They didn't want to see some arty New York band – they wanted to see the Clash…NOW. They weren't prepared to wait, so they threw things and one skinhead jumped on the stage and punched Alan Vega. Suicide did well: they were brave, they finished their set. Alan had a bit of a blpody nose and a red face, but they finished.
Paul Simonon

I figured there should be a female counterpart to

Nils Stevenson, manager, the Banshees

Siouxsie was already becoming a 'face', so I set out on a mission to help her become a significant artist, little knowing how difficult it would be for record companies to accept a strong female character. Although Siouxsie's performance at the 100 Club Punk Festival in 1976 has become legendary, the band's first proper gig didn't take place until the beginning of 1977. After that they toured relentlessly, building up a large fan base and learning to play in the process. Kenny Morris took over the Mo Tucker-style drumming from Sid [Vicious] and, for a short period, Peter Fenton was the guitarist, but was replaced by the darker John McKay. Until they were signed, the group didn't have any equipment, so they borrowed drum kits, amps, etc. from support acts. During that farcical formative period, Siouxsie became a formidable presence on stage, showing no fear in facing up to fucking ferocious audiences. In fact, as the venues got bigger, it became easier for her, as she was further away from the flying bottles and gob. Because Siouxsie looked so stunning there was naturally a lot of interest from the press, and the group matured in the media spotlight. Siouxsie's face launched a thousand looks as fans of the Ice Queen, as she was dubbed in *Sounds* magazine, started copying her style. In a short time not only did Siouxsie become the female counterpart to Rotten in the punk rock stakes, she also became the intimidating English brunette antidote to New Yorker Debbie Harry's pretty, blonde, poptastic punk princess.
Nils Stevenson

We had worked almost non-stop for 18 months up and down the motorway. We played shit clubs, usually borrowing equipment from the support band because we never had any equipment of our own. Nils wanted to build a big myth. He nurtured us, as did Leee

Childers, the Heartbreakers' manager. The Heartbreakers were brilliant; they gave us money, lent us equipment and gave us studio time.
Steve Severin

I was extremely passionate about the group, never doubting that they would be huge, and looked upon their development as a long-term project. At times my obsession with excellence drove the group completely nuts but, for a long period, the two important members of the foursome, namely Siouxsie and Steve [Severin], accepted my neurotic behaviour as par for the course (for which I am eternally grateful). However, defying everyone's advice to the contrary, and denying all my instincts for self-preservation, I flew a little too close to the Ice Queen, and my wings were badly frost-bitten.
Nils Stevenson

Nils always had his eyes set on a bigger deal, a bigger label. He knew you needed real commitments from a label with decent money.
Steve Severin

If a record company did offer a pathetic deal, as Decca did, I turned it down. Many of the punk acts around took whatever was offered. I, on the other hand, refused to accept crumbs off the table for an act I knew would add a significant chapter to the cultural story, and I determined to use our greatest disadvantage to great advantage. Instead of being embarrassed about the lack of interest from labels, I played up the fact that record companies were overlooking one of the biggest live acts in the

Johnny Rotten, and Siouxsie was the ideal candidate.

country. This made a newsworthy story for the music papers, who came out in support of the group, and further increased interest from punters. In the eyes of their fans, Siouxsie and the Banshees were the last outlaws.
Nils Stevenson

We sold out the Roundhouse without having put a single record out, not even a couple of John Peel sessions. We had a large group of fans. They respected us because we were right there at the beginning. Also, the music was different. Siouxsie was the first sexy woman in British punk, and half the audience would be Siouxsie clones. By 1978 there were all kinds of second-division bands, but the Pistols were off to America and the Clash toured Europe. Of course you could see the Stranglers anywhere, but they were the Stranglers. So if you wanted to see a premier league punk band, you could see the Banshees at the Roundhouse.
Steve Severin

All good things come to an end, and in June 1977 Polydor capitulated and signed Siouxsie and the Banshees. Since Siouxsie, Steve and I shared a common vision, I co-produced the group's first single, 'Hong Kong Garden', with the then-unknown and untested Steve Lillywhite (Polydor had a shit fit). This was a perverse love song to a Chinese take-away. It was a delightful piece of nonsense designed specifically for chart success that became a Top 10 hit when it was released in September 1978. Silencing the non-believers and proving to Polydor that we knew our audience, we were given free rein to do whatever we wanted. Sales of the single had, after all,

recouped the whole £20,000 advance. During my tenure as manager, we were never in debt for more than a few months at the beginning of each new option to Polydor because every new single would put us back in the black, which meant they had no leverage. Despite Polydor's misgivings, we even left the hit single off the debut album, *The Scream*, which was released to universal critical acclaim. It went on to become a ground-breaking hit record (Polydor heaved a sigh of relief). We then, in effect, treated the major record company like an indie label. We were totally focused and I was able to build up an autonomous operation in which we had our own agent for live shows, working alongside me in my office. Since the group spent most of their time working, they had full-time roadies and a minder/driver. Everything went back into Siouxsie and the Banshees in the form of wages for staff and equipment, rather than flats, houses or cars. These methods of operation enabled the Banshees to develop, unhindered, a unique sound, stage and media presence, away from the influence of record companies, stylists or any other outsiders. They rapidly evolved into a major musical force, way beyond the stereotypical contrivances of many of their punk contemporaries. Indeed, they invented a whole new style – Goth.
Nils Stevenson

I bought *Juju* [their 1981 album] on the strength of 'Spellbound'. It was definitely their best album and was a defining moment for Goth, marking a real shift in style. When John McKay did a bunk, they replaced him with John McGeoch who was the best guitarist around.
Stephen Colegrave

Above: Siouxsie and the Banshees (John McKay, Kenny Morris and Steve Severin)

No gimmicks, no theatrics, just us – take it or leave it! Public Image Ltd – it's a piss-take, it's ironical.
Don't you understand?
The public image is limited.
John Lydon (formerly Johnny Rotten) in *The Filth and the Fury*

Look, I want to change the music business, right? I want to change all that…but it'll take years. I'll have to do it more skilfully this time. But it'll be with a vengeance. And they won't know.
John Lydon in *The Filth and the Fury*

John was sometimes his own worst enemy. Richard Branson was totally supportive and had lots of loyalty to John from the Sex Pistols' success for Virgin. But John could be a difficult person for a record company to deal with. Once PIL was booked in to do a major TV appearance. Virgin sent a car for John, but he woke up in the morning and said, 'I ain't doing it.' We were all sitting in the studio waiting for him to turn up. It was one hell of a problem because the whole show was based on him.
Dennis Morris

It was in 1978 that this guy Paul, who was John Lydon's minder, found me and said, 'John's been looking for you everywhere.' I went round to John's house one night and that was it, we'd formed the band. 'Are we going to call it Public Image?' he asked. 'Limited,' I said. So we had a name. Three days later he said, 'Wobble's coming over'. And Wobble joined the band too. John Grey, John's best friend, said, 'Don't you think we should call him Jah Wobble?' We thought that was very cool. He couldn't play bass, but he knew about reggae, and music in general, though we particularly loved dub at the time.
Keith Levene, guitarist, Public Image Ltd in *The Filth and the Fury*

Nora Springer and her daughter Ari Upp from the Slits were there from day one. Nora was going out with Chris Spedding [musician and record producer] and John was getting some pretty heavy pressure from Spedding. She was filthy rich and was besotted with John. Of course, John married her in the end.
Dennis Morris

It was really intense. I don't think you'll find many bands like us now. We didn't have a manager, and the band was very naive in its own way. We could never get fucking happening, and because John had been in the Pistols and earned that reputation, we could get away with a lot of stuff other bands possibly couldn't. It was totally anarchic.

It was mad, very intense, a real mixture of feelings, some of them really funny. Some of it was very frustrating. I know we were young and fucking crazy, but we should have played more. We should have got out all over the country. In the end we did something like five UK gigs.
Jah Wobble, bass player, Public Image Ltd in *The Filth and the Fury*

By the time it came to the Metal Box record launch, there was a lot of fighting going on between Keith Levene and the rest of the band. Keith thought he was the leader. He was infuriated when he found out that Wobble, who was quite a clever guy, had managed to do a solo deal. Keith just thought of him as a bass player who couldn't even play properly. By then I had moved to Island Records, but Chris Blackwell agreed I could still work with PIL. John spent most of his time at my office at Island rather than at Virgin, which was quite strange. It was there that I had the idea for the metal box package. Across the road from the secondary school I went to in Dalston [east London] there was a factory called Metal Box. When John came up with the idea to call the album Metal Box, I said we had to package it in a real metal box. When I tried to sell this idea to Virgin, they said 'You must be joking. It will cost too much.' Not prepared to give up, I went to the factory. They had loads of boxes that were a standard size for film, which were just right. In the end getting 10,000 of these from the Metal Box factory worked out cheaper than producing a mainstream sleeve. All we had to do was emboss it and it was a perfect size for the vinyl. It worked out really well.
Dennis Morris

PIL were OK, but not a patch on the Sex Pistols, which goes to show that Lydon was by no means the whole show. He was just part of it, though I'm sure he believes otherwise.
Stephen Colegrave

Nora teams up with Lydon during PIL and they get married. She inherits a Geman publishing empire and the fortune that goes with it. They move to Beverly Hills to live in a mansion with a pool, and they all live happily ever after. So much for anarchy in the UK…
Chris Sullivan

When we returned to London from Jamaica, John said he'd an idea for a new band called PIL or Public Image Ltd. We started throwing ideas around and I said it would be great if the PIL logo could actually be an aspirin. John thought that was great. At the time I was working with Terry Jones from *ID* magazine, so we worked up the logo idea. We all agreed it would be good to get away from the punk look with which John had been so closely associated. We went to Ken McDonald, who had a shop on the Kings Road, to style John. He made all his suits – all those wicked, bright-coloured zoot suits. I designed and shot the first record sleeve with John on the cover with Italian *Vogue* lettering. The reverse featured Wobble in a sharp suit. On the inner bag Keith Levene was in a blue shiny jacket with Jim Walker, the drummer, and the *Mad* typeface. We did crazy promotional campaigns. We were the first to put ads all the way down the escalators at an underground station.
Dennis Morris

Sid fell under Nancy's spell and let her run everything.

Leee Childers, ex-manager, the Stooges and the Heartbreakers

In retrospect, it looks like Nancy and Sid were the only fucked-up people but, you know, Connie and Dee Dee Ramone were the same… They were always fighting… Gyda Gash [of the Transistors] and Cheetah Chrome from the Dead Boys…were always at it too. Sid and Nancy weren't a novelty. They were just another fucked-up couple. Nancy lived on 23rd Street in New York. She had a really nice apartment. We didn't have a shower, so we'd go to Nancy's. I remember her making some scrambled eggs once. She was nice. She wasn't any more fucked up than anyone else.
Legs McNeil, writer on *Punk Magazine*

Sid loved Nancy. On the Pistols' American tour, he wanted to talk to me about her all the time because I had known Nancy before he did. Sid would ask me questions like, was she really a prostitute?… I told him about the time in New York when my friend Dave, Nancy and I were driving around… Nancy was describing the whorehouse she worked in. It was this uptown brothel, where they had theme rooms and…various girls [dressed as] little girls, teachers, nurses.
Bob Gruen in *Please Kill Me*

SID: Hey, do you want to make a pornographic movie? Give us £100.
NANCY: Oh, stop! We made one…
SID: Yeah, it's a real good film.
NANCY: It was great fun on a dirty floor with the *Never Mind the Bollocks* poster under us…
INTERVIEWER: What were you doing? Screwing?
NANCY: Sucking and being dominant and submissive. Sid licking my feet and things like that.
Scene from the film *DOA* by Lech Kowalski

There are so many theories about her childhood, but I thought she was horrible. I should have tried harder to keep her away from Sid, but I was more concerned about Jerry [Nolan of the Heartbreakers] at the time. Before she met Sid in London, I was walking down Carnaby Street on my way to Track Records. All of a sudden I felt this tap on my shoulder. I turned around and it was Nancy Spungen. She said, 'Hi, I'm in London.' I thought, 'Oh, no!' She said, 'I want to see Jerry.' I was determined: 'I'm not going to let you see Jerry. I'm going to keep you away from him and the rest of my band. You can't go near them. Go back to New York where you belong.' She just walked off – you couldn't hurt her feelings. The next time I saw her she was with Sid.

I got to know Sid really well on the bus during the Sex Pistols' US tour. We'd sit together and talk for hours. When he came back to New York, about eight or 10 months later, he showed up with Nancy. He was completely stoned and was like another person. We had almost no conversations during the whole time. He didn't talk to anybody. He just stood there in a stupor. Nancy would take the empty glass out of his hand and give him a new one. He would sip these drinks and be stoned out of his head on whatever they were taking.
Bob Gruen

She was always obnoxious and horrible.
Leee Childers

I have no pictures of the two of them. They were my friends, and I didn't think you should take pictures of friends looking like that. I remember a couple of times Nancy saying, 'Bobby, come over to the Chelsea. Let's take some pictures together.' I'd say, 'Nancy, you look terrible. Get some sleep. Call me in three or four days, and then I'll take some pictures.' They never did get any sleep, so I never did take any pictures of them. I just thought of them as friends, not as people who had a look or style, or who were inspiring a generation.
Bob Gruen

Right: Sid Vicious and Nancy Spungen

STANDARD

Tube crash adds to travel misery

By Frank Draper

WIDESPREAD fog and a derailment on the Underground delayed thousands of commuters today.

With visibility down to zero in many parts of London and the suburbs the motoring organisations warned motorists to use caution and drive slowly.

Woolwich Ferry was not operating because of the fog.

A derailed ballast train on the Piccadilly Line at Holborn has torn up track and caused extensive damage to signalling equipment.

The service has been cut between Kings Cross and Covent Garden.

London Transport said the damage would take most of the day to put right. Commuters were advised to avoid using the Piccadilly Line.

Bus service

Piccadilly line trains are t operating between Covent Garden and Heathrow, Cockfosters and Kings Cross, and between Acton and Rayners Lane.

Season ticket holders are allowed to use their tickets on Eastern Region services, and passengers using the Piccadilly Line for destinations between Covent Garden and Kings Cross can finish their journey by bus.

Southern Region trains from South-east, London, Kent and Sussex were delayed by 10 minutes because of fog. Trains into London from Alton (Hants) were also being delayed and diverted because of a cable fire at Ash Vale, near Woking.

For motorists today was the first bad morning of the foggy season.

In Kent visibility ranged from zero to 100 yards, and the busy A25 road was blocked by a serious accident at Westerham.

Fog covered most of the country and all motorways were operating speed limits of either 30 or 40 miles an hour. The AA advised drivers to drive much slower.

UNDER ARREST . . . Sid Vicious is led away to jail by a New York detective under the glare of cameramen's flash bulbs.

SID VICIOUS IS ACCUSED OF MURDER

Standard Foreign News Desk

SEX PISTOLS punk rocker Sid Vicious has been charged with stabbing to death his go-go dancer girlfriend in a Manhattan hotel room. He will appear in court today.

Police said it was one of the most bizaare cases on the records. The girl, 20 - year - old Nancy Spungen had been stabbed in the stomach.

Police said Vicious—known as John Ritchie and John Simon on their records—was found wandering in the vicinity on one of New York's modest hotels, the Chelsea, in a semi-comatose state asking Where is Nancy?

Nancy was dead in Room 100 at the hotel.

New York policeman Frank Dunn said Vicious told him : " We were having a party last night, went to bed and when I woke up she was dead."

Justice

Vicious, 21-year-old bass guitarist for the way-out Sex Pistols until he broke away from the controversial group, was charged with murder.

A spokesman at police headquarters said : " We understand that the couple were listed as Mr and Mrs John

for months. She had bleached blonde hair in a frizzy style, used heavy eye make-up and often dressed in punk-style black leather.

The couple had occupied a second-storey room in the Chelsea hotel, once a popular gathering place for artists, writers and musicians.

Vicious, with other members of the Sex Pistols group, became a high priest of punk rock which reached a peak in Britain last year.

The group shocked many music lovers with astoishing displays on stage, which included spitting and swearing at their fans. They dyed their hair green and skewered safety pins through their noses. A safety pin stuck through a nostril or earlooe became a cult trade mark.

Formed in 1975, the Sex Pistols shot to notoriety for

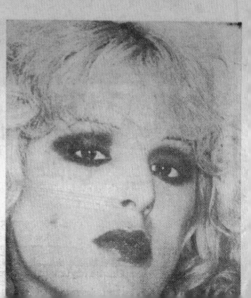

The Connoisseurs' Cognac.

HINE

I don't think he killed her. He wasn't really vicious and he did really love Nancy. Bob Gruen

Sid Vicious, bass guitarist of Britain's spitting and stomping Sex Pistols punk rock band, yesterday was arrested and charged with stabbing his sultry blonde girlfriend to death in their room at Manhattan's famed Chelsea Hotel. His face pale and scratched, the dazed-looking Vicious muttered curses and 'I'll smash your cameras' as he was led from the hotel, where the body of Nancy Laura Spungen, 20, clad in blood-soaked black lace bra and panties, was found crumpled under the bathroom sink. Miss Spungen…had been stabbed deep in the abdomen.
New York Post, 3 October 1978

Sid went all the way. He'd been charged with murdering Nancy at the Chelsea Hotel. I felt creepy.
Nils Stevenson

I was in New York when the murder happened. On the day of the murder, I was with Annie Idols, the publicist for the Rolling Stones, who got them out of all those drug busts. We were down in the El Coyote restaurant at the bottom of the Chelsea Hotel. We were getting drunk on margaritas. There was no particular reason or occasion; there was just nothing to do that afternoon. Annie said, 'Let's go visit somebody.' By this time, being so drunk, we were probably entirely charming and anyone would have been delighted to have us visit. I said, 'Let's go and see Sid and Nancy.' We went to the desk and rang them. We rang and rang, but no one was at home. So we went back to the desk and asked if we could leave some messages for Sid and Nancy. The guy at the desk gave me a little message pad. We wrote all these really rude messages like, 'We were going to come round to suck your dick, but you weren't home,' and stuff like that. We saw the desk clerk stick all these messages in their box. That night Nancy came home and crammed them in her purse. She went upstairs and was murdered.
Leee Childers

Sid didn't look like he was going to get up. He wasn't moving. I said, 'What's wrong with Sid?' Someone said, 'He just ate about 30 Tuinals [barbiturates].' I said, 'Oh, he's going to be fun tonight!' …That's another reason why I didn't want to stay. I mean, I didn't know it was going to be an important night.
Eliot Kidd of the Demons in *Please Kill Me*

I think Sid passed out. I think Nancy had a fight with the drug dealer and he stabbed her. Nancy was the sort of person who fought with people.
Legs McNeil

The first time the phone rang it was John Mackay [of the Banshees] and his wife Linda calling to say, 'What's happening over there? We've just heard Nancy was murdered.' I said, 'I'll make some calls and let you know.' I hung up the phone and it rang again. It was the police. They said that Nancy Spungen had been murdered and that there were all these notes in her purse from me. They wanted to know if I'd seen her the previous night. I said, 'Well, if I'd seen her, I wouldn't have needed to leave her notes.' They said, 'That makes sense. Thank you very much. If you learn anything, please call us.' They never called me again. The police weren't a bit interested.
Leee Childers

Sid definitely didn't do it. People who saw him that night said he was passed out on the bed.
John Holmstrom

I talked to Neon Leon [a band leader] the next day. He said when he left Sid and Nancy that fucking guy was still there. I said, 'Who was that?' He said, 'You know, that…dealer.' Neon Leon told me that when everybody had left, the…dealer was the only person that stayed.
Eliot Kidd in *Please Kill Me*

Sid didn't do it. Afterwards, when he got out of jail, he asked, 'Did I kill Nancy? I don't know.' I said, 'No, you didn't.' He said, 'Good, I'm glad.' It was one of the great privileges of my life to be able to tell him the truth – that he didn't do it.
Leee Childers

There are some conflicting stories about the events of last night and this morning. Here's one uncovered by *Rolling Stone*'s Michael Segell. Apparently Nancy (who handled the couple's finances) had just received a personal cheque from Malcolm on Wednesday, as well as $3000 from Sid's Max's appearances. Nancy then called [one of their friends] for some dilandi [downers]. He visited the couple this morning around 1.30 a.m., staying with them until about 5 a.m. When he left, he saw another drug supplier in the lobby heading for the elevator.
George Gimarc, *Punk Diary 1970-1979*

We know who did it – some drug dealer, who is still around. A moron of a cop could have figured it out, and probably did. But what did they care? They found Sid passed out with a knife beside him. Big deal! Everyone knows he always did stuff like carry knives. The drug dealer must have had a fight with Nancy, who was the most horrible person on earth. So the dealer thought, 'Well, fuck this bitch,' and grabbed a knife, stabbed her and walked casually out of the Chelsea Hotel. Sid was found with the knife, but Sid didn't do it.
Leee Childers

Malcolm McLaren always believed Sid would have eventually been freed. His confidence was shared by most of his friends. Of course this was never put to the test.
Stephen Colegrave

79 *(and onwards)*

In 1979, *as if to signal the end of the whole punk shooting match, Margaret Thatcher was resoundingly voted into power as prime minister of Great Britain. This meant that a percentage of the punk record-buying population actually voted Conservative: in other words, punk and all its intentions were now well and truly finished for pretty much everyone, beggars excluded. The Kings Road still attracted the punk minions but the whole style had transmogrified into an absurd caricature of itself. Now punk meant ridiculous six-inch-high Mohican hair-dos, facial tattoos, fake bondage and steel toecapped boots – and now, for the most part, the swastikas were for real. This was the year when everybody – Westwood and Lydon included – turned their back on punk. It had become the uniform of the stupid.*

Following its brief flirtation with Manhattan, British punk had returned home with its tail between its legs. Punk had holidayed in the UK, dressed up in bizarre clothes, made the headlines first, then a fool of itself second, and now had to sort itself out, return to its day job and grow up. After all, this was the year of Mrs Thatcher's election. Whilst the British punk scene had pushed out the boundaries of fashion and public infamy, the New York scene had quietly chugged along, with a tight circle of bands and fans regularly patronizing Max's, CBGB's and the newly opened Mudd Club, doing what it originally intended to do – making music of a palatable, if controversial, nature.

In Britain, punk, in its demise, had left behind an eclectic music scene, which, although not directly related to it, would probably not have blossomed without punk's assault on the '70s music establishment. Two-tone, New Wave, electro, hip-hop and the New Romantics were all musical forms which in many instances were deliberate reactions against the punk milieu. This book covers these musical forms purely because their very existence was by and large provoked by punk, even if, as in the case of electro, it was diametrically opposed to punk in every way. Of course hip-hop, two-tone and electro were not punk. They never were and never will be.

Along with the offshoots, there was a new generation of highly successful stadium artists such as the Boomtown Rats, U2, the Jam and the Police. It was in '79 that they could shed their punk disguise, only ever a convenient vehicle intended purely to take them where they wanted to go and become who they wanted to be – big stadium rock bands.

More importantly, punk had created a new kind of sensibility, sophistication and even cynicism. No longer were the youth prepared to accept what the establishment, the hierarchy or the powers that be were giving them. They had seen that a certain power was in their grasp and they used it. It showed many people that they could actually be themselves, and it renewed an interest in expressing individuality in all its myriad forms. Many people realized that, as with punk, it is not the number of people involved that matters, but their resolve. The whole British style magazine and nightclub culture was based on the punk ethic of 'We can do it'. Many of the original participants started or embraced the new musical trends with the same confidence and do-it-yourself mentality that had given punk its vitality. Of course there was a huge morass of leftover people who had only recently been seduced by punk. Bands such as the UK Subs refused to believe that they had missed the party, and tried to re-create their own take on 1976, failing miserably. Many believed that the swastika was a viable statement and turned skinhead. Punk had now become the refuge of the uninformed. It was an embarrassment.

The Sex Pistols soap opera still had a couple of tawdry episodes left. No amount of revisionism in The Great Rock'n'Roll Swindle could make up for the sheer drama of Sid Vicious's final overdose or the undignified court case fought over the ownership of the Sex Pistols' future royalties. It was truth well beyond fiction. Fortunately, the Clash managed to resist the temptation to split, and successfully toured and conquered the USA, causing a furore unprovoked by anyone since Frank Sinatra. The Clash had moved with the times. They grasped and understood the meaning of it all, developed, changed and survived the death of punk.

Traditionally, New Wave was seen as an evolution of punk, but this was a fabrication. Few shared or understood the ethic and attitude that created British punk. The New Wave label itself covered such a wide range of musical styles, from Elvis Costello to XTC and the Cars, and was an aberration. Compared to 1976, the sheer variety and number of these bands was impressive, but few could even know or understand the original punk ethic. They relied heavily on the student circuit, and often had the approval of the music press, which was keen to support this newly acquired, pseudo-sophistication that it at last understood. Many of the bands were cynically marketed, of questionable quality and easily fitted the description of shit.

We end this year in New York. That was where the original punk attitude continued to exist in '79, where the spirit of defiance, albeit unintentional, was maintained. It is in the Mudd Club that we find many of the characters and bands that have shaped this story. People from the 1960s, who included Andy Warhol and William Burroughs, gathered alongside the 1970s movers and shakers, such as Jayne County, Debbie Harry and Johnny Thunders, as if to discuss the scene's formation. Many founders of the British punk scene, such as Billy Idol, John Lydon and Malcolm McLaren, moved to New York, as if fleeing the Thatcherite mediocrity at home. New York was where punk as an entity now truly belonged.

The ideology behind punk is elusive to the uninitiated. Easier perhaps to say what it wasn't. It was not a headline on the front page of a tabloid newspaper, nor was it conformity, and it was definitely not stupidity.

MORTUARY

KE

Right: Sid Vicious in a body bag

Smack took away the innocence and the energy.
It's a fucking nightmare smack…a fucking nightmare.

Steve Jones, guitarist, the Sex Pistols

Punk star Sid Vicious was found dead in a Greenwich Village apartment in an apparent suicide, police said today. Police said that Vicious, 21, apparently died of a heroin overdose and was found face-up in the bed of a friend's apartment at 63 Bank Street. Police said the apartment belonged to Michelle Robinson [Sid's new girlfriend]. The former Sex Pistol was released from jail yesterday on $50,000 cash bail. He had been jailed since December 8th, when his bail on the charges he murdered his girlfriend Nancy Spungen was revoked after he assaulted Patti Smith's brother.
The *New York Post*, 2 February 1979

Sid was trying to kill himself at my birthday party. When people weren't keeping an eye on him, he would break a bottle. He would then see if he could scratch up his arm and kill himself somehow. He was like a sick puppy. As I told Tom Forcade [founder of *High Times* magazine], 'That guy is the most self-destructive person I've ever seen in my life.' But Tom said to me, 'No, he's not. I am.' Tom was soon dead. He killed himself within a year too.
John Holmstrom, editor, *Punk Magazine*

In New York, Sid got all wrapped up in the scene. He started to believe it all. He was totally out to lunch. It all ended like…you know.
Paul Cook, drummer, the Sex Pistols

I kicked Sid out of CBGB's three times. He was a mess. He was very destructive. He hit Cheetah Chrome [of the Dead Boys]. Another time he got in a fight. He was a lunatic. He felt everyone was going to cater to him. He always had his crowd. He was bad news. Supposedly, he put out a record which he said he made here. He never did.
Hilly Kristal, owner of CBGB's

At the Speakeasy one night a girl at the bar was really drunk. She had her arms on the bar and was barely listening to the band. Sid was standing next to her. He had a razor blade and started casually slicing little noughts and crosses pattern on her arm. It was not deep, just little cuts, not blood pouring. Finally she noticed something. She turned round and just said, 'Sid, stop that' and went back to her thing.
Leee Childers, ex-manager, the Stooges and the Heartbreakers

Malcolm went out to America after Sid was arrested for killing Nancy. He got him the best lawyer and tried to sort things out for him. Where the fuck was Johnny Rotten, who was supposedly his best mate? Malcolm was hoping to get Sid off somehow, like the O.J. Simpson case of the '90s. It would have been like that and he would have got him off. Malcolm got him bail and he came out of prison.

Then his mum went out there and fucking gave him a load of fear and he overdosed. His own mother! And now his mother owns all his royalties. That's why I think, in the end, I'm sick of seeing interviews with Sid's mum.
Joe Corré, son of Vivienne Westwood and Malcolm McLaren

His mother, who had already purchased more heroin for her detoxed son…went back to a friend's apartment in Greenwich Village to celebrate his release. Backsliding from the seven weeks of detox he painfully endured, Sid immediately jumped back into heroin. The dose wasn't very potent, and he argued that he needed more. His mother obliges him. Twenty minutes later Sid's collapsed on a bed and the friends talk about whether to take him to the hospital, but Sid says he's all right. Some time past midnight, Sid awakes and finds the rest of the heroin in his mother's purse; he uses it and drifts off permanently.
George Gimarc, *Punk Diary 1970-1979*

The mother of Sid Vicious revealed yesterday that she looked after his heroin supply on the night he died. Londoner Ann Beverly…spoke of the fix that led to his death. But she added: 'I know he didn't have any more that night because I had the packet in my pocket…There is no way Sid could have slipped the smack from my pocket. He wasn't like that. He would have waited until next day and said, 'Can I have some more?'
The *Daily Express*, 5 February 1979

His mother was a stupid woman. His dumb mother went to the same drug dealer who killed Nancy to get drugs for her son, for her little boy. They're both legends now.
Leee Childers

I got dressed and ran over there [to Michelle Robinson's apartment], and saw the crowd of reporters… When they saw me, they said, 'There's that girl from the court-house!' And then they started taking my picture. I ran up to the door and the police let me in and then I realized it [Sid's death] was true. Ann, Sid's mother, and Michelle were sitting on the couch crying. But Ann always acted like she knew it was going to happen; she just didn't know when.
Eileen Polk, photographer and Factory muse, in *Please Kill Me*

I can't straighten up. I just can't be straight… I suppose I just have to. I haven't [quite] figured [out]…how I'm gonna do it 'cause I haven't been…straight in four years. I had hepatitis and, when I got out of the hospital, I just really fucked myself up as *badly* as I could. I don't know why, but everybody said you can't do it, so I just went ahead and done it. It's my basic nature…my basic nature's gonna kill me in six months.
Sid Vicious, *Punk Magazine*, 20 January 1978

He seemed to be a very sweet guy who was seduced by the dark side of fame. He became famous for some violent incident. Then he thought, if I keep doing this, I'll be even more famous.
John Holmstrom

I loved Sid. He was very confused. Bear in mind he was just 21 years old when he died. When I was 21 years old I didn't know nothing. He pretty well didn't know nothing either.
Leee Childers

It was tragic. Sid was a contorted, demented soul. He was aggressive. He did have a brain. He was quite aware of things and had something to say, maybe more than Paul [Cook] and Steve [Jones]. But he joined his friend's band and he met Nancy. I'm sure he was still a virgin when he met Nancy. He just couldn't cope with the pressure of being Sid Vicious with his white face, spiky hair, his snarl and the way he walked with his long legs.
Helen Wellington Lloyd, assistant in Sex and McLaren muse

Sid had great style. He had something unique. His version of 'My Way' is brilliant. I think Paul Anka, who wrote the song, was actually asked, 'Of all the many versions, which one is your favourite?' He said, 'Sid Vicious's.'
Leee Childers

Nancy was Jewish, and you can't have non-Jews buried in your Jewish cemetery. That's what they told us, but they really didn't want to have anything to do with Sid Vicious. We're standing at the graveside and it was snowing. We were all crying. We just said some prayers and left some flowers. Then we drove around to the edge of the cemetery. We parked the car and Ann took the ashes, went over the fence, back to the graveside, and dumped Sid's ashes on Nancy's grave…and said, 'Well, they're finally together.'
Eileen Polk in *Please Kill Me*

The mother of notorious Sex Pistols' guitarist Sid Vicious has been found dead from a drugs overdose at her home, 17 years after her son's death. The clothes of 58-year-old Ann Beverly had been neatly bagged up and her credit cards cut in half. A detective said: 'It looks like a straight-forward suicide. We found a note.' Chain-smoking Ann, once a registered addict, had blamed herself for supplying the heroin that killed her punk rocker son at 21 in New York. A neighbour in Swadlincote, Derbyshire, said: 'It's almost as though she wanted to mirror her famous son's death. She was obviously really proud of him.'
The *Sun*, 7 September 1996

SID VICIOUS DIES IN DRUGS DRAMA

Mum finds him in his girl's arms

FREEDOM: Vicious with his mother after his release on bail — just one day before he died.

D VICIOUS, the tormented
ar of punk rock, died of an
verdose of heroin yesterday.

He was found naked in the arms of
s latest girl friend in her New York
t less than twenty-four hours after he
as released from jail on bail.

His mother, Mrs. Ann Beverly, took the
uple a cup of tea in
d and frantically
ed to wake Vicious.

he girlfriend, Michele
bison, was completely
aware that he had
ed while they slept.

Police said last night
at he had taken the
oin overdose by acci-
t.

Vicious, 21, guitarist
th the now defunct
x Pistols, had been
owed £30,000 bail on a
rge of murdering his
mer girlfriend,
Nauseating" Nancy
ungen, last October.
His earlier bail had
en revoked when he

By CHRIS BUCKLAND and STUART GREIG

during a night club
brawl.

After walking from
the courtroom on Thurs-
day, Vicious and Michele
went off to celebrate his
freedom at a party in
her seedy flat in fashionable Greenwich Village.

Later he injected him-
self with heroin and
then had a 45-minute
seizure.

But friends managed

● Continued on
Page Three

Strike-hit Britain . . Strike-hit Britain . . Strike-hit Britain

HOSPITAL CRISIS GROWS

By TERRY PATTINSON and BARRY WIGMORE

LEADERS of the "dirty jobs"
unions last night threatened
to turn the screw on all public
services in Britain next week.

The threat to step up hospital
and town hall industrial action
came as the chiefs of the four
unions involved met at Transport House in London.

They warned that hardly a
hospital would escape disrup-
tion.

But all the union bosses
claimed that no patients would
suffer.

Charles Donnet, national
officer for the General and

make an immediate offer to the
1,500,000 public service manual
workers.

He said: "The 8.8 per cent
everybody is talking about has
not actually been offered.

"Thousands of workers will
be on strike next week in addition to those already operating
overtime bans and work-to-

● Continued on
Page Two

Leyland walkout threat

By GEOFFREY GOODMAN Industrial Editor

BRITISH Leyland boss Michael
Edwardes was fighting last
night to head off a strike that
could finally put paid to the
state - owned firm's recovery
hopes.

Union leaders have threatened to order all the car company's 100,000 production
workers out on strike unless an
efficiency rise agreed last December is paid.

The top union negotiator,
Grenville Hawley of the Transport Workers, said he would
recommend five days' strike
notice to a shop stewards'

meeting in Coventry on Monday.

The UNIONS argue that they
are now entitled to pay rises
averaging about £5 a week
under the productivity package
agreed last year.

Leyland BOSSES have told
the workers that they can't
have the cash yet because production targets have not been
reached.

Production was hit by the
lorry drivers' strike, which
halted deliveries of components,
and a dispute at Leyland's Bir-

Virgin helped John with his court costs and Malcolm lost everything. Joe Corré

Malcolm hoped our record sales would be enhanced if the public were under the impression that we were banned from playing. That was certainly untrue. Some halls wouldn't have us, but others applied to Glitterbest for gigs during 1977 and were either refused or received no replies.
John Lydon, formerly Johnny Rotten, in a statement to court, 7 February 1979

The court case appears to be the moment when relations were severed with Johnny Rotten, or John Lydon as he had become. The original date was in November, but then it was adjourned. I made a statement in February 1979, and the case started a few days later, actually only a few days after Sid died in New York. John wasn't talking to Steve and Paul, and obviously not to Malcolm. John hadn't really talked to anyone on the Glitterbest side since America. Malcolm's allegation was that Lydon was defecting. I was saying things about what had happened in Jamaica, that Richard Branson was interfering; I was persuaded…a bit. Steve and Paul backed Malcolm initially. It seemed more practical to back Malcolm – I guess I didn't really follow where John was going. If I could have got excited about Public Image Ltd…I just don't know. The case was heard and then the receiver was set up, basically to do fresh deals with Virgin. The whole management issue wasn't settled at all, not until much later. And as far as record contracts go, they seemed to be much better deals. Paul [Cook] says how good the deal for *The Great Rock'n'Roll Swindle* was; the Sex Pistols individually were much better off contract-wise than they had been as a band…
John 'Boogie' Tiberi, Sex Pistols' tour manager, 1977-9

Virgin helped John to take Malcolm to court for unpaid royalties. I think every bit of money Malcolm made, including the royalties, went on the film [*The Great Rock'n'Roll Swindle*]. He lost everything because he didn't really fight the court case. Malcolm said he couldn't be bothered with all that shit. He just wanted to finish the fucking movie. He said, 'If John wants to be a pop star, let him go and be a pop star, but don't sue me. He's missing the point.'
Joe Corré

It had to happen eventually. The Sex Pistols/Glitterbest split would spill over into the courts. John Lydon, aka Rotten, was suing Malcolm McLaren for damages for preventing the band from playing live. More importantly, he wanted the Sex Pistols' finances to be put in the hands of and adjudicated by a third party. He also wanted the Sex Pistols' name to be taken out of the reach of Malcolm McLaren so that it could not be used for a band again, even if it consisted of the other band members. Finally, he wanted not to appear in McLaren's forthcoming film, *The Great Rock'n'Roll Swindle*.
Stephen Colegrave, author

Johnny is very much like Malcolm. They both get suspicious. They both get paranoid.
Helen Wellington Lloyd

The court case was partially settled. Although the Sex Pistols had earned £800,000, little of it remained. The court ruled that the Sex Pistols were entitled to this money, minus reasonable expenses. However, as the money had gone, the only way for the Sex Pistols to be paid was to get *The Great Rock'n'Roll Swindle* soundtrack out as soon as possible, and use the profits to settle.
Stephen Colegrave

It all ended in a really messy and sordid way. The lawyers got hold of it and that was that. The receivers came in to sort out all the money. **It was a real mess. We didn't see a penny for 10 years.** Paul Cook

Above: The London courthouse where the Sex Pistols did battle with Malcolm McLaren

If you hate the National Front
as much as you do me, they'll never get anywhere!

Patrik Fitzgerald, musician

You only have to look at the recent riots in Oldham, Bradford and Leeds to understand how virulent the far right, as represented by the British Nationalist Party and the National Front, can be. If you multiply today's problems by a hundred, you will get near to understanding the extent of the racial tension in Britain in 1979. The Front's members, skinheads in tow, were on the streets outside tube stations giving out extremely provocative racist propaganda. Attacks on elderly Asian men and women were very common. That is why Rock Against Racism answered a very real threat. What RAR did was to make bigotry very uncool and old-fashioned. Maybe we need something similar again.
Chris Sullivan, author

I think Rock Against Racism worked incredibly well. It was a very fresh idea and I think it really did glamorize anti-racism and make a lot of people aware of the issue and feel really connected. It engaged the youth of the day and people at school. It was one of those eras where the lines of battle were clearly drawn. I think Rock Against Racism really stayed a vibrant grass roots movement, where people had a lot of fun fighting the good fight.
Viv Goldman, features editor, *Sounds* magazine

I remember the big Rock Against Racism march that started in Trafalgar Square and ended in Victoria Park, east London, where the Clash and Aswad were playing, along with a load of other groups. My most vivid memory is of absolutely dying for a pee as we walked into the East End, but we were surrounded by the police, and beyond them were hundreds, maybe thousands, of skinheads heckling and trying to attack us. So a pee was out of the question and I almost wet myself.
Leah Seresin, former singer, now film director

Millions of lefties, punks, hippies, anarchists and young blacks are hanging around giving out their leaflets, papers and tracts to anyone who'll take them. In the park, Patrik Fitzgerald is booed off stage, canned and spat at by thousands of punks who see the Clash's equipment being set up behind him… My idealism takes a serious battering. What the fuck is going on? He's up there on his own, in front of a massive crowd in some London park, doing his

benefit bit, with all these idiots who look great – colourful, sexy, energetic, committed – treating him like shit, worse than they would a Nazi if they ever bumped into one. He storms off, angry and hurt, shouting: 'If you hate the National Front as much as you do me, they'll never get anywhere!' From then on, and retrospectively, I'm forever trying to cut out the football side of punk, the crummy combination of beer cans and politics, the graceless little Englander in his bondage trousers and boots.
George McKay, professor of counter-culture, University of Central Lancashire

We were invited to do the Rock Against Racism thing and it seemed like a good thing to put our name behind. A lot of students early on thought we were like a fascist group, so it clarified our position, showed where our flag was flying. What I remember most are the arguments our manager, Bernie Rhodes, had with the promoters. Bernie wanted to know how many people were coming, and they said, 'We don't know.' They had this big poster with a picture of a crowd to advertise the march, and Bernie pointed to it and asked, 'Is this how many's coming?' Eventually, they said, 'Well… yes,' so Bernie took the poster and said, 'You don't mind if I count them, do you?' Unfortunately, there were all these hippies running around shaking these big buckets for money: it was for a good cause, but it was really unglamorous. You need something a bit more stylish to attract young people.
Paul Simonon, bass player, the Clash

The National Front were at their height in the mid-1970s. Their marches were reported everywhere, and we used footage from 1976 in *The Filth and the Fury* simply to underline how inflammatory some of these people were. Rock Against Racism, just for a while, caught the mood of the streets – the whole rag-bag of the new punk generation tenuously united under a well-meaning but essentially meaningless banner.
John Shearlaw, music journalist

At one of our first gigs was a speaker with Rock Against Racism on it. I said to Chris, our guitarist, 'Are we playing a Rock Against Racism gig?' He said, 'No, don't be stupid. One of the other bands nicked it from a festival.'
Suggs, singer with Madness

Left: Steel Pulse playing at the Rock Against Racism concert

It was all over
in 18 months. Jock Scott, stand-up poet

You got all these old rock'n'rollers – people with long hair and all sorts of horrible clothes – taking their trousers in. But punk was never hippie, and it wasn't pub rock. It wasn't about spitting, or cutting up a brand-new T-shirt, or the pogo, but it eventually became all of that.
Robert Elms, broadcaster and journalist

The original punks were proud they looked alternative, and they were self-sufficient. I remember some years ago, I was walking down the Kings Road with a friend. We saw a punk family, real hardcore punks, with a cute little child who was only about two or three years old. I said to them, 'My friend would like to take a photo of you, please, if you don't mind,' and the guy said, 'That'll be two quid man.' I wanted to tell the guy, 'Hey, come on! Is this what it's all about? Was that the idea? You dress up like a freak and have someone pay you to take your photograph like a Beefeater at the Tower of London?'
Gene Krell, punk clothing entrepreneur

All that spitting and jumping about like idiots in the name of dancing…wasn't clever, intelligent, stylish, or even attractive. It was really stupid.
Mark Powell, London tailor

Jimmy Pursey [of Sham 69] was always saying, 'We're working class and we're proud of it.' Fair enough, but I remember seeing Sham 69 at the Vortex and they had this whole thing about 'All you plastic poser punks in your punk clothes from Oxford Street,' criticizing anyone who made an effort and tried to look good, and I was thinking, 'What fucking shop is selling punk clothes in Oxford Street? What are you talking about, you oaf?'
Marco Pirroni, guitarist, Siouxsie and the Banshees

That whole spitting thing was so vile…it was disgusting.
Jayne County, singer, actress and DJ

Rat Scabies [the Damned's drummer] started the spitting thing…there you go.
Tony James, bass player, Generation X

I was playing bass with Bazooka Joe and we played at the Vortex one night. By the time I left the stage, I was literally covered in other people's gob. I thought, 'What the fuck is this all about? This is stupid.' After that gig I became a photographer, and I've rarely been spat on since.
Chris Duffy, former bass player, Bazooka Joe

Don't listen to what anyone tells you. The Vortex was better than any other club, better than the Roxy or anywhere else you could care to mention.
Dylan Jones, editor, GQ magazine

Punk started to change from something that was exciting, different, individual and subversive into this oikish thing with blokes drinking beer just as an excuse to be stupid. In the pre-punk days people were restrained from behaving badly, but punk actively encouraged such behaviour. It was like, 'You should be doing that, you should make it worse. You should act like an arsehole, dear boy.'
Marco Pirroni

The whole punk thing became a complete bag of arse. You had all these total and absolute lemons, with their deliberately slashed T-shirts, ridiculous hair and make-up and awful manners, jumping up and down and actually spitting, or rather gobbing, at the acts. It was disgusting. It was just an excuse for a load of wankers, who ordinarily would not have the bottle to break wind in public, to act

up. At the start it was all about being different; at the end it was about acting exactly as the Sun newspaper had told you to…like sheep, bloody sheep.
Chris Sullivan

Live footage of all the punks shows just how daft it was. The memory of punk has become highly stylized, but wearing bin-liners with safety-pins stuck in them was also extremely silly. If you see the girls in the pictures, they were all tremendously ugly; it was a great refuge for the plain girl. That's what was so good about it.
Jock Scott

A lot of people actually denied they were ever involved because it became such a pile of toss.
Frank Kelly, Sex Pistols' aficionado

Punk music actually wasn't very revolutionary and, after a while, it all just sounded the same. It seemed very unsophisticated, especially if you'd grown up listening to jazz and soul, and then things like Lou Reed and the Velvet Underground. Even though the Velvets were raw, they were quite sophisticated. Suddenly, when punk came along, we were all supposed to become dumb and act really stupid. At one point I thought, 'For God's sake, these are 18-year-olds walking around spitting at you. I used to do that when I was 13 or 14 and trying to pretend I was a hard skinhead or something. Why are they doing this kind of thing?' It was totally idiotic in that respect.
Steve Walsh, guitarist, the Flowers of Romance

Punk wasn't about spitting, it wasn't about conformity, it wasn't about being an idiot. It was about playing great rock'n'roll and looking fantastic.
Tony James

Above left and opposite: Postcard punkette

If punk is an attitude rather than a style of music or dress, then two-tone was its offspring. Chris Sullivan

Two-tone's protagonists, brought up on reggae and punk, moulded parts of each to make a new form. They added that 'I can do it' attitude and created two-tone. The lineage isn't obvious, but it is there. They were autonomous and independent, and admittedly used all the doors that punk had opened for them.
Chris Sullivan

The whole punk thing did influence us in that we thought we could start a band too. There were so many bands around that a circuit of live venues had developed and we were able to play them. We were influenced a lot by Kilburn and the High Roads, Deaf School and a strange pub rock, quasi-punk mix. I remember I was so thrilled when I went to see these bands, and being thrilled by the fact that they were so near in the bar. Of course, when we started, none of us could really play that well. It was the 'can do' idea behind it that influenced us.
Suggs

A lot of the people who were into the early punk phenomemon moved in one of four or five directions – electro, rockabilly, a curious rock-dub fusion, a Velvet-inspired goth vibe, and two-tone – until each one of them reached 'Erbertsville and they moved on once again.
Chris Sullivan

The legacy of punk and then Madness was that when you went to a gig, the bloke who had just been performing on stage could now be standing next to you at the bar. He was just the same as you. He had the same common or uncommon accent as you. It was liberating. You were no longer divorced from rock stars; they were just like you.
Clive Langer, songwriter and producer

The whole thing about the punk and two-tone movements was how quickly you could get a record onto the streets. It was just like Jamaica, where guys used to go into the studio, cut a record, get it pressed, go out onto the street, sell 50 copies, then go back and press another 50. That was the greatness of two-tone – people cutting records and getting them out on the street.
Dennis Morris, photographer and record industry figure

It's a different industry now. Music today is clever, but it sounds manufactured. Two-tone had a reality which was raw and natural.
Clive Langer

The two-tone movement became so big and successful that the money men and the major record companies started appearing. That's when the problems began.
Dennis Morris

Above: Madness (Lee Thompson, Mark Bedford, Woody Woodgate, Suggs, Chris Foreman and Mike Barson)

Luckily for Coventry, two-tone happened because, if it hadn't, the town would have exploded. Dennis Morris

I was one of those early punk fans and used to go to Barbarella's. I wasn't into the music that much, but I liked the spirit of it. When we began the Specials, there was a certain punk sensibility, but the music and the clothes were completely different.
Jerry Dammers, keyboard player, the Specials

Coventry was an area which had got really devastated during the Second World War. It was very depressed. There was lots of National Front. It was very heavy. It was lucky that two-tone happened because music has always been the saviour of a divided society, and with two-tone it didn't matter if you were black or white.
Dennis Morris

A lot of bands in the punk thing tried to express the feeling of being unemployed and pissed off in an urban environment, but none of them expressed it as well as the Specials in 'Ghost Town'. One of the reasons two-tone was so valid was that it was multiracial, a true reflection of Britain at the time. I'd like to think that if punk had been left alone and unhindered, it would have developed into this, which is maybe what happened in Coventry.
Stephen Colegrave

The Specials were a fantastic band. It's hard to explain now, but they were absolutely the band of the moment. There was a special energy coming out of their songs and everything they did. The problem was that there were too many strong individual geniuses in the Specials.
Dennis Morris

Being on tour with the Specials was really refreshing because they weren't just another punk group – they were taking it somewhere else, and it was something we were really familiar with, the two-tone suits and all that. A lot of us had been into ska before punk came along, and really it was a direction we could have returned to. Reggae was an area the Clash explored quite thoroughly.
Paul Simonon

The Specials' music is the stuff that turns legs to rubber and plays pinball with your brain. They strike a near-perfect balance between accessibility and attitude.
Dennis Morris

It's not that we're just trying to revive ska. It's using those old elements to try forming something new. In a way it's all still part of punk. We're just trying to show some other direction. …You've got to go back to go forward.
Terry Hall, vocalist, the Specials, *New Musical Express*, 10 May 1979

Above: Neville Staples and Jerry Dammers of the Specials

Bands that came out of places like Liverpool and Belfast were more entertaining than demanding, less depressing and a bit odder. Stephen Colegrave

Liverpool and Manchester didn't really have punk in the sense of kids in leather jackets trying to look like the Sex Pistols. The punk scene was 200 miles away – another world – and people were too free-thinking to categorize like that anyway, although I believe everyone liked the Velvet Underground. It was like a code to get into a speakeasy – mention the Velvets and you're OK. The drugs were different too – southern punk was all speed and energy, whereas Liverpool's New Wave was kind of dreamy and acid-based. The Teardrop Explodes improved markedly after Julian Cope [the lead singer] took acid.
Bill Dunn, senior editor, *Esquire* magazine

A lot of the Liverpool thing seems to stem from Deaf School and their followers, who were around in 1975 and had a big following. 'What a Way to End It All' [from their 1976 album *Second Honeymoon*] was a great track.
Stephen Colegrave

I used to jam with a band called Big in Japan, which was formed in 1977 out of the Deaf School road crew. Various line-ups included Holly Johnson [later of Frankie Goes to Hollywood] on bass, Bill Drummond [who later formed the dance band KLF] on guitar, Budgie [later of the Banshees] on drums, and Dave Balfe [later of the Teardrop Explodes] on bass. The Crucial Three [Julian Cope, Ian McCulloch and Pete Wylie] also came from Big in Japan. Julian Cope went on to found the Teardrop Explodes, Ian McCulloch joined Echo and the Bunnymen and Pete Wylie formed Wah! So it was very

exciting up there, but it took a few years for the Liverpool bands to break through because the London scene was top.
Clive Langer

I was too young to go to Eric's [the Liverpool nightclub], so I used to persuade my mum to give me the money she'd set aside for a new pair of Marks & Spencer's trousers and I'd head off for Probe Records, at the bottom end of Church Street. Pete Burns [who went on to become lead singer of Dead or Alive] would be serving behind the counter. Everything in Liverpool then was about looking cool. I think teenagers today worry much less about making tits of themselves than we did.
Bill Dunn

Liverpool has a history of producing odd, funny, off-the-wall, musical talent. I think the '79–'80 period produced quite a few examples of this – Pete Wylie, Ian McCulloch and Frankie Goes to Hollywood, to name but a few.
Chris Sullivan

Echo and the Bunnymen had an air of mystery. Maybe it was the long coats, or the haircuts, or the production, but the music on *Heaven Up Here* [their 1981 album] doesn't sound like it's made by people who like Ken Dodd or go to the toilet.
Bill Dunn

Above left: Julian Cope of the Teardrop Explodes • Above right: Feargal Sharkey of the Undertones • Opposite: New Wave band XTC

No one who had any sense of style had anything to do with New Wave. It was dreadful, just dreadful.

Nils Stevenson, Sex Pistols' tour manager, 1976

New Wave was a conspiracy between the record companies and the music press to revive the careers of a lot of half-arsed musicians who'd been disenfranchised by punk. XTC and 999 were prime examples – bad clothes, bad shoes, blow-dried hair and insipid music. Awful. Little wonder that New Wave is now, for the most part, forgotten.
Chris Sullivan

I thought New Wave was about being inventive with your hairdryer.
Simon Hinton, journalist and poet

XTC were the top band in the sixth form common-rooms of 1979.
Nils Stevenson

The only New Wave stuff that was in any way interesting was from Liverpool. I feel sorry for the Liverpool bands who get lumped into that category. I think the music

press called anything that wasn't black New Wave, but the press do like a pigeon-hole. It wasn't good.
Chris Sullivan

New Wave was similar to New Labour: totally insincere and dishonest, purely a marketing ploy.
Stephen Colegrave

New Wave was all the weak stuff, the dross, the rubbish.
Paul Simonon

New Wave – that's the student union, real ale, missed-out-on-punk, insipid, pseudo-intellectual stuff…isn't it?
Chris Sullivan

There was that horrible thing called New Wave, which was really just an excuse for failed rock bands to sell a load of records. I mean, all these bands like the Cars were just horrible. If I wanted to listen to a reggae rhythm

I'd listen to Prince Far I rather than that. Most of the real punk thing was suburban but it aimed to be urban, whereas New Wave wanted to stay in the suburbs, where it belonged. Its biggest audience was in Midwest America.
Robert Elms

New Wave – the music loved by journalists because the musicians looked exactly like music journalists.
Tony James

New Wave people were depressives, wandering around in long green coats moaning. I must admit that was never my scene. I'm sure they hated us and I'm sure we hated them.
Robert Elms

Whoever came up with the term New Wave should be shot. I'd have called it shit.
Frank Kelly

Punk was never about big stadiums – it was always a small thing. Robert Elms

The only bands that went on to do the whole stadium rock bit, apart from the Clash, were all the really rubbish bands that in many ways were absolutely nothing to do with the original form. They displayed this fact to great effect by playing in huge stadiums, which was the total antithesis, for want of a better term, of the punk ethic. The bands that by and large perpetrated such heinous acts were the likes of the Police, who just happened to be on the same bill as many of the earlier 'proper' punk outfits and were, in a word, shit. The Boomtown Rats were absolutely hopeless but were loved by misguided folk the world over. Blondie were an admittedly out-and-out pop band, so for them stadiums were fine because that is what pop bands do. You could also lump Billy Idol

in with the stadium acts, but Billy was always rock'n'roll, and that is what you do if you have his success. Anyway, he was an original who defies description. I don't think Billy ever accepted the punk moniker for himself. The rest, the Clash excepted, were just so awful it was untrue. Stadiums were the best place for them.
Chris Sullivan

A few of the bands did go on to play in big stadiums but, to be fair, they were all shit. That is why they ended up playing in a Midwestern football field. That's where they belonged, and they got the audience they deserved.
Robert Elms

The Police were horrible – a fucking nightmare. I remember we did *Top of the Pops* with them. I didn't even know they were on the stage, but Stewart Copeland was in *NME* the next week complaining that we looked down our noses at them, and that we wouldn't even acknowledge them. He said it was obviously a punk elite thing. I remember saying, 'Fucking right it was. You're just rubbish mate.'
Steve Severin, bass player, Siouxsie and the Banshees

Stadiums were different. We did them, but it was weird. We were best in small clubs. That's why we did that tour of seven nights in the same club in the same city – New York and Tokyo. Some bands are better in stadiums.
Paul Simonon

Above: Debbie Harry and Blondie in concert

As the innovators of punk turned their backs on the chaos, they found solace in the Teutonic order of Kraftwerk and electro. Stephen Colegrave

To me Kraftwerk were more important than any of the New Wave bands. They were at least doing new and interesting things.
Caroline Coon, journalist

The electro thing was in effect a direct spin-off from punk in that it was a reaction to it. All the people who were in at the start of the Pistols' phenomenon were there at the start of electro in Billy's – Marco Pirroni, Adam Ant, Helen Robinson and Steph Raynor from Acme, Andy Czezowski, Dougie Fields, Billy Idol. All these people had had their fill of the punk bandwagon and were entirely disenchanted with the pogo-dancing, spitting, sartorially incorrect cartoon character that punk had become. And so they turned against it. Electro music was rather Teutonic and regimented, and the style of dress was almost formal – very neat, very preconceived. Electro was diametrically opposed to what punk had become but, as a statement, it was equally radical for its time.
Chris Sullivan

'Zyclon B Zombie' was a fantastic record by Throbbing Gristle, who were as punk as you could get at one point. Then they made this an electro record.
Dempsey, punk fan

Iggy Pop's *The Idiot* and Kraftwerk's *Trans-Europe Express*, both released in 1977, were, in effect, the first industrial records. *The Idiot* was a landmark record in its time, and the production on *Trans-Europe Express* was absolutely amazing. Later on, I liked the Monochrome Set's early records, and I also loved Cabaret Voltaire, who played with us a couple of times. The Human League track 'Being Boiled' [from their 1979 album *Reproduction*] was also fantastic and very influential.
Steve Severin

The electro thing was important amongst the Billy's scene in London. You'd wear shirts and ties and short manicured hair. The music would be electronic, with drum machines and synthesizers. The younger element of punk, who'd never been in punk bands because we were only 15 or 16 at the time, stood at the back of the events rather than at the front 'cause the other lot were a bit advanced. Eventually we moved up and other kids took our place.
Robert Elms

Punk had to go that way. It had become messy, scruffy and silly. It was time for something a bit more serious, though at times it was a bit too serious.
Mark Taylor, club promoter and early punk figure

Above left: Kraftwerk • Above right: Stephen Mallinder of Cabaret Voltaire

I ain't 'no show' Strummer.

Joe Strummer, guitarist and vocalist, the Clash

Our first gig in the USA was at the Berkeley Community Theater [Berkeley, California] with an audience of toe-tapping, hand-clapping, smiling, scrubbed faces, which reminded us that in California being laid-back is a virtue. The energy went one way, with Strummer striving to push it into their faces, and Jones and Simonon working up into sprints across the huge stage. 'Nice,' said Joe. 'But nice ain't good enough. Who put us on here with this bunch of dozeys?'
Johnny Green, former road manager, the Clash, in *A Riot of Our Own*

The Clash were the one band left who had the spirit of '76 still burning in them and they were ready to take it to America and just watch it ignite. They'd had a whole year flexing their muscles and developing their power on tour, headlining in London and in Europe. Their first album was a huge underground hit in America, even though their record label, CBS, wouldn't actually release it officially, and [Joe] Strummer especially was so steeped in the legends of rock'n'roll. They were just so up for it, they deserved every break they got there. Calling the [first] American tour 'Pearl Harbor, 1979' was a masterstroke worthy of the Pistols. And the Clash even got to share a tour bus with a rock'n'roll legend called Bo Diddley.
John Shearlaw

What we tried to do in America was to get a good roster of bands on the bill. Me and Joe hadn't realized we could get these guys to play with us, so we had Lee Dorsey a lot, Screaming Jay Hawkins, and when we played at Bonds in New York we had Grandmaster Flash. We also brought over the Undertones 'cause we liked them and they were great. At the end of the tour they gave us these toy guns. I suppose that's what people from Belfast give each other.
Paul Simonon

The Undertones were coming up very quickly and it had been arranged for them to play support on some of the Clash's American gigs at the beginning of their second tour. We thought it would be a good idea for both bands to do a photo session for the music press. It would end up with a headline like 'Clash and Undertones join forces for punk invasion'. But the thing that struck me most was just how uncomfortable the Clash were, more nervous and unsure than the Undertones, who were really only just starting out. It was the beginning of the Clash's second American tour, they'd started the whole punk thing off, and they were still jumpy about a photo shoot in a rehearsal room in Camden.
Mick Houghton, Undertones' press officer

The first tour name was good; the second was even better. They called it 'The Clash Take the Fifth', explained away as a reference to Mickey Gallagher [of Ian Dury's band, the Blockheads], who'd joined them on keyboards for the live gigs. But taking on the fundamentals of the Constitution gave Joe plenty of leeway for comment from the stage. For despite all the wrangles with their US record label – in the UK they were on album number three by then, yet the moguls over there didn't even see fit to release the first Clash album until the second visit – they were really enjoying this tour. It gave the Undertones a leg-up, and the range of support acts was fantastic, to the point of being surreal. Soul duo Sam and Dave played the Palladium in New York with the Clash, with Feargal Sharkey from the Undertones singing along in the front row. They also had Lee Dorsey and legendary rock'n'roller Screamin' Jay Hawkins in later. And they still got away with opening the shows with 'I'm So Bored with the USA'.
John Shearlaw

Next day we beat the fog into Cleveland [Ohio]. Joe had a raging toothache. I was surprised it didn't strike more often considering the blackened, rotting stumps in his mouth. The dentists did something – but said the shot would take 24 hours to work. His advice was to cancel the gig. Joe said, 'I ain't "no show" Strummer.' The show went on to a wildly lively crowd and we sussed that the industrial heartland of America was more Clash than California. It had the familiar hard and desperate edge. And then we had Manhattan in our sights.
Johnny Green, *A Riot of Our Own*

Right: Andy Warhol and Joe Strummer (far right) with fans

Detroit was the most outrageous place I've ever seen. As we drove in, there were like bombsites, a bit similar to where I grew up, but more extreme. In the middle of these bombsites there'd be fires and all these black Hells Angels zooming around on motorbikes. I thought, 'Bloody hell.' We were the only white people using the bus. I think our naivety saved us.
Paul Simonon

We knew New York was important. New York claimed to have invented punk. We would show them. That afternoon in the Palladium we did a sound-check and a half. Every light was focused, every speaker double-checked, every spare guitar tuned, every drumstick sanded. That night the Clash looked hard and ripped the joint apart. After I stuffed the sweat-soaked stage gear into holdalls, the famous came to backslap, joined by a chunk of street life I had brought in through the stage door – there was no 'elite only' here. 'Studio 54 tonight, lads?' I shouted. We shot off in a bunch of cabs…that night we had the keys to the city and smoothed our way in past the drooling, star-spotting crowd. 'YMCA' [by Village People] came on and we hit the dance floor. The Clash had cracked New York.
Johnny Green, *A Riot of Our Own*

Two American tours in a year, along with all the other activity back home, would have been enough. The fact that the Clash came back in between and pulled together all the amazing material for *London Calling* [to be released as their third album in the UK in 1979, but, crucially, not until 1980 in the USA] in something like a week must go down as one of the greatest achievements of the punk years. They were back with producer Guy Stevens (who worked on one of the early Clash demos two years previously) at Wessex Studios, but there was something more driving them on that summer. *London Calling* was their greatest statement, culling all the rich American influences along with punk's hard edges and turning the whole thing into Clash rock'n'roll. It sounded great then and it still sounds great now. When it finally did come out in the States, it was rock fans who were buying it by the cartload.
John Shearlaw

The Bonds gig in New York came along because we had released *London Calling*, a double album for the price of a single album. Just to be clever, we then released *Sandinista*, a treble album, and it did us over financially. We even had to take a cut in our royalties. Then Bernie came along and said we were lunatics. But he devised this plan to do seven nights in New York, seven in Tokyo and seven in London. We arrived in Bonds to do seven nights and the fire chief basically said we had to close the show down because there were too many people present. In an effort to accommodate all those who wanted to see us, we did 22 shows. It was mayhem. The whole street was packed and the newspapers said they hadn't seen anything like it since Frank Sinatra. We liked that.
Paul Simonon

They looked hard and they ripped the joint apart …
the Clash cracked New York.

Johnny Green, *A Riot of Our Own*

It might have been subconscious, but both Bernie and Malcolm were prepared to break up their bands rather than do the more difficult thing and deal with the big record companies. If they'd been more determined, they could have taken them to the next stage of success. I wasn't prepared to see the Clash break up like the Sex Pistols and the Damned. To me there was no reason why, like Chuck Berry and other great musicians, the Clash couldn't still be playing in their old age. These musicians had a lot to say and I loved the boys. I knew that if their next album came out and they toured America, they would never have to worry about money again. They would have the freedom to do whatever

they wanted, which is a good position for artists to be in. To see them destroyed by egos would have been such a waste. As the band showed signs of breaking up, with minor disagreements getting all out of proportion, I stepped in and persuaded them that they should go to America. I said this would give them experience as a band that they could never get anywhere else. As I'd known them well since the early days, I offered to manage them temporarily. After all, my reputation was on the line because I'd said this generation of musicians would define music for the next decade, which wasn't going to happen if all the bands broke up.
Caroline Coon

Opposite: Mick Jones and Joe Strummer performing in New York • Above: The Clash (Mick Jones, Paul Simonon, Topper Headon and Joe Strummer)

363

Hip-hop is black punk rock.

Don Letts, film-maker and former DJ

Hip-hop per se came out of the Sugar Hill area of New York and, just like punk, its protagonists had little musical experience but just went for it. They had no musical instruments, so they used decks, cannibalizing other records, cutting and scratching them to make their own brand new form of music. At the start the DJs and rappers were very much influenced by punk. It was all happening in New York at the time and they could relate to it. It talked a language they could understand, it was urban and anti-establishment. As with dub, they rapped over the records, but added the essential scratching and mixing. They wore the studded wristbands, leather trousers and dog collars, and although the music was very party-orientated at the start, it did eventually become very confrontational, Public Enemy and Run DMC being prime examples. Again, the music was so different but the ethic existed in full.
Chris Sullivan

Hip-hop, parody or scratch came from Lee Perry [an eccentric Jamaican record producer] after Bob Marley died. Lee Perry said he knew it was the end of an era, so much so that he completely broke up his studio, flooded it and filled it up with ducks. There were all these ducks quacking away in the studio and he drew crosses all over the place and moved out. He left his family and everything and went to New York. The story is that he was hanging around in New York and started scratching, so he's been recognized as inventing it. Anyway, I rate him as one of the most influential musicians to come out of Jamaica. They all used to go to see Lee Perry in Jamaica, even McCartney, to do some demos with the scratch. Then they'd go back to England to try to catch that Lee Perry thing that only Lee Perry could do.
Dennis Morris

Hip-hop is very much about feelings. It's not sung, it's shouted. Like punk, it's another sort of street music. It's hardcore, tough and real.
Hilly Kristal

The movement of Jamaicans to the Bronx was getting bigger, and they brought with them massive sound systems, the music and the toasting [live voice-over]. Rap developed from toasters like U-Roy and, of course, the Last Poets, but the rap of the Last Poets could not have evolved in hip-hop without toasting and reggae. But hip-hop needed America to develop like it did. Black English kids never really listened to anything other than reggae; they didn't touch rock. Black Americans were different. They listened to everything and took from everywhere. That's why black British music never really moved on to the same degree that American black music did from that period. When punk was ending, black music in Britain just didn't go anywhere. Everything came out of America. For me it was very difficult. Coming from the punk movement, black

people used to look at me as if I was weird. Then, 10 years later, every black kid was having one side shaved off, one lock here, whatever, because they had seen Mr T on television [in The A-Team]. It was as simple as that. If it's cool for Mr T, it's cool. People like myself and Don Letts were at the forefront. We were seen as lepers. Then, suddenly Mr T appeared and every kid in town had gold and stuff.
Dennis Morris

I could see a lot of links between early rap and punk when we played Bonds in New York. We had Grandmaster Flash supporting us, but the Yanks didn't really get it…at all.
Paul Simonon

When they started out with hip-hop, it was very party-down lyrics, and punk never had that. In fact, hip-hop and dub are closer because hip-hop was spoken and toasters spoke, chanted or rapped, so the lineage is sort of clearer there. The connection was also that people from working-class communities were seizing culture for their own use.
Viv Goldman

The rap scene was certainly parallel to the punk scene in the black league. I believe punk is pretty well accepted, but it seems like rap is even more mainstream in America now.
Chris Stein, guitarist, Blondie

I was never really a Beastie Boy fan. Their music was good and I could understand it, but it was a bit like being a kid at school. It felt like you were having parties and wrecking the place when your parents were out.
Dennis Morris

The Beastie Boys mixed the two genres and did very well out of it. Again the people who followed each form at the outset were the same. They were the people who looked for something new. Malcolm McLaren certainly saw the similarities.
Chris Sullivan

Malcolm McLaren got involved with those girls who used to skip: he brought all these American kids over and made a mint out of that. He went to a ship chandler's shop and bought a length of rope and some red gaffer tape, and he had us cutting it up in the office, in like six foot lengths, to make skipping ropes to sell at the gigs. 'Double Dutch'. That's pure Colonel Parker. He just couldn't let the opportunity go to make some money: 'You can sell these at the gig.' Any excuse to make a shilling.
Jock Scott

Opposite: Fab Fine Freddy • Above, left to right: Grandmaster Flash; the Beastie Boys; Run DMC and Russell Symonds (with long hair) of Def Jam

It was only in New York that punk did what it was meant to do — explode and fragment and metamorphose into lots of different musical styles. Stephen Colegrave

Lydia Lunch was in the fantastically monikered band Teenage Jesus and the Jerks. I think that says it all really. She was signed to Ze Records, which was the only label in New York that was saying anything. The band was a mad mix of everything, with a totally punk sensibility.
Chris Sullivan

I saw them at the Vortex and I just thought they were fantastic. Everything was taken down to a minimum. They were so off the wall. The whole band were characters.
Steve Severin

Klaus Nomi was a big part of that New York scene. I think he was Austrian, and he got his start as the singing pastry chef. His music was a mixture of opera and electro.
Gene Krell

Jayne County was maybe the only artist who managed to see the whole thing through from start to finish on both sides of the Atlantic and remain hip.
Chris Sullivan

I played at the Reading Festival [in 1977] and it was awful. We were the only punk band on the bill and went on in between Hawkwind and the Doobie Brothers. Can you believe that? All these real rock types were in the audience. They started throwing bottles, so we threw them back. Then they threw mud and stones and I got hit over the eye. It was awful. We only managed to do three numbers, so I went crazy and said, 'You fucking hippie bastards! You narrow-minded pricks!' and all that sort of thing. John Peel was the DJ and he played my song 'If You Don't Want to Fuck Me Baby, Baby Fuck Off' right to the end. By the end of 1979 I was back in New York.
Jayne County

By the end of '78 the whole punk thing, for those who were there anywhere near its inception, was dead in the water. A lot of the so-called movers and shakers reverted to a more '50s-inspired vibe. Probably the most apparent of all of these manifestations were Levi and the Rockats. They played a residency at the Speakeasy, which was the club where all the bands went after playing. You'd see the Heartbreakers, the Pistols and the Banshees mixing with Ian Hunter of Mott the Hoople... Leee Childers was the Rockats' manager. Jayne County would often duet with Levi Dexter, the singer. In about '79 they moved to New York and became the toast of the town, shagging everything that moved and inspiring a plethora of rockabilly outfits, such as the Stray Cats.
Chris Sullivan

Although the Rockats couldn't play, it didn't matter, they were great and they looked good and had all the attitude. These are people who looked much more likely to be successful mass murderers. It was fantastic but very funny. They'd all been hardcore early punk, then moved on, as many did when it got turned sour, into rockabilly.
Robert Elms

The first time the Rockats ever played they looked good. Levi was out front singing off tune and dancing, Smutty was playing this kind of upright bass shaped like a banana which wasn't even plugged in 'cause he couldn't play, and Dibbs was so terrified that he hid in the wings and you couldn't see him. They were making a complete mess of it, then Johnny Thunders suddenly jumped on the stage, grabbed a guitar and started playing one Chuck Berry song after another, forcing them to join in. The audience went crazy. At the end of the medley he handed the guitar back to Spudhead then turned to Levi and said, 'Let that be a lesson to you. You can't make a fool of yourself as long as you're on the stage.' The band remembered those words and began to learn to play from that point on.
Leee Childers

Above: Levi of the Rockats and Jayne County • Opposite: Lydia Lunch (top); Smutty of the Rockats (bottom left); Klaus Nomi (bottom right)

People forget, but Divine was a huge inspiration on the whole punk thing… just look at the films *Pink Flamingos* and *Female Trouble*.

If that's not punk, I don't know what is. Phillip Salon, club promoter

Sci-fi psychobilly schlock horror – that's the Cramps.
Frank Kelly

The Cramps played New York very early. Our accountant, Tom Holiday, auditioned to be their drummer, and I met Lux Interior [their vocalist] some 25 years ago. They played for a *Punk Magazine* benefit in '77. I remember meeting Lux backstage. He was kneeling down with a bottle of Jack Daniels in his hand, and he was brushing his teeth with the whiskey. We never got to write about them because we were out of business by '77. The Cramps played a lot at CBGB's. I saw them many times. They were great.
John Holmstrom

They sounded and looked like a cartoon, but they were actually like that. At first I thought their sleazy rockabilly image just required a lot of dedication, then I realized they were for real…which is a lot more scary.
Bill Dunn, senior editor, *Esquire* magazine

I loved the Cramps right from the beginning. They just had such great style, and they were funny as well. The whole thing was like a B-movie come to life. There was loads going on with them, and they'd taken it all to extremes, which is always important.
Steve Severin

After Generation X, when I formed Sigue Sigue Sputnik, our main influences were Suicide and the Cramps. I loved them because they were great rock'n'roll groups. Suicide were extraordinary. Here was a group using technology to play rock'n'roll, and it was very visionary of Mick Jones to bring them over to play with the Clash. I think they were the most incredibly innovative group.
Tony James

The B-52's were a mix of pop, punk and '60s movie music with a lot of camp thrown in. They played an important part in the late '70s musical evolution.
Chris Sullivan

Willy De Ville is just symptomatic of the many ways New York went in 1979. They ignored the formula that punk had aquired and went off in hundreds of directions. That total nonconformity is how punk should have developed.
Stephen Colegrave

That first Mink de Ville album wasn't a punk record in anything but attitude. It's kind of latino sou,l but it's great.
Robert Elms

The Lounge Lizards were in many ways not at all punk. They played jazz in the style of Ornette Coleman and Thelonius Monk, and dressed in late '50s suits. But there was something about them that was punk. They were anarchic and had an attitude, and that is what punk is – an attitude and not a musical style.
Chris Sullivan

The Lounge Lizards were superb. They were very anarchic. It was like punk jazz, which was a totally legitimate place for the music to go. The first album was superb, and John Lurie was a great front man. I remember we went to see them at Danceteria in New York. Jim Fourrat, the club's owner, had brought in a piano at great expense, and they didn't even bother playing it.
Robert Elms

Devo were a bunch of crazy guys from Akron, Ohio. They did that song 'Mongoloid'. Devo were just crazy.
Gene Krell

It's nice to see an act whose audience can't relate to them.
Leonard Cohen in *Rock Confidential*

Opposite, main picture: Divine • Bottom, left to right: Lydia Lunch; Poison Ivy of the Cramps; Mink De Ville • Above: The B-52's and John Lurie of the Lounge Lizards

James White and the Blacks
were the personification of the punk ethic.

They were not a punk band and did not look punky at all, and that is the point. The attitude was there in abundance. Chris Sullivan

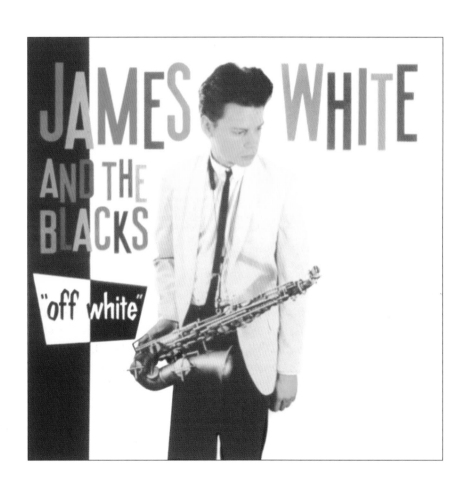

James was really into old-school jazz. He had all those old records – and a saxophone teacher. He wanted to be Ornette Coleman, although he would never admit it… or maybe he would. Jim Fourrat, writer and nightclub owner

In 1979 there was that brilliant rebirth of the New York art scene, with the Lydia Lunches and the James Whites – it was a great scene, really underrated and under-documented. A lot of the music on the Ze record label, owned by Michael Zhilka, such as Teenage Jesus and the Jerks and James White and the Blacks, is fantastic. *Off White* is a great album, and that is truly punk. They were a band that could play.
Robert Elms

James White was really important. He started as part of what was called No Wave by playing at Max's Kansas City. His girlfriend was Anya Phillips, who started the Mudd Club, and he was a big part of that whole New York post-punk fragmentation. He made an album on Ze Records, *Off White*, under the name James White and the Blacks, which was pivotal to say the least. It can only be described as punk funk, and was a massive inspiration to many, including me, on both sides of the Atlantic. He dressed in '60s sharkskin suits and, for a while, was the personification of where punk should have gone.
Chris Sullivan

They were kind of interesting. I wasn't really into the jazzy side of it, like James White, kind of heroin jazz.
Steve Severin

It is interesting that the punk mantle should return to New York with James White carrying the torch. The New York scene was never blown out of all proportion, never reached the tabloids like the UK scene, so it was allowed to grow and develop. James White played anarchic funk, punk, jazz renditions of songs such as 'Heatwave' by Marilyn Monroe, and filled it with scratchy guitars, wailing alto sax and throbbing bass. He realized that the essence of any musical movement is fusion: that's the only way it can grow and attract a new audience. In England punk was full of bands adhering to a set formula that had been hastily assembled some three years before, and no one, apart from the Clash, had really taken it anywhere else. In New York in '79 the scene was thriving in all directions – art, music, clothing, clubs… And even though it was very much divorced from punk as such, it still entertained all its best elements.
Chris Sullivan

The Mudd Club was the quintessential and the centre of the art, fashion and

I opened the Mudd Club. We were trying to find ways of raising some money for *Punk Magazine* and, rather than do a benefit, we figured we'd do an awards show and then all the rock stars would show up from the scene and we could charge money. The event was held at Club Hollywood on Friday 13 October 1978, which was the day after Sid was arrested for killing Nancy. The place was jam-packed. The media tried to descend and interview everybody – they wanted to talk to the real punk rockers and get their

reaction to the killing. But the best part of the night was the party afterwards. I'd arranged for an open bar at the Mudd Club which, at that point, hadn't even got a name, and the official opening was still a few weeks away. This was the first time it opened to the public. It was a disastrous night, but we had opened the club. The place floundered for about three or four months, then there was a write-up in the *SoHo Weekly News* and it was packed from that night on.
John Holmstrom

Anya [Phillips] and Diego Cortez took a punk club with punk sensibilities. [The space] was totally falling apart, but they put velvet ropes outside the front. It was also totally out of the way – nobody had even heard of White Street…Anya Phillips insisted they have a disco ball and a door policy… Steve [Maas, owner of the Mudd Club] would be watching the door from his office through a surveillance camera and he would call us on the walkie-talkie and say 'No black leather', which

Above left: John Belushi, a regular at the Mudd Club

downtown underground nightclub, music scenes in New York. Chris Sullivan

was absurd, or 'American passports only'. Then we'd grill him about exceptions. Once he called down and said, 'No fat people, unless they're famous, like Meatloaf, but charge them triple and tell them why.'
Chi Chi Valenti, club promoter, in *Platinum Blonde*

You'd get to the door of the Mudd Club and there'd be all these bridge and tunnel [suburban] types clamouring to get in, but thank God they never did because you had

either Chi Chi or Gennaro vetting the queue quite severely. Chi Chi was a rather glamorous blonde with a fine line in sarcasm, and Gennaro was a muscular Italian bloke from the Boroughs who, although gay, didn't look it at all. Gennaro's speciality was the one-line put-down. As a pair, they were invincible. Once inside, it was the quintessential nightclub that could only exist in New York. It was fantastic – one of the best nightclubs I've ever been to.
Chris Sullivan

John Lydon was living in New York at that time, and so was Billy Idol. People were there for different reasons. John was escaping the dramas of the court case. Billy went off to be a star, and Malcolm McLaren was there for a while too. When I first went there with the Banshees, we hooked up with all the expats. It was probably the only city in the world that would take the Banshees, and it loved 'em. We all went to the Mudd, of course.
Steve Severin

Above: The Walter Stedding Band, with Debbie Harry guesting on drums • Inset: Anya Phillips

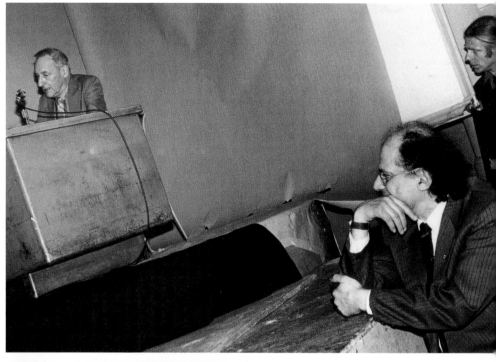

Studio 54 received all the press attention, but the Mudd was the real McCoy.

Chris Sullivan

We all went to the Mudd. All of the original British punks who'd moved to New York went there – Billy Idol, Malcolm McLaren, the Rockats… All the people who were on the CBGB's scene – Richard Hell, the Dead Boys, the Cramps – went there too, and even the people who were left over from the days of Max's. It was great. That was where both the New York and English scene really gelled.
Leee Childers

One of the most amazing things about the Mudd was the clientele. It was there that I met William Burroughs, Allen Ginsberg, Hunter S. Thompson, John Cale, Johnny Thunders, Rick James, Diana Vreeland, and the artists Keith Haring and Francesco Clemente. On any night, even on a Sunday, you might see Iggy Pop, David Bowie, Gregory Corso and Andy Warhol. You don't find such a mix of people frequenting one establishment that often. Studio 54 received all the press attention, but the Mudd was the real

Above left, top to bottom: Steve Maas and friend; Andy Warhol and William Burroughs; (clockwise from top left) Arthur Ferlinghetti, Gregory de Corso, Allen Ginsberg and William Burroughs Top right: William Burroughs reading his work at the Mudd Club, watched by Allen Ginsberg and unidentified fan • Near left: Gregory de Corso

McCoy. It was where your clued-up New Yorker hung out. You'd see punks, rockabillies, drag queens, businessmen, rock stars and strippers. The music, as supplied by Anita Sarko, was an eclectic mix of James Brown, Iggy Pop, Doris Day, the B-52's, James White and the Blacks, as well as a pot-pourri of '60s soul, rockabilly, '60s garage bands and the Ramones. The Mudd also showcased quite a superb collection of live bands. I saw Levi and the Rockats, the Brides of Funkenstein, the Lounge Lizards and Robert Gordon. The Mudd was a complete across-the-board mix of people, music and style, and it influenced me enormously in the creation of the Wag Club in London.
Chris Sullivan

If you knew about the Mudd Club, you were really cool, and if you were press, you were no better than anyone else. Once you were in, you felt like you were part of something that was really special. Now there is no underground. Everything is routinely co-opted and turned into a Gap ad.
Michael Musto, New York's premier nightlife reporter, in *Platinum Blonde*

I didn't like the artists' stuff…I just thought it was bad. And then there were the yuppies and people in suits. But I fucked a lot of girls in the alley from the Mudd Club, so you can't put it down too much.
Legs McNeil

At that time art was in clubs, art was the subtext of clubs, and Mudd was major. Anya invented this new kind of nightlife, which began with Mudd and turned into Tier Three, which became Area, which became Jackie 60. Keith Haring's first job was as curator of the gallery at Mudd in 1982. Keith and Jean Michel [Basquiat] first met at Mudd, and at one point Fred Schneider [of the B-52's] worked the coat-check.
Chi Chi Valenti in *Platinum Blonde*

The Mudd Club was really rather scruffy, with the worst toilets on earth. There was a stage at the back downstairs, and upstairs there was a bit of a lounge area with a bar at the back. On the next floor was Steve Maas's art gallery. Keith Haring was the curator for a while. I saw an exhibition there of Elizabethan-style clothing made out of silver foil and plastic – sort of space-age Elizabethan…as far as I could gather. Steve Maas was rather an odd fellow. He invited people up to his gallery – it was like a sanctuary.
Chris Sullivan

The scene was starting to get arty. People seemed more adult. Things had definitely changed after Nancy was murdered. There was a lot of cocaine around – everybody had white shit hanging out of their noses. Normally, years before, you'd pass out about 3 or 4 a.m. from the drink, but when you had cocaine, you didn't pass out until noon the next day. Steve Maas always had too much cocaine. You'd hang out at the Mudd Club and then go over to Steve's house, do more cocaine and drink more beer. The next thing you knew, it would be noon and you'd be leaving. It was a horrible feeling. The sun would be out, but it was too bright. You'd think, 'Oh God, where are my sunglasses? Have I lost another fucking pair of sunglasses?' That's how it was then – too fucking bright.
Legs McNeil

THE BEST OF PUNK...

The best thing was 'God Save the Queen', one of the best things I'd ever heard, and it wasn't allowed to be number one.
Nils Stevenson

The best thing about punk was hanging out with all those incredible people like Siouxsie and everybody, and the feeling that we were part of something that was actually changing the face of music and standing up to the record industry.
Jayne County

I liked the feeling that you didn't have to be some guitar god to get up on stage. Why not give it a try? It was also quite self-deprecating, which is nice – that sense of 'I'm ugly and crap and useless, but listen to me anyway.' Kurt Cobain took the whole thing too far, though. He turned into 'I hate myself and I want to die.'
Bill Dunn

The best was definitely right at the beginning, when people didn't know what side of the fence to stand. That was really exciting because it was dangerous. We'd do shows and look around the stage covered in broken glass. We had one part of the crowd with us and one that wasn't. It was a tense atmosphere, we were in the middle of it and it was exciting – the best.
Paul Simonon

The best was just a sense of wonder, excitement and inspiration from going to these little places where there was something going on unknown to the world above the pavement. You know, I wouldn't have been in a band if punk hadn't happened.
Suggs

I thought it was the shop Sex, along with the people around it, that promoted anything goes, total decadence, breaking down taboos and putting them more into the mainstream. There had never been provocative clothes before, or clothes that really changed the way you think about things.
Marco Pirroni

The DIY thing, writing your own rules, living outside the law, and that a good idea attempted is better than a bad idea perfected – I still live by all that shit. Hip-hop is black punk rock.
Don Letts

Everyone was encouraged to be completely himself or herself, which is anarchy as well.
Clive Langer

You could do anything, and that really felt possible.
Legs McNeil

The best thing was the sense of possibility. It enabled people to feel free and to go for it, to follow their star. Dub was also another one of the best things about punk.
Viv Goldman

What I liked about the fashion was that it wasn't gay, it wasn't straight. It was just everything thrown together. You never thought, 'Oh, my God, it's a bit gay or it's a bit this or that.' You wore whatever you wanted.
Alan Jones

I loved the sheer crazy brazenness of the thing. It had no generation, no real forethought: it lived for the moment and just exposed itself in front of you.
Andy Czezowski

I think the best thing was that it felt like complete freedom. It influenced people right across the board. Before punk, people were scared to try anything – they were so oppressed and stifled. All it needed was people to say, 'Fuck, just do it.' It was as simple as that.
Paul Cook

I think the best thing of all was the idea that you could do anything. Whatever it is, and the more extreme it is, the more likely you're going to have fun with it and it just might succeed… When I first put on a club in a warehouse, I remember my mum saying to me, 'They have people to do that.' Punk told you that you could be those people, that you could be a musician or a writer.
Robert Elms

Punk said to have confidence in yourself, and if people don't like it, they can fuck off.
Joe Corré

The best thing was the music and all the fun everybody had. Everyone was saying, 'I don't care about my career, I don't care about marching the streets to stop ships polluting the river. I'm just going to a club to have a few drinks and enjoy myself.' That was the best thing.
John Holmstrom

For me, Malcolm McLaren was the best. My mother always used to tell me that society needs artists, artists are the most important things in society, right, culture, things changing, not your academics, but artists. And Malcolm was an artist.
Helen Wellington Lloyd

The best thing was the creativity and the positive effects it had on the future of rock'n'roll.
Tony James

The best thing about it for me was that we put our mark on history.
Steve Jones

THE WORST OF PUNK...

The worst thing about punk for me was Sid Vicious dying. That's the ultimate tragedy.
Alan Jones

The worst thing for me was the complete misinterpretation of punk and the massive hangover that came after it.
Kevin Rowland

The very worst thing was the clichéd nature of the whole thing. Kenny Everett punks, Giles cartoon punks… I remember some TV personalities did a song called 'Part Time Punks', about Mohican-haired trendsetters walking down the Kings Road, which pretty much summed it up for me.
Bill Dunn

I think the worst thing was the way that it was quickly sort of assimilated, and then marketed again, for the second time, flogging it off on the high street.
Jock Scott

I hated all that fucking spitting. I despised it.
Jayne County

The worst thing was that it didn't last very long.
Steve Jones

Once the name was slapped on and it became mainstream, punk became the very thing it weren't supposed to. So it was very short-lived.
Clive Langer

I think it was late '77 when punk started attracting these kinds of people who thought being a punk was about lobbing a bottle into the audience and not caring who's head it hit, or going up behind someone and shoving a Stanley knife into them. It was just getting really kind of stupid.
Nigel Wingrove

The worst bit around it for me was all the violence and the paranoia, the heaviness of it all. People foget that now.
Paul Cook

I hated having to hitchhike home in a leather T-shirt. It had these big holes in it and the weather was so cold that my nipples were going numb. I remember being at the Bristol services for about eight hours. That was the worst thing. I just wished that the fashion had invented something warmer.
Chris Sullivan

There were a lot of fights. It was very violent. These guys coming in from Queens would look to pick on the punks because they took the anarchy thing literally, like everyone else did.
Legs McNeil

I don't think there was a worst thing.
Nils Stevenson

The worst was that the initial enthusiasm was watered down, which was a shame, as at the time everything seemed possible.
Paul Simonon

The worst thing I think was the deaths of Sid and Nancy and their glorification – the fact that kids wanted to be like Sid, taking drugs.
John Holmstrom

The worst thing is that it actually lasted too long.
Chris Duffy

Everybody used to be communal and co-operative until the big record companies started coming round and signing people up. It was sad after that because everybody became very competitive.
Chris Stein

The worst thing about punk was that it was uninformed and became conservative very, very quickly, when it was meant to be the complete opposite. Instead of being a thing that revelled in change, it became a thing that was scared of it.
Robert Elms

The worst was running to catch a train, and the girls would chase after Joey and Johnny. I didn't think they'd be throwing bottles at us, but they were.
Legs McNeil

The worst thing was the laddism. It was very hard, chauvinistic and sexist, even though punk encouraged liberation.
Viv Goldman

The worse thing is that old punks become fat and nostalgic. I should know – I married one.
Hilary Colegrave

The worst thing was finding out you couldn't just do anything.
Legs McNeil

The worst thing was going somewhere like Italy in 1980 and all these blokes with 2-foot spikes gobbing at you years after the event.
Suggs

Punk brought rock'n'roll back to its roots. It brought the rebelliousness and anti-establishment attitude back to music. When it's loud and snotty, that's when it's at its best.

Jayne County

THE LEGACY OF PUNK

The legacy is the fuckin' music industry. There was a huge response from kids, who went out and formed bands – 15,000 of them – and made records: that's the legacy. It's all those records.
Jock Scott

Punk set the scene for a greater revolution within rock'n'roll and we are still feeling the reverberations of it now. It changed the music industry.
Tony James

Before punk, rock musicians had been people at a distance, up on stage, or clothes designers – that was something French people did. Then suddenly there you were, it was your peers and it was blokes just like you, from the same council estates, doing extraordinary things. Punk had told you that you could be those people, and that's the legacy for me.
Robert Elms

The legacy is the rave, trance and dance music that has taken over the world – the whole way that different cultures unite globally through the spirit of music and dance.
Viv Goldman

Pull yourself together and do it. If you've got a good idea, just go and fucking do it. If you believe in it, speak up and just go and do it, see what happens. We can do what we like, you know, and there's not many people doing that these days…
Clive Langer

Punk was a movement which had to hate itself, which had to make itself violent by its own ethos – so it had to fuck itself.
Paul Durden

There have been other music genres since then, but what's happened is that everything since punk has either been a soundtrack or a dance, or a fashion that's been influenced by it. None has been a complete subculture with its own writers, intellectuals, poets, film-makers and fashion designers. It was a complete thing, a complete subculture, and nothing since then has been that complete.
Don Letts

I am the legacy.
Dempsey

Punk took it upon itself to say no, you don't have to do things that way, you don't need this, that and the other. Whatever it is you want to do – play music, write a book, paint a picture, or rave and scream – you can do it your own way. That's what punk was all about.
Paul Durden

The punk movement was kind of like the beatnik movement.
Nat Finklestein

The working class are passionate about it, the middle class are conscientious about it and the upper class make all the money out of it.
Nils Stevenson

Anarchy was the word really, because it became anarchy, and there was no answer.
Clive Langer

The ramifications and the attitudes are still being felt today. The wool can't be pulled over people's eyes as it was before; they have become more aware. It's made people harder, in the sense that they are not easily pushed around.
Paul Durden

Without the legacy of punk there would have been a lot of the same music. People now question authority with a confrontational attitude. The hippies were starting to develop this, but the punks demanded it. It just got a lot more aggressive.
Bob Gruen

The legacy of punk for me is the quote about me from Lou Reed: 'The three worst people in the world are Nat Finklestein and two speed dealers.'
Nat Finklestein

I think it was the 'two fingers in the air' attitude that broke down the barriers… Elvis Presley, Gene Vincent, Jerry Lee Lewis – they were all punks. They were young people who were making statements of their own.
Paul Durden

The legacy is an alternative way of looking at music, which is still followed by a lot of people today. Before punk, it was very regular and organized. Song structures were always the same. I think it allowed people to realize they could make music however they wanted to. I think we had a lot to do with that. People forget how boring it was before.
Steve Jones

Well, it's survived. You can still join punk bands. There seemed to be lots of voices, and that's what's great about it. Patti Smith had a definite voice; Richard Hell had a definite voice… Punk was lots of different points of view. Take, say, a 13-year-old girl, who can learn to play the bass in her bedroom and put together a song: it still seems like a valid way to express yourself when you're a kid.
Legs McNeil

The word 'punk' seemed to fit because most of the kids were rebellious, anti-establishment and against convention.
Hilly Kristal

When we set up Adam and the Ants the legacy became clear: it was like, what do you want? Do you want to be spat on by a thousand punks or do you want roses thrown at you by 10,000 little girls?
Marco Pirroni

The difference is that in a lot of ways nothing was analysed then, but everything is analysed now.
Steven Severin

I think punk made people more politically aware. It criticized people and made them aware of what the real world was like. It marked a decline in the power of the monarch and the government. We don't look at the Royal Family and politicians in the same way. We are no longer deferential.
Paul Durden

Considering the small amount of time punk was actually around, it has left a huge legacy in the areas of fashion, bands and in people's general attitude towards things. Punk was the last great teen movement against an older generation, and since then nothing has been as powerful as that in changing things.
Chris Duffy

It left behind a music industry which will never get too safe and secure again because it now knows that there might just be another time when a bunch of young people come along and shake things up again, just like punk did.
Jayne County

I think punk has had a tremendous impact on British culture. It's funny now when I meet people who were punks. It's a bit like they've survived a war, except in their case they survived radical changes in popular culture. Remember, in places like Wigan you'd get chased up and down the road all night just for having dyed hair.
Suggs

I think punk changed the music industry, it really did. We thought we could storm the barricades and change society. I don't think it changed society, but it certainly changed the idea that you could be in a group without having a manager, without having a record company to make it OK. You could do it yourself. Yes, of course everybody sold out. They became rich and bloated or drug addicts, just like all the old groups, but it set the scene for a greater revolution in rock'n' roll, which we're still feeling the reverberations of today.
Tony James

The sensibility of punk has filtered into everything. There are even elements of punk in wrestling – it's true! It's something there in the culture. I don't think it just came from the musicians in CBGB's. I think it's something intrinsic and it was always going to come to the surface one way or another.
Chris Stein

There are two phrases which sum up the legacy: one is 'No' and the other is 'Fuck off'.
Marco Pirroni

After we'd repackaged and redefined American punk in our own inimitable style, and squeezed the last dying breaths out of rock'n'roll, the Americans reclaimed the initiative with rap. Stealing the remnants of the past and irreverently pasting them together to make something new was as punk as you could get. So, at the beginning of the '80s, I went to New York to manage the World's Famous Supreme Team. The centre of that scene was also a club named, by the tough English punk girl called Blue who ran it, the Roxy. Nils Stevenson

Opposite: Supermodel Gisele brings punk up to date, wearing a Sid Vicious T-shirt

AFTERWORD

Twenty-five years since its birth and punk is still of interest to millions of people all over the world. At its height it had a huge national profile in the UK, less so in the USA, and was a definitive experience for the baby boomers who had missed out on the hippie trip.

Accepted wisdom is that punk had a lasting impact on the worlds of fashion, music and youth culture. This is too simplistic. In many ways the year 2001 isn't radically different from 1976. Most clubs the world over play chart music, just as they did in '76, the only difference being that it is now called house music. People's approach to style is also similar: we still have high fashion victims and high street copycats. As a result, there is no underground. Style magazines once encouraged new ideas; now they exist purely for profit, so the information they deliver is middle of the road, aimed at everyone from bankers to bus drivers. They have lost their cutting edge. DJs have become the new rock stars, spinning out long, self-indulgent sets that all sound the same. In an effort to retain their superstar status, they concentrate on keeping the crowd happy rather than breaking new ground – a recipe for blandness. Culture in all its forms is a marketable commodity. As soon as a new music is heard, it hits one of the magazines and becomes a trend. Manufactured bands get to number one in the charts, boy bands rule to the roost... Nothing is very different from the '70s – only the names have changed: for the Osmonds and the Jacksons substitute Boy Zone and West Life.

The big difference is that punk did make news and move the establishment in ways that youth culture today does not. It set its participants apart and gave them membership of a radical movement. Nowadays, trends have replaced movements. Everybody, especially parents, hated its style; today parents and children dress the same.

Punk is important and will remain so because it was the first and last genuine youth counter-culture. Although the hippie movement had a political context, it was not as single-mindedly anti-establishment as punk. The older generation found the peace and love philosophy relatively unthreatening, but they could find nothing redeeming or understandable about punk. For this reason, it was far more effective at challenging the status quo.

Observed with hindsight, punk seems to have been a very short-lived experiment in counter-culture, but in many ways it is even more relevant today. The original participants interviewed for this book all share a sense of independence and innovation, a free-spirited creativity, which are absent from today's youth culture. For many people, punk represented an opportunity to think for themselves and seriously question the prejudices and elitism of the older generation. It did this in a wonderfully mad and unique way. There was no grand plan or unified manifesto. It didn't even give itself a name till it was almost over, and nobody ever claimed to be part of a movement. Analysts and commentators on counter-culture have found all sorts of hidden agendas and sub-plots. We have not. We set out to compile this book with one simple aim: to reveal the spirit and attitude of the time. We want to celebrate the creative madness that inspired so many kids to stop being passive consumers of music and actually get out there and do it, or write about it in fanzines.

Not all the consequences of punk were positive, heroin, pogoing, spitting, swastikas, violence and bad haircuts to name just a few. Sometimes it was more Carry On than counter-cultural, such as Vivienne Westwood taking her young son, Joe Corré, on *visits to manufacturers of S & M clothing, or the Ramones coming on stage and simultaneously launching into different songs. But this wasn't a political movement driven by a disciplined agenda. It was a group of creative individuals on a voyage of self-discovery fuelled by drugs, sex and loud music. Any attempt to give punk altruistic, social or political motives is futile, even if its lyrics used politics to shock.*

To our surprise, we discovered that punk was both more and less important than we expected. Unwittingly, its commitment to anarchy did have a positive effect on the next decade, especially in London. The best way to assess the true impact and legacy of punk is to pretend that it never happened and then imagine what the 1980s would have been like without its influence. If the early '70s had evolved seamlessly into the next decade without the interruption of punk, the dominance of over-packaged supergroups and a strobe disco culture would have grown unchecked. The relationship between hugely commercial bands, a conservatively compliant music press and a passive fan base would have ensured that the music industry continued to target the core singles-buying market of nine-year-old girls. Music would have been marginalized as a counter-cultural medium and remained in the hands of an ageing group of A & R executives.

If this seems too polarized a view, consider the following. Before punk, the British music business had tight control of its artists and their fans. To be successful, the likes of the Rolling Stones, the Who, Slade and the Bay City Rollers had to be commercially packaged if they were ever to rise above the pub circuit. The advertising revenue from the major record companies ensured editorial control of the music press, and the easily influenced pop charts made sure that only heavily marketed groups were seen on the country's principal TV music show, Top of the Pops.

Punk changed all this. It was not prepared to play by the rules. The very fact that it was always more than just a musical movement meant that it was not going to be boxed into the accepted music industry mentality. In Britain it found a way to achieve a level of PR and national consciousness beyond the imagination of any record company executive, with hardly any actual records being pressed. It had created its own venues, music press and record labels right under the noses of one of the world's most sophisticated music industries. It did this by engendering a DIY sense of self-confidence. Unintentionally, the ensuing anarchy created a real challenge to the established culture, and it did so with a sense of unapologetic confidence.

All in all, the world would have been a less interesting place without punk. It is too easy to forget the backdrop of the '70s – the unemployment, the decaying industrial regions and the dreariness of the suburbs. The media and creative worlds were elitist and tightly closed. The old boy network consigned anyone without further education to a menial job and predestined narrow life. Many people in this book, and many others who started bands in their bedrooms, found the confidence to break out of this confinement and launch themselves in new directions: they became designers, writers, artists, nightclub owners, DJs and film-makers, giving Britain the vital creative spark it so badly needed to shake itself out of its post-war malaise. In this way, punk contributed enormously to the breaking down of the stagnant class system, which wasted so much of the country's creativity and talent. The fact that London became the hippest city on the planet in the late '80s and '90s is due, in large part, to the legacy of punk.

Britain's experience of punk was more vivid and widespread than in the USA. Unlike the later grunge on the West Coast, where Kurt Cobain became a latterday Sid Vicious, punk was largely confined to Manhattan, despite Malcolm McLaren's attempt to convert cowboys in the southern states. Although punk in its pure form lasted longer in Manhattan, it never really broke out from its original scene. In fact, many of the earliest participants were still partying or performing at the Mudd Club well into the '80s.

The impact of punk, however, was probably not as far-reaching in the USA because the scene was more entrenched and sophisticated. In many ways it was more professional and had a longer heritage, so it didn't go through the craziness of British punk in 1976 and '77. American punks in 1979 looked much the same as in 1975: most were cartoon copies of the Ramones rather than sporting the bondage gear of Sex or Seditionaries. Many more British kids set up their own bands and produced records. Many more British parents were appalled by their children's behaviour, attitude, dress and music.

The most significant impact of American punk was actually in Britain. The Heartbreakers, the Ramones, Wayne County, Cherry Vanilla, Iggy Pop and, of course, Debbie Harry were pivotal in inspiring the British scene, and were soon adopted and assimilated as local icons.

Most of the people who helped us with this book believe that the attitude of punk is even more relevant to today's bland society than it was 25 years ago, and that it is time for a similar movement to arise. It is possible that the current renewed interest in punk is a tacit acknowledgement that today's establishment has even more control over youngsters. This control is more sophisticated than in 1976, but perhaps even more effective. Kids are passive consumers of media and pre-packaged music. They graduate from the school run to socially responsible further education, studying courses directly related to future employment. Keeping afloat financially means that extra energy is channelled into part-time work, and graduation is immediately followed by a job. The media, style magazines, and the music and fashion industries have designer-labelled and 'individualized' for the masses every possible trend to ensure there is no more DIY style or music to interfere with the serious business of catering to the youth market.

We hope that the current revival of interest in punk, and this book's part in it, makes people question the new establishment, perhaps even encourages them to create uncomfortable ideas and attitudes that dare to shake the older generation out of its commercial attitude. We also hope this book inspires more than just a few fashion cues for the next Milan catwalk or yet another remix from a well-fed DJ.

LONG LIVE PUNK.

INTERVIEWEES

The authors talked to many people during the course of this book, and would particularly like to thank the following for their contributions.

John Baker, record mogul

Roberta Bayley, photographer and contributor to *Punk Magazine*

Roger Bourton, clothing supplier to the film industry and buyer for Acme Attractions

Sue Catwoman, aka Sue Lucas, McLaren muse and early punk superstar

Leee Childers, ex-manager, the Stooges, the Heartbreakers, and Levi and the Rockats; now photographer and writer

Linda Clark, punk mover and shaker

Paul Cook, drummer, the Sex Pistols

Caroline Coon, journalist, now artist

John Cooper Clarke, Mancunian punk poet

Joe Corré, son of Vivienne Westwood and Malcolm McLaren, founder of the lingerie company Agent Provocateur

Jayne County, singer, actress and DJ

Andrew Czezowski, club promoter (the Roxy, the Fridge) and ex-manager of the Damned, Chelsea and Generation X

Paul Dale, journalist

Jerry Dammers, keyboard player, the Specials

Dempsey, punk fan and Celtic supporter

Howard Devoto, singer, the Buzzcocks

Ian Dickson, rock photographer, *Sounds* magazine

Chris Duffy, former bass player, Bazooka Joe

Bill Dunn, senior editor, *Esquire* magazine

Paul Durden, former Jeff Beck roadie, now scriptwriter

Erica Echenberg, photographer

John Egan, hairdresser at Smile

Robert Elms, broadcaster and journalist

Miles English, art editor, *GQ* magazine

Marianne Faithfull, singer

Danny Fields, ex-manager, the Ramones, the Stooges and Jonathan Richman

Nat Finkelstein, photographer

Jim Fourrat, writer and club owner (Studio 54 and Danceteria)

Viv Goldman, features editor, *Sounds* magazine

Bob Gruen, photographer

Mary Harron, former journalist, director of *American Psycho* and *Who Shot Andy Warhol?*

Gail Higgins Smith, Heartbreakers' tour manager

Simon Hinton, journalist and poet

Steve Holloway, DJ

John Holmstrom, editor, *Punk Magazine*

Brian James, guitarist, the Damned, Eater and Lords of the New Church

Tony James, bass guitarist with Generation X, Sigue Sigue Sputnik, London SS and Chelsea

Alan Jones, assistant in Sex, 1975-7

Dylan Jones, editor, *GQ* magazine

Steve Jones, guitarist, the Sex Pistols

Frank Kelly, Sex Pistols' aficionado and regular customer at Sex

Gene Krell, punk clothing entrepreneur, ex-husband of Nico

Hilly Kristal, owner of CBGB's

Brenda Lamb, punk trendsetter

Clive Langer, songwriter and producer

Don Letts, film-maker and former DJ

Helen Wellington Lloyd, assistant in Sex and McLaren muse

Walter Lure, guitarist, the Heartbreakers

Dan Macmillan, latter-day punk aficionado and heir to the Earl of Stockton

Alf Martin, editor, *Record Mirror*

Glen Matlock, bassist with the Sex Pistols (replaced by Sid Vicious in 1976, rejoined the band in 1996 for their Filthy Lucre tour)

Mark McCarthy, Clash fan

George McKay, professor of counter-culture, University of Central Lancashire

Legs McNeil, writer on *Punk Magazine* and author of *Please Kill Me*

Dennis Morris, photographer and record industry figure

Patti Paladin, punk singer

Marco Pirroni, guitarist, Siouxsie and the Banshees

Ted Polhemus, author of *Street Style*

Mark Powell, punk fan and London tailor

Tommy Ramone, drummer, the Ramones

Roadent (aka Steve Conolly), Sex Pistols' and Clash roadie

Kevin Rowland, Dexy's Midnight Runners

Phillip Salon, club promoter and collector of punk memorabilia

Jock Scott, stand-up poet

Leah Serehsin, former singer, now film director

Steve Severin, Siouxsie and the Banshees

Yvonne Sewall-Ruskin, author and partner of Mickey Ruskin, owner of Max's Kansas City

John Shearlaw, music journalist

Paul Simonon, bass player, the Damned and the Clash

Smutty Smiff, Levi and the Rockats

Daniela Soave, music journalist

Sophie, assistant to Malcolm McLaren at Glitterbest

Chris Stein, guitarist, Blondie

Joe Stevens, photographer

Nils Stevenson, Sex Pistols' tour manager, 1976, and Banshees manager

Ray Stevenson, Anarchy tour photographer

Steve Strange, Visage

Suggs, singer with Madness

Mark Taylor, club promoter and early punk figure

Amanda Temple, film producer

Julien Temple, film director, *The Filth and the Fury*

John 'Boogie' Tiberi, Sex Pistols' tour manager, 1977-9

Steve Walsh, guitarist, the Flowers of Romance and Manicured Noise

Ron Watts, promoter, the 100 Club

Andrew Weatherall, international DJ

Nigel Wingrove, founder, *Stains* fanzine

Bill Wright, promoter at Ivanhoe's

Christos Yianni, bass player, the Doll

PRINCIPAL PEOPLE AND BANDS

Over 500 people and 100 bands are mentioned in this book. The selective lists that follow are intended as a quick reminder of the main figures on the punk scene during its formative years.

THE PEOPLE

A

Gaye Advert, bassist, the Adverts (real name Gaye Atlas)
René Albert, owner of Chaguarama's, London nightclub
Al Aronowitz, first manager of the Velvet Underground; also a journalist on the *New York Post*
Lynda Ashby, one of the Bromley contingent of punk fans
Ron Asheton, guitarist, the Stooges
Scott Asheton, drummer, the Stooges
Martin Atkins, drummer, Public Image Ltd

B

Danny Baker, broadcaster and journalist
John Baker, record mogul
Stiv Bators (deceased), vocalist, the Dead Boys (real name Steve Bators; also in the Wanderers and the Lords of the New Church; died after being run over by a car, 4 June 1990)
Roberta Bayley, photographer and contributor to *Punk Magazine*
Ann Beverly (deceased), mother of Sid Vicious
Big Youth, aka Manley Buchanan, dub reggae singer and DJ
Ronnie Biggs, Great Train Robber and Sex Pistols' film co-star (returned to custody in Britain in 2001)
Dr Bishop, one of the Vitamin Doctors in New York
Chris Blackwell, founder, Island Records

Andy Blade, vocalist, Eater
Johnny Blitz, drummer, the Dead Boys (real name John Madansky)
Reginald Bosanquet (deceased), ITN newsreader
Dennis Bovell, reggae producer
Angie Bowie, performer (ex-wife of David Bowie)
David Bowie, singer, artist and producer
Mickey Bradley, bass player, the Undertones
Richard Branson, founder of the Virgin empire
Tally Brown, Factory regular
Budgie, drummer, Big in Japan, the Slits and Siouxsie and the Banshees (real name Peter Clarke)
Bebe Buell, Factory figure, mother of the actress Liv Tyler (married to Todd Rundgren)
William Burroughs (deceased), novelist
Roger Bourton, clothing supplier to the film industry
David Byrne, Talking Heads

C

John Cale, Velvet Underground (played bass, viola and organ)
Sue 'Catwoman' Lucas, McLaren muse and early punk superstar
Leee Childers, ex-manager the Stooges, the Heartbreakers, and Levi and the Rockats (now photographer and writer)
Terry Chimes (aka Tory Crimes), drummer, the Clash
Cheetah Chrome, guitarist, the Dead Boys (real name Gene O'Connor)

Linda Clark, punk mover and shaker
Stephen Colegrave, author and film producer
Ornette Coleman, jazz musician
Michael Collins, Sex assistant and drug counsellor
Steve Connolly, *see* Roadent
Paul Cook, drummer, the Sex Pistols
Caroline Coon, former journalist, now artist
John Cooper Clarke, Mancunian punk poet
Julian Cope, bass player, the Crucial Three, and lead singer and guitarist for the Teardrop Explodes
Stewart Copeland, drummer, the Police
Don Cornwallis (aka Don Devroe), drummer, Levi and the Rockats
Hugh Cornwell, guitar and vocals, the Stranglers
Joe Corré, son of Vivienne Westwood and Malcolm McLaren (founder of the lingerie company Agent Provocateur)
Gregory Corso (deceased), Beat poet
Diego Cortez, co-founder, the Mudd Club, and also an artist
Jayne County, singer, actress and DJ (born Wayne Rogers; changed name to Wayne County, then Jayne County following a sex change; one-time DJ at Max's Kansas City; performed and recorded with the Electric Chairs, Queen Elizabeth, then the Backstreet Boys)
Alex Cox, screenwriter/director of *Repo Man and Sid and Nancy*
Ian Curtis (deceased), vocalist, Joy Division (committed suicide when the group was at its peak)

Jackie Curtis (deceased), transvestite Warhol superstar and playwright

Ronnie Cutrone, painter and Factory assistant (also whip-dancer for the Exploding Plastic Inevitable)

Andrew Czezowski, club promoter (the Roxy and the Fridge; also ex-manager, Chelsea, Generation X and the Damned)

D

Paul Dale, journalist

Jerry Dammers, keyboard player, the Specials

Candy Darling (deceased), Factory transvestite and performer (real name Jimmy Slattery)

Dorothy Dean, artist and door person at Max's Kansas City

Tony Defries, David Bowie's manager in the early days

Joe Dellasandro, actor and star of various Warhol films

Dempsey, punk fan and Celtic supporter

Jimmy Destri, keyboard player, Blondie

Howard Devoto, vocalist, the Buzzcocks (real name Howard Trafford; also played in Magazine)

Levi Dexter, vocalist, Levi and the Rockats

Dibbs, guitarist, Levi and the Rockats

Ian Dickson, rock photographer (*Sounds* magazine)

Divine (deceased), transvestite actor and performer (real name Harris Glen Milstead)

Terry Draper, co-founder, the Vortex

Laurie Driver, drummer, the Adverts

Bill Drummond, guitarist, Big in Japan and the KLF

Chris Duffy, former bass player, Bazooka Joe (now a photographer and Internet wizard)

Bill Dunn, senior editor, *Esquire* magazine

Ged Dunn, publisher, *Punk Magazine*

Paul Durden, former roadie, now scriptwriter

Ian Dury (deceased), singer, songwriter and actor (formed Kilburn & the High Roads, Ian Dury & the Blockheads, and Ian Dury & the Music Students; died of cancer, 27 March 2000)

E

Erica Echenberg, photographer

John Egan, hairdresser at Smile

Robert Elms, broadcaster and journalist

Miles English, art editor, *GQ* magazine

F

Marianne Faithfull, singer

Mick Farren, lead singer, the Deviants (now journalist and author)

Andrea 'Whips' Feldman, Factory insider

Peter Fenton, guitarist, Siouxsie and the Banshees

Danny Fields, ex-manager, the Ramones (also A & R executive at Elektra Records, and manager of the Stooges and Jonathan Richman)

Nat Finkelstein, photographer and Factory insider

Patrik Fitzgerald, musician

Tom Forcade (deceased), founder of *High Times*

Jim Fourrat, writer and nightclub owner (Studio 54 and Danceteria)

Cyrinda Foxe, a big name on the Max's Kansas City

scene (married David Johansen of the New York Dolls, but divorced him to marry Steven Tyler, singer with Aerosmith; David Bowie wrote his song 'Jean Genie' about her)

G

Mickey Gallagher, keyboard player, Ian Dury & the Blockheads (joined the Clash for their second US tour)

Gyda Gash, bass player, Angel Rot

Dee Generate, drummer, Eater (real name Roger Bullen)

Andy Gill, guitarist, Gang of Four

Charlie Gillett, writer and broadcaster

Allen Ginsberg (deceased), Beat poet

Vic Godard, singer and songwriter, Subway Sect

Viv Goldman, features editor, *Sounds* magazine

Robert Gordon, lead singer of the rockabilly band the Tuff Darts, now a solo performer

Bill Graham, promoter and owner of the Filmore West Auditorium

Derek Green, former managing director of A & M Records

Johnny Green, former road manager, the Clash

Bryan Gregory (deceased), the Cramps

Bob Gruen, photographer

Bill Grundy (deceased), TV interviewer

H

Romy Haag, German singer who ran a transvestite club in Berlin

Eric Hall, agent

Terry Hall, vocalist, the Specials

Rob Hallett, artist and agent

Keith Haring, artist and curator of the art gallery at the Mudd Club in New York

Mary Harron, feature writer, *Punk Magazine* (also director of *American Psycho* and *Who Shot Andy Warhol?*)

Debbie Harry, singer, songwriter and actress, the Stilettos and Blondie

Screamin' Jay Hawkins (deceased), R&B singer (real name Jalacy J. Hawkins)

Topper Headon, drummer, the Clash (real name Nicky Headon)

Richard Hell, bass player, the Neon Boys, Television, the Heartbreakers and the Voidoids (real name Richard Meyers)

Gail Higgins Smith, Heartbreakers' tour manager

Chris Hill, dance DJ at Lacy Lady nightclub in Ilford, Essex

Simon Hinton, journalist and poet

Tom Holiday, accountant for *Punk Magazine*

John Holmstrom, editor, *Punk Magazine*

Mick Houghton, the Undertones' press officer

Chrissie Hynde, guitarist and vocalist, the Pretenders

I

Billy Idol, vocalist, Chelsea and Generation X (real name William Broad)

Annie Idols, publicist, the Rolling Stones

Jonh Ingham, journalist

Tony Ingrassia, playwright (helped stage the musical version of *Ziggy Stardust*, also musical director of Blondie)

Lux Interior, vocalist, the Cramps (real name Erick Purkhiser)

J

Brian James, guitarist, the Damned, Tanz der Youth and Lords of the New Church (real name Brian Robertson)

Tony James, bass guitarist, Chelsea, Generation X, Sigue Sigue Sputnik and the Sisters of Mercy

Derek Jarman (deceased), director of *Jubilee*

Ralph Jedaschek, business partner of Andrew Czezowski

David Johansen, vocalist, the New York Dolls (later performed as a solo artist under the name Buster Poindexter)

Holly Johnson, bass player, Big in Japan (later with Frankie Goes to Hollywood)

Lloyd Johnson, owner of Johnson's, punk clothing shop in Kensington Market, London

Alan Jones, assistant in Sex, 1975-7

Mick Jones, guitarist and vocalist, London SS, the Clash and Big Audio Dynamite

Steve Jones, guitarist, the Sex Pistols

Jordan, assistant in Sex and punk 'star' (real name Pamela Rooke; appeared in the film *Jubilee*; manager of Adam and the Ants, now a veterinary nurse and cat breeder)

Peter Jordan, bass player, the New York Dolls and Jayne County and the Electric Chairs (stood in for Arthur Kane of the New York Dolls when Kane broke his arm)

K

Arthur Kane, bass player, the New York Dolls

Tom Katz, publisher, *Punk Magazine*

Frank Kelly, Sex Pistols' aficionado and regular customer in Sex)

Eliot Kidd, guitarist and vocalist, the Demons

Ivan Kral, bass player, Patti Smith Group

Wayne Kramer, guitarist and leader of the MC5

Gene Krell, punk clothing entrepreneur (former husband of Nico; one-time assistant in Sex; now associate editor of *Nippon Vogue* and owner of Granny Takes a Trip)

John Krevine, co-founder, Acme Attractions

Hilly Kristal, owner of CBGB's

L

Brenda Lamb, punk trendsetter

Clive Langer, guitarist, songwriter and producer (member of Deaf School, under the pseudonym Cliff Hanger; also producer of Madness, Elvis Costello and Catatonia)

Char Latanne, music journalist

Jeanette Lee, assistant in Acme Attractions (later keyboard player on PIL album *The Flowers of Romance* and manager of Pulp)

Don Letts, film-maker and former DJ, one-time manager of the Slits (worked at the Roxy and in Acme Attractions; made *The Punk Rock Movie*, released in September 1977; also made Clash and Bob Marley promos; briefly in Big Audio Dynamite with ex-Clash guitarist Mick Jones)

Keith Levene, guitarist, London SS, which became the Clash (left the Clash to join the Flowers of Romance, then Cowboys International and Public Image Ltd)

Richard Lloyd, guitarist, Television

Helen Wellington Lloyd, assistant in Sex and McLaren muse

Andrew Logan, sculptor (organized a Valentine's Ball in

1976 at which the Sex Pistols played)

Lora Logic, saxophonist, X-ray Spex

Charles Ludlam (deceased), playwright and founder of the Theatre of the Ridiculous

Lydia Lunch, singer, Teenage Jesus and the Jerks (real name Lydia Koch; now a solo artist)

Walter Lure, guitarist, the Heartbreakers (now a Wall St broker)

John Lurie, saxophonist, the Lounge Lizards

John Lydon (see Johnny Rotten)

M

Steve Maas, owner of the Mudd Club, New York

Shane MacGowan, singer and songwriter, the Pogues (also formed the Nipple Erectors and the Popes)

Jim Mackin, member of the Strand, an early incarnation of the Sex Pistols

Dan Macmillan, latter-day punk aficionado and photographer (heir to the Earl of Stockton; has own fashion label Macvillain)

Gerard Malanga, Warhol confidant (also writer and poet)

'Handsome' Dick Manitoba, vocalist, the Dictators (real name Richard Blum; former wrestler)

Bob Marley (deceased), reggae artist (died of cancer, 11 May 1981, aged 36)

Alf Martin, editor, *Record Mirror*

Glen Matlock, bassist, the Sex Pistols (fired before the release of the single 'God Save the Queen' and replaced by Sid Vicious; rejoined the band in 1996 for their Filthy Lucre tour; also in the Rich Kids)

Mark McCarthy, Clash fan

Ian McCulloch, vocalist, the Crucial Three, and Echo and the Bunnymen

Alan McGee, founder, Creation Records

Tony McGee, photographer

George McKay, professor of counter-culture, University of Central Lancashire

John McKay, guitarist, Siouxsie and the Banshees

Malcolm McLaren, manager, the Sex Pistols (also co-owner of Let It Rock/Sex in the Kings Road; leading light in the punk movement)

Legs McNeil, writer, *Punk Magazine* (also author of *Please Kill Me* – see Bibliography)

Russ Meyer, film-maker/director (*Vixens, Supervixens, Who Killed Bambi?*)

Trevor Miles, purveyor of antique clothing and owner of Paradise Garage

John Miller, founder, the Vortex

Nick Mobbs, A & R executive, EMI

Noel Monk, Sex Pistols' roadie

Dennis Morris, photographer and record industry figure (designer of PIL logo)

Kenny Morris, drummer, Siouxsie and the Banshees

Sterling Morrison (deceased), guitarist, the Velvet Underground (died of non-Hodgkin's lymphoma, 30 August 1995, aged 53)

Paul Morrissey, Warhol business manager and film-maker

Billy Murcia (deceased), original drummer, the New York Dolls (died of a drug overdose, 6 November 1972, aged 22)

N

Billy Name, Factory photographer and designer

Neon Leon, leader of eponymous New York band

Nico, Velvet Underground singer and Warhol superstar (real name Christa Paffgen; died of a brain aneurysm, 18 July 1988, aged 44)

Warwick Nightingale (aka Wally), member of the Strand, an early incarnation of the Sex Pistols

Jerry Nolan (deceased), drummer, the New York Dolls and the Heartbreakers (died of a stroke, 14 January 1992)

O

Gene October, vocalist, Chelsea

Ondine, a Factory face

John O'Neill, the Undertones

Genesis P. Orridge, vocalist, Throbbing Gristle

P

Patti Paladin, punk singer

Pete Perrett, vocalist and guitarist, the Only Ones

Lee 'Scratch' Perry, aka the Upsetter, Jamaican record producer (now resident in Switzerland)

Mark Perry, founder of the fanzine *Sniffin' Glue* (later founded the band Alternative Television)

Anya Phillips, co-founder of the Mudd Club, New York

Marco Pirroni, guitarist, Siouxsie and the Banshees and later Adam and the Ants

Ted Polhemus, expert on counter-culture and author of *Street Style*

Brigid Polk, Warhol muse and regular at Max's Kansas City

Eileen Polk, photographer and Factory muse

Iggy Pop (aka Iggy Stooge), vocalist, the Stooges (real name James Newell Osterberg)

Mark Powell, London tailor

Prince Far I (deceased), reggae singer

Jimmy Pursey, vocalist, Sham 69

R

Dee Dee Ramone, bass player, the Ramones (real name Douglas Colvin)

Joey Ramone, vocalist, the Ramones (real name Jeffrey Hyman; died of cancer, 15 April 2001, aged 49)

Johnny Ramone, guitarist, the Ramones (real name John Cummings)

Tommy Ramone, drummer, the Ramones (real name Tom Erdelyi)

Genya Ravan, producer, the Dead Boys

Steph Raynor, owner of the shops Acme Attractions and Boy

Lou Reed, guitarist and singer, the Velvet Underground (real name Louis 'Butch' Firbank)

Bernie Rhodes, manager, the Clash, London SS and Subway Sect (also a former business associate of Malcolm McLaren's)

René Ricard, poet, artist and art critic

Jonathan Richman, singer (leader of the band Jonathan Richman and the Modern Lovers)

Rick Rivets, guitarist, the New York Dolls

Jake Riviera, band manager (the Damned, Elvis Costello, and Kilburn & the High Roads)

Helen Robinson, designer (produced designs for Acme Attractions and Boy)

Michelle Robinson, girlfriend of Sid Vicious at the time of his death

Roadent, Pistols' and Clash roadie (real name Steve Connolly)

Johnny Rotten, vocalist, the Sex Pistols (real name John Lydon; later formed Public Image Ltd)

Kevin Rowland, vocals, bass, guitar and piano, Dexy's Midnight Runners (also in the Killjoys)

Mickey Ruskin (deceased), original owner, Max's Kansas City

S

Phillip Salon, club promoter (also collector of punk memorabilia)

Rat Scabies, drummer, the Damned (real name Chris Miller; also in London SS and the Flowers of Romance)

Jock Scott, stand-up poet

Bobby Seale, founder, the Black Panther Party

Edie Sedgwick (deceased), Factory character (died 15 November 1971, aged 28)

Captain Sensible, bass player, the Damned and King (real name Ray Burns)

Steve Sesnick, former manager, the Velvet Underground

Steve Severin, bass player, Siouxsie and the Banshees (aka Steve Havoc, real name Steve Bailey)

Yvonne Sewall-Ruskin, author (had two children with Mickey Ruskin, the owner of Max's Kansas City, and wrote a book about the club – see Bibliography)

Feargal Sharkey, lead singer, the Undertones

John Shearlaw, music journalist

Pete Shelley, guitarist, the Buzzcocks (real name Pete McNeish)

Paul Simonon, bass player, the Clash (later joined the Pogues as a touring rhythm guitarist; now an artist)

Kate Simons, photographer

John Sinclair, manager, MC5 (left-wing poet and founder of the White Panther Party)

Smutty Smiff, bass player, Levi and the Rockats

Fred 'Sonic' Smith (deceased), guitarist, MC5 (former husband of Patti Smith; died of a heart attack, 5 November 1994, aged 45)

Mark E. Smith, vocalist, the Fall

Patti Smith, singer

Robert Smith (aka Fat Bob), guitarist, the Cure, and Siouxsie and the Banshees

Daniela Soave, music journalist

Valerie Solanis, the woman who shot Andy Warhol

Sophie, Malcolm McLaren's assistant at Glitterbest Ltd (the Sex Pistols' management company)

Chris Spedding, guitarist and record producer

Nora Springer, publishing heiress and John Lydon's wife

Nancy Spungen (deceased), girlfriend of Sid Vicious (died 11 October 1978, aged 20)

Chris Stein, guitarist, Blondie

Joe Stevens, photographer

Nils Stevenson, Sex Pistols' tour manager, 1976, and

Banshees manager

Ray Stevenson, Anarchy tour photographer (and brother of Nils)

Steve Strange, vocalist, Visage

Joe Strummer, guitarist and vocalist, the Clash (real name John Mellor; formed the pre-Clash pub-rock band the 101ers; later bands included the Latino Rockabilly War, the Pogues, Strummerville, and Joe Strummer and the Mescaleros)

Poly Styrene, singer, X-ray Spex (real name Marion Elliot)

Suggs, vocalist, Madness (real name Graham McPherson)

Chris Sullivan, author and founder of the Wag Club, London

Ingrid Superstar, Factory character (real name Ingrid von Scheven)

Syl Sylvain, guitarist, the New York Dolls (real name Syl Mizrahi)

T

Mark Taylor, club promoter and early punk figure

Amanda Temple, film producer

Julien Temple, film director

Marty Thau, manager, the New York Dolls

David Thomas, aka Crocus Behemoth, vocalist, Père Ubu

Gerald Thomas, creator of the *Carry On* films (uncle of Jeremy Thomas)

Jeremy Thomas, film producer

Johnny Thunders (deceased), guitarist, the New York Dolls and the Heartbreakers (real name John Anthony Genzale; died after taking some 'bad' heroin, 23 April 1991, aged 38)

John 'Boogie' Tiberi, Sex Pistols' tour manager, 1977-9

Peter Tosh (deceased), one of the original Wailers with Bob Marley (died from gunshot wounds during a robbery at his home, 11 September 1987, aged 42)

King Tubby (deceased), Jamaican record producer

Maureen (Mo) Tucker, drummer, Velvet Underground

Robin Tyner (deceased), vocalist, the MC5 (real name Robert Derminer; died of a heart attack, 17 September 1991, aged 46)

U

Ari Upp, singer, the Slits (real name Arianna Forster; step-daughter of John Lydon)

U-Roy, reggae singer

V

John Vaccaro, founder, the Theatre of the Ridiculous

Chi Chi Valenti, club promoter

Dave Vanian, vocalist, the Damned (real name David Letts)

Cherry Vanilla, singer and actress (real name Kathy Dorritie; David Bowie's US publicist for three years in the 1970s)

Alan Vega, lead singer, Suicide

Tom Verlaine, the Neon Boys and Television (real name Tom Miller)

Sid Vicious (deceased), bass player and vocalist, the Sex Pistols (real name John Simon Ritchie; drummer in

the Flowers of Romance and the early line-up of Siouxsie and the Banshees; died of a heroin overdose, 2 February 1979, aged 21)

Diana Vreeland, US fashion editor (Factory regular)

W

Steve Walsh, former guitarist, the Flowers of Romance (also in Manicured Noise)

Andy Warhol, artist (founder of the Factory in New York; died 22 February 1987, aged 59)

Ron Watts, promoter, the 100 Club

Vivienne Westwood, fashion designer

James White, singer and musician, James White and the Blacks (also in the Contortions)

Nigel Wingrove, founder, *Stains* fanzine

Jah Wobble, Public Image Ltd (real name John Wardle)

Holly Woodlawn, transvestite character at the Factory

Mary Woronov, dancer with the Velvets (also actress, artist and writer)

Bill Wright, promoter at Ivanhoe's

Pete Wylie, drummer, the Crucial Three and Wah!

Y

Christos Yianni, bass player, the Doll

Z

Jimmy Zero, guitarist, the Dead Boys (real name William Wilder)

Tapper Zukie, Jamaican musician (real name David Sinclair)

THE BANDS

Over 100 bands are mentioned in this book. Those listed below are discussed in some detail in the text. The line-ups given applied during the period covered by this book.

A

The Adverts Gaye Advert (bass), Laurie Driver (drums), Howard Pickup (guitar) and TV Smith (vocals and guitar)

B

Big in Japan Budgie, the drummer (later in the Slits and Siouxsie and the Banshees)), Holly Johnson, bass (later in Frankie Goes to Hollywood), Ian Broudie, guitar (later in the Original Mirrors and the Lightning Seeds; he is also a well-known producer), Bill Drummond, guitar (later of the dance group the KLF), Dave Balfe, bass (later of the Teardrop Explodes), Jayne Casey (later of Pink Military and Pink Industry), Ken Ward, vocalist, Phil Allen, drummer. The band were active for only 15 months. They formed in 1977 and their only record releases were in 1978.

Ian Dury & the Blockheads Ian Dury (vocals), Chaz Jankel (keyboards, guitar), John Turnbull (guitar), Mickey

Gallagher (keyboards), Norman Watt Roy (bass), Charley Charles (drums). Jankel left the band and was replaced by Wilko Johnson, the former lead guitarist with Dr Feelgood.

Blondie Debbie Harry (vocals), Chris Stein (guitar), Jimmy Destri (keyboards), Clem Burke (drums) and Gary Valentine (bass) formed the original quintet. Frank Infante replaced Valentine in July 1977. Blondie later expanded to become a sextet when Nigel Harrison (bass) joined the band.

Bow Wow Wow Malcolm McLaren's next attempt in the pop world after the Sex Pistols. The band featured a teenage singer, Annabella Lewin, and three ex-Ants – Matthew Ashman (guitar), Leigh Gorman (bass) and David Barbarossa (drums). Ashman died of diabetes in 1995.

The Buzzcocks Formed in Manchester in February 1976. The original line-up was Howard Devoto (vocals), Pete Shelley (guitar), Steve Diggle (bass), and John Maher (drums). Devoto quit the band shortly after the release of the 'Spiral Scratch' EP in early 1977 to form the band Magazine. Garth Smith joined the band on bass, Shelley became the lead vocalist, Diggle moved to guitar, with Maher staying on drums. Later that year Garth Smith was sacked and Steve Garvey (bass) joined the band in October 1977. The band split up in 1981 but re-formed in 1989 with a new line-up, which featured Shelley and Diggle, with Tony Barber (bass) and Phil Barker (drums).

C

Cabaret Voltaire Richard H. Kirk (guitar), Stephen Mallinder (bass) and Chris Watson (tape manipulator). Watson left the band in the early '80s, and Kirk and Mallinder carried on as a duo.

Chelsea The original line-up was Billy Idol (guitar), Gene October (vocals) and Tony James (bass), Dave Martin (guitar) and Carey Fortune (drums). Billy Idol and Tony James left the band in November 1976 to form Generation X.

The Clash The original line-up was Joe Strummer (guitar, vocals), Mick Jones (guitar, vocals). Paul Simonon (bass), Terry Chimes (aka Tory Crimes) (drums). Keith Levene (guitar) was also in the early line-up but left the band in September 1976 before the Clash joined the Sex Pistols on the Anarchy tour. Terry Chimes left the band before the release of their second album and was replaced by Topper Headon. Mickey Gallagher (of Ian Dury & the Blockheads) joined the Clash for the second US tour in 1979. Headon left the band in 1981 and Terry Chimes was restored as the drummer. In 1983 Chimes was fired and replaced by Pete Howard. Mick Jones left the band the same year to form Big Audio Dynamite. Vince White and Nick Sheppard subsequently joined the line-up. The group disbanded in 1986.

The Cramps Lux Interior (vocalist), Poison Ivy Rorschach (real name Kirsty Wallace, guitar), Bryan Gregory (guitar), Pam Gregory (first drummer), Miriam Linna (replaced Pam Gregory), Nick Knox (replaced Miriam Linna). Bryan Gregory left the band in 1980 and was replaced by Kid Congo Powers. Later line-up featured a succession of female guitarists and a new bassist, Candy del Mar. Lux Interior and Poison Ivy continue to tour with Slim Chance (bass) and Jim Sclavunos (drums).

The Crucial Three Julian Cope (bass, later of the Teardrop Explodes), Ian McCulloch (vocalist, later of Echo and the Bunnymen, and Pete Wylie (drums, later of Wah!).

D

The Damned The original line-up was Captain Sensible (bass), Brian James (guitar), Rat Scabies (drums) and Dave Vanian (vocals). Lu (real name Robert Edmunds) joined the band in the summer of 1977 as an additional guitarist on their second album. Scabies left the band after the album's release. Jon Moss (ex-London and later of Culture Club) replaced him as drummer for a short while. James left soon afterwards to form his own band, Tanz der Youth. By the spring of 1978 the band had split up but Scabies, Sensible and Vanian were reunited at the end of the year. They joined forces with Henry Badowski (bass) playing under the name Les Punks and the Doomed (Brian James had retained the rights to the name the Damned). They finally regained their name in 1979 from James. In later years the band had various line-ups, which at one time included Paul Gray (former bass player with Eddie and the Hot Rods). The Damned's first single, 'New Rose' (Stiff Records), released in October 1976, was the first ever punk single in the UK.

The Dead Boys Stiv Bators (vocals), Cheetah Chrome (guitar), Johnny Blitz (drums), Jimmy Zero (guitar), Jeff Magnum (bass). The band was initially called Frankenstein. Some of the Dead Boys previously played in Rocket from the Tombs.

Deaf School The band was formed in 1974 by a group of 15 students from Liverpool Art College. The initial line-up was eventually whittled down to an eight-piece band with Bette Bright (née Anne Martin, vocals), Eric Shark (Thomas Davis, vocals), Enrico Cadillac Jr (Steve Allen, vocals), Cliff Hanger (Clive Langer, guitar), Mr Average (Steve Lindsay, bass), the Rev Max Ripple (John Wood, keyboards), Tim Whittaker (drums) and Ian Ritchie (saxophone). Guitarist Paul Pilnick was added to the line-up in 1976. Bette Bright appeared in *The Great Rock'n'Roll Swindle* and married Suggs from Madness. Various ex-Deaf School students also turned up in the Portsmouth Sinfonia.

The Demons Eliot Kidd (guitar, percussion, vocals), Lisa Burns (vocals), Martin Butler (guitar), Martin Rappoport (drums), Robbie Twyford (bass), Bob Jones (guitar, vocals) and Craig Leon (keyboards).

The Dictators: 'Handsome' Dick Manitoba (vocalist and frontman), Andy Shernoff (bass/keyboards), Scott Kempner (guitar), Ross Funicello (guitar), Mark Mendoza (bass), Stu Boy King (drums). Richie Teeter replaced Stu Boy King on drums.

E

Eater Andy Blade (vocals), Brian Chevette (guitar), Ian Woodcock (bass), Dee Generate (drums). Phil Rowland replaced the 14-year-old Dee Generate in June 1977.

F

The Fall The initial line-up was Mark E. Smith (vocals), Martin Bramah (guitar), Tony Friel (bass), Una Baines (keyboards), and Karl Burns (drums). In 1978 Marc Riley (bass, guitar and keyboards) replaced Friel, and Yvonne Pawlett replaced Baines. This new line-up recorded the group's debut album, released in 1979. Mark E. Smith continued to be at the centre of the band during numerous subsequent personnel changes.

Flowers of Romance John Simon Ritchie (later known as Sid Vicious, drums), Viv Albertine, Keith Levene (guitar), Palmolive (guitar), and Steve Walsh (guitar)

G

Gang of Four Jon King (vocals), Andy Gill (guitar), Dave Allen (bass), and Hugo Burnham (drums).

Generation X The original line-up was Billy Idol (vocals), Tony James (bass), Mark Laff (drums), Bob Andrews (guitar). Terry Chimes and John Towe were in later line-ups.

H

The Heartbreakers Formed in 1975. Johnny Thunders (guitar), Jerry Nolan (drums), Richard Hell (bass), Walter Lure (guitar). Hell left the band in 1976 to form the Voidoids and was replaced by Billy Rath.

J

Joy Division Ian Curtis (vocals), Bernard Albrecht (guitar), Peter Hook (bass), Stephen Morris (drums). The band was previously known as Warsaw.

K

Kilburn & the High Roads A band formed by Ian Dury in 1970. Band members included: Dr George Butler, Terry Day, George Khan, Keith Lucas, Roderick Melvin, Davey Payne, David Newton Rohoman, Charles Sinclair, Edward (Ted) Speight, Charlie Hart, Louis Larose and Russell Hardy. Disbanded in 1976.

Kraftwerk Formed in 1970 by a pair of classical music students at Dusseldorf Conservatory – Florian Schneider (vocals, keyboards, drums) and Ralf Hütter (vocals, keyboards). The duo were at the centre of the band through numerous line-ups. Wolfgang Flör (vocals, keyboards) was one of the most enduring members of the group.

L

The Last Poets The original trio was Omar Ben Hassen, Jalaluddin Mansur Nuriddin and Abiodun Oyewole. Oyewole was imprisoned before the release of the band's eponymous 1970 debut album and replaced by Nilaja. Suliaman el Hadi, a jazz drummer, joined the line-up in 1971.

Levi and the Rockats see the Rockats

London Riff Regan (singer, real name Miles Tredinnick), Steve Voice (bass), Jon Moss (drummer, who later joined Culture Club), Colin Wight (guitarist).

London SS Mick Jones (guitar), Nicky 'Topper' Headon and/or Terry Chimes (drums), Keith Levene (guitar), Tony James. Paul Simonon replaced Tony James, who went on to form Generation X. London SS joined forces with Joe Strummer and the 101ers to form the Clash. Brian James (later of the Damned) was also in London SS but left to join the Subterraneans with bassist Captain Sensible. With the addition of the then-unknown Chrissie Hynde, the Subterraneans changed their name to the Masters of the Backside and Malcolm McLaren became their manager. Hynde left to join the Pretenders, and the remaining threesome went on to form the Damned, while McLaren went on to manage the Sex Pistols.

The Lords of the New Church Stiv Bators, Brian James

Lounge Lizards John Lurie (saxophone), Evan Lurie (piano), Arto Lindsay (guitar), Steve Piccolo (bass) and Anton Fier (drums) were in the line-up for the band's 1981 self-titled debut album.

M

Madness Graham 'Suggs' McPherson (vocals), Chris Foreman (guitar), Mike Barson (keyboards), Mark Bedford (bass), Lee 'Kix' Thompson (saxophone, vocals), Woody Woodgate (Dan Woodgate, drums, percussion), Chas Smash (backing vocals).

MC5 (Motor City 5) Rob Tyner (vocals), Wayne Kramer (guitar), Fred 'Sonic' Smith (guitar), Pat Burrows (bass) and Bob Gaspar (drums). Michael Davis (bass) and Dennis Thompson (drums) replaced Burrows and Gasper in 1965. Steve Moorhouse (bass) replaced Davis in 1972. The group disbanded at the end of 1972.

Jonathan Richman and the Modern Lovers The original quartet who recorded the demos that constituted the band's eponymous debut album were Jonathan Richman (vocals, guitar), Jerry Harrison (keyboards, later joined Talking Heads), David Robinson (drums, later joined the Cars) and Ernie Brooks (bass). The original band broke up in 1973. Richman then formed a new acoustic version of the band retaining Robinson on drums but bringing in Leroy Radcliffe (guitar) and Greg Keranen (bass).

N

The Neon Boys Richard Hell (bass), Tom Verlaine (guitar, vocals) and Billy Ficca (drums).

The New York Dolls Formed in late 1971. The original line-up consisted of David Johansen (vocals), Johnny Thunders (guitar), Rick Rivets (guitar), Arthur Kane (bass), Billy Murcia (drums). Syl Sylvain replaced Rivets in 1972. Murcia died in 1972 during the Dolls' first tour of England and was replaced by Jerry Nolan. Malcolm McLaren was appointed the band's manager after the commercial failure of their first two albums. By mid-1975 Thunders and Nolan had left the Dolls. Johansen and Sylvain then fired McLaren. The band continued to perform with a new line-up (including Chris Robison and Tony Machine) until they broke up permanently in 1977. Peter Jordan (ex-Jayne County and the Electric Chairs) stood in for Arthur Kane on bass when Kane broke his arm.

O

The 101ers Joe Strummer (vocals, guitar), Richard Dudanski (drums, later played in Public Image Ltd), Dan Kelleher (bass), Clive Timperley (guitar). The group was named after Joe Strummer's house number at the time (according to Keith Levene). The 101ers disbanded in early 1976 when Joe Strummer joined the London SS, which became the Clash.

The Only Ones Pete Perrett (vocals, guitar), Alan Mair (bass), Mike Kellie (drums), John Perry (keyboards, guitar).

P

Père Ubu The original line-up was David Thomas (ex-Rocket from the Tombs, vocals), Peter Laughner (ex-Rocket from the Tombs, guitar), Tom Herman (guitar), Tim Wright (bass), Allen Ravenstine (keyboards), Scott Kraus (drums). Peter Laughner left the band in June 1976 and died a year later. Tim Wright departed to join the No Wave band DNA and was replaced by Tony Maimone. The latter line-up featured on the band's debut album. The group disbanded and reformed several times in later years with varying line-ups.

Public Image Ltd John Lydon (vocals), Keith Levene (guitar), Jah Wobble (bass) and Jim Walker (drums) were the original quartet. Walker left the band in 1980. Other band members include Martin Atkins, Allan Dias, Richard Dudanski (ex-101ers), John McGeoch, Bruce Willie Smith, Jebin Bruni and Mark Schulz.

Q

Queen Elizabeth A band formed by Wayne County.

R

The Ramones Joey Ramone (vocals), Johnny Ramone (guitar), Tommy Ramone (drummer) and Dee Dee Ramone (bass). Tommy Ramone left in the spring of 1977 and was replaced by Marky Ramone (Marc Bell). Marky left in 1983 and was replaced by Richie Ramone (real name Richard Reinhardt, aka Richard Beau). In later years C.J. Ramone (Christopher Ward) joined the band as a bass player. Clem Burke (Blondie's drummer) at one time played with the Ramones under the pseudonym Elvis Ramone.

The Rockats (aka Levi and the Rockats) Levi Dexter (vocals), Eddie Dibbles (aka Dibbs, guitarist), Smutty Smiff (bass)

S

Sex Pistols Glen Matlock (bass), Johnny Rotten (vocals), Steve Jones (guitar) and Paul Cook (drums). Sid Vicious (John Simon Ritchie) replaced Glen Matlock. Glen Matlock rejoined the band in 1996 for the Filthy Lucre tour.

Sham 69 The original incarnation of the band in 1977 was Jimmy Pursey (vocals), Dave Parsons (guitar), Dave Tregenna (bass) and Mark 'Dodie' Caine (drums). Other band members include Billy Bostik, Johnny Goodfornothing, Neil Harris and Albie Slider.

Sigue Sigue Sputnik Tony James (bass), Chris Kavanagh (drums), Martin Degville (vocals), Ray Mayhew (drums), Neal X (drums). Kavanagh went on to join Big Audio Dynamite and Neal X later played with Marc Almond (ex-Soft Cell.)

Siouxsie and the Banshees The line-up of the band when they appeared at the 100 Club Punk Festival was Siouxsie Sioux (vocals), Steve Severin (bass), Marco Pirroni (guitar), who had replaced Billy Idol, and John Simon Ritchie (aka Sid Vicious, drums). Soon afterwards Vicious left to join the Sex Pistols and Pirroni joined Adam and the Ants. Peter Fenton briefly took over on guitar, but was replaced by John McKay, and Kenny Morris (drums). McKay and Morris left the band two days into the start of the 1979 tour. Robert Smith (guitarist, ex-the Cure) and Budgie (drummer, ex-the Slits, who later married Siouxsie) then joined the band. Smith returned to the Cure and John McGeoch (ex-Magazine) took his place. Siouxsie continued to lead the Banshees through various line-up changes until they split up in 1995.

Slaughter and the Dogs Wayne Barrett (vocals), Mike Rossi (guitar), Howard Bates (bass), Mad Muffet (drums). When Barrett left the band, Rossi became the vocalist and Billy Duffy was recruited to play guitar.

The Slits Formed by Ari Upp and Palmolive (Paloma Romero, drums) with Kate Kaos and Suzy Gutz completing the initial line-up. Gutz and Kaos left the band (Kaos went on to form the Modettes). Their replacements were Tessa Pollitt (bass) and Viv Albertine (guitar). Budgie (who later joined Big in Japan and Siouxsie and the Banshees) replaced Palmolive as the band's drummer before the release of their first album.

Patti Smith Group Patti Smith (vocalist), Lenny Kaye (guitar), Richard Sohl (guitar), Ivan Kral (bass, guitar, keyboards) and Jay Dee Daugherty.

The Specials Jerry Dammers (keyboard), Lynval Golding (guitar, vocals), Terry Hall (vocals), Neville Staples (vocals, percussion), Roddy Radiation (guitar), Sir Horace Gentleman (bass) and John Bradbury (drums). Hall, Staples and Golding left the Specials to form the Fun Boy Three.

The Stilettos Debbie Harry, Elda Gentile and Rosie Ross. Chris Stein was the guitarist.

The Stinky Toys A French punk band who recorded an eponymous debut album in 1977. Elli Medeiros (vocals), Bruno Carone (guitar), Jacno (guitar), Albin Deriat (bass), Herve Zenouda (drums).

The Stooges Formed in 1967. Iggy Pop (vocals), Ron Asheton (guitar), Scott Asheton (drums) and Dave Alexander (bass). Dave Alexander left the band after their second album. James Williamson joined as a guitarist and Ron Asheton moved to bass. The group disbanded in 1973, but Iggy Pop went on to enjoy a successful solo career.

The Strand Steve Jones and Paul Cook formed this band with Warwick Nightingale, Jimmy Mackin and Steve Hayes. Warwick Nightingale left the original line-up of the Strand

The Stranglers Hugh Cornwell (guitar and vocals), Jean-Jacques Burnel (bass and vocals), Dave Greenfield (keyboard and vocals), Jet Black (real name Brian Duffy, drums and percussion).

The Stray Cats Brian Setzer, Slim Jim Phantom, Lee Rocker

Subway Sect Vic Godard (vocals), Paul Myers (guitar), Steve Atkinson (keyboards), Mark Laff (drums).

Suicide A New York punk band formed in 1971, comprising the duo Martin Rev (keyboards) and Alan Vega (vocals).

T

Talking Heads David Byrne (guitar, vocals), Jerry Harrison (ex-Modern Lovers, keyboards), Chris Frantz (drums), Tina Weymouth (bass).

The Teardrop Explodes Julian Cope (vocals, guitar), Dave Balfe, Alfie Agius, Gary Dwyer, Michael Finkler, Alan Gill, Jeff Hammer, Paul Simpson, Troy Tate.

Teenage Jesus and the Jerks Lydia Lunch, James Chance, Reck, Bradley Field, Gordon Stevenson.

Television Tom Verlaine (guitar), Richard Lloyd (guitar), Richard Hell (bass), Billy Ficca (drums). Richard Hell left to form the Heartbreakers and was replaced by Fred Smith.

Throbbing Gristle Genesis P. Orridge (vocals), Chris Carter (keyboards), Cosey Fanni Tutti (guitar), Peter Christopherson (tapes and special effects).

U

The Undertones Feargal Sharkey (vocals), Mickey Bradley (bass), Billy Doherty (drums), Damian O'Neill (guitar) and John O'Neill (guitar).

V

Velvet Underground Lou Reed (guitar, vocals), John Cale (bass, viola and organ), Sterling Morrison (guitar), Angus MacLise (drums) and Nico (vocals). Maureen (Mo) Tucker replaced MacLise on drums very early on. Doug Yule replaced John Cale.

Visage A band that emerged in 1978 from the London nightclub Billy's. The original trio were Steve Strange (vocals), Rusty Egan (former DJ and ex-Rich Kids, drums) and Midge Ure (ex-Rich Kids, guitar). The group then expanded to take in Billy Currie (ex-Ultravox, keyboards) and three members of Magazine – Barry Adamson (bass), John McGeoch (guitar) and Dave Formula (keyboards). The band started to disintegrate in 1982 when Midge Ure left to focus on Ultravox.

W/X/Y/Z

James White and the Blacks James White (saxophone), Don Christensen (drums), Pat Place (slide guitar), Jody Harris (guitar), George Scott (bass)

X-ray Spex Poly Styrene (vocals), Jak Airport (real name Jack Stafford, guitar), B.P. Hurding (drums), Lora Logic (real name Susan Whitby, saxophone). Lora Logic left to form the band Essential Logic and was replaced by Rudi Thompson.

BIBLIOGRAPHY

Andy Warhol: The Factory Years 1964-1967, Nat Finkelstein
(Canongate Books, Edinburgh, 1999)

Beat Punks, Victor Bockris (Da Capo Press, New York, 2000)

British Greats, ed. John Mitchinson (Cassell & Co, London, 2000)

Deborah Harry: Platinum Blonde, Cathy Che (Andre Deutsch, London, 1999)

Destroy – Sex Pistols 1977, Dennis Morris (Creation Books, London, 1998)

Doing It with Style, Quentin Crisp & Donald Carroll (Franklin Watts, New York, 1981)

England's Dreaming – Sex Pistols and Punk Rock, Jon Savage
(Faber & Faber, London, 1992)

Flash Bang Wallop! Photographs of the Punk Explosion, Ian Dickson
(Abstract Sounds Publishing, London, 2000)

High on Rebellion: Inside the Underground at Max's Kansas City,
Yvonne Sewall-Ruskin (Thunder's Mouth Press, New York, 1999)

Iggy Pop, Modern Icons series (Virgin Publishing Ltd, London, 1997)

Instant Art of the Punk Rock Movement: Fucked up and Photocopied,
Bryan Ray Turcotte & Christopher T. Miller (Gingko Press Inc, Corte Madera, California, 1999)

Intransit: The Andy Warhol–Gerard Malanga Monster Issue (magazine)

I Swear I Was There, David Nolan (Milo Books, Bury, 2001)

I Was a Teenage Sex Pistol, Glen Matlock with Peter Silverton
(Virgin Publishing Ltd, London, 1996)

Johnny Thunders – In Cold Blood, Nina Antonia (Cherry Red Books, London, 2000)

Juxtapoz (magazine), Vol. 9, issue 2, ed. Jamie O'Shea
(High Speed Productions Inc, San Francisco, Mar/Apr 2001)

Lobotomy – Surviving the Ramones, Dee Dee Ramone with Veronica Kaufman
(Thunder's Mouth Press, New York, 1997)

The Look, Paul Gorman (Sanctuary Publishing, London, 2001)

Lou Reed: The Biography, Victor Bockris (Vintage, London, 1995)

Man Enough to Be a Woman, Jayne County and Rupert Smith
(Serpent's Tail, London, 1995)

The New York Dolls: Too Much Too Soon, Nina Antonia
(Omnibus Press, London, 1998)

Nico: The Life and Lies of an Icon, Richard Witts (Virgin, London, 1993)

Photo Past 1966-1986, Ray Stevenson (Symbiosis, London, 1988)

Please Kill Me: The Uncensored Oral History of Punk,
Legs McNeil and Gillian McCain (Penguin Books, New York, 1997)

Popism: The Warhol '60s, Andy Warhol and Pat Hackett
(Harcourt, Brace, Jovanovich, London and New York, 1980)

Psychotic Reactions and Carburetor Dung, Lester Bangs, ed. Greil Marcus
(Serpent's Tail, London, 1996)

Punk: The Illustrated History of a Music Revolution, Adrian Boot and Chris Salewicz,
(Penguin Books, London, 1999)

Punk Diary 1970–1979, George Gimarc (Vintage, London, 1994)

Punk Magazine, Vol. 2, ed. John Holmstrom (John Holmstrom, New York, 2001)

Punk: The Original, ed. John Holmstrom (Trans-High Corporation, New York, 1996)

A Riot of Our Own: Night and Day with the Clash, Johnny Green and Garry Barker
(Faber & Faber, London, 1999, and Onion Paperbacks, 2000)

Rock Confidential – A Backstage Pass to the Outrageous World of Rock'n'Roll,
Coral Amende (Plume, London, 2000)

Search & Destroy #1–6: The Complete Reprint, ed. V. Vale (Re/Search
Publications, San Francisco, 1997)

Sex Pistols: The Inside Story, Fred and Judy Vermorel (Omnibus Press, London 1989)

Sniffin' Glue – The Essential Punk Accessory, Mark Perry, Mark Petty and Danny
Baker (Sanctuary Publishing, London, 2000)

Take It Like a Man: The Autobiography of Boy George, George O'Dowd and
Spencer Bright (Pan Books, London, 1995)

Uptight: The Story of the Velvet Underground, Victor Bockris and Gerard Malanga
(Omnibus Press, London, 1983)

Vacant – A Diary of the Punk Years 1976-79, Nils Stevenson and Ray Stevenson
(Thames & Hudson, London, 1999)

The Velvet Underground, Dave Thompson (Omnibus Press, London, 1989)

Vivienne Westwood: A Fashionable Life, Jane Mulvagh (Harper Collins, London, 1999)

What's Welsh for Zen: The Autobiography of John Cale, John Cale and Victor Bockris
(Bloomsbury Publishing, London, 1999)

USEFUL WEBSITES

www.allmusic.com
The All Music Guide is a huge on-line rock encyclopedia, which can be searched by artist, song title, album title, music style or record label. Artist information includes line-ups, biographies, discographies and album reviews.

http://ubl.artistdirect.com
The Artist Direct Network features links to 175,000 fan sites. The site contains biographies from the All Music Guide, but also has details about concert dates and on-line events, collectables, song samples and message boards.

www.buzzcocks.com
The official Buzzcocks website.

www.cbgb.com
The official CBGB's site.

www.cyperspike.com/clark
John Cooper Clarke's website contains an index of his poems with hyperlinks to the lyrics.

www.gimarc.com
The website of George Gimarc, author of *Punk Diary 1970-1979,* provides the complete index from his book, which lists important dates, events and bands from the punk era. Also includes a punk chronology for the years 1970-76.

www.johnnymoped.free-online .co.uk/frontpage/webwelcomepage.html
A comprehensive collection of articles about US and British punk rock, and biographies of all the major punk bands and artists.

http://londonsburning.org
A Clash fan site.

www.luminist.org/Archives/wpp.htm
The manifesto and 10-point programme of the White Panther Party, which was first published inside the gatefold of the MC5's eponymous album.

www.lydialunch.org
The official Lydia Lunch website.

www.malcolmmclaren.com
McLaren's official site includes a chronology of his career to date.

www.maxskansascity.com
The official Max's Kansas City site.

http://members.aol.com/clashcshow
The Clash City Showdown is an on-line Clash fanzine.

http://members.aol.com/olandem
A comprehensive Velvet Underground site with detailed listings of all the books and magazine articles which have ever been published about the Velvet Underground.

www.missingchannel.com
Keith Levene's website

www.officialdamned.com
The official Damned website

www.officialramones.com
The official Ramones website.

www.punkmagazine.com
The official website of *Punk Magazine.*

www.punkrock.org
A punk rock directory with links to the websites of punk bands and artists, fanzines and stores.

www.punk77.co.uk
This site provides a complete history of punk rock in the UK from 1976 to 1979. Includes detailed biographies of virtually every UK punk band from this era, reviews of punk books, and even an on-line punk novel.

www.sex-pistols.net
An unofficial Sex Pistols' site crammed with useful information about the Sex Pistols, and the latest news about the band.

www.sham69.com
The official Sham 69 website.

www.trashsurfin.de
The website of the 1970s punk magazine *Search & Destroy:*American punk 1978-9.

http://members.aol.com/Siouxsie
A Siouxsie and the Banshees fan site.

www.velvetunderground.com
An unofficial website for the Velvet Underground, with biographies, essays and quotes.

www.warhol.dk
An informative site about Andy Warhol, with a biography, lists of books and movies, and a gallery of his art.

www.warholfoundation.org
The official site of the Andy Warhol Foundation for the Visual Arts.

www.worldwidepunk.com
A big feature of this site is the database of films with punk connections, e.g. films with a punk rock theme, punk rock soundtracks or punks as actors. The site also includes links to punk fanzines.

INDEX

Page numbers in *italic* indicate photographs

PICTURE CREDITS

Every effort has been made to trace copyright holders. The publishers invite readers to notify them of any errors or omissions.

Associated Newspapers Ltd 338

Roberta Bayley 71, 76, 78-9, 302, 369, 373

Roger Bourton 84-5 (l, tc, r), 86-7, 127, 130 (all except third from top), 136, 140-1, 149, 280-1, 283 (all except bc), 285

Leee Childers 27 (bl, br), 44-5, 46, 47 (bc), 48-9, 50-5, 57, 58, 60-1, 72-3, 74 (main), 77, 92, 175 (c), 176, 179, 311 (br)

Stephanie Chernikowski 273 (l), 318-9, 334, 366, 368 (all except br), 369, 372

Ian Dickson 56, 212 (l)

Erica Echenberg 156 (r), 192, 194 (all except tr), 195-6, 198-9, 208, 232, 235, 238, 240, 243, 251 (inset)

Danny Fields 38, 40-1, 47 (t), 68-9, 70, 210 (tl, r), 211, 213

Nat Finkelstein 21, 22, 23, 24, 25, 26-7 (main, bc), 28-9, 30-1, 32-3, 34, 35, 36, 37, 39

Ronald Grant Archive 271, 272, 273 (r)

Bob Gruen 62, 64-5, 148

Hulton Archive 152, 154, 344-5

Matt Jones 381

Kobal Collection 316, 317

Don Letts 267

Helen Wellington Lloyd Collection 84 (br), 86, 113 (r), 114-5, 123, 130 (third from top), 131, 144-7, 160, 189 (inset), 191, 251 (main), 265, 282, 283 (bc)

London Features International 274, 276, 321, 357

Mirror Syndication 166-7, 230, 260, 347

Dennis Morris 99, 100, 102-3, 116, 132, 188-9 (main), 200-2, 216-23, 225-7, 229, 252-5, 259, 262 (l), 263 (main), 264, 278, 284, 308-11, 339

Michael Ochs Archive/Redferns 42-3, 320

PA Photos 349

Pearson Television 162-3

Pictorial Press 268-9

Redferns 212, 323, 324-5, 354, 365 (br)

Marcia Resnick 80-1, 330, 331, 335, 361, 367, 368 (br), 372 (l), 373 (inset), 374-5

Retna 261, 275, 322, 337, 356, 359, 362-3, 365 (bl and c)

Rex 94-5, 134, 138-9, 231, 314, 315, 352-3

Ebert Roberts 212, 323, 365 (br)

Sheila Rock 126, 137

Graham Smith 246-7

Ray Stevenson 55, 75, 83, 88-9, 90-1, 93, 97, 98-9, 100 (tl, bl), 101, 102-3, 107, 112-3 (l), 117, 119, 120, 121, 122, 124-5, 129, 142, 156 (l), 157, 158-9, 172, 174, 175 (l, r), 177, 180-3, 190, 193, 194 (tr), 206-7, 209, 210 (c, l, bl), 214-5, 234, 241, 244-5, 249, 286, 312, 313 (all except br), 332-3, 350, 355, 358

John Tiberi 256-8, 262 (r), 263 (inset), 293-300, 304-7, 326-9

Permission to reproduce the following posters and record and magazine covers has kindly been granted by the copyright holders:

63 *Live in New York,* Receiver Records
74 *Horses,* Arista Records
82-3 *Punk Magazine,* John Holmstrom
91, 113, 114, 115, 123 Gig flyers, Helen Wellington Lloyd and Nils Stevenson
150-1 *Sniffin' Glue,* Mark Perry. Photography by Michael Beal
170-1 Anarchy tour brochure, Jamie Reid
191 Roxy Club flyer, Barry Jones
200 *Natty Cultural Dread,* Trojan Records
204-5 'Spiral Scratch', The Grey Area
239 *Time's Up,* The Grey Area
370 *Off White,* Ze Records under licence to Infinite Zero